Age of Obama: A Reporter's Journey with Clinton, McCain and Obama in

THE MAKING OF THE PRESIDENT 2008

By Mark Curtis

www.MarkCurtisMedia.com

NIMBLE BOOKS LLC

Nimble Books LLC

ISBN-13: 978-1-934840-82-5

ISBN-10: 1-934840-82-3

Copyright 2009 Mark Curtis

All images copyright Mark Curtis.

Version 1.0; last saved 2009-01-14.

Nimble Books LLC

1521 Martha Avenue

Ann Arbor, MI 48103-5333

http://www.nimblebooks.com

The cover font, heading fonts and the body text inside the book are
in Constantia, designed by John Hudson for Microsoft.

Contents

NIMBLE BOOKS LLC

FOREWORD

*by Ronn Owens, KGO Radio talk show host and author of
"Voice of Reason: Why the Left and Right are Wrong"*

No one knows politics like Mark Curtis! The long-time anchorman for KTVU-TV2 struck out on his own this year, covering the Presidential campaign from start to finish as a freelance reporter and political analyst. He was a guest on KGO AM-810 quite often throughout the year from the frozen plains of Iowa in January; to the Texas Two-Step primary in March; to the Democratic National Convention in Denver in August. We called on him often during "The Ronn Owens Program." Often funny and always engaging, he had a knack for explaining the sometimes complicated world of politics in a way every listener could easily understand. Now, with his popular website[1] he has mastered the art of internet reporting in the new media age. His daily blogs from all over the nation are insightful, educational and entertaining.

This was one of the most historic elections in U.S. history, with the first viable African-American and female candidates. Having covered every Presidential campaign since Ronald Reagan's victory in 1980, Mark has encyclopedic knowledge of the process and has an endless volume of facts and political trivia crammed into his head.

This book is a great chronicle of this year's campaign. Mark traveled from coast-to-coast with all the candidates. Along the way, he spoke with average Americans in small towns and big cities alike. This book is about their hopes and dreams now that the voters have made their decision. It gives everyone the opportunity to relive this historic era from a new, informative and entertaining perspective. Politics has been a mainstay of my program for years;

---

[1] www.markcurtismedia.com

you'll hear Mark as a guest often in the future. He is a top political analyst who understands the American political psyche.

—*Ronn Owens, San Francisco, January 2009*

ABOUT THE AUTHOR

Mark Curtis is a 30-year professional in Radio and TV, all over America.

Mark covered the entire 2008 Presidential campaign, traveling the country with all of the candidates as a blogger and freelance political analyst.

Mark is well known from his many years with KTVU, from 1993 to January 2008.

From 1993 to 1998 he was the Capitol correspondent in the Washington, D.C. bureau for all Cox Televisions stations, including KTVU.

In January 1999, he moved to Oakland, to become co-anchor of the "KTVU Morning News," which became the # 1 local early morning newscast in the Bay Area for the past 6 years.

Mark left KTVU in January 2008, to start his own freelance news reporting, public relations and political analysis agency: www.MarkCurtisMedia.com. It is a full service, multi-media company.

He grew up in Milwaukee and graduated with a degree in Broadcast Communication from Marquette University in 1981. While there, he received a Distinguished Student Service Award for his work as Program Director at WMUR Radio. In 1986, he received a Masters Degree, with honors, from the University of Florida in Gainesville. He is currently working on his Doctorate in Educational Leadership at St. Mary's College of California, in Moraga.

Curtis worked in Gainesville, FL at WCJB-TV20 as a general assignment reporter and as bureau chief in the Central Florida regional news bureau.

In 1987, he moved to WEAR-TV3 in Pensacola, Florida—Mobile, Alabama, where he served as investigative reporter covering police and court beats, county commission and state and local politics.

He spent 1992-93 as a Congressional Fellow, working in the House Judiciary Subcommittee of Rep. Charles Schumer, (D) New York, as well as for Senator Herb Kohl, (D) Wisconsin. His duties included planning for Congressional hearings, budget and issue research, developing press contacts and legislative strategies.

Mark returned to broadcasting in 1993 at the Cox Broadcasting bureau in Washington. In his five years as Capitol Correspondent, he provided daily live coverage of Congress, the White House, and the Supreme Court for eight television stations.

He's received numerous awards for his work, including the Florida Motion Picture & Television Association's "1989 Best Documentary" award in 1989 for a report on sightings of Unidentified Flying Objects. And the Florida Associated Press Broadcasters Association honored him with three awards including "Outstanding Spot News Coverage" in 1990 and 1992, and "Outstanding Enterprise/Investigative Report" in 1991.

NIMBLE BOOKS LLC

DEDICATION

This book is dedicated to my dearest family and friends

who supported me and gave me hope during

the most difficult year of my life.

May God Bless you all.

Introduction and Acknowledgements

I was only 5-and-a-half years old, but Election Day 1964 altered the course of the rest of my life.

You see, I was a kindergartener at Leland Elementary School in Elm Grove, Wisconsin. My school also doubled as the community polling location, so school was cancelled that day so people could vote. Democrat Lyndon Johnson was running for reelection against Republican challenger Barry Goldwater, to be President of the United States. It was a big deal.

Now, normally a kid who had his school day cancelled would be in heaven. I could stay home all day and watch my favorite TV shows including, "Leave it to Beaver" and "The Mickey Mouse Club." The problem was, there wasn't much for kids to watch that day. Just about everything on TV was election coverage. My mom was a news junkie and loved politics. She would watch it all on TV as she ironed our clothes, mended our torn shirts, or cooked dinner. I was one of seven kids, so she was a busy lady.

My mom, Mary Beth, loved Walter Cronkite on CBS; and she loved "The Huntley-Brinkley Report" and the "Today Show" on NBC. Bob Herzog, the man who lived across the street, was the anchorman for Chanel 12 in Milwaukee. Needless to say, she watched a lot of news in our house.

I never really paid much attention until Election Day. With little else to watch, I lay on the couch and watched election reports throughout the day and night with my mom. It was fascinating. My parents and grandparents were Republicans and they voted for Barry Goldwater. I told my mom that I kind of wanted Lyndon Johnson to win.

Now at that age, I did not know anything about what a Republican or Democrat was, nor did I care. What I did know very well was that Lyndon Johnson became President because John Kennedy was killed in Dallas the year before. I remember how sad everybody felt. I remember lots of people crying and going to St. Mary's Church on our street. I remember that President Johnson tried to make people feel better. So, he seemed nice and I thought he should win. That was my assessment of U.S. politics as a five year old.

I was fascinated how the results came in from each state. We never traveled as a family, so I had never been outside of Wisconsin. Hearing about far away places like New York, Florida and California intrigued me. My mom got me an atlas, so I could find where they were. Suddenly, I was hooked on politics and geography!

The TV thing puzzled me to no end. How did those people get inside that box near the end of our couch? Why did Mr. Herzog look so big in person, but so small on TV? How did they know what to talk about? How could we get radio in the car, when there were no cords to plug in? Suddenly, I was hooked on news and broadcasting.

My interests took off like the NASA space program (which hooked me, too), and I never looked back. In 1967 Apollo I tragically caught fire on the launch pad, and three astronauts died; by summer, many of the nation's biggest cities, including Milwaukee, had erupted in riots. In 1968 Martin Luther King Jr., was assassinated and then Senator Robert Kennedy, too. The images coming back from Vietnam prompted protests all over the nation. Then, it was time to choose a President again and the Democratic and Republican National Conventions came on the air, and all my favorite shows vanished for a week. I didn't care. I was a political junkie and news hound, hard core. At the age of nine, I watched the conventions in Chicago and Miami, from gavel to gavel.

On Election Night in 1968, I stayed up until midnight, watching the gripping, air-tight race between Republican Richard Nixon and Democrat Hubert Humphrey. Finally my parents sent me to bed, which was wise since I had school the next day. It worked out okay, because Nixon wasn't declared the winner until morning. We've had several cliffhangers since.

Forty years later, I am still at it. God bless my late parents, Dr. Bill and Mary Beth Curtis, for instilling in me their love of current events, news and politics.

Other people I wish to thank include my sister Tierney Curtis, who donated thousands of frequent flyer miles so I could make all these crazy campaign trips. The book was edited by my mother-in-law Shirley Davis Ware, my wife Kathi Curtis, my youngest sister Tyler Curtis, and our good friend Victoria Lorrekovich, all of whom are excellent writers and grammarians.

The people at KGO radio had me on-air from all corners of the country, with thanks to Ronn Owens, Mark Silverman, Brian Copeland, Lynne Slone, Harry Hall, Mel Baker, Greg Jarrett, Rosie Allen and Kim McCallister. My dear friend Aimee Allison from KPFA Radio and Comcast TV had me on often. Stephanie Kelmar and Ross McGowan kept my voice alive on KTVU for most of the campaign. The true geniuses who built KTVU's morning news, Kevin O'Brien, Fred Zehnder, Rosemarie Schwarz, Frank Somerville, Tori Campbell, Pam Cook, Tom Vacar, Brian Banmiller, Diane Dwyer, Andrew Finlayson, Melinda Tichelaar, and the ultimate political junkie Sal Castaneda—all have my deepest appreciation. Tribune Broadcasting's Scott Warren brought me into KTLA in Los Angeles, along with Paulette Bleam at KTXL Fox 40 News in Sacramento. KQED-TV9's Belva Davis and Robin Epstein booked me, too. Newspaper columnists Tim Hunt, Lisa Vorderbrueggen, Chuck Barney, Susan Young, Carla Marinucci, C.W. Nevius and Dolores Fox Ciardelli praised and promoted my work. Mike James of Newsblues.com and Michael Bille of CollectiveTalent.com did the same on the internet. Thanks to Andrew Johnson and the whole gang at Comcast. A very special thanks to former San Francisco Mayor Willie Brown for telling me that I was "one of the best political analysts on TV in America."

Paul Fifield and Vibol Peou taught me more about "new media" than I could ever thank them for. Doug de Urioste and Mark Elster at Dagaz Solutions are the best web site builders ever. Karen Alvarez of Tribute Video is my video editor; Jinah Jo Manly is my photographer; Blake and Diane Shoemaker at J. Blake Designs are my graphic artists. Rich Ware, Diane Baker and Tom and Carrollee Moore gave me free room and board, and lots of support. Helen Mendel, Penny Warner and Kenny Wardell gave great public relations advice.

Jamie Dupree from Cox Radio and the University of Florida has been my professional mentor and best friend for 25 years and is the wisest political reporter I've ever known.

Some people, who inspired and encouraged me along the way, sadly left this world before this project was complete. They are Dr. Bill Curtis, Tim Russert, Tony Snow, Mark Eastman, Congressman Tom Lantos and Congresswoman Stephanie Tubbs Jones. May they rest in peace.

My brothers and sisters, my mom Helen and my many lifelong friends supported me along the way, especially when things got tough. Classmates and teachers from St. Mary's Grade School, Marquette High School, Marquette University, the University of Florida and St. Mary's College of Califronia, all had my back. Their e-mails, IMs and phone calls at all hours of the day, while I was in far-flung places across America were priceless and kept me going.

To my many, many friends in the San Ramon Valley especially the Kiwanis and Rotary Clubs, the Veterans groups and Community Presbyterian Church, thank you for all the prayers.

Most of all, thanks to my wife Kathi and our children Alexandra and Patrick, for putting up with me being on the road most of this year. I'm home!

God bless you all!

Mark Curtis, Danville, California, January 2009

NIMBLE BOOKS LLC

Chapter 1: The Iowa Caucuses

It is minus six degrees outside, and politicos and media are coming from everywhere. As I ponder why we are all here, it strikes me that the only thing falling faster than the mercury is President Bush's approval rating. Both threaten to drop still lower. But just as autumn has yielded to winter, this presidency is about to end, so we embark as a nation on the search for our new leader. It's America's quadrennial ritual, and frigid Iowa is always the first stop.

I come fearing everyone is already sick of us (and by "us," I mean the press corps and the candidates). The campaigns began so very long ago. But we are potentially making history this year. First of all, this is the first time since 1952 that there been no incumbent president, vice president or former vice president on the ballot. In other words, it is open season, a free-for-all battle for the White House.

Second, we expect some kind of "first" this time. "First woman President," "first black President," "first Mormon President," "first 'First Lady' President," "first ex-POW President," "first President who was "America's Mayor" first," "first Baptist preacher-turned-bass-player-turned-Governor President," and the list goes on. So we expect this "first something," as we arrive in Iowa in droves and as we freeze.

Covering a "first" is a big deal for a reporter and a historian. You are *there* when this first thing happens, so you are *there* for history. I was only there for the "second" impeachment of a President, so that had been done before. Iowa would to take us places we've never been before, besides West Des Moines!

I made my first mistake assuming people would be sick of the traveling campaign circus. They were not. Iowa welcomed us with a big, warm bear hug; and, given how cold it was, we loved it. Nice place, Iowa. Nice people, too.

Since 1964 when Lyndon Johnson ran against Barry Goldwater, I have been fascinated about how a country chooses its president. Just what is it people are looking for? Is the president supposed to be some kind or "savior?" What qualities do the people want in their leader? And why are the press and the public so fascinated by the process?

The fun thing about being a reporter is that it gives you license to start talking with anyone, even complete strangers. I was waiting for my photographer to arrive on a later flight from San Francisco; and, since I was freezing, I went in search of coffee.

No, not Starbucks. You can't have coffee made by a chain. That wouldn't be authentic. What I was in search of was a real honest-to-goodness local coffee shop, filled with local people and local color. I found it not far from the airport at a place called, "Coffee and Comics." This was kind of a "Spiderman Meets Mrs. Olson" place. It was much like a bar, but serving coffee, no booze; and they sold vintage comic books. It was reminiscent of a beatnik-type place you might expect to find in San Francisco, but we were in Des Moines.

The owner was Matt Johnson, who was backing Democratic Senator Chris Dodd, of Connecticut, and had even hosted a fundraiser in the coffee shop for Dodd. Like many Iowans, Johnson defended his small state's "super sized" influence on the national election process. "Iowa has... " and he stopped a moment to ponder. "We're not too fundamentalist when it comes to religion," Johnson said. "We're not too crazy when it comes to left—wing issues," he added. "We're very, very passive. We're very nice people." He could have added, "We make good coffee!" Johnson is a former TV producer turned barista. We talked, and I thought perhaps he missed the madness of television news. Then he contentedly sipped his coffee again, and it was apparent he didn't really miss the insanity of TV at all.

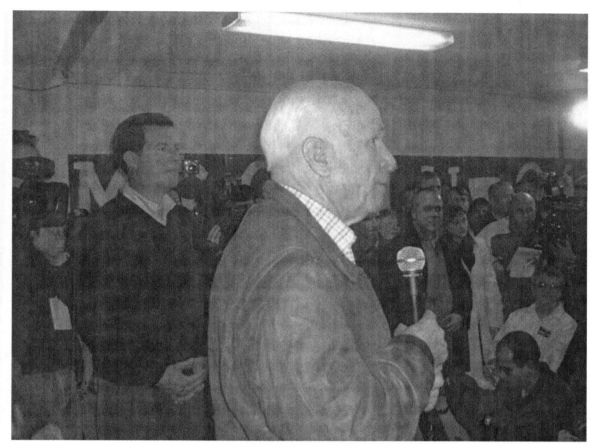

Figure 1. John McCain campaigns in Des Moines, Iowa, Jan. 2, 2008.

The first night in Des Moines was a scene from the "Wild West." My photographer, Paul Fifield, arrived from San Francisco. Paul had grown up in Des Moines and knew his way around. With events all over town, we decided we would try to catch John McCain, John Edwards and the Clintons, all in the span of about two hours. With apologies to the Iowa State Police, we made them all.

First stop was a John McCain "thank the volunteers" rally in West Des Moines scheduled for 7:30 p.m. We arrived at 7:25, perhaps the last crew there. We edged into a spot, stage right, smack dab under the U.S. Flag. We were warned McCain would be an hour late, waiting for his plane to de-ice somewhere else in Iowa.

With an hour to kill and pressed up against the stage, my only choice was to talk with a group of white- and gray-haired men surrounding me. What a godsend! Among those in the group were Tom Moe and Orson Swindle, both former POWs who spent time in the "Hanoi Hilton" with John McCain. We talked the full hour about what made McCain presidential material. Moe, who used to live in Arlington, Virginia, where I had lived for six years, was particularly chatty. He was now back in Iowa; and since we had both grown up in the Midwest, we really hit it off. Swindle is best remembered as Ross Perot's running mate in 1996, so this was great stuff.

As we all chatted, I glanced around the room and realized we were in a "Who's Who" of the national media: Tim Russert of "Meet the Press," George Stephanopoulos of "This Week" on ABC, Andrea Mitchell of NBC, Judy Woodruff of PBS, Carl Cameron of Fox News, and the list went on. "Why are they all here?" I wondered. McCain was polling in about fifth place and seemed to have no chance in Iowa. In fact his whole campaign was on life support. After the rally I briefly spoke with Russert about why so many top reporters were there and said, "Do you guys know something we don't know?" Russert too, seemed surprised at this media attention, given McCain's disappointing poll numbers.

Figure 2. NBC's Tim Russert at McCain rally in Des Moines, Iowa, Jan. 2, 2008.

McCain's Iowa State Chairman, Dave Roederer, was standing next to me, so I asked him whether the campaign's internal polling told them a surprise might be coming, thus explaining the presence of all this national media.

"Internal polling?" said Roederer, laughing slightly. "We can't afford that. This campaign is broke. We have no money for polling."

I was stunned. I had no idea McCain's campaign was that badly on the ropes. A crushing loss in Iowa, could mean a quick exit from the campaign for John McCain.

The room was about as big as a phone booth, with two hundred of us packed in. It was bitterly cold outside, so we were just glad to be inside where it was warm. It was a good thing there was no fire marshal around. This had to violate code, but no one seemed to care.

Finally, after an hour's delay, McCain arrived, with Republican Senators Lindsey Graham, of South Carolina, and Sam Brownback, of Kansas, in tow. McCain stood on stage right, next to me, and we said hello. As a reporter in DC and San Francisco, I've known McCain for almost fifteen years. He always seems to remember me. His face lit up, and I appreciated his warm greeting.

I have to share a funny story about the very first time I met John McCain. It was 1993, and I was a legislative aide, working in the U.S. Senate. Many people probably don't know this, but there is a small subway system which runs under the U.S. Capitol complex. It makes stops at six Congressional office buildings. Senate and House members—along with their staffs—use the subway to get to and from the Capitol for votes or other urgent business. There is one protocol, though: If you are a staffer who is seated and the train stops for a Member of Congress, you must stand up and offer your seat. I was sitting with Jim Borland, a friend from our days as

Congressional Fellows, and up walked Senator John McCain of Arizona, whom I greatly admired but had never met.

Nervously we stood up, and I said, "Senator McCain, please have a seat."

"No, no, guys, that's not necessary, " McCain said. "I don't mind standing."

Then, just as I sat down, McCain sat right down on my lap. He swung his legs up and placed them across Jim's lap. He put his arm around my shoulders, looked us dead in the eyes and said, "So, gentlemen, how are things going today?"

I honestly don't recall what we told him, probably just small talk. It was bizarre and funny at the same time. I wanted to burst out laughing, but I didn't dare. Fortunately, it was a quick ride to the Russell Senate Building. McCain stood up, smiling, shook our hands and left. Jim and I were in stitches, but I suspect McCain was laughing harder at our embarrassed reaction to his practical joke. I said, "You know, if McCain ever becomes President of the United States, I am going to have one hell of a story to tell!"

After McCain shook my hand in Iowa fifteen years later, he turned to face the crowd. We were packed so closely together that, as he talked, he kept jostling my notebook with his right elbow, causing my pen to scrawl wildly over the page. I was thinking that I might have a memento for the Smithsonian should McCain actually become president, but then I realized any kindergartener could have made those scrawls all over my notebook.

McCain was funny, by the way—a side of him one doesn't often see—as he greeted this overflow crowd: "I'm very grateful for you being here. I'm grateful for this expression of support. And I can tell you we've come a long way since I met the 1,203-pound pig named 'Big Red' at the Iowa State Fair and then enjoyed a pork chop on a stick, followed by a delicious deep-fried Twinkie," McCain said to huge laughs from the crowd.

The fact that key surrogates showed up in the bitter cold meant a lot to McCain. Lindsey Graham joked that it was in the 80s in his native South Carolina and that he was the only person on the plane to frigid Iowa. McCain joked that they had brought a translator so Iowans could understand Graham's southern accent.

McCain electrified the crowd here and then promised to stay around and shake hands with every volunteer and to pose for pictures, as long as it took. When you have no money, you have to get creative in securing votes. Indeed, McCain greeted everyone present.

An hour later, we had to bolt to a Des Moines banquet hall to see John Edwards and hear a free concert by his supporter, singer John Mellencamp. Celebrity endorsements generally bore me to tears, but a free concert isn't a bad gig in a campaign where you hear a lot of the same speeches over and over again.

Finally, after Mellencamp sang and after Edwards's cancer-stricken wife Elizabeth spoke, the candidate delivered his speech. You got the feeling the former Senator had been upstaged, but he made his case like the seasoned trial lawyer he is. "Beginning in the heartland of America, right here in Iowa, you're going to rise up, stand up and say to America, 'Enough is enough. We want our country back. We want our democracy back'," said Edwards to nearly three thousand people gathered in the Val Air Ballroom, a classic bowling-alley-type wooden ballroom, where you could imagine union meetings being a popular attraction. It was packed. We had to park four blocks away and climb five-foot snow banks in the freezing cold, but we got in. This was classic small-town, big-time Americana politics.

Then it was off to see Bill and Hillary Clinton at the State Historic Society in downtown Des Moines. As fast as we drove, we got there just as it was wrapping up. The crowd was huge; and, not too surprisingly, more people were lining up to shake Bill Clinton's hand than Hillary's. Despite the impeachment, despite whatever other White House "baggage" he has, Bill Clinton is tremendously popular in Democratic circles, even more so than his wife. I wondered about this. We had just seen Elizabeth Edwards unintentionally upstage her candidate husband, and now Bill Clinton was doing the same thing to Hillary. I wonder if we just have a natural empathy toward political spouses. Their jobs, in many respects, are tougher and less rewarding than those of the candidates.

As we left the building by a side entrance, we found a garage with its door open and two big SUVs backed in. We assumed it was the Clinton motorcade, so we set up the camera and got ready to videotape. With that, a swarm of Secret Service and police descended upon us and told us to stop filming or be arrested. They didn't want the Clintons' security detail made public. Our protests got us nowhere and, rather than spend the night in a freezing Des Moines jail, we just packed up and left. It was pretty heavy-handed treatment, though, in a country that prides itself on the First Amendment. That said, tonight a frigid hotel room sounded much better than jail. Who would bail us out anyway?

Thursday morning we got up and did a number of TV and radio appearances; and then we had a whole day to kill. The actual caucuses would not meet until 7 p.m. The Iowa Convention Center in downtown Des Moines was the pulsing heart of the state. The Democratic Party was headquartered there; and, in some of the smaller rooms, members of the GOP were gathering for TV-watching parties. This was great for us, because there was no shortage of people to interview, including the candidates.

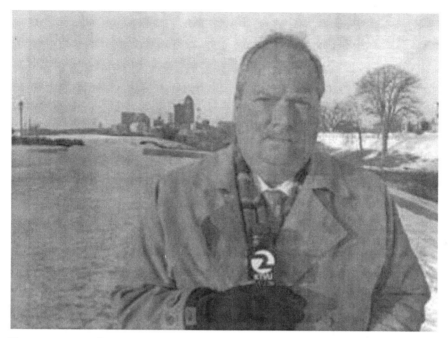

Figure 3. Mark Curtis reports "live" from Des Moines, Iowa, for KTVU, Jan. 3 2008.

Our station, KTVU, in Oakland, wanted us on "The 10 O'clock News," which is the station's marquee newscast. Of course, that meant we would be on at midnight Central Time, and by then the caucuses would be long over. The station would do the "nuts and bolts" of the results, while our job was to focus on why the small state of Iowa has such a huge impact on the national election, and whether that is fair.

Not a minute after we received our assignment by cell phone, I saw Iowa's Democratic Governor, Chet Culver, walking our way. He was all alone. No security, no entourage, no "Arnold Schwarzenegger aura" that we get in California. In fact, Iowa was so "folksy" I just yelled out, "Hey, Governor, can you talk to us right now?" He smiled and headed our way. It was just amazing! Had I tried a similar stunt in downtown San Francisco, I would have been laughed at by fellow reporters or pounced upon by security, or both.

9

I explained that we were doing the "small state, big influence story," a theme that is controversial, but nothing new to him. He answers questions about it all the time. Iowans are very proud of their role in elections, even if the rest of the country is angry about it.

"We vet the candidates. This is kind of like spring training [in baseball]," Governor Culver said. "You've got to put these candidates through the test to see if they are ready to compete on the national stage," he added.

Many candidates "die" here and never get beyond the Iowa voters. Many Democrats said this year, "There are only three tickets out of Iowa," meaning the top three vote getters would make the cut, and everyone else would be gone. Republicans had a bit of a wider field; and some, like former New York Mayor Rudy Giuliani, did not even bother to compete here. So was it fair that Californians and Pennsylvanians never got to give Senator Chris Dodd or Governor Bill Richardson a fair shot? Probably not, but that's the system we have.

The caucus itself was fascinating. I had never seen it before. We showed up at a community center on the fringe of downtown Des Moines, and it wasn't long before the action was underway. What started out looking like a civil PTA meeting, looked more like a professional wrestling "battle royal" twenty minutes later.

The rules were fairly simple. You needed at least 15 percent of the voters present to remain viable. In other words, if there were a hundred delegates in all, but only eight for Senator Dodd, he would no longer be viable; and people from other campaigns could lobby those eight to join their sides. Think of the classic kid's game, "Red Rover, Red Rover, let Barb come over," when that player would run from one side of the yard to her new team.

As soon as each camp announced the number of delegates present, the "bidding" began. It was clear from the start that Obama, Clinton and Edwards each had enough delegates to stay in the race for good. For them, it became more a matter of winning the whole thing, so those sides were very vocal in wooing delegates from candidates who were no longer viable.

It looked like absolute chaos and bedlam, but organizers in Iowa clearly knew what they were doing. "Iowans take this very, very seriously," said John Edwards's supporter and caucus organizer Andrea Vitzthum. "I think that—unlike in many states—it isn't who has the most money. It isn't who runs the most commercials," she added.

She was right. Organization was king! After months and months of candidates' coffees in people's living rooms or at union halls, tonight was "where the rubber met the road." Campaigns had to get their delegates out to caucuses, or it was over.

As soon as the caucus was underway, the shouting began. An Obama organizer began looking in the Edwards campaign for people to switch sides. Two Edwards supporters shouted him down. "That's the wrong way," yelled one. "Get outta here. Bye!" shouted the other.

Twenty minutes later, the Obama supporter was standing on a chair yelling to others that he had some new converts to their side. "Four! Four!" he shouted, telling his helpers how many new delegates they had. "One more after that," he yelled, as another turncoat joined the Obama camp.

Within about ninety minutes, it was all over; and the precinct captains called in the totals to party headquarters. This was hard for those running the show, and it was hard work just trying to observe and to keep track of who was ahead. At 9 p.m. we still had a long night ahead of us. For those who finished poorly, it was frustrating.

Many Iowans get to meet the candidates face to face, and they believe that if more people had such an opportunity some of the "dark horse" candidates would have a better shot. In person, a candidate can go from being a name on a bumper sticker to being a fellow human being. "Absolutely, you do get a sense of that when you meet them face to face," said Ron Paul supporter Sebastian Villarreal. We caught up with him at a Ron Paul rally at Des Moines College, where the candidate gave a health care reform speech and really worked the crowd. "I've met Ron Paul twice, and he's a very genuine person," Villarreal said. "I think he's for real, and you do get that sense when you meet him," he added.

In the end, Iowa sent a shock wave through the political world. Not only did Mike Huckabee upset Mitt Romney here, but John McCain actually finished fourth. With his campaign on the ropes, New Hampshire now became a "do or die" state for McCain.

The same was true for the Democrats. With Barack Obama's bruising victory in Iowa and a second-place finish by John Edwards, Senator Hillary Clinton had to do well in New Hampshire in just five days, or her campaign would be done, too.

One of the central questions, at least for the Democrats, was whether the Iowa winner would be a runaway nominee. Obama's win was historic, and his victory speech one of the best ever I heard in thirty years of covering politics.

Before a rousing crowd, the Illinois Senator said, "They said this day would never come. They said our sights were set too high," he added to wild cheers! He continued: "They said this country was too divided, too disillusioned to ever come together around a common purpose! But on this January night, at this defining moment in history, you have done what the cynics said we couldn't do." The crowd cheered wildly.

Obama didn't have to state the obvious—that Iowa, a state that is 97 percent Caucasian, had just given 38 percent of its Democratic vote to an African-American. It was, in fact, historic and had everyone wondering whether he could recreate this amazing phenomenon across America. There's an old adage in the world of radio and marketing: "If it will play in Peoria, it will play anywhere."

Granted, we were a few hundred miles away from central Illinois; but—trust me—Peoria and Des Moines have a lot in common. Tonight everyone was wondering if we, as a nation, were on the verge of picking a black President.

The racial and gender issues aside in this campaign, we were also seeing the emergence of one of America's great new political orators. They don't come along very often. In the twentieth century we heard the likes of Franklin Roosevelt, John F. Kennedy and Ronald Reagan—men who could seemingly move mountains with words. Now Obama was on the horizon as another great political speaker in the infancy of a new millennium.

There was unity and symmetry and even poetic tone to his speaking style. This was a man who had spent a lot of time in church, listening to preachers speak in cadence. It's a style not unique to the African-Americans, but they probably use it more often and better than others. Call it the "preacher-politician" style of speaking, if you will. Martin Luther King, Jr., was the best at it. Jesse Jackson had the knack, too. But in 2008, the nation was suddenly captivated by Barack Obama, "the son of a black father and a white mother," as he often described himself, who could spellbind the public with his speaking style, as well.

"In lines that stretched around schools and churches, in small towns and in big cities, you came together," Obama said, "as Democrats, Republicans and Independents, to stand up and say that we are one nation, we are one people, and our time for change has come!" The crowd cheered loudly again. Obama had to wait a full fifteen seconds for calm before he could continue. His supporters were in a frenzy.

"We are choosing hope over fear. We are choosing unity over division," he said. "We are sending a powerful message that change is coming to America!"

John Edwards, Hillary Clinton and Bill Richardson promised to fight on, but word came that Senators Chris Dodd and Joe Biden were "hanging it up" after Iowa. A Reuters-C-Span-Zogby poll taken January 5 had Obama up thirteen points in New Hampshire. A CNN-WMUR TV poll had him up nine points. A runaway victory by Obama on January 8 could mean the end of Hillary Clinton and the rest of the Democrats. The "one-two" punch of Iowa and New Hampshire wins could make an Obama nomination inevitable.

At this point, it looked more as if the Republicans would have the epic primary battle that could lead to a brokered convention. McCain was up in the New Hampshire polls, perhaps surging ahead of Mitt Romney. The former Utah resident turned Massachusetts Governor, was still popular out west. Polls had him up in Nevada.

Heading into New Hampshire, we were facing the possible end of the Democratic race and the possibility we would have a different GOP winner in each of the first three contests. The long-term prospect was unity for Democrats, division and disarray for Republicans. Little did we know the political world (also known as the voting public) was about to turn all of us pundits on our heads.

The day ended for me with a glass of wine at 2:30 in the morning, and a 6 a.m. "wake up" call on the way. When I did arise three-and-a-half hours into my "nap," Hillary Clinton was already "live" on CNN, speaking at a rally in Manchester, New Hampshire. She must have flown the "red eye" from Iowa. Here she was, undaunted by a third-place finish in the cold Midwest. She was now in New Hampshire, hoping for a comeback, even though another poll showed her behind by seventeen points.

I don't know what drives the candidates, or how they do it. Hillary Clinton's day was just as long mine and probably a lot more stressful. I was exhausted and barely able to get out of bed in West Des Moines. She was already in New Hampshire, with fire and energy in her speech, to boot.

You have to really want to live in the White House to submit yourself to this self-torture. I wouldn't run for the job, but I love watching and writing about those who do! On to New Hampshire!

Chapter 2: The New Hampshire Primary

I woke up in Des Moines, Iowa, on Friday, January 4, after only three and a half hours of sleep. I was exhausted! It had been a two-day marathon of campaign coverage in freezing temperatures; and I was beginning to think the candidates, their staffs and the press corps that covers them were all completely nuts.

My opinion seemed justified when I turned on the TV. Hillary Clinton was already speaking "live" at a campaign rally in New Hampshire! She appeared fresh, looked good and was really hitting her stride as she delivered her stump speech before an enthusiastic outdoor crowd. She certainly did not look like the candidate who just had her "butt kicked" the night before in Iowa. So many people had presumed that Clinton was the inevitable nominee—the heir apparent—that her stunning loss in Iowa sent shock waves through her entire campaign. Various polls had Clinton in the lead around Thanksgiving, 2007; but six weeks later her momentum had vanished. In fact, Obama had won by eight percentage points over John Edwards, with Hillary Clinton a razor-thin, third-place finish. This was supposed to have been a coronation, not a nomination, and Barack Obama had just interrupted the procession.

The morning after the caucuses many of us were struck by a profoundly unexpected thought. Iowa is a state that is 95 percent white. Despite this, 38 percent of Iowans had chosen Obama, an African-American Senator from neighboring Illinois. Was this the start of something revolutionary in American politics? David Gergen, a former advisor to Presidents Nixon, Ford, Reagan and Clinton, thought so. "For Barack Obama, this is a personal triumph," Gergen told CNN. "For an African-American to go into a state that's 95 percent white and win against Mrs. Clinton is an absolutely remarkable victory," he added.

I, of course, was stuck in Iowa for another day. I felt as though the train had left the station without me. I needed to be in New Hampshire, but my flight wasn't for another twenty-four hours. I also had to make TV and radio appearances wrapping up the Iowa Caucuses, a story that already seemed stale mere hours after the vote. This taught me an important lesson. It was the first and the last time during the campaign that I would be caught a day behind, seemingly in the "wrong" town. The campaigns just surge ahead at lightning speed. They seem to be in their own time zone and on their own momentum.

The news was not good for Hillary Clinton, despite her energy and enthusiasm. Post-Iowa polls in New Hampshire now showed her trailing Barack Obama, including one by Reuters/C-SPAN/Zogby that had her down by thirteen points. Even CNN had Clinton behind Obama by nine points. The primary was just four days away.

On the other hand, things looked better for John McCain. Despite his finishing a distant fourth in Iowa, polls were showing him pulling ahead in New Hampshire, where he simply had to win, or his campaign was probably over. The ever optimistic Reuters/C-SPAN/Zogby poll had McCain up by nine points over former Massachusetts Governor Mitt Romney, who had hoped his neighboring-state status would help his cause. The Rasmussen Poll had McCain ahead of Romney by just one point. This was going to be another showdown!

I left Iowa for New Hampshire on Saturday, with a stopover in Chicago to change planes, and I ran into friends from Fox News Channel and CNN on the connecting flight. It was like a reunion from my days working in Washington and added to my excitement as we headed for New Hampshire. The number of foreign reporters also on our flight was staggering.

The Granite State was a welcome sight. While temperatures had hovered near zero in Iowa, it was a balmy fifty-seven degrees my first day in Manchester. Deep snow was on the ground, but streets were nicely plowed; and it looked everywhere like a New England postcard, except that volunteers and campaign signs were seemingly on every corner. When I ducked into J.W. Hills Sports Bar and Grille for a bowl of authentic local clam chowder, the campaigners were there in force, also.

Here I met Jim Stevens, a Steelworkers' Union rep from New York City. When I told Jim I was from the San Francisco area, he told me he had grown up in San Jose. Either way, Jim was a long way from home. So why was he in Manchester in the dead of winter?

Stevens was here supporting Democrat John Edwards for President. "He's right on the issues for people who work for a living," Stevens said. "Pensions, health care, tough restrictions on NAFTA. It rings true to us." Stevens told me that his daughter is a schoolteacher and a union member. "I'm up here because of my daughter," he said.

At the very next table was a Republican contingent surrounding South Carolina Senator Lindsey Graham, who was there to back John McCain for President. Noting their competing T-shirts, the two tables playfully sparred back and forth, with me standing in the middle like a referee. I was glad they were courteous and not throwing things!

On a more serious note, Senator Graham explained why he was backing John McCain. "He's just the right person, at the right time, with the right qualities for this country," Graham told me. Both Senators are military veterans; and Graham said McCain's Navy experience, including his five years as a POW, made him uniquely qualified to run the war on terrorism, including the ongoing conflicts in Iraq and Afghanistan.

I had just spoken to Senator Graham four days earlier in Iowa. The accessibility reporters had to the candidates and to their top surrogates was tremendous. Graham had just happened to sit down at the table next to mine in a restaurant, but he was more than willing to interrupt his own lunch to talk with a reporter and to pose for pictures with other patrons. This was a good example of the "retail politics" to which Ronald Reagan often referred. The folksy, cordial, intimate campaigns of Iowa and New Hampshire certainly couldn't be duplicated in big states such as California, Florida or Texas, but I appreciated the relaxed informality while I had the chance.

Despite New Hampshire's small size, getting around wasn't exactly easy. Thank God, a friend had given me a portable GPS as a gift. I ate my delicious hot clam chowder, chased it with a cold beer, and said my goodbyes to Senator Graham and the union boys. I had to get to an afternoon Barack Obama rally at the famed Pinkerton Academy in Derry.

After driving around in circles—lost, despite the GPS—I finally found the school. It seems the New England "roundabouts" even confuse a high-tech satellite tracking system (or maybe the problem was just the operator!).

In any event, cars were parked along the streets and in lots stretching for several blocks around. I walked at least a mile, but fortunately the day was mild and partly sunny. When I entered the school, two things struck me. This was the first rally for any candidate where I was searched by Secret Service agents, and my briefcase full of computer and electronic gear was checked by bomb-sniffing dogs. The very real possibility of an African-American candidate winning the Presidency had elicited threats, and they had to be taken seriously. At this point in the race, no other candidate was getting this kind of protection. The security measures were both frightening and impressive.

Inside the gymnasium, the atmosphere was electrifying. The audience was jam packed, shoulder-to-shoulder. Many people had waited inside for an hour and a half, as Obama was running late. Once he arrived, the roar of the crowd was deafening. "In two days time, New Hampshire, it is your turn to stand up and create a different kind of politics," Obama said, to wild applause. He was clearly hoping his momentum from the win in Iowa would carry him to victory here, as well.

I was blown away by the Obama rally, both by its massive size and by its contagious enthusiasm. It was the first time in the campaign when I genuinely thought, "This guy might just win!"

Figure 4. Barack Obama campaigns in Rochester, New
Hampshire, Jan. 7, 2008. (Jamie Dupree, Cox Radio)

The contrast could not have been sharper hours later at a rally for Hillary Clinton at Winnecunnet High School in Hampton. The place was only about two-thirds full; and the crowd—by comparison with that at the Obama rally—was almost lethargic. Surprisingly, Clinton began criticizing President Bush, and not her main challenger, Barack Obama. "Bush really premised so much of our foreign policy on his personal relationships with leaders, and I just don't think that's the way a great country engages in diplomacy," she said.

The partisan crowd applauded her criticism of President George W. Bush and Russian President Vladimir Putin, but this struck me as an odd tactic for a woman on the ropes in her political bout with Obama. It was Obama that she needed to defeat, not a termed-out, unpopular president. The reporters with whom I was gathered were in agreement. This was a very weak showing compared to Obama's rally a few hours earlier. Clinton seemed tired and unenthusiastic. She needed something huge to change the momentum. As the sun set on Sunday's campaign blitz across the state, little did we realize that we were less than twenty-four hours away from a "game-changing" event.

Monday morning, just a day before people in New Hampshire would cast their votes, Hillary Clinton gathered with a small group at Café Espresso in Portsmouth. With TV cameras rolling, one of the women asked Senator Clinton how she keeps up with the day-to-day campaign grind. "It's not easy, it's not easy," Clinton said shaking her head. At that point, her eyes became watery, as she appeared to fight back tears. "I couldn't do it if I didn't just passionately believe it was the right thing to do," she said. "I have so many opportunities from this country, and I just don't want to see us fall backwards as a nation. This is very personal for me. It's about our country; it's about our kids' futures; it's really about all of us together," she added, with her voice cracking.

This was a Hillary Clinton we had not seen before. Stoic through her husband's indiscretions and impeachment, she had never cracked. "Some of us put ourselves out there and do this against some pretty difficult odds; and we do it, each one of us, because we care about our country," Senator Clinton said. Perhaps the tough loss in Iowa was still on her mind, as she went on: "As tired as I am—and I am—and as difficult as it is to try to keep up what I try to do on the road," she said, "I just believe so strongly in who we are as a nation.... so I'm going to do everything I can to make my case and leave it to the voters to decide."

This was a huge and unexpected development. Hillary Clinton, choking and holding back tears, was showing one of the rare emotional moments of her public life. Was this the beginning of her comeback, or the end?

That video was all over the place. Word of the story and Clinton's emotional reaction spread across New Hampshire like wildfire. The video was played over and over on local TV, not to mention the networks and cable news channels. This was high drama. There was speculation that she was acting; there was speculation that it could bring her down like Senator Ed Muskie's emotional defense of his wife back in the 1972 primary; and then there was speculation that this could be the event that showed Hillary Clinton's humanity, launching her to victory here and perhaps beyond. Hillary's "cry" would be simply the talk of New Hampshire for the ensuing twenty-four hours, right through primary day.

Hillary Clinton's final New Hampshire appearance was Monday night inside a huge airplane hangar at the Manchester International Airport. It was clear that the momentum from the tearful incident earlier in the day had energized her. She was also on stage with daughter Chelsea and husband Bill. The hangar was rocking, and the sound boomed and bounced off the metal walls. While her Sunday event that I had attended in Hampton had seemed flat and uninspired, this was just the opposite. As I would often observe, she was different when her family was present. In many respects, Bill Clinton is still the more popular politician, somewhat overshadowing his wife. Chelsea is fascinating, simply because we knew so little about her growing up. Sometimes they dwarf Hillary; but more often they energize her. Given their volatile family history, this just blows me away.

When Senator Clinton finally addressed the crowd, she talked about the qualities needed in the next President. She started to say, "I know what it will take...," and suddenly a man yelled from the previously quiet crowd, "A woman!" The audience erupted in raucous cheers! The place just went bananas! It was the line of the night, and anything else Hillary said after that just paled. I thought, "This just might mark the eve of her comeback!"

For Barack Obama, all of a sudden, Hillary was a tough act to follow. The Clinton story was now dominating the headlines, and Obama needed to regain the momentum. There was little time left. Obama's last appearance of the day was a 10 p.m. rally at Concord High School, near the Capitol. He did not disappoint!

The whole point of timing the rally at 10 p.m. was to get local TV stations and those from Boston to carry the event live on their late-night newscasts. The big cable news networks would also be broadcasting live. This was intended to be the last, lingering impression many New Hampshire voters would have before going to bed, waking up, and voting the next day.

When I arrived just minutes before the rally, the building was jumping. The Secret Service was not amused that I was so late getting there to be searched and cleared, but it appeared I was the final reporter who would be allowed in. This would become a common occurrence for me throughout the campaign. It's tough working as a freelancer without the luxury of being chauffeured around like the big-media people.

Figure 5. John McCain campaigns in Concord, New Hampshire, Jan. 7, 2008. (Mark Curtis)

I didn't care. To get to Obama's rally, I had to race from the Clinton rally at the Manchester Airport, where my rental car was parked a good mile away. My heart was pounding. I raced to Concord like a scene from "The Rockford Files" and paid a convenience store clerk $10.00 to let me park in his lot, right across the street from Concord High School. Had we not forged a bargain (I filled up my tank and bought snacks, too), I would have had to park miles away again and walk! You do what you have to do to succeed in the new media world. This was the road trip of a lifetime!

As I approached the school, there was a cute, but melting, snowman. He was wearing a red T-shirt that said, "Make Global Warming a Priority!" An "Obama for President" sign stood to his right. This was a great photo op! Click! Flash! That picture would go on my blog. The ability to instantly upload pictures onto the internet was really catching on with me. I loved it!

James Brown's classic, "Living in America," was blasting on the public address system, and people in the crowd were singing along. Finally, with a large "Change We Can Believe In" banner behind her, Michele Obama introduced her husband. As Barack Obama took the stage, the place went crazy. "We can come together as Democrats, Independents and Republicans. Cast aside the same old polarizing politics of the past," he said firmly, as the crowd cheered in approval.

The Illinois Senator noted that young people in Iowa had voted in the same percentages as senior citizens. Historically in America, older folks turn out at the highest rate; those in their teens and 20s, at the lowest rate. If this new trend continued and if younger voters continued to show up at the polls, it struck me that Obama could ride that wave to the White House. All he had to do was sustain the interest, enthusiasm and momentum of young voters. That's no easy task!

Monday was also a busy day for the Republican candidates. I caught up with Mitt Romney's campaign at a Rotary Club meeting at the Nashua Country Club. Once again I had to park a mile away and walk in, but it was a beautiful day, albeit a bit chilly. I ran into a lone protester outside, dressed in a porpoise outfit with a sign identifying him as "Flip Romney! – Say Anything to Win!" It was a hysterical satire, based on the old TV show "Flipper," and was clearly intended to suggest that Romney "flip-flopped" on various issues—once again, good political theatre.

Inside, Rotarians welcomed Romney with their traditional "Hello Song!" The place was packed with Romney supporters, curious club members and droves of reporters, many of them from overseas. I asked a reporter from Hungary why she was there; and she said, "This is the greatest election ever. People overseas really care about this. What happens here matters in Europe."

Romney went through a very methodical power-point presentation, with slides changing on a big screen as he spoke. He talked of his experience as a businessman, in government, and in the nonprofit sector.

"In business you either change and improve, or you go out of business," Romney said. "Change is a lot harder in government," he added. "If ever there was a time we need a change in Washington, it's now. Washington's broken." His comments were met with polite applause; but the presentation struck me as more suitable for a college lecture than a campaign rally.

Highly noticeable was the number of times Romney used the word "change." Ever since Barack Obama won Iowa just days earlier on the theme, "Change You Can Believe In," all the other candidates were working the word "change" into their campaign mantras. Signs at Hillary Clinton rallies now read, "Ready for Change." To me, they all sounded like copycats. Why couldn't they do something original? Why was there this propensity to mimic the frontrunner? I've yet to see that work in thirty years of covering politics.

Romney said that in all the town hall meetings he had attended, people kept asking the same question: "Why does Washington, DC, fail to act?" Romney's response: "I'm going to Washington to change things." Romney was clearly counting on the people in New Hampshire to remember his days as Governor of neighboring Massachusetts, as well as his successful stint as President of the Winter Olympics in Salt Lake City.

Meanwhile, this was a crazy day for me and my one-man news operation. I was done with the Romney event in Nashua, but had to get to Concord, about fifty minutes away, for a McCain rally on the steps of the Capitol building. My entire campaign coverage was like this, ricocheting from rally to rally, from town to town in my rental car, like a pinball in an arcade game. I also had to eat lunch, which usually meant visiting a "drive-through" and speeding up the Interstate with double-cheeseburger and fries precariously resting on my dashboard. Thank goodness for the "blue tooth" in my ear, as my phone rang constantly.

My network friends did not have to work like this. At CNN and Fox, for example, each candidate was assigned a network reporter. Not me. I had to cover "all candidates, all the time!" It was the "Wild West," of "new media" coverage on the internet. It was a bit stressful and dangerous, but exciting and exhilarating at the same time.

On the lawn of the New Hampshire Capitol, I was greeted by my longtime friend and colleague, Jamie Dupree, of Cox Radio. The two of us had attended the University of Florida together twenty-four years earlier. We had also worked together at Cox in Washington and on various campaign stops over the course of the past fifteen years. We kept in constant contact on the trail by cell phone and email. With radio stations in Atlanta, Orlando, Jacksonville, Hartford, Dayton and Tulsa, Jamie had his hands full. Like me, he was blogging daily and posting internet articles and photos. We literally worked on about four hours of sleep per day, if that much. We were insane to work like this, but we also had a front-row seat to history. We were getting an amazing ride!

The McCain rally was packed with his supporters and with hecklers from the Ron Paul campaign standing on six-foot-high snow banks behind us. It was McCain's last broad pitch to voters here. He had won the New Hampshire Primary in 2000, only to lose the nomination to George W. Bush. A loss this time, on the heels of a fourth-place finish in Iowa, would likely doom his campaign.

A poll in October 2007, had Mitt Romney ahead in New Hampshire by thirteen points, but by early January McCain had pulled slightly ahead in most polls. Romney was spending millions of dollars of his personal fortune on the race. McCain, who was broke by the summer of 2007, was still on a shoestring budget, but had high name recognition. This was a fight to the finish. Mike Huckabee, who just days earlier won in Iowa, was not really a factor in New Hampshire. The man known after September 11 as "America's Mayor," Rudy Giuliani, was nearly invisible. This would haunt his campaign to the end.

McCain stood with his wife Cindy and a flock of supporters on the Capitol steps in Concord. He touted his military service and foreign policy credentials as his biggest assets. "I can lead this nation in difficult times," said McCain, who spent five years as a prisoner-of-war in Vietnam. McCain cited recent international problems, including the assassination of Prime Minister candidate Benazir Bhutto in Pakistan and a recent U.S. clash with the Iranian military, as examples. "I know how to handle the Iranians," he said. The partisan crowd cheered its approval.

Tuesday morning the voting began. Historically in New Hampshire, voters in the tiny northern town of Dixville Notch cast their ballots at midnight. It's high drama and great political theatre, but it really has no bearing on what the rest of New Hampshire does. Still, it's a fun ritual. Barack Obama took seven votes in the Democratic Primary, with two for John Edwards and one for Bill Richardson. Hillary Clinton was shut out. On the GOP side, John McCain won with four votes; Mitt Romney received two; and Rudy Giuliani, one.

Elsewhere across the state, people were voting in droves. The weather was sunny and unseasonably warm. With a wide-open race on both sides of the aisle, a record turnout was likely.

Voting day also marked the beginning of the controversial role Bill Clinton would play in this campaign. At a Monday rally at Dartmouth College, the gloves came off as the former President launched the first of his well-publicized attacks on Obama. Clinton complained that reporters appeared spellbound by Obama's charisma and did not question Obama's claim that he was the only Democratic presidential candidate consistently opposed to the war.

"It is wrong that Senator Obama got to go through fifteen debates trumpeting his superior judgment and how he had been against the war," Clinton said. "There's no difference in your voting record and Hillary's, ever since," Clinton said. "Give me a break. This whole thing is the biggest fairy tale I've ever seen."

In an earlier speech, Bill Clinton also referred to Obama as a "kid," a reference that offended some African Americans. As I watched CNN for reaction on primary day, I was struck by comments from Donna Brazile, who once ran Al Gore's Presidential campaign. "For him to go after Obama, using "fairy tale," calling him "a kid," as he did last week— it's an insult," said Brazile, "and I tell you, as an African-American, I find his words and his tone to be very depressing," she added.

I later spoke with former White House Press Secretary Tony Snow for his take on why Hillary Clinton's campaign struggled so in the early months. He blamed her troubles on former President Bill Clinton. "Her rapscallion husband. He should shut up." Snow said, "*She's* running for President." Later he added, "Bill Clinton is a wedge politician," and suggested the Clintons were subtly playing the "race card" against Barack Obama.

This was the first public injection of racial politics into this campaign, and I was stunned. However, at the time this video was broadcast, about 4 p.m. Eastern Time, many in New Hampshire had already voted. Many others were at work, and likely did not see the clip. My sense was that if this video had aired twenty-four hours earlier, it might have sunk Hillary Clinton's chances. Now, because it aired so late, it could still be a factor in other states, but not New Hampshire. My observation would prove to be true later on in the campaign.

Trying to figure out which election night rally to cover was a real coin toss. Obama was going to be at Nashua South High School. McCain was also going to be in Nashua at the Crowne Plaza Hotel. Maybe I could hit both. Hillary Clinton was going to be at the Southern New Hampshire University in Manchester. Mitt Romney was in Bedford. As I've said, I cover everything on my own. Sometimes the schedules work out; sometimes they collide head-on. Tonight was the latter!

I decided that Nashua was my best bet. Both Obama and McCain were going to be in the same city, and both were the leaders in most polls. Trust me; it's always best to go to a political victory rally. A losing rally is like a funeral, especially if it spells the end of a campaign. I arrived at South Nashua High School by about 6:30, an hour before the rally was to begin. There wasn't a parking spot to be found. I looked everywhere, up and down side streets. Nothing. I searched for at least a mile and found nothing. I knew if I tried much longer and had to walk all that distance, I would miss one of the later rallies. For the first time in the campaign, I gave up and left. It turned out be a great stroke of luck.

I headed for the McCain rally, which was across town, just a few miles away. It was dark and getting colder, and I didn't feel like another mile-long hike carrying a bag of heavy equipment. My GPS promptly led me to an abandoned restaurant in Nashua. As I was driving in circles around the building, the Nashua Police pulled me over. This was not my night. People acting odd within a mile of a Presidential candidate get extra scrutiny. Driving circles around a closed and dark building qualified me for some of that special attention. Fortunately, the officer told me I was not the only lost soul. It seems that someone had published the wrong address online. The Crowne Plaza Hotel was right across the street, and he pointed the way.

Luckily, I found a parking spot really close. When I got inside, the party was in full swing, even though the results were not in yet. Bartenders were pouring drinks, and people were having a festive time. I thought, "What if McCain loses?" Well, the bartenders might be doubly busy then. The ballroom was packed. I was jammed in with the other reporters like sardines near the main door. Since I was at the end of the row, I could open my laptop computer, and many others gathered around me as the "live" streaming results came in on the internet.

The technology we have now is amazing. Years ago, we'd be up all night watching people biting their nails. Now, the office of the Secretary of State can hook up a direct feed to major media outlets and, in some places, to the general public. Watching the vote totals and precinct counts update every thirty seconds is pretty amazing. Since I was one of the few with an open laptop and a wireless internet card, I was very popular. I was surrounded by a throng as I kept calling out the returns even faster than the networks could get them on the air.

It wasn't long before John McCain was declared the Republican victor. John McCain won with 37 percent of the vote, to 32 percent for Mitt Romney. Mike Huckabee, who had won in Iowa, was way back in third place with 11 percent. The rest of the pack was in the weeds. On the Democratic side, it was dead even. It was just too close to call, and we were heading for a late night.

The best part of this is that John McCain realized the networks were all his, since they would not be cutting to Clinton or Obama any time soon. After a concession speech by Mitt Romney from across the state, a jubilant McCain took the stage in Nashua.

"My friends, I am past the age when I can claim the noun 'kid,' no matter what adjective precedes it. But tonight we sure showed them what a comeback looks like," said the 71-year-old McCain, as the crowd broke into cheers. "When the pundits declared us finished, I told them, 'I'm going to New Hampshire, where the voters don't let you make their decision for them'," McCain added.

And so New Hampshire chose McCain. He ended his speech with references to his arduous military service and noted that the nomination was far from won—that a long, hard fight lay ahead. "So, my friends, we celebrate one victory tonight and leave for Michigan tomorrow to win another," McCain said, "but let us remember that our purpose is not ours alone. Our success is not an end in itself. America is our cause—yesterday, today, and tomorrow."

Confetti cannons exploded, as balloons fell on the crowd. This was a raucous comeback victory for McCain, whom many pundits had written off months earlier, when he backed the controversial troop surge in Iraq. If that had seemed to signify his political death, New Hampshire marked his resurrection. People in the crowd were beside themselves. This was a mighty celebration.

With my earpiece plugged into my laptop computer, I was walking around the back of the ballroom keeping an eye on the Clinton-Obama race online. Suddenly, someone tapped me on the shoulder and asked who I was and what I was doing. No, it wasn't the Secret Service; it was a producer from French TV. After answering a few questions, I was asked to appear on the French news channel as an American political analyst.

My three years of French classes in high school had long faded from memory. Fortunately they had a translator. The downside was

I had no time to put on makeup, and it had to be a hundred degrees in the crammed ballroom. I was sweating profusely and probably resembled Niagara Falls when the interview began. No matter. I was just glad someone was using my expertise. I had lobbied in vain to be on CNN, Fox, MSNBC and C-SPAN. They were all polite and took my business card, though no one ever called. But hey, French TV? I said, "Oui!" Thus began a longstanding campaign joke. I would tell people I was just like entertainer Jerry Lewis—beloved in France—but unappreciated in America!

The glamour for this star struck reporter did not last long. With the Clinton-Obama race a real nail-biter, I had to get to Manchester as fast as possible. As I was running out of the Crowne Plaza Hotel, I literally ran into my old DC friend, Carl Cameron, from Fox News Channel. We exchanged pleasantries; I handed him my new business card; and I asked to be considered as an analyst on Fox. "Who else have you worked for?" Cameron asked. "I was just on French TV, doing analysis on McCain's win," I said, as a puzzled expression crossed his face. We shook hands, and off I went, knowing that French newscasts are probably not a popular staple in Carl's newsroom. Oh well, I was having a great time.

The ride to Manchester was smooth, and I listened to all-news radio all the way, getting updates on the Clinton-Obama cliffhanger. My heart was pounding, and I was probably driving faster than I should. Southern New Hampshire University is in kind of an odd location. Instead of being downtown, it's seemingly surrounded by miles of residential neighborhoods. As I arrived, police waved me away from the driveway, saying there was no more parking.

I drove a mile and a half down the road across the freeway and found a place to park in a quiet neighborhood. It was dark, but I could tell the area was beautiful. A woman who parked behind me walked with me to the campus. "I know the way," she said. "My daughter goes to school here." The woman was exuberant. By now, the networks had declared Hillary Clinton the winner, 39 to 36.4 percent over Barack Obama. "I can't believe it," she said excitedly. "We might actually have a woman President. I've wanted that for so long, and now I want it for my daughter."

I could tell she was fighting back tears, when our conversation was suddenly interrupted by the wild blare of police sirens seemingly from out of nowhere. As we were about to walk up the University driveway, police stopped us. Senator Clinton's motorcade, including the former President and Chelsea, was arriving. No one was allowed in until after they arrived. It was quite dramatic. Police car after police car sped onto the campus. Huge SUVs pulled in, and their doors flew open, with security agents leaping out everywhere. The Clintons were whisked into the building with all the urgency of a fire drill.

Finally, police allowed the rest of the public and reporters into the building. We were told the gym was filled, and those who arrived late had to go to an equally-packed overflow room downstairs to watch on a giant television screen. I ran into longtime California Democratic Committeeman Bob Mulholland on the way downstairs. The often-quoted and normally chatty partisan would not stop for long. "This is unreal," Mulholland told me, as he pressed to get back inside the main auditorium.

He wasn't kidding. This was a monumental comeback win for Hillary Clinton. She came to the stage just minutes after I got in the building. The crowd was so boisterous and energized that Hillary Clinton could not get a word in edgewise for minutes, except "Thank you! Thank you so much!"

Finally the crowd settled down. "I come tonight with a very, very full heart," Senator Clinton said. "And I want—I want especially to thank New Hampshire. Over the last week, I listened to you; and, in the process, I found my own voice." And with that the crowd erupted in wild cheers again.

"I felt like we all spoke from our hearts, and I am so gratified that you responded," Clinton said. "Now together, let's give America the kind of comeback that New Hampshire has just given me!" The applause rocked the building for another thirty seconds, with chants of "Hil-la-ry, Hil-la-ry," before she could finish.

Now the word "comeback" had been mentioned twice tonight, both by Hillary Clinton and by John McCain. Its significance dates back to 1992, when Bill Clinton came back from a bad defeat in Iowa to finish second in the New Hampshire Primary. He dubbed himself "the comeback kid," knowing his strong finish had saved his campaign.

History was repeating itself tonight for both Democrats and Republicans. I knew, when I walked out of that building, that we were possibly in for one of the greatest, most dramatic, most historic Presidential races in American history.

New Hampshire had in essence decided nothing - except to foreshadow the high drama that would mark this primary battle to the bitter end. I decided, at that moment, I was in for the long haul. The next stop for me would be the Nevada Caucuses on January 19.

CHAPTER 3: THE NEVADA GAMBLE

I am not much of a gambler. I will make a friendly wager on a football game, or put a dollar in a slot machine, or buy the occasional lottery ticket; but, aside from that, I am not a gambler. I lose too much as a matter of course. It's who I am; so Las Vegas is the last place you would probably find me, except that I love the buzz of entertainment, color, neon lights and drama. I won't bet my money on it, mind you; but I love to watch it all play out. So, too, is my love for and fascination with the world of politics.

As my plane landed at McCarran International Airport on January 17, I thought, "When was the last time Nevada played a major role in Presidential politics? Probably never." But 2008 was shaping up as a year like no other. All of a sudden, it appeared that every state mattered, every vote counted.

Two days before I arrived here, Mitt Romney had won the Michigan Republican Primary, with a vote of 39 percent to John McCain's 30 percent. We were on the verge of a standoff. So far there had been three GOP contests: Mike Huckabee won Iowa; John McCain won New Hampshire; and Mitt Romney won Michigan. Romney, a Mormon, who made his name to a large degree in the neighboring Mormon-dominated state of Utah, was a favorite to win Nevada. A victory here could mean big momentum.

For Democrats, the scenario was similar. Barack Obama won Iowa; Hillary Clinton won New Hampshire; and John Edwards might have great appeal in Nevada, where the power of organized labor was growing rapidly. Michigan's primary had essentially been disqualified for Democrats after state officials had violated party rules and moved up the date of its primary. So, Nevada could be the break-out state, at least west of the Mississippi.

South Carolina would be holding its Republican primary the same day, with McCain leading polls there, so the overall momentum was anybody's guess. Democrats in South Carolina would vote the following Saturday, January 26. At this point in the campaign, there was no clear national frontrunner in either party. That meant every state, every vote truly counted more than ever. All of a sudden, Nevada wasn't just a bet maker; it was a deal maker and a potential kingmaker, too!

I got lucky, just by being there. It was freezing when I landed. There had even been some uncharacteristic snow in the desert. I didn't care. This is where the political action was, and I was right in the heart of it.

My flight was an hour late arriving because of the weather, but my luck changed at the car rental counter. I had reserved online and had selected a cheap compact car. None was available. Instead, they took me out in the lot, where the clerk said, "You get a free upgrade. Take your pick." When he waved his arm, he pointed at two Econoline stretch vans that could probably hold ten people each, and then pointed at a fire-engine red Dodge Daytona, with a black convertible top. Oh my! Can you imagine what I picked?

Honestly, the charge was $40 dollars a day. I took the convertible, even though the temperature was below freezing. I knew I'd never put the top down; but, sorry! I was not driving the Las Vegas Strip in a stretch van. No, I was taking the car that reminded me of the ride made famous by Dan Tanna, the private detective in the old TV show "Vegas." I had places to go, people to see. I was going in style!

The first stop was a town hall meeting held by John Edwards in Henderson, just outside of Las Vegas, where he was speaking mostly on economic issues. This was a day that the Dow Jones dropped another 300 points, and concerns were raised again about a recession. "In the richest country in the world, it's just wrong that we have 47 million Americans without health care and millions more worried about losing the care they have," said Edwards. "Most families are one bad break, such as a lost job or a serious illness, away from going right off a cliff."

That sentiment hit home for many in the crowd. Nevada had the highest rate of home foreclosures in the nation. Despite the massive growth of Las Vegas, unemployment was up here, too. There was also a large migrant, minority workforce, many of whom would be voting for the first time.

"I'm working for John Edwards because of his stance on the war, health care and women," said precinct captain Norma Price, of Henderson, whom I interviewed after the rally.

Edwards had to leave immediately for a fundraiser in Los Angeles. Hillary Clinton was at campaign fund raisers in Northern California. While Nevada was crucial right now, most of the candidates were focusing on raising money for "Super Tuesday," February 5, when big states—such as California, New York, New Jersey and Illinois—would all be voting.

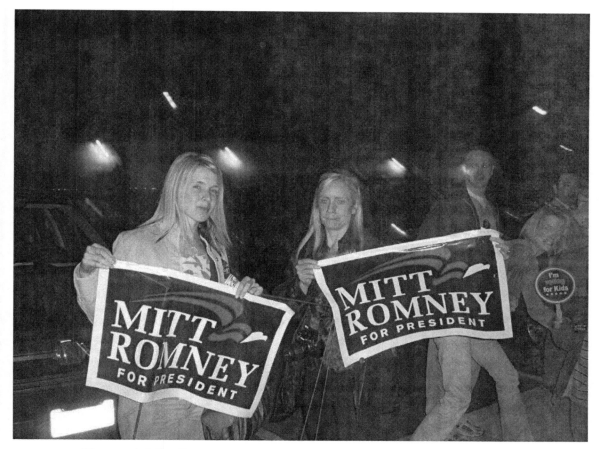

Figure 6. Mitt Romney supporters outside a rally in Las Vegas, Nevada, Jan. 17, 2008. (Mark Curtis)

Polls in Nevada were a mixed bag, confusing the candidates and reporters even further. The latest *Las Vegas Review-Journal* poll had Hillary Clinton at 41 percent, Barack Obama at 32 percent, and John Edwards at 14 percent. That left a critical 12 percent undecided. This poll was somewhat suspect since a *Reno Gazette-Journal* poll this week had it Obama 32 percent; Clinton 30 percent, and Edwards 27 percent.

How could two polls in the same state have such different results in the same week? Well, it has a lot to do with "sampling" and the poll's "population." Reno and Northern Nevada have a more rural, conservative population than Las Vegas. If the papers sample their own markets, but not the entire state, the sample can be skewed. Polls are good only if they pick a representative sample of the entire population.

The lesson for the candidates was that this race in Nevada was wide open! That message was not lost on Barack Obama, who appeared at a rally at Rancho High School in Las Vegas in the late afternoon. In honor of his wife's forty-fourth birthday, he led the crowd in singing "Happy Birthday" to Michelle; but then the rally got more serious.

In a direct attack at Hillary Clinton, Obama mocked her performance in a recent debate. "Folks, they don't tell you what they mean!" Obama said. He was referring to Clinton's comment during the debate that she was happy that a bankruptcy bill for which she had voted in 2001, never actually became law.

"She says, 'I voted for it, but I was glad to see that it didn't pass.' What does that mean?" Obama asked, drawing laughter from the crowd. "No, seriously, what does that mean? If you didn't want to see it passed, then you can vote against it! People don't say what they mean." The crowd laughed more.

This was the first time in the campaign that Obama really took on Clinton, even mocking her. His supporters loved it; I suspect her campaign did not. Clearly, the tone of this Presidential race was getting harsher, as the votes got closer.

On the GOP side, the Las Vegas paper had it Romney 34 percent, McCain 19 percent, Huckabee 13 percent. This was stunning, since the paper's last poll in December had Rudy Giuliani in the lead. Today's poll had him in sixth place! Romney had shifted a lot of his campaign resources to Nevada at the last minute, since it was felt that he could fare poorly in the South Carolina GOP Primary to be held the same day. A Nevada win would "counterpunch" a possible loss to John McCain in South Carolina.

So, Mitt Romney was the only Republican candidate to cover while I was in Las Vegas. He was attracting lots of supporters, including people from neighboring California, who came to help register voters. The interstate travel of campaign workers amazed me and was something I would see eventually at every stop on the campaign trail. Both parties wanted badly to win, and campaign volunteers were willing to travel far and wide to make it happen.

People from around the nation, including the Bay Area of California, were pouring in to help get out the Nevada vote. Claudia Bermudez, a well-known politico from Alameda, California, was here trying to help Republican Mitt Romney. She joined an enthusiastic crowd estimated at one thousand people at Brady Industries Thursday night. She was helping organize, getting people registered, and then planning to work as a poll observer on Election Day.

"He's got a strong economic background, and he has experience in both the public and private sectors," Bermudez told me. She noted Romney's tenure as Massachusetts Governor, his leadership of the 1992 Salt Lake Olympics, as well as his successful private business ventures.

For his part, Romney, fresh off his first primary win in Michigan, told the crowd that many issues were universal to all Americans, not just regional: "People of that state (Michigan) said we do want a middle-income tax cut, and we want our border secure."

One of the big issues simmering in Las Vegas was where people could vote and when. Since the gaming capital of the world is a city that never sleeps, measures were underway to ensure that all workers on the Strip got to vote. These measures proved so controversial, they even divided union workers.

On one side was the Culinary Workers Union, which backed a plan to set up polling places in nine casinos and restaurants on the Strip. That way, workers could easily vote during breaks on their shifts. The Culinary Workers Union was heavily comprised of Hispanics and African-Americans, who—polls indicated—favored Obama.

On the other side was the Nevada State Education Association, which heavily favored Hillary Clinton. The teachers' union felt that if you make special voting provisions for one group, you must make them for all. It wanted a level playing field and took the matter to Federal court.

On Thursday, two days before the caucuses, the judge ruled against the teachers. The special voting locations inside the casinos would be allowed. This was high political drama in a place that usually has very little.

After working all day, I grabbed a quick dinner and then headed for the Stratosphere Casino and Hotel on the Strip, not far from where I was staying. As I said, I am not a big gambler, but I love simple games like slots and video poker. To me, if you have to think about it, it's work and, therefore, no fun. I also had learned that if you looked "busy" enough gambling, drinks would be on the house. As I sat at the bar, playing video poker and sipping Chardonnay, Rick, the bartender, and I talked politics.

"It's amazing to me that you are even here," he said. "In the past, the political parties and the press didn't care about us. We didn't matter." He was really excited and animated as we spoke. Like many others across the nation, he was upset that Iowa and New Hampshire always go first and always wield disproportionate influence. "For the first time that I can ever remember, the votes of Nevada will really count," Rick said.

He was right on the money, and I encountered a similar sentiment in almost every state along the campaign trail. Oftentimes the nominees were chosen very early in the process, after only a handful of states voted. Now, in a very close race in both parties, this was a primary season that could stretch into summer. Every vote, every state might matter!

Figure 7. Barack Obama campaigns at Dillon, South
Carolina high school, Jan. 23. 2008. (Jamie Dupree, Cox
Radio)

I was having the time of my life. This was like a dream, being on the presidential campaign trail with such color and high drama, and driving a low-priced convertible on the Vegas Strip, to boot! I even won $23 dollars in the slot machines and got three free glasses of Chardonnay.

The bubble had to burst, of course. The next morning, as I was getting ready for a TV broadcast in downtown Las Vegas, the cameraman casually asked me where I was staying.

"I'm at the Econo Lodge at the end of the Strip," I said. "Only thirty-five bucks a night!" He turned white as a ghost and said, "Do you know the history of that hotel? That's where the 9-11 hijackers stayed in the weeks before the attacks. They spent their whole time there, ordering pizzas and hookers."

I was pretty "creeped out." It just gave me chills. A *Los Angeles Times* article I found online later confirmed most of the details of what he told me. It had nothing to do with the election, of course, but suddenly my Vegas trip wasn't so glamorous after all. All of a sudden, I looked forward to moving along on the campaign trail.

When the vote was counted on Saturday, the result was mixed. Hillary Clinton won the Nevada Caucus popular vote on the Democratic side, 52 to 45 percent; but, because of the way votes were proportioned geographically, Barack Obama wound up with thirteen convention delegates to Clinton's twelve.

Mitt Romney won on the Nevada Republican slate, but his victory was tempered by John McCain's victory the same day in South Carolina.

As mentioned, the Democrats' primary in South Carolina wasn't until the following Saturday, so whatever perception of victory Hillary Clinton was claiming in Nevada, would likely be short-lived.

John Edwards fared poorly in Nevada, with just 4 percent of the caucus vote. A big loss in his birth state of South Carolina the following week could end his campaign.

The big winner was simply the State of Nevada, itself. It was playing a critical and pioneering role in electing the next President. As we would find out later, that would prove true not only in the primary season, but also in the general election.

CHAPTER 4: THE FLORIDA PRIMARY:

Florida determined the outcome of the 2000 Presidential race, and it generated a controversy that will not soon be forgotten. The Sunshine State is now the nation's fourth most populous and is becoming a "must have" in any race for the White House.

In 2008, controversy was revisiting Florida again. Like Michigan, Florida had decided to move its primary up by a week, so that it might be more influential in the Presidential selection process. That was fine with Republicans, but the national Democratic Party had long warned states that if they violated party rules they would be punished. Having their primary votes thrown out would be the punishment for Michigan and Florida.

Michigan's Democratic primary on January 15 was simply a "beauty contest." Hillary Clinton won the popular vote, but no convention delegates were awarded. In fact, Barack Obama's name did not even appear on the ballot.

Democrats in Florida now faced the same dilemma, and candidates pledged not to publicly campaign in Florida. Yes, the primary vote was still on the ballot; but no delegates would be awarded. Florida's Democratic primary was rendered as meaningless as Michigan's, though this would all become a huge fight again down the road.

My trip to Orlando on Sunday, January 27, was almost exclusively to cover the Republicans. That was okay. There was plenty to talk about.

One of the things that struck me in the early stages of Campaign 2008 was the number of young people who were out volunteering for the campaigns, and voting. It was very apparent in my visits to Iowa, New Hampshire and Nevada, and now it was happening again in Florida. I decided to visit my alma mater, the University of Florida, hoping it might shed some light on why young people were becoming politically active.

Back when I started graduate school in 1984, Ronald Reagan was running for reelection. The popular President was so far ahead of Walter Mondale in the polls that the election seemed almost a formality. It was over before it began. Reagan crushed Mondale 59 to 40 percent. The Republican incumbent took home 525 electoral votes, to Mondale's 13. It was one of the most crushing defeats in U.S. political history. Because it seemed a "done deal" so early in the race, the University's forty thousand students had seemed generally indifferent.

Fast forward twenty-four years and, boy, had things changed! When I arrived at the Reitz Student Union on January 29, 2008, it was a hive of activity. Tables were set up on the outdoor concourse for a variety of candidates.

The Obama table was extremely popular. Marcus Dixon, an African-American public relations and political science student, was manning the volunteer operation. Dixon was trying to sign up fellow supporters. He admitted that he had been torn between Obama and Hillary Clinton, saying they were very close on the issues; but Dixon had settled on Obama. "He's more of a unifying figure and is inspirational," he explained.

Another candidate who really caught the eye of many young voters this year was rebel Congressman Ron Paul, a Republican from Texas. In fact, early in the primaries, it appeared to me that, among the GOP Presidential field, Paul had the most youthful supporters.

Electrical engineering sophomore Eric Maclean was very enthusiastic in his support of Ron Paul and was trying to convince other students. "He's for limited government," Maclean said. "He's for personal freedom, libertarian values, and a free market economy."

There was at least one nonpartisan student in the campus crowd. Political science major Frank Bracco was dressed as "Uncle Sam," while registering fellow students to vote. Reflecting his college major, Bracco simply said, "I believe in it [our American political system]!"

The students all agreed that there appeared to be more enthusiasm among young people this year. Friends and classmates were all talking about politics, a subject many of them had paid little attention heretofore. Now, it was just about all they were talking about.

So far, every state in the primary season was reporting record turnout for voters aged 18 to 24. This fascinated me because the U.S. Constitution was amended at the height of the Vietnam War in 1971, lowering the voting age from 21 to 18. Despite that, youthful voters had turned out in relatively small percentages over the ensuing thirty-seven years. Now that was all changing. The big question in 2008 was whether young people would maintain their enthusiasm and turn out in the same large numbers for the general election in November.

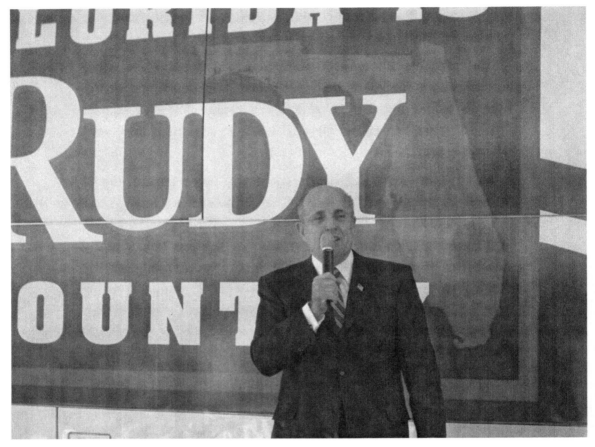

Figure 8. Rudy Giuliani campaigns in Sanford, Florida, Jan. 28, 2008. (Mark Curtis)

In Florida, there was no shortage of issues to talk about, whether you were young or old.First and foremost was the fate of New York City's popular ex-Mayor, Rudy Giuliani. The man, who went from relatively quiet success running the nation's largest city, was thrust into the national spotlight by his handling of the September 11 terrorist attacks. He became a national hero. Indeed, "Time Magazine" had made him its "Man of the Year" for 2001. Pundits started touting Giuliani as a future U.S. President.

It was an amazing revival for the often mercurial Giuliani. He had made his name prosecuting mobsters as a U.S. Attorney; but then he faltered badly in 2000, after a bout with prostate cancer and a very bitter, public divorce. That year, Giuliani had been planning to challenge Hillary Clinton for the open U.S. Senate seat in New York. It was the marquee national race, aside from the race for President. Instead, he opted out of the Senate race, citing his personal problems. Because of term limits, he was in his final year as Mayor. It appeared his career was about to fade into the sunset, but then his response to the September 11 attacks changed all that.

Fast forward six years, and now people were talking seriously about President Giuliani. By the summer of 2007, John McCain's hopes were fading fast; and other candidates, such as Mitt Romney and Mike Huckabee, were not very well known nationally. Rudy Giuliani, on the other hand, was now an American icon. Many polls in 2007 had Giuliani as the clear national frontrunner. In many states, such as Nevada and California, he was way ahead near the end of the year.

Then Giuliani's campaign took a calculated and dangerous political gamble. His handlers decided that Giuliani was probably too moderate-to-liberal a Republican to do well in Iowa, which was fairly conservative. The same situation existed in New Hampshire. So, instead of running a serious campaign in either of the first two states, Giuliani made just a token effort. He decided to pour all of his energy into Florida, a key state that was now home to hundreds of thousands of New York retirees.

Five days before the Florida primary I had dinner with former White House Press Secretary Tony Snow at the annual Contra Costa U.S.A. Dinner in Concord, California. I was the "emcee" and Tony was the keynote speaker. We talked a lot about Rudy Giuliani's risky game plan. Snow called Rudy Giuliani's strategy "a roll of the dice in Florida, a riverboat gamble." Ultimately, Snow thought Giuliani would fail, because he took himself out of the critical Iowa and New Hampshire contests and ultimately out of the media spotlight glaring on both states. "He (Giuliani) made himself irrelevant," Snow said.

The Giuliani plan was to win Florida, hoping the momentum would carry over to "Super Tuesday" the following week, when New York, New Jersey, Connecticut, California and Illinois would be among the states voting. He and his handlers thought he would just surge to victory in many other states, following a tidal wave in Florida.

The problem was that, by the time Giuliani arrived in Florida, the strategy was already backfiring.

To many people, politics is about money. Certainly that's a critical factor; but I have always said that name recognition and momentum are factors that can trump money. There have been plenty of instances where the wealthiest candidate did not win. Raising and spending the most money is not a guarantee of winning public office.

Now, Giuliani had name recognition, but he let it fade. By not participating as a serious candidate in Iowa and New Hampshire, he essentially removed his name from the headlines. He did not run as a viable candidate in Michigan, Nevada or South Carolina, either. Romney, Huckabee and McCain were getting all the press attention. People and reporters were talking about them because they were actively engaged and campaigning. They were at coffees in people's homes; and they were in front of TV cameras on the news at night. You couldn't miss them.

Giuliani, on the other hand, was "out of sight, out of mind!" It was proving to be a disastrous strategy. Instead of looking strong, visible and decisive, as he had in the wake of September 11, Giuliani now looked weak, tenuous and vulnerable. It was one of the most stunning mistakes I had ever seen in all my years of covering politics. He was potentially committing political suicide.

It was with this as a backdrop that many reporters, including me, flocked to the Sunshine State. It was a homecoming for me, too. I had received my Master's Degree from the University of Florida twenty-two years earlier and had worked in radio and TV across the state for nearly nine years. While I hadn't lived there for sixteen years, I visited often. In many respects, Florida is as much home to me as Wisconsin.

One of the first things that impressed me when I attended a rally for Rudy Giuliani on Monday was how many young people were there. It was an impression that would hit me again and again across Florida, and then across the rest of the nation. Something was changing on the American political landscape, and it appeared to be a dramatic rise in political interest and activism among the youngest voters, a trend which I mentioned earlier.

Of course, I was struck by the impact of the celebrity culture, too. The Giuliani rally featured Academy Award-winning actor Jon Voight and Texas Governor Rick Perry, who came to publicly endorse and campaign for "America's Mayor." Voight, a fellow New Yorker, reminded the crowd how Giuliani led his city after the terrorist attacks. "All the world was watching this guy, and we were behind him as Americans," Voight said to loud cheers.

Rick Perry, who had succeeded George W. Bush as the Republican Governor of Texas, praised Giuliani for turning New York City around, saying "He took New York to a jewel from a cesspool." Florida Attorney General and former Congressman Bill McCollum was here, as well, praising Giuliani as a crime fighter. "He cleaned up the mob," said McCollum.

This all sounded good, I thought, but was it a case of too little, too late? Giuliani's campaign bus arrived forty-five minutes late, and many of us in the press corps wondered out loud if this was a metaphor for Giuliani's dying campaign. Many of the reporters at the rally were from New York and were just dumbstruck at how the campaign of their once vaunted Mayor was on the verge of collapse.

Perhaps the most telling sign came from the candidate himself. Giuliani told the crowd, "I am the only one who has reduced taxes." That may have been true, but he was touting his economic record in the wake of a big tumble on Wall Street the previous week. He wasn't talking about fighting terrorism or prosecuting crime figures, the two issues for which he was best known. In an uncertain economy, Giuliani was denied the chance to show off his best assets. That was another devastating blow to his campaign.

There was at least one funny moment. When Giuliani promised to send the first American to Mars, someone in the crowd shouted, "Hillary!" and the rally erupted in laughter. It was the only light moment of the day.

As Giuliani ended his morning speech, he said, "In the past, I've done the impossible, or what people thought was impossible." To win the Florida primary, he was asking the public's help to do the impossible just one more time.

A few hours later, Mitt Romney arrived in Sanford to rally his troops. Approximately six hundred boisterous backers packed an airplane hangar, cheering loudly for the former Massachusetts Governor, who said he cut a $3 billion dollar deficit in his state and created sixty thousand jobs. While praising John McCain as an American war hero, Romney said the Arizona Senator was too much of a Washington insider to get the job done as President. "They said they'd cut back on earmarks and pork-barrel spending. They haven't; we will," said Romney. He then listed a host of other problems Washington needed to address, and the crowded joined in loudly with the call and response, "They haven't; we will."

The immediate irony was that Representative Tom Feeney (R-FL) was standing right next to Romney. The Congressman was there to endorse Romney, while Romney was blaming Congress for many problems. But, that's the art of politics; and Feeney, a former Florida House Speaker, was undaunted, touting Romney's experience as Governor and as President of the Winter Olympics in Utah. "We need somebody like Governor Romney, who turned around a disaster in Salt Lake City. We need a turnaround artist, and that is Governor Romney." The crowd cheered its approval again!

Figure 9. Mitt Romney rally in Sanford, Florida. Jan. 28, 2008. (Mark Curtis)

Romney promised a "Reagan approach to the economy," a reference to former President Ronald Reagan, who remains immensely popular in Florida.

As with my previous campaign stops in Iowa, New Hampshire and Nevada, there was a lot of territory to cover in Florida, with the candidates and rallies spread out everywhere. After the Giuliani and Romney rallies north of Orlando, I met up with my "partner-in-crime," Jamie Dupree, from Cox Radio. There was no point in both of us driving to Tampa to see John McCain and Mike Huckabee, so we rode together. Both of us started our day before sunrise, and we probably would not get back to our hotels until 2 a.m. But who was complaining? This was a political road trip like no other.

John McCain knew it was a fight to the finish in Florida. Various news polls in recent days showed him and Mitt Romney dead even. McCain led in some polls; Romney led in others. The most telling was a composite poll by Real Clear Politics, which was an average of several recent polls. It had the race at 30.7 percent for McCain to 30.1 percent for Mitt Romney. This was about as close as Bush versus Gore in the 2000 General Election and had every possibility of producing another cliffhanger.

As Mitt Romney did earlier in the day, Senator McCain made reference in his speech to the razor-thin margin in the latest polls. "We need you to get out and vote," McCain said to cheering supporters in a dinner-time rally at the Tampa Convention Center.

McCain chose not to attack his GOP rival Romney. Instead his words of anger were directed at Al-Qaeda and Islamic terrorists. "This is the greatest force of evil this nation has ever faced," said the one-time Vietnam prisoner of war. McCain once again promised to "chase Osama bin Laden to the gates of hell" to capture the world's most wanted terrorist. The crowd erupted in cheers. It was a line McCain used often on the stump, and it always brought down the house. No other candidate dared to make such a bold promise, but no other candidate knew evil like John McCain. Those torturous five and a half years he spent as a Vietnam POW were never far from memory.

Florida Governor Charlie Crist invoked them when he introduced the Presidential hopeful. "Ladies and gentleman you know what the facts are. This is an American hero," Crist said of McCain.

"He fought for his country, unlike many of his opponents," said former longtime Tampa Republican Congressman Michael Bilirakis, who also shared the stage.

McCain wrapped up the rally with Ronald Reagan-like optimism. "America's greatest days are ahead of us," he said, knowing that a Florida primary win could propel him with great momentum into

Super Tuesday just eight days away. Super Tuesday featured twenty-four state primaries, and anyone who began that day as a clear frontrunner in either party, might just have the inside track to the nomination. Having lost a tough nomination fight to George W. Bush in 2000, McCain knew a lot about the importance of momentum.

Our next stop in this all-day campaign marathon was a rally for Mike Huckabee inside an airplane hangar near the Tampa airport. This was a typical location. I attended four rallies that day, three of them at airport facilities. Why? Well, in a big state like Florida, candidates have to be virtually everywhere. They might have stops at 8 a.m. in Orlando, 10 a.m. in Tallahassee, 1 p.m. in Miami, 4 p.m. in Pensacola, and 7 p.m. in Tampa, ending the night with a 10 p.m. rally in Jacksonville. The only way you can do that is with what's known as a "fly-around" campaign. Rather than risk getting stuck in traffic, the candidates hold their rallies at the airports and then fly off to their remaining stops. Aviation has literally put the traditional "whistle-stop" train campaign out of business.

Such campaigning has also become a bit more dangerous, with the number of candidates dying in plane crashes on the rise. In recent years, Missouri Governor Mel Carnahan and Minnesota Senator Paul Wellstone both died during campaign fly-arounds. However, the fly-around has become a necessary part of campaigning; and it's not going away.

I was excited to go to Mike Huckabee's rally. Because of all the conflicting campaign schedules, I had yet to see him on this year's Presidential campaign trail.

Figure 10. Mike Huckabee shakes hands in Tampa, Florida. Jan. 28, 2008. (Mark Curtis)

Despite the advantage of being able to fly from rally to rally around the huge state of Florida, Huckabee was still running late. It was the last campaign rally of a very long day, and finally the former Arkansas Governor strolled into the hangar met by a cheering crowd of three hundred supporters. Denying some media reports, Huckabee said flat out, "We have not pulled out of Florida." His supporters went crazy; because there had been rumors he was quitting the campaign. Ever the populist, Huckabee stirred more cheers when he proposed creating a so-called "fair tax" and abolishing the Internal Revenue Service. He spoke of the Tax Code and the IRS being roadblocks, especially to small, start-up businesses. "It's crushing their dreams, crushing their hopes," he said of the Federal tax system.

Huckabee worked the crowd like the Evangelical minister he once was—friendly and warm, with some touching, engaging anecdotes. He mentioned his stands against gay marriage and abortion—positions popular with his followers. Not afraid to speak of his own faith, Huckabee cited the work of the Founding Fathers and how the nation was formed. "It was the hand of a Provident God," he said. "And we should never be ashamed of the heritage of this great land of ours," he added, as people in the crowd shouted enthusiastically.

I was impressed. He was a guy on the ropes, fighting for his political life. Yet he was stating his positions on controversial issues, stances that could cause him more trouble in some quarters. He wasn't afraid to wear his faith on his sleeve, and I found that pretty courageous in the 2008 political environment. He wasn't preachy, though; he was fun and engaging.

Huckabee can work a crowd with the best of them. The fact that both he and Bill Clinton grew up in Hope, Arkansas, and that each later became Governor just astonished me. Were they putting "charm pills" in the drinking water there, or what? Tonight was a critical night for Huckabee. If he could finish well in Florida—perhaps even ahead of Rudy Giuliani—he would survive through Super Tuesday, when Arkansas and many nearby states were holding primaries. After Fred Thompson dropped out, Huckabee was the only true Southerner left. That was "gold," given this nation's political landscape. If Romney dropped out, Huckabee would be the only true conservative left and could mount a challenge to the moderate McCain. This all was very intriguing.

Of course, the biggest challenge to any Republican was winning enough convention delegates. Florida, like many other states, was a "winner-take-all" primary for Republicans. In other words, the first-place finisher took home all fifty-seven delegates, even if the second place finisher lost by only a few votes.

Tuesday was a beautiful day for voting. It was sunny and warm under clear blue skies, and turnout was likely to be huge, at least on the Republican side. Even though the Democrats were holding a "beauty contest," with no delegates at stake, a win in a state as big as Florida offered potential momentum for November, when the votes would actually matter.

After a variety of TV and radio appearances in the morning, I made stops at the University of Florida in Gainesville, and then the headquarters of Newsblues (www.newsblues.com), near Ocala. Newsblues is the TV news industry's leading "gripe" site, where people in the TV business trade all kinds of news, gossip and other happenings, good and bad, on the internet. It is the "water cooler" of the TV news media, and a daily joy to read. For better or worse, I had been featured a number of times; and, even though we had never actually met, I had become acquainted with Mike James and Mona Scott, the husband-and-wife team who run the site. Many TV General Managers and News Directors loathe them, but Newsblues has "given voice to the voiceless" in a very rocky industry.

"Oh my God, you really do look like a political analyst," said Mike James, laughing, as I exited my rental car. I think he was referring to my rather portly figure, not my intellect. I had, over the years, come to resemble some of those frumpy guests on "Capitol Gang" and the "McLaughlin Report," and I wasn't yet fifty. Oh well, I earned it. We all laughed and talked politics over a couple of glasses of wine. Mike and Mona are both former TV anchors, and we lamented how the industry has dramatically changed from good, solid journalism, to rank amateur show business in many markets. Of course, we dissected the Florida primary, too, and the looming downfall of Rudy Giuliani.

Speaking of Giuliani, I had to get back to Orlando for his rally. While I usually go to the winner's rally, McCain was in Fort

Lauderdale; and that was too far to drive. Besides, the possible end of Rudy Giuliani's campaign was the big story of the night.

Racing back to Orlando was another adventure. In a matter of days, I was racking up easily a thousand miles on my rental car—crisscrossing another state, with only a few hours sleep and a long Starbucks tab. It was some kind of ride!

I mentioned earlier that political victory rallies are the best; but losers' rallies are the worst. There are exceptions, though. Giuliani's concession speech was scheduled at the swanky Portofino Bay Hotel in Orlando. It was luxurious and beautiful. It was the nicest hotel of the entire campaign, in my opinion. After rubber-chicken box lunches and airplane hangars smelling of fumes, this was nice!

White-tuxedoed bartenders were setting up portable bars around the ballroom lobby. This looked more like a debutante's wedding than a campaign funeral. I suspected more than just a few Giuliani diehards needed a stiff drink. This was a political meltdown of monumental proportions.

You have to understand: A Florida composite poll from Real Clear Politics on the same day as the New Hampshire primary had Giuliani leading Florida with 27 percent; Huckabee 21 percent; Romney 19 percent; and McCain at 14 percent. That had been only three weeks before the Florida primary; yet tonight the entire poll virtually flip-flopped. In the end, McCain won with 36 percent to Romney's 31 percent. Giuliani finished third with 16 percent, followed by Huckabee at 14 percent.

What happened? I maintain that Giuliani just torpedoed himself by not participating in the Iowa, New Hampshire, Michigan, Nevada and South Carolina contests. The other candidates dominated all the news coverage, and Giuliani was shut out of the headlines. In three week he went from being "America's Mayor" to "Rudy who?" His poll numbers plummeted like a barrel over Niagara Falls. He must have been in absolute shock when he spoke to the Orlando crowd.

"I'm proud that we chose to stay positive and to run a campaign of ideas in an era of personal attacks, negative ads and cynical spin," Giuliani said, as he stood on stage with his wife Judith.

"The responsibility with leadership doesn't end with a single campaign if you believe in a cause. You continue to fight for it, and we will," he said, as teary-eyed supporters applauded. He never actually said he was dropping out, but the handwriting was on the wall.

Now, I had learned a trick along the way in these campaigns. The mainstream press corps is supposed to be in a roped-off area in the back of the room; but I was a guy in a nice suit, with a laptop and tiny digital camera. I looked like a rank-and-file political supporter, so I just hung out in the front of the room near the rope line at most rallies. I would stuff my credentials in my jacket pocket and mingle with the crowd. This gave me great quotes and, best of all, close-up pictures.

When Giuliani was done speaking, I slid up to the rope line, as he and Judith greeted sad supporters. Giuliani shook my hand and thanked me for being there, as I snapped some great close-ups. The guy next to me asked, "Rudy, are you going to California?" This was another way of asking, "Are you staying in the race?" All Giuliani said was, "I got my ticket." After the Mayor moved on, I asked the man what Giuliani meant. "He's going out west to endorse McCain and, at that point, will drop out," he speculated. It was a great tip and something I got online before most network reporters. This was the fun and intrigue of working in "new media." I loved it.

There was a downside to all this, too. No matter how you slice it, it was a sad night. He may have been "America's Mayor," but Rudy Giuliani was a human being, just like the rest of us in that room. Failing at any endeavor can be heartbreaking. I felt very, very sorry for him.

Out in the hall, bartenders were doing a booming business. I was writing my story at a table, having a glass of wine and chatting with the wait staff and Giuliani supporters who came by. Actor Jon Voight came by, too; and one of the waiters (who obviously wanted to be in show business) sang an impromptu Broadway show tune as a kind of mini-audition for Voight. The legendary actor was so impressed that he had the waiter call his parents and then got on the phone himself: "Ma'am, this is Jon Voight calling. I just want to tell you what a talented and wonderful son you have," he said. Either the lady flipped, or just thought it was a prank call. The waiter finally got back on the phone to confirm to his folks that "Yes, it was the real Jon Voight." For those of us within earshot, it was just one of those special fun moments on the campaign trail.

Voight posed with me for a photo, and I asked him if he had any regrets about being so active in Giuliani's failed campaign. "Not at all. It was fun," Voight said, as he made his goodbyes and departed.

McCain made his acceptance speech in South Florida and was starting to look like the Republican frontrunner heading into Super Tuesday the following week.

Perhaps the oddest moment in Florida on this night came when Hillary Clinton addressed a rally in Miami to declare victory. This was a sudden, surprise move by the New York Senator, given that all the Democratic presidential candidates had agreed to boycott Florida; but technically the boycott was over since the primary was done.

Clinton said, "Thank you for this tremendous victory tonight!" as the crowd cheered. Yes, technically she won with 50 percent to 33 for Barack Obama and 14 percent for John Edwards; but no convention delegates were won by any Democrats. It was a symbolic victory for Clinton and a nice public relations coup at the last minute.

Clinton dearly needed some form of victory, though—any victory—to grab onto. Just a day earlier, Senator Ted Kennedy and his niece, Caroline Kennedy, had stunned the Democratic establishment by endorsing Barack Obama for President, blindsiding Hillary. The political drama was never ending!

The next stop was Super Tuesday on February 5, as twenty-four states would hold primaries or caucuses. We were going to get to the real meat of the campaign in just one week.

CHAPTER 5: SUPER TUESDAY

The nice thing about Super Tuesday is that California is the largest state with the most delegates at stake. It also means that instead of traveling, I got to stay right here at home. I love the travel, mind you, but week after week, living out of a suitcase and dealing with airports can get old. Besides, with twenty-four states holding primaries, where else would I go?

A lot was at stake Super Tuesday. In the week leading up to it, two candidates dropped out. Republican Rudy Giuliani bowed out and endorsed John McCain. Democrat John Edwards dropped out, too, but made no endorsement. McCain was emerging as the Republican frontrunner, but the Democrats were in a standoff, with Hillary Clinton holding a slight lead. What happened on Tuesday could change everything.

Politics, of course, is more than just about who got how many votes. It's about issues, too. And when you talk issues, you have to talk about how issues affect ordinary people.

On the day before Super Tuesday, I decided to drive to Stockton, California, which is about an hour from my house. Bill Clinton would be headlining a rally there for Hillary, but she would not be present. This strategy became an effective tool for the Clintons, especially on days with multiple primaries. Whether you like him or not, Bill Clinton was, and still is, a great campaigner.

I was going to Stockton for another reason. Stockton is the county seat for San Joaquin County, the fifth largest agricultural producing county in the United States. Sadly, as the economy continued to turn sour, San Joaquin County ranked thirteenth in the United States for the number of home foreclosures. While Barack Obama and Hillary Clinton were starting to exchange a lot of harsh words, folks in places like Stockton, Tracy and Mountain House had more to be concerned about than a Democratic Party "family feud."

San Joaquin County became a rapidly-growing bedroom community for some suburbs of San Francisco, where real estate prices were out of sight. Many folks built homes in communities such as Mountain House, which literally "popped up" overnight. The mortgage deals were good, and you could get a lot of house for the money. Sure, the commute to the San Francisco Bay Area was long and slow, but at least you could pay for a roof over your head—at least for the short term.

Many of the adjustable mortgages had low teaser rates at first. But years later, higher rates kicked in, and many people could not pay the differences. Some simply abandoned their homes and moved out. The number of foreclosures was staggering.

So, Bill Clinton came here to outline his wife's plan. The Clinton plan would freeze all foreclosures for ninety days. Those who refused to pay or who skipped town would be foreclosed upon. Those with late payments, but a job and a willingness to keep paying to save their homes, would get help. They would have five years to get locked-in and caught up on their payments.

The former President admitted it would be costly, with taxpayers footing the bill for $30 billion dollars. The alternative, though, was much worse, he said. Unemployment, foreclosures and a decline in property values would hurt the economy even more. He said Hillary's plan was designed to "stave off a calamity in the real estate market."

The crowd applauded politely, but this issue had still not hit critical mass with most voters, as it would by September. The economic warning signs of spring would almost literally hit the fan by fall.

Catherine Rivera, of Stockton, and Bernie Giva, of Modesto, spoke to me after the rally. They were supporting Hillary Clinton, but not because of the foreclosure crisis. Rivera said, "Number one, because of universal health care. Plus she's a woman. It's her time." Rivera admitted being very tempted to vote for Barack Obama.

"Obama's time will come," she said, noting he's only been in the U.S. Senate two years.

Bill Clinton's strong emphasis on the economy the day before Super Tuesday was an indication of what was to come for the rest of the campaign. That's because the housing mess threatened to worsen and plunge the nation into a recession.

It wasn't just bad for homeowners. Construction firms, developers, mortgage brokers and real estate speculators were all in peril. Whether they could solve the problem was debatable, but the Clintons knew the political impact of a bad economy. Remember the Clinton election mantra he rode to the White House in 1992? "It's the economy, stupid!" This was sounding like the "same song, but different verse."

I have always said, "Politics is as much about math, as it is about ideology."

My point is, you may have the greatest idea in the world, but if you don't have enough votes, it's not going to happen. This was the reality Barack Obama and Hillary Clinton faced on Super Tuesday. A Democratic candidate needed 2,025 delegates to win the nomination. Right now, Clinton had 256; and Obama 181.

I analyzed polls from the twenty-four states up for grabs on Super Tuesday. By my count, Hillary Clinton led in states with 1,499 delegates; Obama led in states with 389 delegates. Since Democrats awarded delegates based on the proportion of popular vote, there was no "winner-take-all" system such as the Republicans had. Hillary Clinton would have to win 85 percent of all delegates awarded on Super Tuesday to win the nomination that night. Barack Obama faced even tougher odds.

So, even days before the big event, it was clear Super Tuesday would not produce a nominee for the Democrats, as many had hoped. But it did offer high drama. Many of the nation's biggest states were up for grabs, including California, New York, Illinois and New Jersey. This could at least give us an indication of which candidate was strongest in which region. It could also give us some indication of which candidate might be strongest for the general election in November.

On the Republican side, things were equally as dicey and here's why: Republicans needed 1,191 delegates for the nomination. Before Super Tuesday, it was McCain 93; Romney 59; Huckabee 40. There were 1,004 delegates up for grabs Super Tuesday; and even if he won them all, McCain would still be just shy of the nomination.

Figure 11. John McCain greets voters in Stockton, California. May 22, 2008. (Mark Curtis)

It was pretty clear to me there would be no Republican nominee on Super Tuesday either. This must have been a shock to both parties. They had set Super Tuesday up as something akin to a national primary. Their hope was to include as many states as possible and make the party nominee clear early on in the process. That way, the nominees could gear up and focus more on the November election, rather than having an expensive, bruising and long primary process. The plan looked as if it was about to backfire. The primary season was scheduled to run through June. What was designed to look like sprint to the nomination was beginning to look like a marathon.

Tensions were high, and that was reflected in some of the debate sniping. It was starting to get tough out there. For example, when Hillary Clinton and Barack Obama debated in South Carolina, it got downright ugly. When Obama accused Hillary Clinton of "sending jobs overseas" when she was on the Board of Directors of Wal-Mart, she countered that he once did legal work for a "slum landlord" in Chicago. Ouch! This was turning into high drama.

By the time they reached California, they were the only two Democrats left. Debating side-by-side at a table, they still differed, but were more civil. When debating health care reform on CNN from Los Angeles, Clinton said, "I believe absolutely passionately that we must have universal health care. It is a moral responsibility and a right for our country."

Obama countered sharply and said, "She believes that we have to force people who don't have health insurance to buy it ... that's a genuine difference."

On foreign relations, it got even harsher as Hillary Clinton attacked Obama for suggesting diplomacy with certain U.S. enemies. "I don't think that the President should put the prestige of the Presidency on the line in the first year, to have meetings without preconditions with five of the worst dictators in the world," Clinton said.

Obama, again disagreed sharply, especially concerning Iran. "I think, and the National Intelligence Estimate ... the last report suggested that if we are meeting with them (Iran) and talking to them, and offering them both 'carrots and sticks,' they are more likely to change their behavior," Obama said.

Their differences aside, both Obama and Clinton recognized that one way or another the Democrats were now down to a woman or an African-American as their nominee this year. "It is a testimony to the Democratic Party, and it is a testimony to this country that we have the opportunity to make history, because I believe one of us two will end up being the next President of the United States of America," Obama said, as the debate hall echoed in cheers and applause.

"The Republicans were in California yesterday debating. They are more of the same. Neither of us—just by looking at us, you can tell—we are not more of the same," said Hillary Clinton to both hearty laughter and applause from the audience.

The differences among the candidates certainly were clear this year on the campaign trail, but there was another big difference in this campaign. The internet was now playing a huge role in marketing the campaigns, spelling out the candidates' positions on issues, raising money, and recruiting volunteers. As a reporter, traveling from coast to coast with the candidates, it was invaluable to me as well.

This was especially evident the week of Super Tuesday with twenty-four primaries on tap. Candidates were jetting all over the country, and it was hard to keep up with their schedules. I wrote a column about it, saying keeping track of candidates was like finding the title character in the kids' book *Where's Waldo?* Here's what I said about Mike Huckabee's schedule: "With a lead in the Georgia polls, Mike Huckabee spent all of Sunday crisscrossing Georgia, where he faces a 'must win' situation to stay in this race. Today he campaigns in Tennessee and Arkansas, two states he could also win on Super Tuesday. We assume Huckabee has already bought his wife a nice Valentine's Day gift, after she was dispatched to campaign in Anchorage, Alaska."

"BBBBBBBBrrrrrrrrrrrrrrrrrrrrrrrrrrrrrrrrrr!!!!"

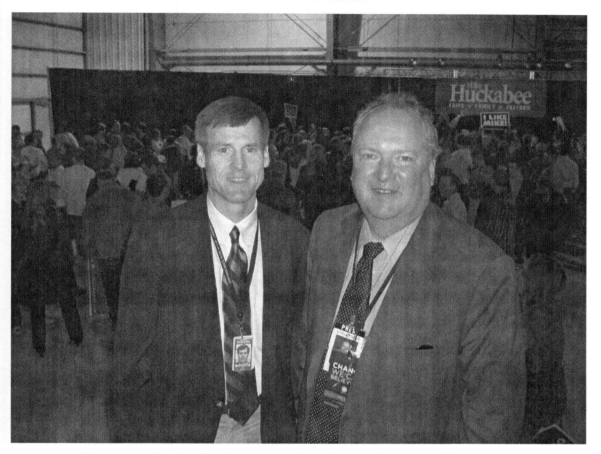

Figure 12. Cox Radio Correspondent Jamie Dupree with Mark Curtis, Tampa, Florida. (Pat Pugliese)

How did I keep track of all this? The internet of course! I received constant email updates from all the candidates with their daily schedules, issue positions, differences with other candidates, etc. I could research their past votes, or I could apply for press credentials to their next rally online. If I wanted to see how the public was reacting, I could check any number of blogs or chat rooms. If I missed a news conference or a candidate's gaffe, you can bet I would find the video posted on YouTube or could download the audio as a Podcast. I, of course, was writing my own daily blogs, with videos and photos, too.

I live on the fringes of Silicon Valley, and I could tell that what we saw online from the candidates this year has absolutely revolutionized politics in terms of how the politicians campaigned, how the reporters covered it, and how the public discussed it. It was truly eye-opening.

On Super Tuesday primary night, I did a combination of traditional and "new media" coverage. I was on the nationwide Pacifica Radio Network with host Aimee Allison, from the KFPA radio studios in Berkeley, California, for an hour. When I was done there, I set up shop at "Jordan's Restaurant" at the famed Claremont Hotel in Oakland. I was "live" for an hour on KGO Radio AM-810 doing political analysis for Brian Copeland's show. All the while, I was online monitoring real-time election returns from several states, as well as blogging and chatting with my own readers. I was media multi-tasking like crazy, and the nice part was I could order dinner and drinks, too!

The election results were pouring in; and the way I covered it, and the way it turned out, just amazed me.

What a night! The Democrats were now "neck and neck" in victories and delegate counts! Hillary Clinton won Arizona, New Jersey, Massachusetts, New York, Oklahoma, Arkansas, Tennessee and California. Barack Obama won Alaska, Minnesota, Connecticut, Colorado, Idaho, Kansas, Utah, North Dakota, Alabama, Delaware, Illinois, Missouri and Georgia. That meant the latest delegate count was Clinton 783; Obama 709. With 2,025 needed to win the nomination, this was anyone's race.

Hillary Clinton spoke to cheering supporters in her home state of New York. "Tonight we are hearing the voices of people across America," Clinton said, "people of all ages, of all colors, all faiths and all walks of life."

Obama sounded similar themes while addressing his supporters in Chicago.

"This campaign for the presidency of the United States of America is different," Obama said to cheers and chants. "Our time has come. Our movement is real, and change is coming to America."

It was equally as wild for the Republicans. John McCain won Arizona, Oklahoma, Missouri, New York, New Jersey, Illinois, Connecticut, Delaware and California. Mitt Romney won Minnesota, Alaska, Colorado, North Dakota, Montana, Utah and Massachusetts. Mike Huckabee won Tennessee, Georgia, Alabama, Arkansas and West Virginia. The delegate totals were: McCain 559; Romney 265; Huckabee 169. With 1,191 needed to nominate, McCain's lead was widening, but this was far from being a done deal.

In Phoenix, the crowd was chanting "Mac is back! Mac is back!" as John McCain entered the ballroom. It was the continuation of a stunning political comeback from someone who had been counted out and called politically dead months earlier. "Tonight, my friends," McCain said, "we've won a number of important victories in the closest thing we've ever had to a national primary." As the crowd applauded and cheered, McCain added, "We've won some of the biggest states in the country."

Even more enthusiastic was the rally for former Arkansas Governor Mike Huckabee, who won five state primaries in the South. "Over the past few days, a lot of people have been trying to say, this is a two-man race (between McCain and Romney)," said Huckabee, as he was interrupted by some jeers, before he continued. "Well, you know what? It is!" Huckabee said, and people in the crowd roared, knowing their candidate was right in the thick of it and was not dropping out.

As for Mitt Romney, he rallied his troops in Massachusetts, where he had served as Governor. They celebrated his wins in seven primary states. "One thing that's clear is this campaign is going on," said Romney. The crowd interrupted with applause and chants of, "Mitt! Mitt! Mitt! Mitt! Mitt! Mitt!" Romney then continued, "I think there are some people who thought it was all going to be done tonight, but it's not all done tonight. We're going to keep on battling ... and we're going to get to the White House." It was indeed shaping up to be a titan, three-way Republican battle for the nomination.

The morning after Super Tuesday, I was at the State Capitol in Sacramento doing my usual round of TV and radio appearances and blogging during my breaks. One of the things I researched was how many people voted in each party. Again, this is information you can now find readily online, from most Secretary of State or Registrar of Voters Office sites. I found some new numbers that were bound to make Republicans worried.

So far in the 2008 primaries and caucuses, Democrats had received almost 21 million votes to just under 13 million for Republicans. That's a split of 59 percent to 38 percent and a troubling trend that could hurt Republicans in November. That said, there are a few possible explanations for the disparity.

The party out of power tends to draw larger numbers, especially if it's a contested primary. The Clinton vs. Obama showdown matched "Ali vs. Frazier" in boxing. Simply put, right now the Democrats were selling more tickets.

The GOP race had trended toward McCain for a few weeks. Some Republican voters may simply have stayed home, assuming another win for McCain. Right now, GOP voters were less motivated. That could easily change by November.

Independent votes are skewed. Some states do not allow independents to vote in partisan primaries. McCain tended to draw big numbers of independents. It was possible that people would come out to vote for him in November, who could not vote for him now. The Wisconsin primary on February 19 could prove revealing.

Wisconsin is one of only a few states that allow an "open primary," where any voter may vote for any party. It is totally nonpartisan. Exit polling would tell us how many independents voted and for whom.

While in Sacramento, I spoke with California Republican Party Chairman Duf Sundheim about the disparity in total voters. He said he was not worried. "We still have nine months before us," Sundheim said, "We've got a long way to go." But a voter ratio of 59 percent Democrat to 38 percent Republican had to be giving some GOP strategists a sleepless night, or two.

I also asked California Democratic Lt. Governor John Garamendi. Having been elected to statewide office three times, he knows something about the importance of voter turnout, especially with a lot of independent voters out there. "There are still many people undecided about this election," Garamendi said.

No, Super Tuesday did not settle anything, even though it was designed to. The next round of primaries was the so-called "Potomac Primary," in which Virginia, Maryland and Washington, DC, would all vote on the same day, February 12. That was just a week away. This is the region where the next President would live, breathe and govern for the next four years. It only made sense that this would be my next campaign stop, too!

Chapter 6: The Potomac, Wisconsin, & Texas Primaries

I was excited about returning to Washington, D.C. I had lived there for six wonderful years. As a fairly young reporter, I moved to the nation's capital in late 1992, the day after Bill Clinton was elected President. I was going because I had been awarded a Congressional Fellowship through the American Political Science Association. The Fellowship allowed journalists to come to Washington and work as Legislative Aides in the House and Senate. The primary goal was to see how politics operated from the "inside." As journalists, we were always "on the outside, looking in" at the legislative and government process. It was a fascinating year in which I worked for then-Representative Charles Schumer (D-NY) and Senator Herb Kohl (D-WI).

The experience was akin to going to the best graduate school for political science. I learned so much, some of it was wonderful, while some of it exposed me to the seamy underbelly of politics. But I learned a lot and made many great contacts and friends with whom I still connect today. Still, I was a reporter at heart, not a politician, and I wanted to get back to my chosen profession.

To my luck, my good friend Jamie Dupree from Cox Radio called me to say that Cox Broadcasting had an opening for a TV reporter in its Capitol Hill Bureau. I went for an interview with Andy Cassells, who had been the legendary Bureau Chief at Cox for many years. It was one of the best—but also one of the strangest—interviews I ever had. Cassells liked me immediately because of my experience on Capitol Hill. I knew how the system worked. "I don't have to teach you Congress 101," Cassells said. "You know where all the bodies are buried."

At the end of the interview, he asked me the most bizarre question I have ever been asked in a job interview. "Mark," Cassells said sheepishly, "would you be comfortable saying the word 'penis' on television?" I was floored, but before I could inquire, Cassells explained that the Bureau would be covering the trial of Lorena Bobbitt, in nearby Manassas, Virginia.

She was the woman charged with assault for cutting off her husband's penis during a domestic quarrel and then throwing the offending organ out her car window. The police found it and it was miraculously surgically reattached to her soon to be ex-husband, John. It was all over the headlines and was the talk of the nation.

It seems that Cox had a former reporter who was a bit squeamish about such things and thought broadcasters should not be saying "penis" on television, especially at the dinner hour.

Now I risked being turned down by making a joke, but I couldn't resist. I looked at Andy Cassells and deadpanned, "I guess this gives a whole new meaning to the name Cox Broadcasting." He roared with laughter, offered me the job and I was hired. Honest to God, it's a true story!

I became a Washington, D.C. correspondent for Cox's chain of television stations, which at the time numbed nine across various parts of the United States, including WBS-TV2 in Atlanta and KTVU-TV2 in the Oakland-San Francisco-San Jose TV market. For the next five years I covered Congress, the White House and the U.S. Supreme Court for the Cox TV stations. I also covered elections, including Presidential and Congressional campaigns. Life was good!

My final year in D.C. was marked by the impeachment of President Clinton—the biggest story of my career. I spent so much time on the air with KTVU that General Manager Kevin O'Brien asked me to transfer to the West Coast to co-anchor "The KTVU Morning News." It was a great promotion, but I was sad to leave Washington and the 24-hour a day political buzz.

So, going back to cover the Potomac Primary was a thrill. I'd get to see old friends and visit old haunts, but most of all I'd be covering what was turning out to be one of the greatest Presidential campaigns in U.S. History.

I took the "red-eye" from Oakland to Dulles, jumped in my rental car and immediately headed on a three-hour drive to Virginia Beach, Virginia. Republican Mike Huckabee was speaking there at noon, and John McCain was holding a rally in Richmond late in the day. I could backtrack my way to D.C.

Virginia was a fast-growing state and was changing. It had been a Republican stronghold for many years, due in part to the huge military infrastructure in the Norfolk-Newport News-Virginia Beach area. Both John McCain and Mike Huckabee were trying to capitalize on this, now that Mitt Romney had dropped out of the race.

In addition to a solid showing on Super Tuesday, Huckabee was coming off wins on Saturday in Kansas and Louisiana. He was the only true conservative left in the GOP contest, and he wasn't quitting. "We are in this race for you and every other conservative American," he told cheering audience members in Virginia Beach. Huckabee then attacked the U.S. Senate where the other three remaining candidates—Clinton, McCain and Obama—were employed. Huckabee seethed over a compromise immigration bill that ultimately failed. "What has the Senate done lately other than try to put before you an immigration bill you hated so much you burned and melted their phone lines until they finally got the message?" said Huckabee. "They work for us; it's not the other way around." The large crowd cheered his populist message. McCain might eventually win the nomination, but Huckabee is going to give him headaches, I thought.

The place was packed and I got there late, so I tried to take notes and photos from the lobby outside the overflowing ballroom. At this point in the campaign, I had collected at least a dozen press credentials and they hung around my neck with a photo ID. I still wore all of them—even ones from Iowa—because security people and campaign staffers recognize you are in the press corps and let you in. You have to look official, even if it's a bit overdone. Anyway, as I was working, some woman saw a "Hillary Clinton" credential around my neck and went ballistic on me. "Hillary Clinton?" she shouted at me, "What are you doing here? You don't belong here." Honestly, I thought she was going to attack me, assuming I was a spy. "Ma'am, it's just a press credential. Calm down!" I yelled back. I got as far away from her as I could.

After lunch with old friends at a nice Mexican restaurant, I headed for Richmond and the McCain rally. I had a continuing problem with which I had to contend. Since I had no wireless Internet card for my computer, I signed up for a T-Mobile account. That meant I could only get online in places that had T-Mobile access. That usually meant Starbucks. So, on more occasions than I could ever count, I plugged the name "Starbucks" into my GPS, and the car would magically find one. I began to refer to any and all Starbucks as "my office." It is where I wrote most of my blogs, uploaded pictures and posted it all on my website for the world to see. Like I've said, it was the "Wild West" of "new media" journalism, but you do whatever works. I loved it!

The McCain rally in Richmond was at the Virginia Aviation Museum. With military jets hanging from the ceiling and stationed on the floor, it was a great backdrop for the former U.S. Navy pilot, turned U.S. Senator. He was flanked by a "Who's Who" of Virginia Republican politics. Senator John Warner, former Senator and Governor George Allen, former Governor Jim Gilmore and one-time Presidential candidate Gary Bauer, just to name a few.

Figure 13. John McCain at Richmond, Virginia, Aviation Museum, Feb. 11, 2008. (Mark Curtis)

With a Navy plane similar to the one he flew in Vietnam behind him, McCain attacked his Democratic opponents. "I want to continue this surge [in Iraq] which, as you know, is succeeding," McCain told the crowd, before chastising the Democrats. "They want to set a date for surrender. I will never surrender."

The real goal of this rally was to paint McCain as conservative enough to be acceptable to the right wing of the party. For weeks, talk radio hosts had been attacking him as a "closet liberal" for his stances on immigration and campaign finance reform. McCain was a Senator who liked to forge compromises with Democrats on occasion. That did not endear him to the most conservative elements on the right. Tonight he tried to appease them by promising Federal Court appointments in the mold of Antonin Scalia and Samuel Alito, two of the most conservative justices. McCain promised more judges who "won't legislate from the bench," which has been a conservative rallying cry.

After the rally, I dined on Big Macs with my long-time cohort, Jamie Dupree, of Cox Radio. We agreed that this was a good event for McCain. The backdrop made for a great photo op, and enough Virginia conservatives gave a "wink and a nod" as if to say, "McCain's okay with us. He's safe to vote for."

It worked. The next night, McCain made a clean sweep, winning the Virginia, Maryland and Washington, DC, primaries. It wasn't easy, though. Mike Huckabee was strong in Virginia, carrying 41 percent of the vote, to McCain's 51 percent. The bad news for Huckabee was that Virginia was a "winner-take-all" state, meaning McCain won all sixty convention delegates, no matter how well the second-place finisher did. This would be a continuing problem for Huckabee and was certainly a reason why Mitt Romney had already quit.

The biggest problem for all was the weather. A steady and chilly rain most of the day turned into an ice storm by mid-afternoon. I barely got out of the District of Columbia by 3 p.m. and headed to my brother-in-law's home in Arlington, where I was staying. The entire Washington area was in gridlock by rush hour. Cars spun out on the ice, and the Capital Beltway and main roads looked like an old-fashioned Demolition Derby. In all of this danger and chaos, people were still trying to vote after work. A judge in Maryland ordered all polls to remain open until 9:30, providing an extra 90 minutes for people to vote there; but Virginia polls closed firmly at 7 p.m.

Of course, I still had to get to McCain's rally in historic Old Town Alexandria. What should have been a twenty-minute ride took me almost two hours. Thank God I knew the area well and had lots of experience driving in icy storms. It was a mess. Even when I got to Alexandria, I had to park a good six blocks from the hotel. The roads and sidewalks were caked with a quarter-inch-thick layer of black ice. I lost count of how many times I slipped and fell down. This was scary!

The good news was that everyone was trapped in this mess and the event was running late. Once inside, you never would have known there was an ice storm outside. The victory celebration was packed, and McCain's rhetoric was on fire. By now he was assuming he'd be the nominee, even though he was still short of the magic number of delegates needed. Instead of criticizing Mike Huckabee, McCain took dead aim at the Democrats. "We know where either of their candidates will lead this country, and we dare not let them," he said. "They will paint a picture of the world in which America's mistakes are a greater threat to our security than the malevolent intentions of an enemy that despises us and our ideals." The crowd loved it and cheered heartily.

It was a huge night, too, for Barack Obama. He swept Hillary Clinton in all three primaries and by wide margins. In Virginia, for example, it was Obama 63 percent, to 36 percent for Clinton. It was a landslide, and the margins in Maryland and D.C. weren't any better for Clinton. All of a sudden, Barack Obama was on a roll.

On the Saturday before the Potomac Primary, he also beat Senator Clinton in Washington State, Nebraska and Louisiana. He had won six straight primaries since Super Tuesday and was showing strength in all regions of the nation. As a matter of fact, the Potomac Primary finally put him ahead of Clinton in the overall delegate total. He had 1,215; she had 1,190. With 2,025 needed for the nomination, this was going to be a fight to the finish.

After a raucous Monday afternoon rally before twenty thousand people at the University of Maryland, Barack Obama headed to Wisconsin, the site of the following week's big primary. He gave his Potomac Primary victory speech from Madison, Wisconsin, and took aim not at Clinton, but at John McCain. "Understand this:

John McCain, the likely Republican nominee, is an American hero; and we honor his service," said Obama. "We honor his service, but his priorities don't address the real problems of the American people because they are bound to the failed policies of the past." By ignoring Clinton and attacking McCain, Obama was essentially declaring that he would be the Democrats' nominee. That was a pretty bold gamble with a lot of big primaries left.

Hillary Clinton missed the ice storm in the nation's capital, too. She was in El Paso, campaigning for the Texas primary on March 4. It seemed odd at the time that she was so far away, but there would be a big payoff weeks later. Still, she spent her primary night speech attacking the soon-to-be retiring President, rather than attacking her real challengers, Obama and McCain. "There's a great saying in Texas—you've all heard it: 'All hat and no cattle.' Well, after seven years of George Bush, we need a lot less hat and a lot more cattle," she said. Sure it was a funny line, as we watched from Virginia, but George W. Bush wasn't running again. Clinton's campaign and message seemed like a train that derailed. She needed to get back on track, or she was doomed.

It was a triumphant night for John McCain and Barack Obama in the bitterly icy nation's capital, from where they each hoped to govern as President. Nothing was settled, and now the campaign trail led to my home state of Wisconsin.

The Badger State has had a unique political history. The people of Wisconsin have picked mavericks and people who liked to tip over the political apple cart, if you will. This was the state that sent "Fighting Bob" Lafollette to the U.S. Senate and then later the eventually disgraced Senator Joseph McCarthy. Wisconsin also loved Senator Bill Proxmire and his famed "Golden Fleece Award" for government waste. Then there was the jolly and red-vested professor, Lee Sherman Dreyfus, who became Governor in 1978, beating three famous and well-heeled professional politicians. Yep, my home state liked to mix it up.

I had mixed feelings about being back. It was a bittersweet trip. I had hundreds of family and friends there and was glad to see so many of them. But we had also buried my dad just eight weeks earlier, and the pain was still pretty raw. When my contract was not renewed after nine years at KTVU, my dad was as stunned as I was. My team, after all, had the number one early morning newscast in the market, six years running. I told my dad of my plans to cover the Presidential campaign all year as a freelance reporter and analyst. He knew what a political junkie I was (as was he), and he encouraged me to "go for it." He was really excited. Sadly, less than a month after we hatched this crazy plan, he was gone.

My dad left his kids a lot of wisdom and, fortunately, he also left us an old Ford Taurus station wagon. Sure, it had a lot of miles on it and two badly deflated tires, but this was going to be my campaign "war wagon." Caked with street salt from an already snowy Milwaukee winter, this car would get me everywhere like a Sherman tank! It had shuttled us to Lambeau Field and back a number of times. My sister Tracy used it to cart flowers to weddings as part of her job. And, lo and behold, my dad's medical kit was still buried under the back seat, because he had still been seeing the occasional patient in his sixty-first year of practicing medicine. If this car could only talk!

First stop was Beloit College near the Wisconsin-Illinois border. Chelsea Clinton was speaking at a campaign rally for her mom, and I wasn't about to miss it. Chelsea, whose privacy was rightfully guarded by her parents when she was a child in the White House, was now all grown up. At twenty-seven, with a degree from Stanford in hand, her mother's campaign had been her coming out party. While she politely declined questions from the press, she was quite candid in this forum. Students applauded every time Chelsea said her mother would end the Iraq war. It was the issue that received the most response today.

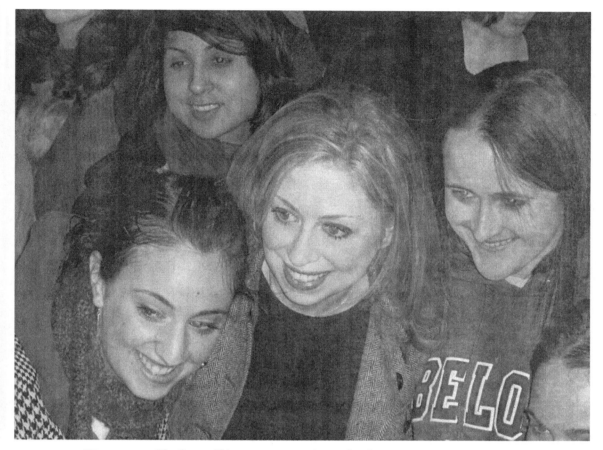

Figure 14. Chelsea Clinton campaigns for her mom at Beloit College, Beloit, Wisconsin, Feb. 18, 2008. (Mark Curtis)

The first student to question her called her "Hillary," and the crowd burst out laughing.

"My grandmother does it too, its OK," she said graciously. She spoke completely off the cuff, with no notes. Her jokes were spontaneous, and she had the packed Campus Center laughing often. She made no speech and just took questions for well over an hour. "Oh gosh," she said repeatedly to the huge number of student questions. If that was her only nervous tick, she could be quite a candidate somewhere down the road.

Finally, a male student asked, "As early as eight years from now, would you consider running for President?" The young Clinton will be old enough then at age 35, but was diplomatic in her response. "My political aspirations stretch to my mom becoming your president," she said.

She didn't shy from controversy. Chelsea said of her mother "She certainly supports opening diplomatic relations with everyone. She won't go to Tehran (Iran) on January 21, but she will talk to everyone." It was a direct slap at Barack Obama who supported diplomatic talks with Iran.

Beloit student Alex Brown seized on that after the rally, because Hillary Clinton has criticized Obama for making similar statements in the past. Brown said the New York Democrat was trying to have it both ways. "She'll try to appease the far left as much as possible, then move to the right [in opposition to Iran]," he said.

Chelsea posed for pictures with students for quite some time after the rally. Her mom was campaigning elsewhere in the state, but would have been proud of her daughter's job as her stand-in.

Aside from the fact that she refused to speak with the press, I was impressed and thought she was quite a remarkable young lady, perhaps a candidate someday, too.

To my good fortune, Barack Obama was also speaking at Beloit College, but his rally was at 9 p.m. I had time to go to "my office" and write and upload my story and photos to the blog.

It was good to be back in Wisconsin, but it was cold. Beloit College has a beautiful campus, but the area is pretty flat; and a strong Midwestern wind could about cut you in half this time of year. At one point, the wind-chill factor reached minus twenty degrees. I joked during a morning TV interview with KTVU's Ross McGowan that Hawaii was also holding a primary today and that maybe I had picked the wrong state to visit. Oh, well.

I was bundled in multiple layers of clothing, with a sweater, a heavy coat and thermal gloves. Still, I was freezing. I assumed when I got back to campus, the crowd would be smaller due to the frigid weather. Boy, was I wrong.

The Beloit Memorial High School Pep Band kept the crowd warm for an hour. I was not surprised that they were recent State Champs. What a great band to warm us up—and we needed it! Good thing it was not halftime at a football game. We were inside at the college's Flood Arena. My hope was that the arena was named after some college donor named Flood and not after a natural disaster. The cold and snow were enough to handle!

Barack Obama walked onto the stage at 9:43 p.m., making a great backdrop for the 10 p.m. newscast on every station in the state, plus Chicago and Rockford, Illinois. It was great planning to maximize his media coverage on the eve of the primary. While some polls showed a tight race in Wisconsin, Obama never mentioned his opponent Senator Hillary Clinton by name until nearly the end of the rally. He didn't have to. When he said, "I am not running because of what I think is owed to me!" the crowd cheered and knew to whom he was referring.

The crowd was easily three thousand strong, dwarfing the three hundred who showed up for Chelsea Clinton this afternoon on the very same campus. Granted, one was a candidate; one, a candidate's daughter. Still, the contrast was pretty stark.

Yet, I was left to wonder about the candidates' real differences on the issues. Today, both the Obama and Clinton campaigns were cheered the loudest when they spoke of the war ending; they both spoke of health care for all Americans, but letting people who like their current insurance keep it; and they spoke of annual college tuition tax credits ($3,500 from Clinton; $4,000 for Obama). Both spoke of public service jobs to pay back student loans. The agendas were nearly identical. It was like comparing Pepsi and Coke. In the end, after all these weeks of watching both, the differences were hard to discern. Likability could turn out to be the most crucial issue. More people seem to like him, than her. We would see what the polls would say on Tuesday!

One difference might matter. "This was an unwise war. I opposed it," Obama said to the loudest cheers of the night. Senator Clinton supported the war initially, but now opposed it. Obama might have the edge, even though he was not in the Senate when the original vote was taken. "I will not just meet with our friends. I will meet with our enemies," Obama had said to loud cheers, but Chelsea Clinton pledged that on behalf of her mother today, too.

Of course the more stark comparison would come when one of these candidates finally faced off against John McCain. It was unlikely that question was to be resolved this Tuesday.

Finally, Obama addressed the recent criticism from Hillary Clinton that his inspirational message was not a public policy road map. "She is right that 'speeches don't put food on the table,' but for the past twenty years I've worked at it," he said. When he finally mentioned Senator Clinton by name, there was a smattering of boos.

"Sometimes a speech can help people find what they have in common with each other," he said. "I don't apologize for inspiring people!" The crowd cheered wildly! Then he talked about a November opponent. "I respect John McCain for his service to this country. He's a genuine American hero," Obama said, "but he has defended George W. Bush and he wants to continue Bush's economic policy. I want to have a debate with John McCain. He can debate the politics of the past, because I want to debate the politics of the future," the Illinois Senator said. The crowd roared again.

"I talk about hope a lot, because the odds of me standing here were low," he said. "Hope. That is how this nation was founded. That's how the greatest nation defeated Hitler and lifted us out of the Great Depression. That's what hope is." Obama spoke for forty minutes, much longer than his normal stump speech.

The roar of the crowd was long and unmistakable as Obama plunged into the audience to shake hands. I had seen him speak on many occasions, but this may have been one of his best performances ever. He was going to need it. The latest Real Clear Politics composite poll showed the race 46 percent Obama, and 42 percent for Clinton, with 12 percent undecided. Those last-minute voters could swing this primary.

Hillary Clinton spent much of her time in central and northern Wisconsin and even had to cancel one last campaign rally due to bad weather. More snow was in the forecast, and that was bound to affect voter turnout. On Sunday, she did manage to make it to Miss Katie's Diner—a legendary Milwaukee restaurant. That's where President Bill Clinton and German Chancellor Helmut Kohl held the so-called "Sausage Summit" in 1996, when the two men ate everything in sight. I missed Hillary's campaign visit, but stopped in on Monday for a great breakfast and a chance to chat with the locals.

Wisconsin was shaping up to be another battleground state, as it has been in many elections. It could go either way. In 2004, President Bush lost Wisconsin to John Kerry by just five thousand votes, the closest state margin in that election.

The sharp divisions were evident the morning I dropped in. Sitting at the bar having lunch next to me were Nancy and Dave Strehlow, who've have been married for fifty years. She is a Democrat. He is a Republican. Dave had voted for Senator John McCain. How did that go over with his wife? "I'm trying to straighten her out, but it's hard," Dave said.

Nancy voted for Hillary Clinton. "I think it's time for a woman President. I like what she stands for," said Nancy. That's when World War III nearly broke out!

"You are voting for her just because she's a woman," Dave shouted.

"I am NOT voting on gender," Nancy snapped back.

"Yes you are!" Dave retorted. "No I'm not," she insisted.

This went on for a few minutes and then calmed down. Finally, Nancy turned to me and said if Barack Obama wins, she's okay with that, too, and could even live with the moderate John McCain as President.

You see, she admitted, when they got married fifty years ago, she was a Republican, and Dave was a union worker and the family Democrat. Somehow, over the years, they each switched parties.

Their sparring, while fierce, was playful and not mean-spirited. They finished their drinks and lunch, shook hands with the bartender and me and left all smiles! Nice people! The kind "Miss Katie's" is filled with!

It was a busy day in Wisconsin. Despite the frigid temperature of three degrees above zero in Milwaukee, it was partly sunny; and snow did not seem to be a real threat. As with every other state I had been to, people were out voting in what appeared to be record numbers.

Turnout would be crucial in this very close race. John Hallanger was the Milwaukee County Chairman for the Clinton campaign. I visited his office early this morning to watch the "get-out-the-vote" effort in full swing. "We've got people calling from the office. We've got people calling from their houses," Hallanger said. Having phone banks in people's homes was probably a really good idea, given the freezing temperature.

John McCain held a mid-morning voting day rally in the Milwaukee suburb of Brookfield and then left the state to campaign in Ohio. McCain, who was trying to ban Congressional budget earmarks, got one last dig in at his Democratic opponents before leaving Wisconsin. McCain said, "Senator Clinton, in the last year, got $340 million worth of earmark projects for the state of New York. Senator Obama got some $92 million worth of pork for the state of Illinois." McCain said he never accepted an earmark for a special project during his twenty-four years in Congress. If elected President, he said, "I will veto every single pork barrel earmark bill that comes across my desk." The crowd shouted in approval.

McCain was not the only one to leave town, and this was becoming a trend. Hillary Clinton and Barack Obama were long gone, too. With Ohio, Texas, Vermont and Rhode Island holding primaries in two weeks, the candidates had to move ahead on the trail. It was disappointing because they would give their acceptance or concession speeches from states far away from those that were voting.

There were still campaign rallies to attend; and, to the surprise of many, the results came in early and they were stunning. While he only had a four-point lead in the final polls, Barack Obama beat Hillary Clinton 58 to 41 percent. He crushed her by a whopping seventeen-point margin. The large block of independent voters went largely his way.

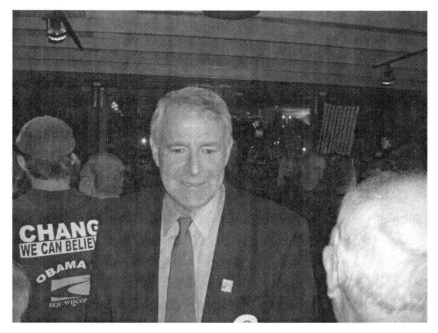

Figure 15. Mayor Tom Barrett hosts Obama victory rally. Milwaukee, Wisconsin, Feb. 19, 2008. (Mark Curtis)

At the victory party, I spoke with Milwaukee Mayor Tom Barrett, who was an old family acquaintance. He was one of Barack Obama's earliest marquee supporters, having endorsed the Illinois Senator a full year before the Wisconsin primary. "I think I was the first big city mayor outside of Illinois to endorse him," said Mayor Barrett. "It was his message of hope and unity," he added. Barrett also noted that Obama was a community organizer in Chicago, the nation's third largest city. "I need a President who understands urban issues," said the Milwaukee Mayor.

The mood was more somber across the Milwaukee River at a bar where Hillary Clinton supporters gathered. "I am sick to my stomach," said Kaela Zielinski, a teacher at Cass Street School in Milwaukee. She backed Clinton and told me, "I can't believe Wisconsin would pick someone with so little experience compared to Senator Clinton."

Zielinski believes an early GOP win by John McCain forced Democrats to pick someone like Obama, who might be more electable on a national level.

She was on to something, and it was very apparent to everyone now. Hillary Clinton's back was against the wall. She had to win some big primaries, or this race was over. The biggest state was Texas, and I was headed there next.

My plane landed in Dallas on March 2, but I was not traveling alone this time. Out of nowhere, my 16-year-old daughter, Alexandra, begged me to go on the campaign trail. Unbeknownst to me, she had decided she wanted to follow in her father's footsteps and become a TV journalist. I was surprised and reluctant, at first. But with two years left in high school, Allie had to make college and career choices soon. I thought what better way to learn than on-the-job training. "Consider this an internship," I said. "You're going to be working long, tiring days with lots of travel. This isn't a vacation." I assigned her my digital camera and made her my staff photographer with official press credentials and all!

I wasn't kidding. Once we landed in Dallas, Allie and I had to drive two and a half hours across the Texas plains to Wichita Falls. Bill Clinton would be campaigning there for Hillary. The earth is as flat as can be in this area, and you can see for what seems like forever. Way off in the distance we could see lightning, but it seemed too far away to pose any threat.

The drive to Wichita Falls was boring and uneventful. I found campaign updates on an all-news radio station. It was Sunday, but the candidates were busy bees. Bill Clinton had ten rallies to attend for his wife. That's right—ten in one day in mammoth Texas! Hillary Clinton and Barack Obama were in Ohio, which also had a Tuesday primary. So did Vermont and Rhode Island, so the campaign travel schedules were just nuts. Once again I kept track via the internet, which was a godsend.

Figure 16. My daughter, Press Intern Allie Curtis, covering Bill Clinton. Wichita Falls, TX, Mar. 2, 2008. (Mark Curtis)

Bill Clinton was two hours late for his 6 p.m. rally inside the Wichita Falls Convention Center. He was always notoriously late for events when he was President, but this time it was not his fault. Severe weather, including a tornado warning, was upon us. The pouring rain, wind and lightning were scary. Somehow, Clinton's helicopter managed to land in this dangerous weather, and the rally was on. The press people credentialed my daughter, Allie, and put her in the photo pool with Associated Press, Reuters, *Time*, *Newsweek* and the *Washington Post*, among others. They were right up onstage, off to the side, when President Clinton spoke. I was so proud of her!

The long wait was worth it for the fifteen hundred patient supporters. "The American people are determined to change this country," Clinton said, as he stood next to a large red tractor covered with "Hillary for President" signs. He promised his wife would end U.S. dependency on foreign oil and bring the troops home from Iraq. He received lots of "Texas sized" applause. With polls showing Hillary slightly ahead in Texas, 49 to 46 percent over Obama, Bill Clinton pleaded to undecided voters to choose his wife based on her experience.

Roberta Price was a senior citizen who drove here from St. Joe, Texas, three counties away. She supported Senator Clinton, "because I think she's the best person for the job. She's the smartest, has the most experience. She'll stick to her guns. I think she's brilliant," Price said. The former city employee also wore a button saying, "Bill Clinton for First Dude" and hoped he would play an active role in a Hillary Clinton administration. "Well, I heard he might be named Ambassador to the World. I don't think there's a better person for it. We need to get some of the world's respect back that we lost," Price said.

The Clintons were also targeting the Hispanic vote in Texas, where Hillary was showing strength. Lydia Sanchez from San Antonio was a longtime Clinton supporter who traveled the country for Hillary's campaign. She may be one of the few people in America who has the autographs of Bill, Hillary and Chelsea Clinton—all on one "Hillary" baseball cap. She collected the signatures along the trail.

Strong Latino backing meant Clinton would be a better November candidate than Obama, she argued. "She understands much about Latinos. We think she's going to be able to do something for us," Sanchez said, hoping that health insurance, new educational initiatives for kids, and better worker benefits would top Clinton's White House priorities.

Bill Clinton departed Wichita Falls by 10 p.m. He was still flying to one more rally despite the severe weather. This man was like the "Energizer Bunny" campaigning for his wife. You got the sense he wanted to move back into the White House just as badly as she did.

Allie and I drove back to Dallas in a blinding thunderstorm. The Interstate had almost zero visibility, unless the sky was lit up by lightning, which happened often. The tornado warning continued, and there were funnel clouds sighted. We felt like storm chasers in a scene from the movie, "Twister!" Fortunately, no cows flew past our car.

It was 2 a.m. when we got back to our hotel in Dallas, and we had to be at a Mike Huckabee rally at Southern Methodist University by 8 a.m. We overslept! We woke up at 7:40, and the event was in just twenty minutes. Yikes! Fortunately, SMU was only a few miles away. So, brush the teeth, comb the hair and out the door. So much for journalism being a glamorous business.

Mike Huckabee was already speaking when we got there. A small but dedicated group of about two hundred supporters was there. They were ever faithful, carrying campaign signs and chanting, "We like Mike." His most famous supporter, TV actor and martial artist Chuck Norris joined Huckabee on stage. The former Arkansas Governor even joked, "If you don't vote, Chuck will roundhouse kick you." Norris posed for pictures with people in the crowd, including my daughter Allie. It was a fun event, but you got the sense that this might be Huckabee's last round. If he lost Texas and Ohio, John McCain was likely going to be the nominee.

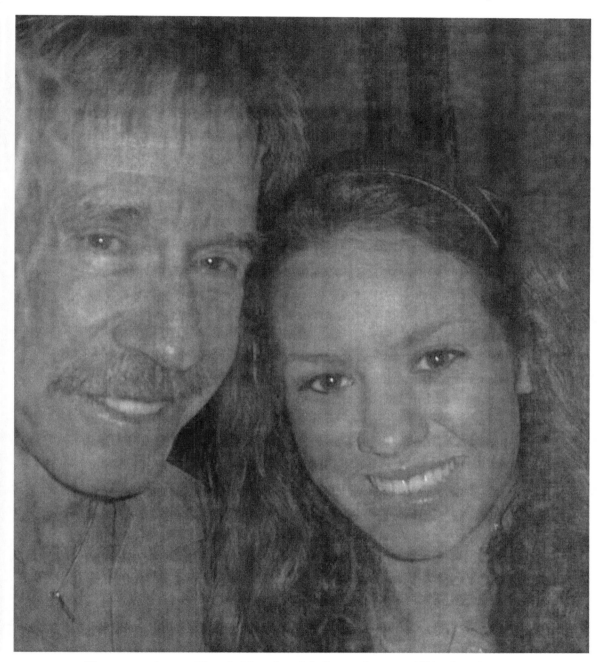

Figure 17. Actor Chuck Norris with Press Intern Allie Curtis
at Mike Huckabee rally. Dallas, Texas, Mar. 3, 2008.
(Allie Curtis)

Allie and I had lots of work to do. Aside from TV and radio interviews, we had to get the blog written and upload our pictures. Part of me was trying to keep very busy, because I was avoiding something I dreaded. I knew we needed to visit Dealey Plaza, where President John F. Kennedy was assassinated almost forty-five years earlier. I had never been there, but given the historic nature of this Presidential election, we could not avoid it. It was still a living history lesson for my sixteen-year-old daughter and me.

Following a "live" interview at the Fox News Bureau in downtown Dallas, we drove to the assassination site. It was eerie, and I got chills. Standing on Elm Street below the Texas School Book Depository, you got the same perspective as seen in the famed Zapruder film—the home movie of the assassination as captured by private citizen Abraham Zapruder. I was only four-and-one-half years old when Kennedy was killed, but I remember it so well. I didn't really comprehend the magnitude back then, but I remember the enormous sadness and grieving in my own home and neighborhood in Wisconsin. This brought it all back, and I almost began to cry. We spoke with people gathered there and took our notes and pictures. I said a quiet prayer for the safety of our current candidates and leaders, and then we left.

Our next stop was an Obama town hall meeting at Newman Smith High School in Carrolton, Texas, just north of Dallas. It was raining fairly steadily now, and there were predictions of freezing conditions and possible snow for primary day. This was sounding like the messes I had encountered in Washington and Wisconsin all over again.

Senior Emmanuel Ayala introduced Obama and excitedly announced he would vote for the first term U.S. Senator the following day. "The old ways of doing it just don't cut it anymore," Ayala said to cheers. The audience was comprised of high school students most of whom were ineligible to vote. Within the press corps tonight, it begged the question: "Why campaign here?" Every state poll had the Clinton-Obama race in a dead heat on election eve. Obviously there would be lots of TV coverage, but this was one of the weakest performances I had seen from Obama. He seemed flat with his stump speech and was perhaps tired from the endless campaigning, but who wouldn't be? The schedule and pace for these political candidates was grueling.

The teens liked his message, especially when he talked of pulling troops out of Iraq and giving tuition tax credits for college. This was stuff they cared about. It was their future. "We've got to have high standards in our schools. Especially in the area of math and science," Obama said to cheers. "One thing that we know works is after-school programs for kids. And summer school programs for kids," Obama added.

A big piece of the puzzle was missing. The candidate never stated how he would pay for his promises. "All this stuff is going to cost something," he said, "but it's a worthy investment if we are going to keep our economy competitive." His lack of specifics didn't seem to matter. The students wildly applauded his message of hope and optimism. "Your voice matters. You can have an impact," the Illinois Democrat said. "Change always happens in this country when young people act."

I was glad my daughter got to be at this rally and see how her high school peers in another state reacted to the Presidential race in general and Obama in particular. She was missing three days of school for this internship, so I wanted it to be a learning experience.

We headed out in the cold rain, and I feared the weather would affect turnout in tomorrow's primary. Allie and I stopped at "Bob's Steak and Chop House," the famous Dallas eatery. We had been working hard. It was time to ditch the fast food and have a real steak dinner treat. We earned it!

Primary day brought the predicted snow and cold. In some parts of Dallas, one or two inches had fallen overnight. Still, heavy turnout was already being reported at the polls and 1.2 million Texans had already participated in early voting.

There was also a real oddity. This Democratic primary was known as "the Texas Two-Step." Democrats would vote in the normal primary election, and that would determine about two-thirds of the convention delegates. Then many voters would gather again after polls closed to have a precinct caucus and to select the final one-third of convention delegates. So, there were two votes; and it was possible Hillary Clinton could win the popular vote in the primary; while Barack Obama won more convention delegates via the caucus system. Former President Bill Clinton even joked, "Texas is the only place you can vote twice in the same day, without getting arrested!"

Yes, he was right, and it was confusing. Essentially it could be just like the 2000 Election where Al Gore received more popular votes, but George W. Bush won the most Electoral College votes. It was further complicated because the final delegate selection for the Democrats would take place at the state party meeting in June.

The drama was everything we had anticipated when the votes finally came in primary night. Hillary Clinton won the popular primary vote by a close margin of 51 percent to Barack Obama's 47 percent. She also beat Obama in Ohio, 54 to 44 percent. Clinton won the Rhode Island primary, but lost to Obama in Vermont. All in all, it was a huge comeback for her. Had she lost either Texas or Ohio, I don't think her campaign could have gone on. This was a political resurrection of the first order, and she knew it.

With thousands of supporters gathered at her rally, cheers and applause interrupted Clinton often as she spoke. "For everyone here in Ohio and across America who has ever been counted out, but refused to be knocked out; and for everyone who has ever stumbled, but stood right back up; and for everyone who works hard and never gives up, this one's for you!" Clinton said, as she pointed excitedly at the crowd. The place just went nuts. Honestly,

I think it was the best line Hillary Clinton ever delivered in all the years I've seen her speak. And she was right on the money. To use a boxing analogy, she had been "down for the ten count," but got back up just before the referee counted her out—just in the nick of time. It may have been the greatest political comeback I had ever seen.

John McCain had an equally triumphant night. He won all four primaries and now had enough delegates to be the Republican Party's nominee for President of the United States. Thousands of red, white and blue balloons cascaded from the ceiling of the Fairmont Hotel ballroom in Dallas. Cannons on the floor exploded with millions of pieces of red, white and blue confetti. This was an amazing comeback victory for McCain, as well, having been counted out of the GOP race last summer. "Mac was back," as the saying goes.

McCain was humbled by the nomination. "I owe my country every opportunity I ever had," said the former Vietnam POW, who was held captive and was tortured for over five years. I was thrilled my daughter was there to witness this with me.

One of his cellmates was in the Dallas ballroom to see McCain's nomination victory secured. Texas Republican Congressman Sam Johnson had been a prisoner of war with McCain, and he told me how that shaped McCain to lead the nation. "Well, it's a challenge, not the kind you get every day," Rep. Johnson told me. "He came through the thing with flying colors. Nothing prepares you for that. He's a real patriot." As we shook hands and said goodbye, the Congressman grabbed my shoulder to assure me this is not just about McCain's military service. "He's fiscally sound!" Johnson said. Supporters such as Johnson wanted to make sure wary conservatives were onboard. Many didn't trust the moderate Arizona Senator.

As for November and a possible Obama-McCain showdown, Texas Congressman Pete Session told me Tuesday night the GOP was ready. "We've got a candidate who can run a fifty-state race," Sessions said. "Name one 'Red' state Obama wins?" he asked. Of course, he was assuming that Obama was the nominee, but Hillary Clinton was far from being done after her huge comeback tonight.

My daughter Allie and I had the time of our lives. She really learned a lot. "It was good because I got to experience an historic election. It was really cool to see all of the candidates in person," Allie said, "and to get the feel of what the whole political process is really like." She plans to study mass communication and political science in college.

Now we had the longest break of the campaign. There were no major primaries or caucuses for seven weeks. In essence, it was halftime at the Super Bowl, with the score tied. We had a Republican nominee, but the Democrats were in a standoff. It was basically dead even between Obama and Clinton, and the next big prize was a whopper. The Pennsylvania Primary was April 22, and I would be there.

Chapter 7: Pennsylvania—A "Must Win" State

It has been almost ten years since I lived on the East Coast; and I was reminded of this as I got off the plane in Philadelphia. The humidity hit me like a slap in the face. It was jarring and nostalgic at the same time.

I love the "City of Brotherly Love!" I was last here for the Republican Convention of 2000. The city just drew me in. Maybe it was its history as the birthplace of a nation; maybe, its politics and protests. Then, of course, there was the food! Philly may be known for its cheese steaks, but there was so much more here to savor. It's an American urban buffet, and now I was back. Like many other big cities, Philly has its own unique heartbeat, a certain pulse you can feel.

The drama of such an airtight presidential race playing out where it all began seemed truly ironic. It made me wonder whether Ben Franklin might be spinning in his grave over our tumultuous elections, or whether he might jump from his coffin with joy to see that, somehow, our crazy system actually works and has worked for two hundred and thirty plus years.

Reflecting on that, I hopped in my rental car and headed towards the University of Pennsylvania, a school I always forget is part of the Ivy League. Tonight they would get an Ivy League political performance from the Clinton team: Hillary, Bill, Chelsea, Governor Ed Rendell (D-PA), Michael Nutter, the Mayor of Philadelphia, and others.

But first things first and there was a lot of waiting before the "show" would begin. Penn is right next door to Drexel University, so this is "college central." Given the importance of the youth vote this year, especially for Barack Obama, this was to be a real showdown, as the Clintons would try to reclaim some of their youthful charm. However, it had been a long time since 1992.

99

The Palestra, the Penn Arena, was packed with ten thousand people, many of them students. Mixed in were hundreds of union members and senior citizens - both strong coalitions for Hillary Clinton. She was now at war with Barack Obama, and in a state where many battles of the Revolutionary and Civil Wars were fought, the setting couldn't be more appropriate.

My arrival here and, indeed, my stay in Pennsylvania were largely a comedy of errors with the Clinton campaign, but it worked out better than I could ever have dreamed. I arrived at the Palestra very late, with a contingent of foreign reporters and photographers. Somehow I got lumped in with them and had to wait an eternity for a Secret Service dog search.

Once inside, though, I was directed to go sit in the bleachers right behind the stage, literally twenty-five feet from where the Clintons would be. This was a mistake, of course. I was supposed to be in the press riser, about a hundred yards away. Instead, I was seated practically in the Clintons' laps. I was surrounded by grannies, union members, minorities, hippies, thrilled college students, and a human potpourri that included every other demographic.

If I were in the barnyard, I think I would have been in what they call "hog heaven." I say this because I was not here just as a reporter. I've been working on my Doctorate at St. Mary's College of California, and my dissertation is focusing on the communication skills of our leaders. Why do some leaders inspire us? Why do some bore us? Why do we vote for some based simply on how they talk to us? What exactly do we want from our leaders?

Yes, it's an academic discipline, but it's also a very practical American exercise. We do this every four years; and, in some sense, it is autobiographical or, at least, "self defining" for us as a nation. I remember covering the Reagan campaign in 1980 and not fully "getting it" until election night, when the landslide came. I loved Reagan as a speaker (though I voted for John Anderson). I had supported Carter in 1976 for his idealism; but within his four years as President, I had learned the stark difference between idealism and reality. It's like fiction vs. nonfiction.

The reality of Reagan, though, was not just within him. It was a part of us. Our nation was getting its tail kicked by some thugs in Iran holding American hostages, and many people voted for Reagan because they knew he would "kick some ass." It was the nation collectively beating on its chest and proclaiming: "We're not going to take this any more!" That's what I mean by the vote being "autobiographical." The vote is often not just about the candidate; it's about ourselves. It is our national, collective "reflection in the mirror" exercise we do every four years.

For me to be thrown in the bleachers with "America," instead of with the press corps, was a blessing. I now had access to my own personal cross section of the electorate. I had the security folks and their misdirection to thank for that. I started handing out questionnaires to anyone willing to take the twenty-question survey It was a good mix of folks, too—different races, ages, and genders. If it skewed in any direction, it was heavily blue-collar and almost exclusively Democrats. Not to worry! The same surveys would be taken at Obama and McCain rallies yet to come.

As I've said, being a reporter gives you license to start talking to anyone; and, with two hours to kill before the Clintons were to arrive, people were in a friendly, chatty mood. The young man next to me, I concluded, was probably a student at either Penn or Drexel; but, as we often find out in life, it's a mistake to jump to conclusions. Daniel Aubry, nineteen years old, actually came here from New Hampshire to campaign for Hillary Clinton. Why?

"I am a cancer survivor," Aubry told me. "I am in remission." He told me that he was diagnosed with lymphoma at sixteen, but that since there was no pediatric hospital in New Hampshire for that affliction, he was forced to go elsewhere. "Thank God, I had a teacher in middle school who knew people at NYU (medical center), pulled some strings, and got me in." He wants Clinton's brand of health care reform because "the average person doesn't have the strings," he said. So for Aubry, his choice of backing Hillary Clinton was easy. "**Personally, for me, it's health care!**" he declared. Given his plight, that was not hard to understand.

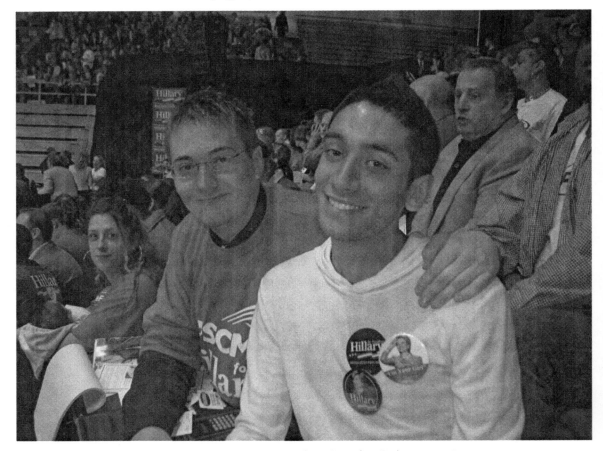

Figure 18. Cancer patient Daniel Aubry (right) campaigns for Hillary Clinton in Philadelphia, Pennsylvania. April 21, 2008. (Mark Curtis)

The choice, I suspect, was not so simple for the family of Mindy and Allen Jeter, of Philadelphia. He's black; she's white; and they have two biracial children. It was interesting to note that—despite the presence of both a female and an African American candidate on the ballot— their decision seemed void of race or gender preference.

Mindy Jeter said that she was supporting Senator Clinton "because she is the best choice. She's what the country needs right now. She has the experience." I assumed Allen Jeter might be more inclined to Obama since both he and the candidate are African-American; but, like his wife, Jeter said he was voting on political experience, not race or gender. I even asked him whether he favored a "Clinton-Obama" ticket. "I'll support that only if she (Clinton) is at the top of the ticket," Allen Jeter insisted.

Hillary Clinton would love to hear that story. She had been selling herself as the candidate with the most experience, best prepared to walk into the Oval office January 20, 2009. (This proved to be a winning strategy in Pennsylvania because, when all the votes were counted, a "USA Today" exit poll indicated that 60 percent of undecided voters who made up their minds in the final week voted for Clinton because of her experience.)

Finally, after many of us had been in the Palestra for almost three hours, the rally began shortly after 10 p.m. It was like a "three-act play." First on stage was a triumvirate of members of Congress. Representative Joe Sestak, of Philadelphia, is a former Navy Admiral who served in Bill Clinton's White House. He was joined by Representative Allyson Schwartz, also of Philadelphia.

However, the local folks were upstaged by a firebrand from Cleveland, Ohio. Representative Stephanie Tubbs Jones had been a loyal stalwart for Hillary Clinton in the African-American community. It is possible that Jones may have brought in enough voters to guarantee Senator Clinton's significant margin of victory in the Ohio primary, just six weeks earlier. This lady could work a crowd into a frenzy! With her shouts that it was time to "Step up, PA," Jones had the building rocking.

The next act must have felt like a "garage band" opening for the Beatles, but Governor Ed Rendell (D-PA) and Philadelphia Mayor Michel Nutter took the stage, undaunted. Nutter, one of the nation's leading black politicians backing Clinton, told the audience

"You've got to be ready day one," touting Clinton's experience for the Presidency as greater than that of Obama.

The governor took a different tack, trying to sell Clinton as a tireless fighter, who came back after being way down, near defeat. "The media tried to count her out after Iowa, and she came back," said Rendell. The crowd erupted. Then Rendell delivered the punch line: "We all better get ready to say two new words: 'Madame President'." The building shook with excitement.

Now you should understand one thing here. In politics, timing is everything. This event was scheduled for 10 p.m., so that it would be the lead story on the 11 o'clock TV news in Philadelphia, the fourth largest media market in America. What we in the audience didn't understand was that all these speakers were killing time.

Perhaps the most fascinating was Chelsea Clinton, who had become something of a secret weapon in this campaign. After being a "wallflower" much of the campaign, they brought her out during the Wisconsin primary. Why they hesitated to use the 27-year-old Stanford graduate is beyond me. She was sharp, chatty, funny, and intelligent, and she toed the campaign line well.

Now Chelsea was in something of a "pickle" this night, because she had recently said in the press that her mom would be a better President than her dad. This was okay when she was campaigning on her own; but tonight her dad was standing beside her, and her mom was on the way. Undaunted, she explained to the partisan crowd just exactly why her mom would be better than her dad. "She's more progressive," Chelsea said, "and I think she's more prepared than he was." With that, Bill Clinton nodded his head up and down, and the crowd burst into a torrent of laughter.

This was great political theatre! Then Chelsea became serious and made her case. She believed the foreign policy experience her mom had gained in the Senate was something her dad just didn't have as Arkansas Governor. She may have had a solid point.

As well as she performed, Chelsea Clinton couldn't upstage her dad. She introduced him, and the crowd went wild. As with Ronald Reagan, the man is so popular you get the feeling he could have won a third term, if only the Constitution allowed it.

The former President wisely saluted Philadelphia when he began his remarks. "America was born in this city, and we should never forget it," Clinton told the cheering mob. He noted the irony of this race in the birthplace of the original Constitution, which did not grant voting rights to women and most blacks. "Two people running in this race could not have voted (back then)," he said. "This is a profoundly significant time."

The ex-President said his wife would "take the good intentions of the campaign and turn it into real change in other people's lives." He was just getting warmed up. Clinton mentioned that Hillary's plane was running late, but he seemed unfazed. Like the "Energizer Bunny," he just kept on going.

This was where he got most candid, too. He shared what he calls "Clinton's Laws of Politics." For a man who first ran for office unsuccessfully thirty years ago, he has learned some lessons along the way. Perhaps most pertinent tonight was rule number two: "If someone tells you to quit, it's because they are afraid you won't." Certainly that was a message to the Obama campaign and to party leaders. On that note, Mr. Clinton laid out his fourth law: "If someone tells you 'You can't win,' it's because they are scared that you can, or will!" The crowd applauded loudly because they knew he was right. Being positioned as an underdog and being urged to quit the race was probably the best place Hillary Clinton could have been at that time. She could present herself as a fighter, not a quitter. This is simply a trait the American people want in any president, of any party. We want them tough as nails; we don't want them to fold under pressure.

Hillary Clinton was going to be late, and the entourage of speakers had to filibuster. Well, no one does this better than Bill

Clinton. The man could talk about a phone pole and make it interesting. He took the stage at 10:20. The candidate finally arrived at 10:44. He had just filibustered twenty-four minutes with no notes, no teleprompter, no script, and no nothing. In my thirty years of covering politics, I've learned he's the master at this. He has no peer.

Finally, the former President introduced his wife. "She is the ablest candidate I have ever supported for President of the United States," he said. With that, the music hit a crescendo; and the junior Senator from New York emerged from backstage. The Philadelphia crowd was at full throttle.

Above the roar of the crowd, Senator Clinton shouted into her microphone, "Are you ready to pick a president tomorrow?" The crowd shouted a loud and collective, "Yes!" Intermittently there were loud chants of "Hil-la-ry, Hil-lar-ry" from nearly ten thousand throats. It was deafening.

The name of Senator Barack Obama was never spoken that night, although there were veiled references. The closest candidate Clinton came was when she mocked one of Obama's signature rally lines. "It's not enough to say 'Yes, we can'," she said in a clear shot at her opponent. "We need to say *how* we can." The subtlety was not lost on this crowd.

Senator Clinton promised a whole litany of items: Starting to bring the troops home in sixty days; ending the "No Child Left Behind" law; providing health care coverage for all Americans; and growing the "green" or environmental sector of the U.S. economy.

These were all items that sounded good to this crowd, whether they would be doable, or not. Many military experts doubt the wisdom of a rapid troop pull-out. "No Child" was not just the education bill of a Republican President; it had strong support from Congressional Democrats. Providing health coverage and a healthy environment have mass appeal, but no one mentioned a word about how it would all be paid for.

This is fairly typical of presidential politics. We want to hear all the good ideas; we don't want to hear how difficult or costly they might be. This may explain why we so often are disappointed and disillusioned with our leaders. They simply don't (or can't) deliver what they promise.

But tonight was about euphoria and momentum. The sordid financial details of public policy would have to wait until after November. Hillary Clinton hit the nail on the head best when she told the crowd that this was really more like a job interview, and not an election. "Who would you hire to turn this economy around?" she asked; and the crowd cheered wildly for her. It was also clearly an appeal to undecided voters. Some polls had Clinton up by nine points, while another showed Obama surging and perhaps winning. He spent an estimated eleven million dollars, double what Clinton spent on TV ads; and many wondered if his huge money advantage would lead to an upset.

Still, the Clintons and their entourage, including the Pennsylvania Governor and the Philadelphia Mayor, were not even about to entertain the idea of defeat. As they left the arena with the "Theme from Rocky" blaring in the background, they were clearly ready to fight to the finish.

Philadelphia awoke to a sunny primary day on Tuesday morning. With projections of another record voter turnout, the weather did not disappoint. I stopped by a polling place at a church near the Liberty Bell, and the lines were long. As always, one of the best places to take the public pulse was at the local eateries. I stopped in for lunch at Fork Restaurant, a place I had found popular with political types back in 2000, during the Republican Convention. Great food, too!

Sitting with me at the bar was 82-year-old Lura Reisman, a lifelong Philadelphia Democrat. When she found out I was a reporter, Lura was ready for conversation. She's an admitted news and political junkie. She compared the excitement of this race to

1960, when Senator. John F. Kennedy narrowly beat Vice President Richard Nixon. "The year 2008 has something in common with 1960," she said, "because it has the young people interested. Finally the young people are getting off their butts."

She had a good point. When the Constitution was amended in 1971 during the Vietnam War, lowering the voting age from 21 to 18, many people thought it was a privilege that would bring millions of young people to the polls. To the surprise of many political observers, youthful voters never materialized in any great numbers until this year. "They were more interested in lowering the drinking age," Reisman said of college students back then.

Reisman said that she sees a lot of Kennedy in Obama. "I hope that he remains as he is now," Reisman said, "and doesn't get corrupted by politics." As for President Kennedy, Reisman said he had a similar trait to Obama when it came to public speaking. "Kennedy made you feel good. He was an optimist," Reisman added.

Despite her passion for Obama, Reisman was in the minority today. When the primary results were tallied in Pennsylvania, Hillary Clinton beat Obama by more that 220,000 votes and won by nearly 10 percentage points. Obama won the Philadelphia and Harrisburg areas, but that was it. Clinton won every other county in the state, including the home county for Pittsburgh. That she won all the rural areas was not a surprise. A week earlier, Obama had made some surprising (not to mention self-damaging) comments about voters in rural America who are disillusioned by the political process. At a private fundraiser in San Francisco, he said: "So it's not surprising then that they get bitter, they cling to guns or religion or antipathy to people who aren't like them or anti-immigrant sentiment or anti-trade sentiment as a way to explain their frustrations."

While no reporters were present, someone taped Obama's remarks and shared them with the *Huffington Post* website. New media has changed the landscape and the rules, and Obama's remarks were shortly heard throughout the land. On the eve of the Pennsylvania primary, this was not what Obama needed. He had already lost Texas and Ohio to Clinton six weeks earlier, and she was hammering him on the fact that he could not win in states needed for a Democratic victory in November.

Now with her win in Pennsylvania (a landslide in rural areas), Senator Clinton strengthened that argument. "Some people counted us out and said to drop out, but the American people don't quit," Clinton told the packed crowd gathered at her victory rally, "and they deserve a President who doesn't quit."

By now Clinton had won California, New York, Ohio, Texas and Pennsylvania. She had also won Michigan and Florida, even though their delegations were disqualified. Even so, with seven of the nation's largest states in her back pocket, she made a strong case that she could win those states in November. Any Democrat would need every one of those states, except Texas, to become president. This was certainly an argument that she was making to hundreds of undecided Super Delegates across the nation who, in many respects, held her nomination in their hands.

"The road to the White House does go through Pennsylvania," Clinton said, noting that without the Keystone State Democrats might be doomed in November. Besides, Pennsylvania has one of the highest concentrations of military veterans in the nation; and that meant John McCain could be competitive and might even win here. So, instead of listening to calls for her to quit the race, Clinton shot back at the frontrunner, Obama. "I think the question ought to be 'Why can't he (Obama) close the deal?' " she said.

Many Clinton backers believed that her nomination could be sealed by two things: Convincing many undecided "Super Delegates" that she had a better chance than Obama of winning in November, and getting the delegates from Michigan and Florida reinstated.

There were strong sentiments on that latter point, so much so that an interesting group of "lobbyists" from Florida showed up in Philadelphia. Diane Mantouvalos ran a website, www.hireheels.com. One of its main goals was to lobby for Hillary Clinton and get her into the White House. The Democratic National Committee had already announced that a meeting in late May would decide the fate of those two state delegations. Mantouvalos blamed the chaotic dispute on Democratic National Committee Chairman Howard Dean. "When it comes to seating Florida and Michigan, it is clouding his (Dean's) judgment," Mantouvalos said. "I'm not even a Democrat," she added. "I'm an independent."

On this night when Hillary Clinton won Pennsylvania, she also surged ahead in the national popular vote, (if you count Michigan and Florida). So, while the race was close and Obama had more committed delegates, Clinton had more popular votes. "Everyone is consumed by the margin," Mantouvalos said, believing that electability in November was the more important issue. She and her cohorts worked the crowd, trying to organize more folks on behalf of candidate Clinton.

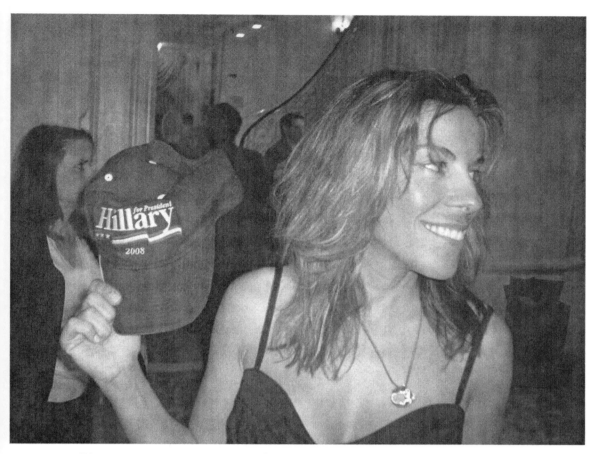

Figure 19. Diane Mantouvalos supports Hillary Clinton's
disputed delegates from Florida and Michigan with
www.HireHeels.com in Philadelphia, Pennsylvania,
April 20, 2008. (Mark Curtis)

There were more conventional political strategists in the crowd, too. Ann Lewis was White House Communications Director under President Clinton and a longtime party mover and shaker. With Pennsylvania behind them, Democrats were facing a two-state showdown in two weeks, as North Carolina and Indiana would hold primaries on May 6.

"Our strategy is simple," said Lewis. "She's the candidate who can win in November. We've just got to get out there and prove it." Lewis admitted that Clinton had to win at least one of the May 6 primaries to keep her argument (and her campaign) viable. It would be a daunting task. Recent polls showed Obama ahead in North Carolina by as much as sixteen points. On the other hand, Clinton was polling just barely ahead in Indiana, with a mere three-point margin.

The Clinton campaign was also getting help from another strong ally. Democratic Congresswoman Stephanie Tubbs Jones represented Cleveland, Ohio, in Congress. Her support for Clinton was key in Ohio's African-American communities. As one of America's leading black politicians who supported Clinton over Obama, Jones carried some weight. She was in Philadelphia campaigning for Clinton, hoping her sway, especially among women voters, would pay off. Now with Pennsylvania in the victory column, Jones was not stopping her crusade. "My philosophy is we just take these one state at a time," she said. "I will be campaigning with President Clinton in North Carolina. Then I'm going to Indiana." Being from Ohio, a state that borders Pennsylvania and Indiana, Jones felt she had a unique role in helping Hillary Clinton.

Needless to say, after Pennsylvania, Texas and Ohio, it appeared the tide was indeed turning for Hillary Clinton. According to CNN, Obama had 1,694 delegates, to 1,556 for Clinton, meaning she was within striking distance. She also won over 60 percent of the votes among whites, senior citizens, blue collar workers, and people who had made up their minds within the past week. Her case as the better "November candidate" was getting stronger.

Perhaps sensing another defeat, Obama chose to deliver his primary night remarks from Indiana, where voters would cast ballots in two weeks. Sounding optimistic and upbeat, Obama told supporters gathered in Evansville, "There were a lot of folks who didn't think we could make this race when it started, but we worked hard." Obama reminded supporters he was still in the lead.

It was befitting that the rest of us were still gathered in Philadelphia, home to boxing great Joe Frazier. That's because the Obama-Clinton battle was becoming an epic reminiscent of the Joe

Frazier-Muhammad Ali trilogy of boxing matches. Clinton played the "Rocky" theme to death in Philly, but "Rocky" was fiction; Frazier vs. Ali was the real deal. They slugged it out for months, and no one could nail the knockout punch. Hillary Clinton's tenacity in the face of adversity also drew notice from Republicans. Former White House Press Secretary Tony Snow told me a funny joke. He said his old boss, President George W. Bush, might describe Hillary as "somebody who you should never mis-underestimate!" It was funny, but true!

Now for Obama and Clinton, it was on to North Carolina and Indiana; but we knew it wouldn't end there either. A long, hard, bumpy campaign road was still ahead.

CHAPTER 8: NORTH CAROLINA & INDIANA

"It's not over 'til it's over;" and "It's not over until the fat lady sings."

These are two of the most overused clichés in the news business, but I won't need to use them when describing the never-ending high drama of the Democratic primary season in 2008.

Instead, Hillary Clinton has now re-coined the phrase: "It's not over until the lady in the pantsuit says it is." It may have been a funny, self-deprecating remark about her own wardrobe, but her point in early May was clear: Hillary Clinton would not drop out of the Presidential race, despite calls from some factions in her party to quit.

Fresh off her decisive 10 percentage point victory in the Pennsylvania primary, Hillary Clinton was on a roll. She was closing the gap on Barack Obama in the total delegate count. Obama led with 1,489 delegates while Clinton had 1,337. The winning candidate had to have at least 2,024 delegates to claim the Democratic nomination.

The week of May 6, all eyes of the political world were on Indiana and North Carolina, both of which were holding Tuesday primaries. Polling indicated the contest was going to be very close. The Real Clear Politics composite poll the day before the North Carolina primary had it Obama 50 percent, Clinton 42 percent, with the all important undecided vote at 8 percent. In Indiana, it was 49 percent Clinton, 44 percent Obama, with 7 percent undecided. In other words, the two states were literally reverse images of one another, and both campaigns were in high gear. If one candidate swept both states, the fight would likely be over. If Clinton and Obama split the states, the campaign would march on.

With more delegates at stake in North Carolina, I chose to fly to Charlotte. Since I had been the Washington correspondent for WSOC-TV9 in Charlotte for five years, I knew more about this state than about Indiana; and I still had media connections in Carolina, too.

North Carolina is a beautiful state, but it's a long stretch from one end to the other. This was going to be a long trip in the car. My usual "partner-in-crime," Jamie Dupree, from Cox Radio, chose to cover Indiana, so I was going it alone.

My first assignment was a campaign stop that Bill Clinton was making in the small town of Kernersville, about ninety miles from Charlotte. It was at a high school gymnasium. I just loved events like this one because, not only did you have better access to the candidates, but the folksy townspeople were so genuine and quotable. I loved the feel of small-town U.S.A.

Bill Clinton had been elected President, in part, because he understood small-town and rural American politics. Coming from little Hope, Arkansas, had proved a blessing, not a handicap. His insight into small-town life was precisely why Clinton wowed a crowd of about two thousand at Robert Glenn High School on this Sunday night.

One of the keys to understanding the psyche of small-town America is to recognize that the people want to be heard. They want a voice, too. New York City has a voice; so does Chicago. California has a voice; so does Florida. To have a say in American politics, bigger is better, because there are more voters and they get a larger media microphone.

Still, rural America can carry considerable weight if it speaks with its collective voice. Barack Obama had given the Clinton campaign a break a few weeks earlier in San Francisco, when he remarked that many rural voters were "bitter" and "clung to guns or religion." The Clintons seized on the remarks as elitist and trumpeted them to rural voters in Pennsylvania, where Hillary then beat Obama by 10 percentage points. Now, the Clintons were taking the same tack in North Carolina.

Debbie Hollowell is a disabled mother of two. She came to the rally with her sixteen-year-old daughter, Bree. They supported Clinton, mainly on the issue of health care. But Hollowell's eighteen-year-old son, Alex, supported Obama. "It makes for interesting dinner conversation," Debbie said with a laugh. "He takes voting very seriously. He wants his voice heard."

Hollowell said that people in the community did take offense at Obama's rural criticisms. "A lot of people do stand behind their religion here. It is the 'Bible Belt.' But they are smart," she added. "We are in an economic crisis. We need help. We are paying all kinds of taxes, but it's getting us less benefits." She pointed out that religion is an important part of life here all the time, not just something people run to in a crisis. Bottom line: She supported Hillary Clinton based on her many years in public service. "I feel like she has the experience to do the job," Hollowell said.

Marshall Nance is a longtime local resident. He and I really hit it off when we both recalled being at Bill Clinton's inaugural in 1992 – a day that was bitterly cold, but a moment in history you just don't forget. After all, how many people have ever seen a Presidential Inaugural in person, even with frozen feet?

Nance, too, said that people were angry about Obama's criticism of rural America, but now, weeks later, Nance was willing to forgive and forget. "I have no comment. None of us are perfect," he said. "Sometimes we say things we don't actually mean." I asked Nance whether he had now forgiven Obama. "Yes," he said, "and if Hillary Clinton does not succeed, I am supporting Mr. Obama."

Bill Clinton knows how to work a crowd like this. There were about two thousand of us in the hot, humid high school gym. He talked about health care reform, about the environment and about eliminating the "No Child Left Behind" education program, which got the biggest cheer of the night.

However, it was his talk of eliminating the federal gas tax for the summer that may have resonated most. The economy was in a downturn, and people were hurting. Now, gas prices near four dollars a gallon were slapping them in the face. Senator Hillary Clinton wanted the oil companies to pay the gas tax for consumers from Memorial Day to Labor Day, while Senator John McCain simply wanted the tax suspended during that time. Senator Barack Obama had accused them both of creating a political stunt—a "shell game" he called it. Bill Clinton disagreed.

"Hillary knew she would be derided if she offered short-term relief from gas prices," the former President said. "She thinks the oil companies ought to share a tiny smidgen of their profits with you."

Mr. Clinton said the attacks on his wife had been unfair, and he knew the tax cut would have populist appeal. "She just said people are having a hard time, and we ought to help them," he said of his wife, "You won't have anybody calling her a panderer who is having trouble filling up their gas tank."

Sixteen years ago, Bill Clinton had won the presidency when his campaign used the catchphrase, "It's the economy, stupid!" He recognized that more than anything else voters care about their own pocketbooks and economic wellbeing. If Hillary Clinton should win Indiana and North Carolina on Tuesday, it could be because her gas tax idea simply appealed to voters, especially in rural areas.

Much as he had in Texas, Bill Clinton was bouncing all over North Carolina, from rally to rally. I believe he had six stops that first day, and more the rest of the week. Hillary Clinton was spending a lot of time in Indiana, though she would be in North Carolina on Monday. But as we saw in the Texas and Ohio showdowns, it was a great strategy to have Bill Clinton work one state, while Hillary worked the other.

Many people have speculated about the Clintons' relationship over the years. Some pundits have called it more of a "business arrangement" than a marriage. Following Bill Clinton around for months on the campaign trail, I really got the sense that he deeply respected Hillary and believed she would, indeed, be a good President. He was working too damned hard for her, to be feigning sincerity. She had stood by him in his toughest times, despite his disloyalty to her. Now, he seemed honestly trying to pay her back. At least, that was my take.

In a scene reminiscent of Harry Truman's "Whistle Stop" tour, Hillary Clinton made a campaign stop at the historic train station in High Point, North Carolina, on Monday. Okay, she arrived by motorcade and not by train, but the scene was a beautiful backdrop. Her speech was interrupted by two trains and two noisy track cleaners, so we had the ambience. She started her speech by talking about prayer and her Methodist faith. The crowd was warm and receptive. Every now and then her voice would slip into a slight southern accent, something many of the candidates have been guilty of every time they visit the South. It was a little jarring, but the audience didn't seem to care.

Where the New York Senator really scored some points was in discussing her idea to freeze the federal gas tax for the summer. This issue, first proposed by John McCain, had grown "legs" after seeming at first like a campaign gimmick. Now that people really liked it, the Clinton campaign was seizing upon it. "These high gas prices are directly causing an increase in our food prices," Clinton said. "I want the oil companies—out of their excess profits—to pay the gas tax this summer," she added.

She differed from McCain in this regard. He simply wanted the federal gas tax repealed from Memorial Day to Labor Day. Obama wanted the gas tax left as is, referring to the freeze as a campaign gimmick. "Senator Obama wants you to pay the gas tax this summer, instead of the oil companies paying it out of their record profits," Clinton said. "I'm ready to take on the oil companies. This is part of a larger difference between my opponent and me."

The idea had broad populist appeal. Voters I spoke with that day echoed the concerns about fuel prices. Moneka Smith is the mother of two kids in High Point. She was backing Clinton, especially on the gas tax issue. "I thought it was a great speech," she said. "I just love what she is talking about, with the gas prices and the troops coming home. I'm all for that." Some economists had estimated that the average taxpayer might save only $28 per month from cutting the gas tax. Smith said that even that small amount was fine with her. "Hopefully, it will help a little bit and will make a difference," she said. It would help her at the grocery store, too, she added. "Oh God! Yes! Milk, eggs, even bread's gone up."

The crowd seemed to like the speech and the railroad station backdrop. When two noisy trains barreled through, Senator Clinton was undeterred and even ad libbed that high-speed rail was a way to ease our dependence on foreign oil. Some undecided voters left the rally convinced that Clinton was their candidate. Evelyn Hohn, of High Point, even took home a campaign sign for her front yard. "I think she's wonderful," said Hohn. "I just think she does her own self, nothing 'put on.' I just like her!"

Once the forty-five minute rally was over, Clinton sped away in her motorcade to board a plane for Indiana, which would also be holding a crucial primary the following day. Clinton went by plane, not train, because with a campaign this intense, the candidates practically need to be in two states at once.

This was going to be a busy day for me. John McCain and Michelle Obama both had speeches in Charlotte late in the afternoon. If I played my cards right, I could make at least parts of both. This was an especially tough time for McCain. He had the Republican nomination sewn up two months earlier. While he continued to campaign, it was hard for him to get any press coverage, let alone to make headlines. The epic struggle between Clinton and Obama was so monumental, that any other political story paled by comparison. Unless you were New York Governor Elliot Spitzer getting caught with a hooker, you were old news.

Maintaining visibility was challenging for the McCain campaign, and they knew the lack of it had helped destroy Rudy Giuliani's campaign. Still, there were some upsides. First, McCain could get some rest. At age 71, with people questioning his fitness for office, (he was fine!) McCain could at last relax a bit. Second, he could strategize for the November election. Since he had started with little money and against all odds had won the nomination, this was a time to create a game plan, think about cabinet nominees and let the Democrats beat each other up.

On the downside, the lack of drama on the GOP side meant minimal press coverage; and it was critical that McCain try to get his message out there and keep it out there. So it was wise strategy that he came to North Carolina Monday for a town hall meeting at the Charlotte Chamber of Commerce. Tuesday he was scheduled to speak at Wake Forest University, in Winston-Salem. With all the press here, the trip was a wise move, even if only to remind the country, "Hey, I'm still a candidate for President, too!"

McCain was all business before the Chamber of Commerce in the heart of downtown Charlotte. His first topic was the economy. "Thank you for everything you do for the economy here," he said. "It's a high growth economy!" McCain mentioned a commonly-held belief that manufacturing is not coming back as a great force in this economy. He commended North Carolina for expanding into the high tech, banking and education sectors. "We should not fear that change," the Arizona Senator said. "We should never fear that change. I know these are tough times," he added, "but the fundamentals of our economy are strong." He pledged to keep taxes low and to lessen the nation's dependence on foreign oil.

McCain also addressed the issue of health care reform. He believed it is better for employers to provide health insurance, instead of having a government-run system. This was perhaps where he differed most from the two Democratic candidates. "There will be a stark difference," he said. "I want the families to make the decisions about their health care. Senators Obama and Clinton want the government to make those decisions."

He also talked about immigration reform and the bill he led that had failed to pass Congress. "This is a burning issue. Our borders are broken." McCain said. "Twelve million are here illegally, and two million of them are criminals who need to be deported. The rest must be offered a guest worker program, but can't skip ahead of those in the citizenship line who came here legally. We are a Judeo-Christian valued nation, and we must address it in that fashion."

McCain talked international issues—the need to stop Iran from creating nuclear weapons and the need to provide aid to Myanmar, which had recently been devastated by a cyclone, killing maybe ten thousand people.

On a lighter note, the Arizona Senator remained the funniest candidate on the trail. Today he said, "We now have a pro-American President of France, which shows that if you live long enough, anything can happen!" The crowd loved it and laughed.

I raced across Charlotte, hoping to catch Michelle Obama's speech at the civic center. She had recently been keeping a low profile in the campaign, but that was about to change. The Obamas were a dynamic team together, but they also saw how effective the Clintons were when they split up and took on two states. I believed the Clintons owed their same-day wins in Texas and Ohio to that strategy. Now, with Barack Obama attempting to win North Carolina and Indiana the same day, Michelle really had to play a more visible role.

I have written before about political spouses and how sometimes they are so dynamic that they steal the limelight from the candidates. Elizabeth Edwards could upstage husband John; Bill Clinton still has so much star power in some circles that Hillary gets dwarfed; and first lady Betty Ford often made more headlines than President Gerald.

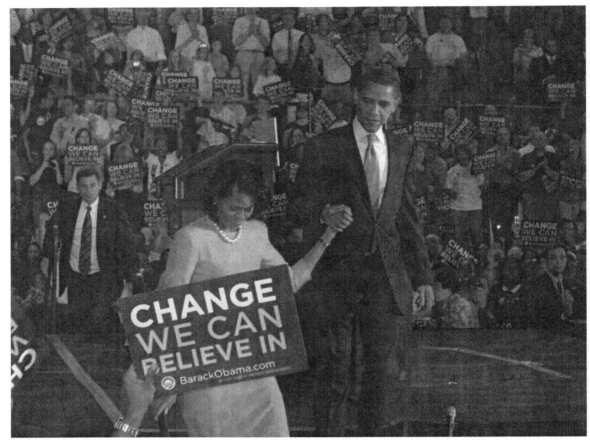

Figure 20. Michelle and Barack Obama walk down stage at
North Carolina State University in Raleigh. May 6,
2008. (Mark Curtis)

Why was this? I don't know! My friend Doug Sovern, from San
Francisco's KCBS radio, and I were pondering this after we watched
Michelle Obama simply blow the doors off a campaign event in
Charlotte—one that was not attended by her husband. I wondered
whether candidates' spouses are simply more liberated because
they can say pretty much anything they want without major
repercussions. Maybe that's it, we agreed. Who knows?

To say Michelle Obama was spectacular would be an
understatement. I had never heard her speak in public before,
and—quite honestly—I was blown away. So was the crowd, and this
event had a pretty impressive marquee. Former Charlotte Mayor

Harvey Gantt and longtime civil-rights leader the Reverend Joseph Lowery spoke before Mrs. Obama. Those are tough acts to follow.

Gantt talked about Obama's ability to be a unifier, appealing to a lot of people, "black, white, young, old, rich and poor and bring them together to solve our problems."

He received the loudest applause when he said, "We need to send someone to Washington who is not beholden to the special interests." The crowd went wild!

The Reverend Lowery said Obama could, "Move America from the dark valley of doubt to the mountain top of hope."

When Mrs. Obama took the stage, she took command of the audience. In rapid fire she laid out her husband's case for the nomination: "Barack Obama has raised more money, has broken records. Barack Obama has won more of the popular votes. Barrack Obama has won more pledged delegates. Barack Obama has won more states. And let's be clear, Barack Obama has won in all kinds of states," she said, barely coming up for air. "Barack Obama has won in big states and small. He's won primary and caucus states."

She then added, "He's won red states and blue states and purple states." With that, the crowd burst into laughter; but the point was made.

Michelle also talked about her modest upbringing on the south side of Chicago. "There's a whole lot of talk in their race about elitism and being out of touch," she said. "The life I had growing up was not miraculous." Michelle's father was a disabled city worker in Chicago, yet worked hard enough to get two of his kids educated at Princeton.

"He got up and went to work every day without complaining. He knew hard work could lead to a better future for his kids. That's what kept him going," she said; and the crowd cheered her personal story. "Barack's upbringing was tough, too. His mother was eighteen and single, a white woman trying to raise a black child in the 1960s. You know she was a dreamer!" The crowd laughed again; but it was a poignant story, and people were touched by that. Obama said she and her husband tried to teach their two little girls the values that her parents and Barack's parents and grandparents had taught them.

One person who was especially touched by the story was retired schoolteacher Lula Glover. She tried to teach her students similar lessons. "When I was teaching school, I taught just this thing—that they could be what they wanted to be, as long as they persevered," she said, "and I especially taught that message to young boys."

Glover admires the Clintons, but has doubts about whether there should be a Clinton-Obama ticket, no matter who is on top. "I have a problem with that. I was hoping for it in the beginning, yes. Now I may have to calm down," Glover said. "I'm not feeling it again."

The crowd was completely aroused. Many had already voted by mail, and they were urged to make phone calls and emails to help get out the vote. Michelle Obama clearly inspired them, despite her husband's absence. One campaign worker led the crowd in a repeated chant: "Fired up; Ready to go!" On Tuesday we would know whether all the inspiration had paid off!

Primary day had arrived in North Carolina and Indiana, and there was nervous anticipation in both camps. Would today be the day Hillary Clinton or Barack Obama was finally dealt a knockout punch? We didn't yet know, and there was still plenty of campaigning to cover, including another rally with the seemingly tireless Bill Clinton.

For many reporters, it's a once-in-a-lifetime opportunity to meet a President (or a former one), let alone to ask him some questions. I've actually met Bill Clinton twice before when he was President, but today was our first encounter since he left office. It was also my first Presidential interview!

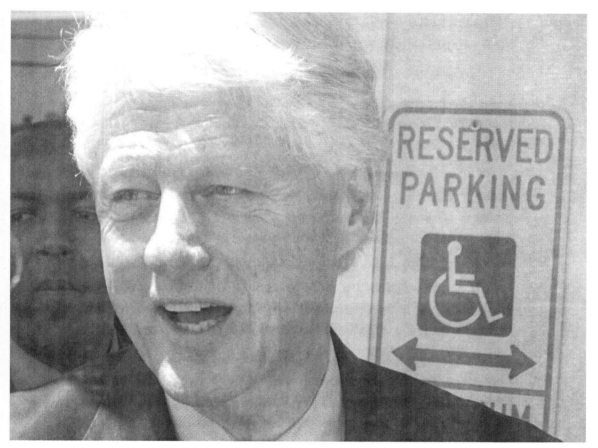

Figure 21. Bill Clinton dines and campaigns for Hillary at Lexington BBQ, Lexington, NC, May 6, 2008. (Mark Curtis)

The location was the "Lexington BBQ" out on U.S. Highway 64, west of Interstate 85. Clinton and supporters gathered there at 11:30 in the morning. He shook hands and posed for pictures with about two hundred people, all the while imploring them to go vote for Hillary in the North Carolina primary.

Then the ex-President headed in for lunch, and we knew this would be a long wait, even though he was scheduled to be in Winston-Salem at 1 p.m. Finally, at about 1:20, Mr. Clinton emerged from lunch, shook hands, and signed books for some people, then stopped to greet me. As he shook my hand, I inquired, "How was the barbecue, Mr. President?"

"It was unbelievable," he said. "The barbecue was good. The hush puppies were good," he added.

"Anything else?" I asked.

"If I had the ice cream, I'd need a nap," Clinton said. He walked a few steps farther and—still waving to the crowd—got into his Secret Service van.

At first I wondered, "What was I thinking? This is the most critical election in sixty years, and I ask the ex-President and husband of one of the candidates about food?" Then I thought, "Lighten up, Mark. Campaigns are supposed to be fun, too!"

Truth be told, small-town America is a great place to stop and kvetch about politics. People here were thrilled to be put on the map. Polls had been open since 6:30 a.m. in North Carolina, and turnout was heavy. A half-million people had already voted by mail.

Lee, a laborer from nearby Thomasville, told me by late morning he had yet to vote. He was still undecided between Clinton and Obama. "Tell you the truth, I don't really know," he said. "Both of them have good points on stuff, but pretty much it's a tough choice."

Kitty Craver, a lifelong resident of Lexington, was more certain. She voted for Hillary Clinton. "She's the most qualified person that's running," Craver said. Craver wore a button suggesting the key issue for her was gender and having the first female president. "In this election, it's number one. We also have a woman running for governor," she added, "and I am for her. I think it's time for women. I think we have more to offer than people realize. We are the backbone of the household. We can be the backbone of this nation."

This kind of community gathering makes small-town America feel that it counts and that the politicians are here because they care. It's also a great place to get a good meal and chat politics.

Wayne Monk has owned the Lexington BBQ for forty-five years. Clinton was the first President to visit, although Monk once fed Ronald Reagan and six other world leaders at a summit in Williamsburg, Virginia. Not bad for a great barbecue joint!

Monk sported an "I voted" sticker, so I asked him whom he picked. Wisely, he kept it a secret! Because he's a prominent businessman in a small, close-knit town, Monk told me, "I don't argue politics, religion or Carolina basketball!" I laughed out loud at the last part, knowing college basketball is king in this state!

Monk had the perfect line to describe this gorgeous primary election day with sunny, clear skies and highs in the 70s. "Hectic, but everyone's in a good mood. Smiles everywhere," he said.

Record turnout continued throughout the day, and then the ballots were counted. After three tough primary defeats in three of the nation's biggest states, Senator Barack Obama won a "Top Ten" state tonight, as he defeated Senator Hillary Clinton in North Carolina. The latest tally had Obama up in North Carolina 56 percent, to 42 percent. Clinton clung to a slight 51 to 49 percent margin in Indiana.

Obama delivered a rousing twenty-minute victory speech at North Carolina State University's arena in Raleigh. He told the crowd that stories about the Democrats being too "bloodied" to win in November were not true.

"Well, I am here to tell you tonight, I don't believe it," Obama said. "Yes, there have been bruised feelings on both sides, but ultimately this race is not about Hillary Clinton, Barack Obama, or John McCain. It's about you, the American people!"

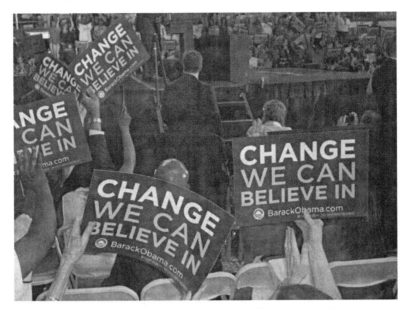

Figure 22. Barack Obama supporters rally at North
    Carolina State University, Raleigh, North Carolina, May
    6, 2008. (Mark Curtis

Figure 23. Cheering Barack Obama supporters after North
    Carolina Primary. Raleigh, North Carolina, May 6,
    2008. (Mark Curtis)

The crowd roared in approval and shouted the now familiar campaign chant, "Yes, we can! Yes, we can!" One of those in the crowd tonight was Sammie Whiting-Ellis, who was fully backing Obama because of how he inspired people. "I think he makes people think of themselves at a higher level," she said, "and he respects the fact that they can think."

Figure 24. Barack Obama addresses supporters in Raleigh, North Carolina, May 6, 2008. (Mark Curtis)

The race was not over. While Obama had widened his delegate lead slightly, he and Clinton were to square off the following Tuesday in the West Virginia primary.

Chapter 9: West Virginia, Oregon and Kentucky:

"Tonight we've come from behind, we've broken the tie, and thanks to you it's full speed ahead, on to the White House!" said Hillary Clinton, as the crowd cheered her Indiana primary victory.

It was a campaign-saving moment. Clinton noted a prediction made by her opponent Barack Obama just weeks earlier. He said Clinton would win Pennsylvania; Obama would win North Carolina; and Indiana would be the tiebreaker. Say what you want about Obama, but the man must own a crystal ball. His prediction was right on the money, but it would be a cliffhanger!

Hillary Clinton held a steady, if not comfortable, lead in Indiana all night long. But the last precincts to report were in the heavily populated Gary-Hammond region in Indiana's northwest corner. Those were essentially Chicago "suburbs," and Obama was bound to get the vast majority of those votes. He did, and almost snatched victory at the last minute. The big race in Indiana in May 2008 was not the "Indianapolis 500." It was the Clinton-Obama race to the nomination.

Figure 25. Barack Obama shakes hands with supporters. Raleigh, NC. May 6, 2008. (Mark Curtis)

I was in North Carolina, as this played out, covering that state's primary, which Obama just won. It was well after midnight as I made the three-hour drive from Obama's victory celebration in Raleigh back to my hotel in Charlotte. Late at night you can get radio signals from all over the nation after many low-power AM stations go off the air. I was listening to WABC radio in New York, WSB in Atlanta, WSM in Nashville and KMOX in St. Louis, just to name a few. I was punching the radio buttons like a teenager searching for his favorite song. The buzz about Indiana and the closing of the lead was all over the airwaves, and the drama was gut wrenching.

In the end, Hillary Clinton won Indiana, but just barely. The final total was Clinton 50.7 percent to Obama 49.3 percent. Out of 1.2 million ballots cast, Clinton won by just over eighteen thousand votes. Had she lost, it would have been over.

With Clinton hanging on, the race moved to West Virginia where she had an enormous lead in the polls. All she had to do was keep winning, and she stayed in the game. If she took West Virginia, there would be Oregon and Kentucky to look forward to next week. If she won at least one of those, there would be Puerto Rico, South Dakota and Montana two weeks later, with the final primaries.

As I said earlier, politics is about ideology, but politics is also about math.

Hillary Clinton was trailing Barack Obama by about 160 delegates at this point, and she was bound to gain some ground by picking up more primary wins; but she also had another weapon. While Republicans had the quirky "winner-take-all" system for delegates in many states, Democrats had an equally bizarre system of "Super Delegates."

"Super Delegate" status was usually reserved for elected officials and party bosses. In California, for example, every Democrat in Congress was a Super Delegate. So were the Mayors of San Francisco and Los Angeles. Regular delegates were the folks elected in the primary or caucus process and were distributed by a candidate's proportion of the popular vote. They had a sense of obligation to vote for their candidate.

Super Delegates, on the other hand, could vote for whomever they wanted. San Francisco Mayor Gavin Newsom was a big Hillary Clinton supporter, and he could have cast his ballot for her, even if Barack Obama had received every single popular vote in San Francisco!

The point is, if you lobbied enough Super Delegates, you could secure the nomination regardless of what the voters said. As with the Republicans' "winner-take-all" system, the "Super Delegate" system is not very democratic. Both parties would be well advised to change their unfair rules, in my opinion. Be that as it may, Hillary Clinton was working Super Delegates hard on her hopeful journey to the White House.

That journey took her next to West Virginia, so I bought a plane ticket to Charleston as well.

West Virginia is a state of contradictions. In many places it is lush, green, mountainous and breathtakingly beautiful. On the other hand, it is one of the poorest states in the nation, with pockets of heartbreaking poverty. The state is fairly conservative and usually votes Republican for President. Even many of the Democrats here are moderate-to-conservative. Some polls indicated Clinton led Obama by a staggering forty points, which I found hard to believe. Still, Obama's recent comments about "bitter" rural Americans who "clung to guns or religion" were not playing well here; and people were still talking about Obama's now former pastor, the Rev. Jeremiah Wright and his famed, "God Damn, America" sermon. In short, this was not "Obama Country."

Hillary Clinton was now making the case that she could win in places in November that Obama could not. She had won three of the biggest states: Texas, Ohio and Pennsylvania; and she had been arguing that she could beat John McCain in places such as West Virginia and Indiana. It was a pretty compelling point, even if she was still behind Obama in overall delegates.

For now, the immediate task was West Virginia, where polls had Clinton way ahead. Despite that, the Obama campaign folks were working hard to get people to the polls. When I arrived on Monday, both candidates were still campaigning in other states. No matter, there were still plenty of voters and volunteers to speak with.

Now the news media and the general public have an obsession with polls. When I speak at luncheons during a political season, two questions are always asked: Who is ahead in the polls? And, why are there so many polls? The questions contradict each other. Personally, I love polls ... and I hate polls! They can be a road map to what is about to happen, and they can be incredibly wrong. In 1983, the night before the Chicago Mayor's race, polls showed Richard Daley, Jr., and Jane Byrne way ahead of an obscure black Congressman from Chicago named Harold Washington. Washington won (as I predicted at the time, saying that polls inadvertently under-survey minorities).

Even this year in New Hampshire, one poll had Barack Obama up thirteen points, fresh off his win in Iowa five days earlier. Hillary Clinton won, going away. So, polls indicating a thirty-to-forty-point Clinton lead for Tuesday in West Virginia made me suspicious. We would see!

With the candidates out of town tonight, I stopped by their respective state campaign headquarters in Charleston. Both were busy with last-minute phone banks and door-to-door canvassing.

Obama spokesman Tom Bowen was not giving any quarter, based on the polls. "It's a clear choice," Bowen said. "Senator Obama or four more years of Bush's policies."

Hard at work canvassing door-to-door today was Obama supporter Ahmed Mongi. Ahmed just became a U.S. citizen on April 7, after emigrating here from Tanzania in 1983. "I came here to get an education," Mongi said. "I'm a college grad of West Virginia University." Why did he choose Obama for his first vote as an American? "The message of hope resonates with me," Mongi says. "The fact that he is new in Washington means he has a better chance of changing business." Mongi's big concerns were ending the war in Iraq and providing better health care for veterans. All that aside, he just plain liked Obama: "I think he's got charisma," Mongi said.

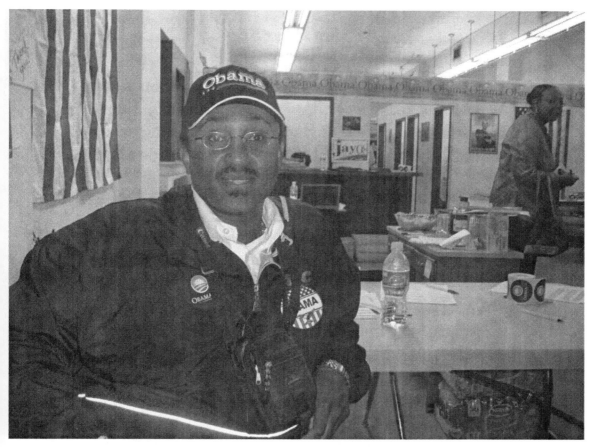

Figure 26. Obama supporter Ahmed Mongi prepares to
vote for the first time as an American citizen.
Charleston, West Virginia, May 12, 2008. (Mark Curtis)

About five blocks away at Clinton headquarters in downtown
Charleston, it was just as busy, as volunteers and staff worked
phone banks urging people to get out the vote. Organizer Cory
Waldron was just twenty years old and was taking time off from
college to work on the Clinton campaign. "She has intelligent, well-
thought-out policies," Waldron said. "Obviously, she has a true
concern about the middle class and the state of our nation," he
added, "and I truly believe she is a once-in-a-lifetime candidate."

It occurs to me that now, at age 20, Waldron was just four years
old when Clinton's husband was elected President. Does he even
remember? "For some reason I remember the saxophone (Bill

Clinton played) on Arsenio Hall," he says. I told Cory that I was four years old when John Kennedy was killed, and I remembered it pretty well. Even at age four, the political junkie thing can start!

I asked Waldron whether the staff is supporting Hillary for VP yet, should she fall short of the nomination. "We're not entertaining that possibility right now," he said. "We're still playing to win!" Echoing that thought was Clinton volunteer Angela Reed, from Fayette County, West Virginia. She said Clinton had much more experience than Obama, and that is what truly matters. "I believe she's qualified. She can take care of our problems," Reed said. "It's (experience) a big factor," she added. "I think she's a good problem solver. I think she has particular experience in foreign policy. I don't think Obama has that," Reed said.

Both campaign offices promised to be open until midnight, doing any and all last minute work.

West Virginia polls opened promptly at 6:30 Tuesday morning; and, if the lines at Chamberlain Elementary School in Charleston were any indication, this could be another record turnout in one of the most contested primary seasons in American history. Among those voting today was Daryl Huffman, age twenty, who was voting for the very first time. "I voted for Hillary," Huffman said. "I just really like her views, especially on the environment. That's what I am studying in school." Huffman attended the nearby University of Charleston and was majoring in environmental biology.

Her vote was not an easy choice. "I like Obama as well," she said, "but I feel like she has a better chance running against McCain."

The debate over McCain, and whom to support if Clinton did not win, was weighing on others today. There was concern within the Obama campaign that he could not attract enough white "blue collar" voters who might bolt the Democratic Party for John McCain if Obama was the nominee.

The Obama campaign would have mixed feelings meeting retired coal miner Thomas A. Ward, Sr. Today he voted for Hillary Clinton, saying "I think personally, myself, if we get Obama in there we got a lot of problems down the pike." Ward said Obama lacked experience. Ward thought Obama was trying to be another John Kennedy, who made inspiring speeches, but couldn't follow through. Clinton had far more real experience, according to Ward; but if Clinton failed to win the nomination, Ward would support Obama. "No, I won't back McCain," Ward said. "I'll support Obama, and my union will, too." Ward was a member of the United Mine Workers; and if that union endorsed Obama, there promised to be far more white voters in blue-collar jobs backing Obama, as well.

Democratic Party leaders knew Obama needed that support to win West Virginia in November. West Virginia almost always picks the White House winner, and no Democrat has won the presidency without it since 1916.

Young George Chamberlain came out to vote with his dad that morning in Charleston. They were Obama supporters. Chamberlain, a student at the University of Notre Dame in South Bend, Indiana, was home on summer break. Of Obama, he said, "I feel like he's a great candidate for change. He's a real honorable guy, a person who can change America in a positive direction."

Turnout was described as record breaking; and when polls closed at 8 p.m., the results did not take long to come in. I was at the Charleston Civic Center awaiting the returns at Hillary Clinton's planned victory rally. When she was declared the winner, the crowd began chanting: "It's not over! It's not over!"

Clinton captured the West Virginia Democratic primary by a huge margin; and, while her campaign for the presidential nomination remained a statistical long shot, she was still in it. Clinton won West Virginia by a whopping 67 to 26 percent over Barack Obama.

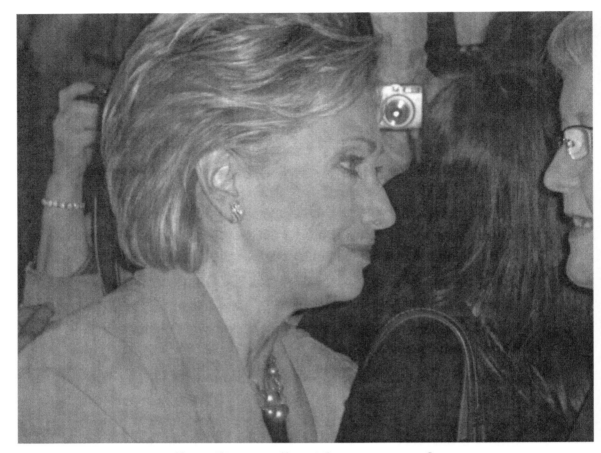

Figure 27. Hillary Clinton talks with supporters after winning the West Virginia Primary. May 13, 2008. (Mark Curtis)

According to CNN exit polls, Clinton won over 70 percent of female voters; she also won over 72 percent of white voters without college degrees. In other words, Clinton won a landslide of working class "blue collar" white voters. She did the same thing in Ohio and Pennsylvania, raising serious questions about whether Senator Barack Obama could capture those same voters should he win the nomination. There were concerns among Democrats that some of those "Reagan Democrats" would bolt the party as they did in 1980 and 1984 and would support the Republican—in this case, the more moderate Senator John McCain.

To a roaring crowd, Clinton laid out her case as to why she would be the better candidate in November. "We won in states that we must be prepared to win in November," she said, alluding to key states such as Michigan, Ohio, Pennsylvania and, yes, West Virginia, "if the Democrats want to take back the White House." Clinton won all four of those primaries and by decisive margins. "I am strong enough for this challenge," Clinton said. "You know I never give up!" And the crowd roared again!

Clinton did not speak ill of her opponent, Barack Obama, who was still the front-runner. "I deeply admire Senator Obama, but our case is stronger," she said. She also commended Obama on the quality of his campaign. She added: "I will work my heart out for the Democratic nominee of our party, so we have a Democratic president." Whether this was all to position herself for a possible vice-presidential selection should her run for the top job fail, only Senator Clinton knows.

Jim Cochran, a 61-year-old Vietnam veteran who backed Clinton, hoped for a brokered convention in Denver in August. "I hope it gets to the (convention) floor, like the old days," Cochran said. "That's when the Clintons will bring out their charm!" Cochran's scenario was possible, though not likely. However, if neither candidate had enough delegates and Super Delegates by August, there could be a floor fight at the convention. Much of this rested on the five remaining primaries and the disputed Michigan and Florida delegations. Clinton needed many in those groups to go her way if she was to win. Again, it was possible, but not probable at this point.

Cochran was supporting Sen. Clinton because West Virginia saw better economic times when Bill Clinton was in office from 1993 to 2001. "We need someone to bring the budget back," he said,. "and I am a Vietnam veteran, but it's time to end this (Iraq) war."

As for Clinton taking the VP spot on the ticket should she lose the nomination, Cochran said, "I think it would be a 'dream ticket,' but he (Obama) has got to make that decision."

The night rang with shouts of "Madame President! Madame President!" throughout the crowd of hundreds of Clinton supporters.

I was starving. Charleston will probably never make the cover of *Bon Appétit* magazine as a culinary scene, nor were many restaurants open late. My only real choice was a twenty-four-hour IHOP located next to my hotel, which was essentially a truck stop. When I arrived about 11 p.m., I got one of the last seats available. The restaurant was packed to the max with long-haul truck drivers and a lot of other people in "Clinton for President" T-shirts. Most of the patrons were white.

A short time later, twenty more customers showed up. All were in "Obama 2008" T-shirts, and most of them were African-American. Now, things were already tense in the packed restaurant, because it was short staffed. I suspected they weren't normally so busy this time of night. At best, there were two waitresses and two people in the kitchen. Orders were slow, and the IHOP employees were shouting at each other. While some tables were clearing after people finished eating, it was all moving quite slowly. Some people were getting a bit impatient.

What happened next? Nothing.

Forty years ago, this might have been a real powder keg, with a mix of racial and political tension. You add in the fact that people were tired, hungry and perhaps emotional over the primary, and it had all the potential for lighting a short fuse.

Suddenly, someone from the Obama camp saw a friend in the Clinton group and went over and gave a congratulatory handshake. That broke the ice. Then someone cracked a joke, and suddenly everyone was laughing. Strangers were greeting strangers. People started chattering about what happened at a certain precinct or a phone bank or on a newscast—and on and on it went. I was kind of sad to finish my meal and leave, but some kind folks in the Obama group needed my table, plus I had more stories to write. This was turning into a very friendly party, and I wished I could have stayed.

After all the racial tension and political violence I saw on TV as a child, especially during the 1968 convention in Chicago, I was so pleased to witness what was playing out before my eyes in West Virginia. I say that because earlier in the day, I spoke with two white men who were backing Hillary Clinton, but were not planning to support Obama if he won the nomination. "I can't vote for no black man," one of the men said, as the other shook his head from side to side. It was the only time in the entire yearlong campaign that I encountered this attitude. The times have changed a lot!

The nomination was by no means settled after West Virginia, and the Oregon and Kentucky primaries loomed just one week away.

On Monday, May 19, I arrived in Portland, Oregon. Various other business, including helping my son Patrick's Little League team, kept me off the campaign trail for a couple of days. Sadly, I had missed Barack Obama's Sunday rally, which drew an estimated seventy thousand people. This large turnout was becoming a regular occurrence, and it was impressive that he could sustain such energy and momentum. Everyone was still talking about the enormous rally, and there were still plenty of people around to talk politics.

Even though I've lived in Northern California for ten years, I had somehow never made it to Oregon. I was looking forward to my first visit there, as well as into Washington State. Some of the best fun of this whole campaign was simple geography—going places on the map where I had never before visited.

I usually started an Election Day blog by saying something like, "Polls open at 7 a.m." But things here in Oregon were very different. People had been voting for weeks. Oregon has the only 100 percent mail-in elections in the nation, though the trend is likely to spread. Neighboring Washington State plans to do the same. By 8 a.m., 40 percent of Oregonians had already cast their ballots, according to the Secretary of State. He believed that, when all was said and done, 60 percent of state voters would cast ballots by 8 p.m., and that would be a record.

This is fascinating, because it's not just "mail-in" voting. It's more like "drive-through" voting. People pulled up to metal boxes along certain streets and slid their ballots into the election box, just as they would with mail. There was even a voting box at a McDonald's drive-through. Turnout was greater, as was efficiency, so expect more states to join this trend.

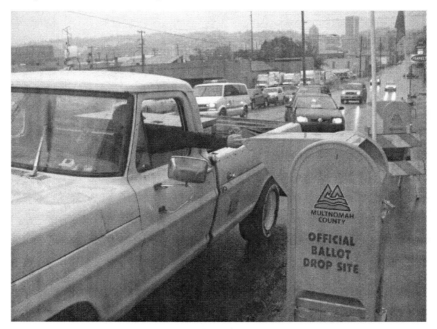

Figure 28. Most people cast their ballots by mail in the State of Oregon on primary day. Portland, Oregon, May 20, 2008. (Mark Curtis)

There were very few traditional polling places left in Oregon. The only one I found was actually at the Multnomah County Elections office in Portland, where people could drop in to vote. We should note: This was not just the contest between Barack Obama and Hillary Clinton for the Democratic presidential nomination. Thirteen people were vying for Mayor of Portland, and there was a flurry of candidates running for State and Congressional offices. Election fever, as it were.

Time now for an embarrassing confession: I showed up in one of the world's rainiest cities with no raincoat and no umbrella. What was I thinking? Newsflash! I'm in Portland, and it's raining! Okay, so it's not a 7.9 earthquake, I know; but it rains all the time here, so why should my first visit be any different? What was I thinking?

Thanks to the kindness of convenience store clerk Jagdish Singh, I stayed relatively dry. Singh lent me her umbrella to use during my broadcast to KTVU. She's an interesting woman. She holds both U.S. and Canadian citizenship, but chose not to vote in this election. "I just feel guilty if I choose the wrong person," Singh said. "I don't like the three of them anyway. They are not too strong for running for the President." Singh was born in India, but came to the U.S. twenty-five years ago.

It was kind of like "old home week" here, too. Mark Glyzewski, a reporter from KPTV-Fox 12 in Portland, assisted me in my broadcast. It turned out both Mark and I grew up in Waukesha County, Wisconsin. Small world! It just proved no matter where you go in this country, there always seemed to be another Packer fan nearby!

We were all quite busy, and there was a lot of ground to cover. If you ever wanted to visit a political nerve center, then visit a campaign headquarters on Election Day; but be careful! You might get run over in the process. Such was the case today at Barack Obama's main campaign office in Portland. People were working the phones and people were coming in for lists to be used canvassing the neighborhoods. Despite a big lead in most polls, Obama's communications director told me there was no time to talk with me. "It's Election Day and every vote counts!"

While driving through a nearby neighborhood, I found a volunteer doing a door-to-door canvass, and she was not even from Oregon. Sara Eckhouse was here from Iowa helping out. She had been away in Europe most of the year, and so this was the first chance for her to work directly on the Obama campaign. "Well, I've been out of the country. Oregon was the place to go!" she told me. As for why she chose Obama from the originally crowded field of Democrats? "I like that he brings people together," she said. "I like that he is really intelligent and not a divisive figure." She added, "He's something the country needs right now, because we are so divided and polarized."

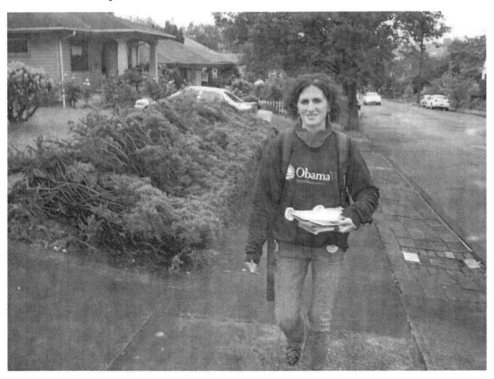

Figure 29. Sara Eckhouse campaigns for Obama, door-to-door in Portland, Oregon, May 20, 2008. (Mark Curtis)

Across town, at Hillary Clinton's headquarters, a phone bank was set up, and dozens of people were on the lines in a last-minute effort to get out the vote. While most polls have had Clinton down by twelve to eighteen points, a more recent poll put the margin at four points. So, the political troops were in high gear, dialing for votes. "We always knew it was going to be an uphill fight," said communications aide Frank Rothman. "We're just working as hard as we can."

A sign said the phone banks would be open Wednesday, even though Oregon's primary would be over. The volunteers would be calling voters in Montana and South Dakota, which would hold the final two primaries on June 3. "We have the (telephone) infrastructure," said Rothman, "so we're going to use it."

Think Joe Frazier and Mohammed Ali. They split the first two fights; and they split the first 12 rounds of bout number three. There were three rounds left in the nomination fight, too: June 1 in Puerto Rico and June 3 in South Dakota and Montana.

Tonight it was a split decision, again! Hillary Clinton won the Kentucky primary, 65 percent to 30 percent; but Barack Obama won the Oregon primary, 58 to 42 percent. As of tonight, Obama had now gained a majority of the pledged delegates, which he believed made him the all-but-certain nominee. The Clinton team was not giving up. Campaign Chairman Terry McAuliffe said, "This thing goes on. I don't know why people say it's over. It's another 2-to-1 victory tonight in Kentucky."

You'd have a hard time convincing the Obama campaign rally in Portland, though. The crowd went wild when CNN projected Obama the winner shortly after 8 p.m. Democratic Congressman Earl Blumenauer spoke to the hundreds gathered, saying that the Sunday rally here that approached seventy thousand people was the clincher for Obama. "It was the largest rally in the country for any candidate," said Blumenauer. "We've got 1.6 million people who financed this campaign," he added.

Despite all the euphoria, I spoke with former Governor Barbara Roberts (D-OR), who offered a more sobering outlook. "All the enthusiasm we feel tonight has to start tomorrow morning, and the day after, and the day after that," Roberts said. At 71, Roberts is a lifelong politician who has seen the Democratic Party's enthusiasm in the spring fade by the fall election. She cautioned against that tonight. Whether the Obama legions heeded her advice remained to be seen. "This is the first time in forty years our votes mattered," she said of Oregon's role in the 2008 presidential primary.

Governor Roberts told supporters they should even forego their summer vacations to work on the Obama campaign. That's when Huma Pierce, a 33-year-old local chiropractor shouted out, "We can't afford the gas (for a vacation)," and the crowd erupted in laughter.

Later when I spoke with Pierce, her reasoning for supporting Obama was bereft of any humor at all. "I just can't afford my father's health insurance," she said. "He has Parkinson's." Pierce's father is 73, and she supports Obama's plan for national health care for him and others like him.

As the night came to an end, it was another split decision, with Obama triumphant in Oregon, while Clinton won in a landslide in Kentucky. We now had two weeks off before the final round of primaries, but I just couldn't keep still. With neither candidate having enough delegates for the nomination, the issue of what to do with the disqualified delegates from Michigan and Florida came to the forefront again. Having been in Florida twice this year already, it was time for me to visit Michigan.

Chapter 10: The South Dakota and Montana Primaries

It's a seemingly simple question: How do you get to South Dakota and Montana from San Francisco's Bay Area? Why, by way of Michigan, of course! That's how wacky air travel has become these days

I was planning a trip to the final two primary states, and I was excited because these were two states I had never visited. I was excited, too, expecting the conclusion of the primary campaign. However, when I did the math, I realized it was possible that we might not have a Democratic nominee even after South Dakota and Montana. Yes, Obama was likely to be near or over the top, but Hillary Clinton might be able to overcome that lead by claiming hundreds of disputed delegates and the Super Delegates.

You may recall that back in January, Florida and Michigan had defied the Democratic National Party and moved their primaries forward on the calendar. For their punishment, delegates from the two states would not be certified for the national convention. Residents in both states were furious! How could their votes not count? If the national party stuck to its guns, there was a more practical problem: How could any Democratic nominee win the White House, if voters in two of the largest states felt disenfranchised? Winning the Presidency would be tough without Florida or Michigan.

The Democrats needed to make a decision about the fate of the delegates from Michigan and Florida, and time was growing short. Hillary Clinton had won both states and was counting on their delegates as her last, best shot at winning the nomination.

I flew to Wisconsin for a quick family visit and then, borrowing my dad's old Ford Taurus station wagon, I traveled to Michigan on Tuesday, May 27, to speak with voters and party officials about their hopes for the upcoming Democratic National Committee

(DNC) meeting in Washington. Not only were the primary delegates at stake, but turnout in November could be affected, too. First stop was the South Berrien County Democratic Club headquarters. That's where I met up with Jess Minks and John Klimek, two active party leaders who were both candidates for the County Commission. Both were busy watching what was happening in Washington. "We want to make sure our votes count," said Minks. "The delegates will be seated when this is over," he said optimistically.

Various ideas had been kicked around, including the possibility that each delegate from Michigan and Florida would be counted as only a half-vote. Critics said that violated the principle of "one man, one vote" and could open the door to a legal fight by the Clinton campaign.

The bigger issue to many was what would happen in November if Florida and Michigan were not counted. If angry voters in both states stayed home, John McCain would likely win the White House. John Klimek, who makes his living as a contractor, worried about turning off the young voters who had turned out in record numbers this year. "The fear is that our children and grandchildren will be disenfranchised," he said. "Those young people, who we need to step forward in years to come, will say, 'I'm not getting involved'."

For Jess Minks, that prospect meant only one thing. "The candidates will sit down [to reach an agreement]," he said. "We'll see if Hillary Clinton is vice-president. They'll work this thing out. Neither one of the candidates wants to see the party split or divided."

Despite Minks's optimism, the phone had been busy at the Democratic headquarters. One woman called while I was there, promising never to donate to the party again. She was one of the local voters angry at the national party. Minks, who is a retired coal miner turned political organizer, tried to calm her down and explained that the situation would be fixed. "She was very upset," he said. "She called the DNC in Washington to find what's going on." He added hopefully, "She'll go back to making donations."

Democrats here had an idea which they believed would prevent these fights in the future through a system of rotating primaries. Buchanan may have been the birthplace of a plan that could change American politics. The goal was to finally remove Iowa and New Hampshire from always holding the "first-in-the-nation" caucuses and primary elections. This year Michigan and Florida, as two of our nation's largest states, had broken the party rules and tried to leapfrog the other early primaries in an effort to exert greater influence on the presidential process. Like many people in other heavily populated states, Michiganders and Floridians were tired of having less say in choosing the nominees of both parties.

"Look at the state of Iowa," said Jess Minks. "It is a very small minority (of the U.S. population)." Only three serious Democratic candidates survived Iowa, and only four Republicans. By Super Tuesday, when twenty-four states cast ballots, such earlier favorites as John Edwards and Rudy Giuliani were already gone. Millions of voters never had a chance to have their opinions count.

The issue of "which states go first" is not entirely political either. Some of it is economic. "Iowa gets ten million dollars each year," said Klimek. And he had a point. The early primaries and caucuses were front loaded with media, delegates, party activists, etc. That was a lot of hotel rooms and restaurant receipts. States with later primaries did not enjoy that economic boon, especially if a nominee had already been selected.

Some in the Michigan delegation wanted to see a staggered primary season. The nation would be divided into three regions: East, Central and West. Each region would hold a lottery to see which four states would vote first, and then the other regions and states would rotate over the course of weeks, if not months. Every primary season would begin with a different region.

Imagine in January 2012 that New Mexico, Oregon, Montana and Utah had the first four primaries. The following week, it rotated to Michigan, Delaware, New York and Kentucky. The next week, Wisconsin, Oklahoma, North Dakota and Texas would vote.

Then in 2016 the primaries might start in the East, and perhaps New Hampshire would get to go first again. The idea had two overall goals: Variety and change. Every election cycle the regional and state order would be determined by party lottery.

"Finally, everyone would get an opportunity to go first," said Jess Minks. His Democratic Party cohort John Klimek said the idea of a more equitable system was crucial to retaining all the young voters who got involved this year - young voters who had appeared indifferent in the past. "This young, vibrant group that is now involved is going to walk away," Klimek said, "if the primary system is not fixed."

"What Michigan and Florida are doing is the right thing," said Minks. We would know within days what the DNC decided on the disputed delegates. In the meantime, I wanted to see how other Michigan voters felt.

I drove down to the tiny coastal town of New Buffalo. Although I lived in Wisconsin for the first twenty-five years of my life, I had never set foot in Michigan, except to change planes. I had always wanted to stand on a beach on the "other side" of Lake Michigan, and—at age 49—I finally reached that goal.

The view was breathtaking! But it was cold, and a thirty-knot wind was blowing from the west across the lake. The waves were at least ten feet high. Michigan was angry—the lake, that is—but many of the voters, too!

The weather was a fitting analogy for where Michigan stood in this year's presidential campaign. Many voters felt a "chill wind" had swept away their attempt to be "kingmakers" or "queen makers" in this year's campaign. Without the Florida and Michigan delegates, Hillary Clinton could not win the nomination; and even if they were counted, she remained a long shot! If Barack Obama was the nominee, he faced the daunting task of trying to win both states in November with many Democrats potentially staying home.

Cherie Heyn worked in the booth at the beach parking lot in New Buffalo. She had voted for Hillary Clinton in the primary and was disappointed at how this dispute was affecting her candidate's chances. "I think she should be the president," Heyn said. I broached the prospect of Clinton's being Obama's vice presidential running mate, and I got a reaction chillier than the wind. "I doubt that, too," Heyn said, clearly not hiding her bitterness.

She was a very kind, friendly lady, and she smiled when I mentioned how beautiful her town was and that I wanted to come back for a vacation. However, I could tell my questions reopened a wound that had really hurt people in Michigan. They wanted to make a difference, but felt their voices were not being counted.

I didn't dare ask Heyn if she was prepared to support Obama. I made that mistake before when talking to Clinton supporters and got stares more piercing than the Lake Michigan wind. Instead, I asked if she was concerned about Democrats staying home in November. To my surprise, she said, "I don't think that's so, but only time will tell."

This whole day in Michigan stunned me. People here were numb, angry or indifferent. Every other state I had visited was wildly enthusiastic about the Presidential race. This was night and day. It was as if Michigan had been punched in its collective gut.

Four days later, the Democratic National Committee decided to recognize only partial delegations from Michigan and Florida. Some delegates were still disqualified, and Clinton backers were furious. Clinton strategist and high-powered lawyer Harold Ickes, Jr., threatened a floor fight at the August convention in Denver, or legal action. Ickes angrily informed the party's Rules Committee that Clinton reserved her right to debate the matter publicly at the convention in August.

"There's been a lot of talk about party unity: Let's all come together and put our arms around each other," Ickes said angrily. "I submit to you, ladies and gentlemen, hijacking four delegates ... is not a good way to start down the path of party unity."

The Democrats were now facing an internal "family feud," and it could get really ugly. How all this played out was weighing heavily on the final primaries, too. So, I headed to South Dakota and Montana.

Because of the DNC decision to seat some disputed delegates, the overall math had changed heading into the final weekend. Now, 2,118 delegates were needed to win the nomination. Hillary Clinton had just won the Puerto Rico primary and was closing the delegate gap. Barack Obama needed just forty-nine more delegates to go over the top, but Clinton needed two hundred and two. She was a long shot; but a Clinton win was still possible, depending on the Super Delegates, who were free to announce their allegiance at any time.

That question loomed over South Dakota and Montana, as they got set for the final two primaries on Tuesday. I spent time with both Clinton and Obama supporters at their respective offices in Rapid City. Even though it was a Sunday, the offices were beehives of activity, as people worked phone banks or prepared to go out and canvass neighborhoods.

Whitney Dinger was a nineteen-year-old student at the University of Central Oklahoma, who flew in to help the campaign even though she had never been on a plane before and was scared to death of flying. "A little bit of tears," she said about getting on the plane. "I was nervous about the plane ride, but excited to be here." So why did she brave her fear of flying for Hillary Clinton's now long-shot bid for the nomination? "I believe in health care coverage for every American," Dinger said, "and her plan - in my opinion - is the only plan that can accomplish that."

Also in the Clinton office was retired Methodist minister Lin Jennewein. She believed Clinton's vast experience greatly outweighed that of Obama, a first-term Senator. "Tremendous! The experience that she has, that would take her into the Presidency," Jennewein said. "For me, I always hear her speak to the problem, here is the solution, and how we're going to get the money," added Jennewein. Oddly enough, she wasn't hoping for Clinton to be named the VP running mate. "I don't think so," Jennewein said. "I would like to see her get a marvelous position on the U.S. Supreme Court." Jennewein opined that the high court carries more weight than the vice presidency. "She would make the important decisions affecting Americans over the next twenty years," the retired minister said.

Across town, the Obama campaign headquarters had characters every bit as interesting and every bit as busy. Dean Henderson was a Harley-Davidson-riding former Republican. He switched parties after meeting and hearing Obama in Sioux City a year ago.

"I think he represents a change that we've been looking for with the loss of honesty in Washington," said Anderson. He added that he had a lot of disappointment in the disconnect of the Republican Party." Anderson said Washington had too much focus on protecting large corporate entities, while farmers in South Dakota and elsewhere were ignored. "These are people who have worked the land, and the Republican Party has forgotten them," Anderson complained.

Also helping out at Obama headquarters was retired Washington lawyer Ed Gerwin. He flew out to South Dakota to volunteer for Obama. He wanted government reform. "In Washington, you get to see the mess close up," Gerwin said. "It's such a mess. People aren't working together. People are playing political games." Gerwin said he knows it will take time. "No one person can fix this in four to eight years, but you have to start somewhere," he said.

My plans were also to visit the Republican Party headquarters here this week, as John McCain had yet to open a full-time campaign office. South Dakota had voted Republican in presidential elections for many decades.

I had wanted to see Mount Rushmore since I was a little kid. Somehow, covering Campaign 2008 made it seem like a "must stop," as I crisscrossed America. The fact that South Dakota, along with Montana, held the final primaries Tuesday made my wish come true. Apparently, lots of others had the same idea. The presidential race was the talk of the large crowd which came to see the oversized Presidents of the past.

The Pelton family was visiting from Colorado Springs. Bradford was an attorney, who came here with his wife Jenny and their ten-year-old daughter Amy. They were simply awestruck. "When we first drove by, I almost started to cry," said Jenny. "It's really cool."

I asked Bradford, as someone in the legal profession, for his reflections, considering that the four Presidents depicted were so instrumental in shaping this country's Constitution and legal system. "If you think about why, and how, and how long, and how well it has worked, in spite of overwhelming opportunities for it to go bad—including the Civil War—it is truly inspiring," he said.

I did not intend to ask people here for whom they were voting; I was more curious about their reflections on what this monument represented amid the current campaign. "There seems to be a fundamental disconnect between what these guys intended and what we're hearing today," Bradford said. "But because of this [what the monument represents], we will survive." His daughter Amy volunteered that she wanted Barack Obama to win. "That's because his name sounds cool," she said. I recalled that I had a similar opinion of the name "Spiro Agnew," when I was ten, and they laughed.

The next four people I spoke with were quite spirited, to say the least! Beverly Smith was here with her husband Ron, and they were joined by Pat Pierson and her husband Park. The couples are senior citizens from New Jersey and Pennsylvania. When I mentioned that I was a reporter, they did not hold back.

Beverly Smith launched a harsh criticism of the Electoral College system. "Why do we vote, if someone else is going to choose the President?" she wondered. Pat Pierson looked up at the Mount Rushmore monument and spoke thoughtfully, "In light of this, I don't think we have presidents with this much character nowadays." She was not a fan of Hillary Clinton, either. "I don't have a problem with a woman president," she said. "I just have a problem with Hillary." Then her husband Park chimed in, saying, "Obama hasn't said much." Ron Smith then bemoaned what he felt was a lack of good choices. "Anyone any good, is a CEO," he lamented. The four kept up a lively debate for quite some time after I had bid them farewell.

Another couple I met at Mount Rushmore was Terry and Christina Townsend, from Seattle, Washington. Both served in the military; and they were driving from Tennessee to Washington State, when they decided to visit Mount Rushmore. He is African-American; she is Filipino and awaiting her U.S. citizenship. Both are fascinated with the current campaign, and Mount Rushmore only fueled the discussion. "If you think about it, it's possible to have the first black president or the first female president," said Christina. "It's history."

Terry, who served in the Marines, was reflective, too. "To me, I am just curious to see how America adjusts to whoever wins," Terry said. "How will people accept it? Is it going to pull us together, or tear us apart? It's interesting." Christina lamented that she would not be able to vote, since she was not yet a citizen. Despite this, she served in the U.S. Army, including duty in Iraq. That seemed ironic and, perhaps, quite unfair, as we stood at Mount Rushmore.

I was spellbound by Mount Rushmore. A man I met in Rapid City urged me to go to the night time ceremony and the lighting of the monument after dark. It was a stunning tribute I will never forget. The best part was that veterans in the audience were invited on stage for the retiring of the colors. Each was asked his name and branch of service, as he touched the flag that had been folded thirteen times in the shape of a triangle. The crowd erupted in applause after the final veteran spoke. We were also treated to all four stanzas of "The Star Spangled Banner."

President Teddy Roosevelt was the "Father of the National Park System," along with his good friend John Muir. Looking down from the mountain tonight, T.R. must have been proud of a job well done! It was a beautiful national park and was now being showcased by one of the most dramatic American elections ever.

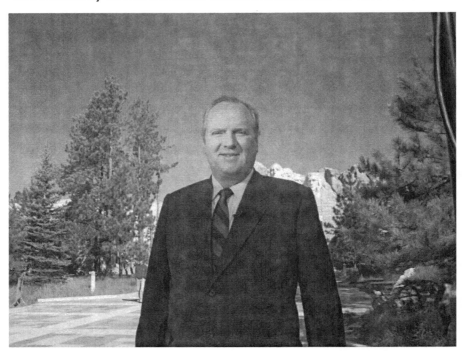

Figure 30. Mark Curtis reports "live" from Mount Rushmore, South Dakota, June 3, 2008. (MarkCurtisMedia.com)

Hillary Clinton would cross the finish line with Tuesday's vote. She might not win the general election, but she ran the gauntlet, and never faltered. That was apparent as hundreds of supporters lined up inside and outside Tally's Restaurant in downtown Rapid City, South Dakota, Monday morning to see the former First Lady-turned-Senator-turned-presidential-hopeful.

Clinton had flown all night from Puerto Rico, where she had won that primary in a landslide Sunday. She had not arrived in Rapid City until 3 a.m., so she was an hour late for this morning's rally. She may have been late, but she did not disappoint.

Lillian Letner and her adorable four-year old daughter Lauren waited patiently outside. Mrs. Letner was supporting Clinton based on her stands on fiscal policy, health care reform and the environment. Despite Clinton's being down in the polls, Letner was fully behind her. "Actually, I am surprised it is such a close contest," said Letner. "She has the experience and qualifications. To me, you go with the proven 'horse.' I think you go with those most qualified...."

Letner worked in a hospital for ten years as a health care director. "From an insider's perspective, it's definitely a broken system," she said. "It needs more than just a little tweaking."

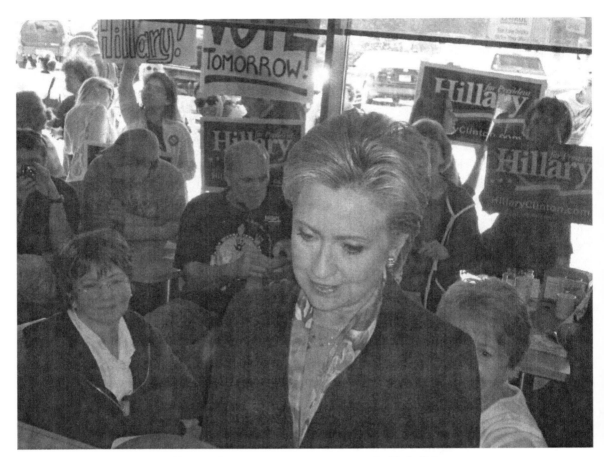

**Figure 31. Hillary Clinton greets voters at Tally's Diner.
Rapid City, South Dakota, June 2, 2008. (Mark Curtis)**

Inside, the restaurant was buzzing. All the tables and counters were packed with breakfast diners. One whiff and you could tell the food was really good here. I was pinned in a corner with other press photographers, wedged next to the last booth, where four people were sitting. Harold Hansen, of Rapid City, was a Vietnam veteran supporting Clinton. "I supported her husband. We need total change," Hansen said. "A lot of men have trouble with a strong woman, but that's what this country needs."

Hansen's wife was at a booth across the room. One of the people sitting with him was Nancy Sutterer—up until now a total stranger; but when the Secret Service tells you to sit down and to stay where you are, you tend to obey. Anyway, new friends were being made all around the room, and Rapid City was one of the friendliest places I have ever been. Sutterer had been unemployed for the past ten months. "We need massive economic changes in the country," she said. "I've had to move in with my mom, the economy is so bad."

Sutterer wanted Hillary Clinton to be President, but I asked whether she would be okay with Hillary as Vice President. "I think it would be better for her to be on the bottom of the ticket, than not at all," Sutterer said. "We need a woman's perspective in there."

Both Hanson and Sutterer got to meet Mrs. Clinton when she finally arrived. "Thank you for your service!" Clinton said to Harold Hansen, who wore his Vietnam Veteran hat. He told me later that when he came home from the war, he was told not to wear his uniform, or people might spit on him. Today he wore the Vietnam hat proudly and was thrilled when Senator Clinton thanked him. "It feels good. It really feels good," Hansen said. "It makes me feel like what I've done was important."

Clinton shook hundreds of hands and signed autographs. In a brief appeal to those in the crowd who might still be undecided, she said, "Look at the record of what I've achieved over a lifetime."

She talked about being ready to be President from day one and urged voters to think about that when they went into the voting booths Tuesday. "Who would you hire to do the job?" she asked. Then it was off to her final stop in Sioux Falls to campaign with Bill and Chelsea, before heading home to New York.

She ran one hell of a race! She never quit! She may not have ended up as her party's nominee, but she was the first serious female presidential candidate from any party to cross the finish line. That, in and of itself, was remarkable. I had a feeling we had not seen the last of Hillary Clinton.

By the way, Senator Clinton did not leave Tally's Restaurant empty-handed. Hillary wanted a "to go" order. "They made her breakfast," said co-owner Kathy Johnson, "It was an 'everything' omelet." As I said, the smell of the food here was intoxicating - which explains why Rachel Ray taped a feature on Tally's for "The Food Network." When everyone else cleared out, I stayed for the best meatloaf lunch in America.

On Tuesday, polls opened at 7 a.m. in South Dakota and Montana, and it was likely that we would see a record turnout in both states, as we have in most others. There was a steady stream of voters before noon at the Community Center in Sturgis, the western South Dakota town now famous for its annual motorcycle rally. These were the final two primaries and we could have a Democratic nominee by later Tuesday night. South Dakotans were thrilled. One in Rapid City, who has voted since 1973, was overjoyed at all the excitement and all the time candidates had spent there. "This is the first time since I was eighteen that voters in South Dakota mattered," said Nancy Sutterer. "We've never had this many candidates here."

One of the families I enjoyed meeting were the Mesteths of Rapid City. They are Oglala Sioux and have lived on reservations. Lori Mesteth was backing Hillary Clinton, no matter what. "She's a woman, and she and her husband have both visited the reservation," said Mesteth. "They were doing a good job when he was in office," she added. Mesteth said her concerns go well beyond Native American issues. She liked the fact that the federal budget was balanced during Bill Clinton's presidency and that health care was improving.

"She's a strong woman, and that is one of the very first things I see about her," she said. "She's a good role model for my daughters." Her fourteen-year-old daughter had talked her into attending a Clinton rally. Mesteth and her two daughters supported Clinton, but her three sons were backing Obama. So was it a family feud at home? "No," she said. "It's a split family, but as long as they are interested, I don't care," she added.

Malcolm Chapman was President of the Rapid City Council. He was thrilled by the turnout and having a strong final primary. "I've been telling people, we're just as important as the other forty-nine states," said Chapman, as he urged people to get out and vote.

Another Clinton backer heading out to cast her vote was Judy Hansen. "I think she's the real deal. I think she's honest, and she knows what she's doing. I think Obama will be a great president in eight years, maybe twelve," Hansen said.

It was easy to lose track of the Republican Party in the clamor over Hillary Clinton and Barack Obama and their down-to-the-wire nomination fight; but South Dakota and Montana are very conservative states. No matter how the Democrats fared today, it was quite possible that both states would land in the GOP column in November.

Figure 32. Voters go to the polls in Broadus, Montana on primary day. June 3, 2008. (Mark Curtis).

While I spent a lot of time in South Dakota, I had never been in Montana before; and I wanted to take the pulse of local voters there, as well. I drove to the small town of Broadus, about two-and-a-half hours away. When I arrived, the Powder River County Courthouse was a busy place as voters cast ballots. County Clerk Karen Amende ran the elections here. "It has been steady, and we always have a good voter turnout here," said Amende. "It's been fun watching the news and having the politicians know Montana is here and that we have a voice."

The local bowling alley, Powder River Lanes & Cafe, was busy at lunchtime, too. Local contractor Rick Higgins was eating with his kids. He backed John McCain. "I guess I believe in the war we're in," said Higgins. "I believe we are doing good over there. I feel like as soon as we leave, they (the terrorists) are going to come after us again." Higgins was also upset with federal environmental policy that has protected certain species of wolves that attack and kill livestock, hurting local farmers.

At Hoofer's Laundromat and Ice Cream Parlor, they advertised "gossip" on the sign, as well. That's where I found people talking politics, including Danny Johnson, who was running for County Commission, along with Ty Brewer and his dad, Tom Brewer. "I like the Republican stance as far as less government intrusion," said Johnson. "Traditionally, the Democrats follow government programs and have more intrusion, especially on agriculture and farming here." Johnson said Washington policies were keeping Montana from mining more than twenty-seven billion cubic feet of coal under its soil—a resource that might help ease the nation's energy crunch.

Tom Brewer was pretty vocal, too. "I would definitely support McCain," he said. "You can document this. I will never, ever, in my lifetime vote for a Democrat for President." Brewer supported McCain on Iraq policy and believed the U.S. effort will prevail.

No matter what happened that night, people in Montana were thrilled that their votes counted in this primary process. All too often in the past, the nomination had been decided in Iowa and New Hampshire, long before Montanans cast their ballots. The headline in the "Billings Gazette" nailed the situation perfectly. It read simply, "All Eyes on Montana."

I drove back to Rapid City, all the while listening to news-talk radio KBHB-AM from Sturgis, South Dakota. I was also in constant cell phone contact with reporter Jamie Dupree from Cox Radio in Washington, with whom I traveled on much of the Presidential campaign trail. A significant story was developing. As the week rushed by and the drama steadily heightened, many of the undecided super-delegates began announcing their commitments. Most were breaking for Obama, and many were doing it as a simple act of party unity. While the Clinton-Obama standoff was exciting, if it left the party fractured and wounded, Republicans could seize on that and win in November. It was becoming clear that we would have a nominee—at least "on paper"—by the time polls officially closed in South Dakota and Montana.

It was a night to be nice. Hillary Clinton, John McCain and Barack Obama all congratulated one another for a hard-fought campaign and for inspiring their various constituencies. They noted they were all still friends in the U.S. Senate. We didn't expect the love fest to last long. This was politics—a hardball sport. That's the way it is.

Now that it was McCain vs. Obama in November, the gloves would come off. Already, Tuesday night McCain mocked Obama, saying that direct talks with the President of Iran were "not the kind of change" people wanted. He also said that Obama, twenty-five years his junior, "has fallen for failed ideas of the past." Obama later praised McCain's heroic service to this country, and then counterpunched: "I respect his (McCain's) many accomplishments, even if he denies mine."

In Rapid City, the seat of Pennington County, local Republicans gathered to watch the election returns and speeches on TV. All the candidates had already left the state. Barack Obama won the Montana primary, but Hillary Clinton's surprise upset in South Dakota was the real shocker of the night. Obama had been ahead by 10 percentage points in at least one poll. It was fitting to end on another dramatic split decision.

"Oh, I believe that Obama does not represent the demographic of this state," said Marli Erickson, who will be President of the Pennington County Republican Party in 2010. "He comes from an urban population area in Illinois. I don't see the commonality with South Dakota," she added. As for how John McCain can carry South Dakota, a traditionally Republican state when it comes to the presidency, "McCain has to do a balancing act," Erickson said. "With the economy at home in the doldrums and the war in Iraq, his platform has equally to address both." Erickson works in the financial industry.

Obama was the last person to speak on the TV that night. He commended his primary opponent. "Senator Hillary Clinton made history in this campaign," Obama said from St. Paul, Minnesota. "She has made history, not just because she's a woman ... but because she's a leader who inspires millions of Americans." Obama congratulated Clinton for her surprising South Dakota victory and for her overall hard-fought campaign. There were no hints yet whether she would be his VP choice.

A local Republican leader I spoke with, who asked that his name not be used, had some big concerns. While he was voting for McCain, he worried the GOP had a tough road ahead with Obama. "He's young; he's articulate; and he has enormous appeal to young people," the man said. "Even in South Dakota, people have flocked to hear him speak." Of McCain's speech that night, the same Republican expressed more concerns. "It was almost pathetic. It seemed canned," the man said. "There was very little passion in it."

Nevertheless, he thought South Dakota was still Republican enough to be safe for McCain in November. The rest of the nation was his concern.

One of the many fascinating people I met election night was an African-American man named Dana Jones. Jones, a mortgage banker, is a military veteran. He moved here from Orange County, California. He got to meet Obama at a recent rally, where Jones said he told the candidate that his biggest concern was the nation's high school dropout rate. Jones, who is forty-four and working on his MBA, said the two had a good talk. "He fully understands the implications on a global economic standpoint," Jones said. He was also excited that Obama made history. "I feel proud that he's a great candidate who just happens to be black," Jones said, adding, "Even if he was white, I'd be proud of him." Jones said he supported Obama for his stand on the issues, not because they were both black.

I ended my trip to South Dakota at Mount Rushmore on Wednesday morning. Each day I had done my TV commentary in the shadow of those four great Presidents - Washington, Jefferson, Lincoln and Teddy Roosevelt. To me it was a fitting place to end the primary campaign in one of the most historic and groundbreaking primary election campaigns in U.S. history. As I looked up, I wondered, "If those stone faces could talk right now, what they would say?"

I think as a nation, we did them proud!

Chapter 11: Denver & the Democratic National Convention

"Look, a tornado!"

That was my welcome to Denver, Colorado. I was driving down the highway near Parker, a suburb of Denver, with Tom and Carrollee Moore. The Moores were friends from California, who built their retirement home in Colorado. They kindly invited me to stay with them during the convention.

The weather was already bad when Tom suddenly spotted a tornado touching down about a mile south of our car. Then Carrollee spotted a second twister. This was scary! Fortunately we were in a fairly wide-open area; nobody got hurt and there was little, if any, damage. It was bizarre, though. I had only been in Colorado a few hours, and had already been caught in an anti-war protest downtown, and now we had the tornadoes. This was an awful lot of drama, and the Democratic National Convention hadn't even started yet.

It promised to be an interesting week inside the Pepsi Center, where the convention was being held. Joe Biden had already been selected as Barack Obama's Vice-Presidential running mate. But there was lingering drama between the campaign of Hillary Clinton and Obama's camp. Plus, this was a political convention and there were bound to be surprises. The culmination was to be Thursday night when Obama gave his acceptance speech before eighty-four thousand people at Mile High Stadium.

Some of politics, of course, is designed to be great theater. Often times it is staged and scripted. That was what they were planning for Mile High Stadium. At other times, there are spontaneous moments that offer great drama and surprise. On the first day of the convention, we had *all of the above.*

The networks long ago, gave up on gavel-to-gavel coverage. So now, in order to get the attention of TV and the Internet, the show is tightly scripted. I sat behind the stage part of today and watched as the speakers read from a teleprompter. Above it was a bright red digital countdown clock, telling them how much time they had left. These early speeches were usually reserved for relatively unknown state and local officials or an occasional member of Congress. It made me wonder if there was a trap door that opened up behind the podium, to swallow any speaker who went overtime! It was a funny prospect.

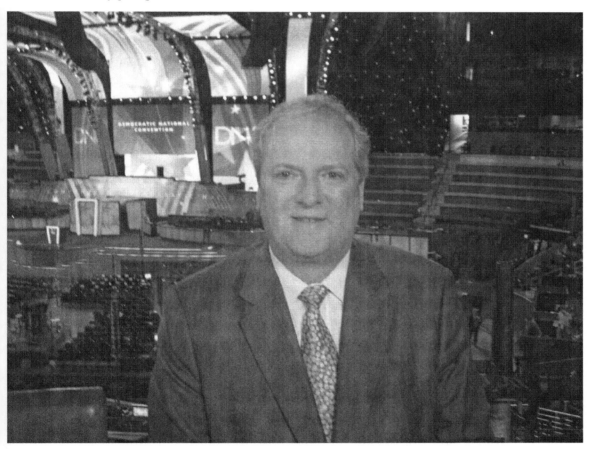

Figure 33. Mark Curtis reports from inside the Pepsi Center in Denver, Colorado, at the Democratic National Convention. August 26, 2008. (Trish McHenry)

The biggest drama of the night was the tribute to Sen. Ted Kennedy, who had had surgery for brain cancer just three months ago. Kennedy had endorsed and campaigned for Barack Obama for several weeks before he fell ill. The convention featured a beautiful film tribute that chronicled his life and career, but no one knew if Kennedy was healthy enough to address the crowd. To everyone's surprise, he not only waved to the cheering delegates, but he went to the podium.

"It is wonderful to be here tonight," said Kennedy. His voice broke with emotion when he thanked people who had journeyed with his family's triumphs and tragedies. These have been "the happiest days and the hardest days," Kennedy said, and he'd had plenty of both. "For me, this is a season of new hope," he said, likely referring to his cancer, his medical treatment and this election. It was some of the longest sustained applause I've ever heard at a political speech and I saw several people crying. It was quite a dramatic opening night for this convention.

Tuesday night promised more drama as well. Hillary Clinton was scheduled to address the convention, but there was lingering bitterness between her campaign and Obama's. One issue was whether the nomination process would have the traditional roll call, where each state announces its delegate vote. In the past, this was always the fun and colorful moment when you would hear, "Iowa, the Potato State, home of Sun Valley, proudly casts its 25 votes for the next President of the United States, Jimmy Carter." It was ceremonial and full of boasting, as each state tried to top the others. It was political Americana and many people loved it, including me.

Hillary Clinton received eighteen million votes in the primary season and just missed winning the Democratic nomination. No woman had ever come this close and her supporters wanted her historic achievement noted through a full roll call of the states.

This was a real concern, though, to Barack Obama's campaign. A roll call of the states would show the convention goers and a national TV audience of millions, just how close this race had really been. That could make the Democrats appear sharply divided, when Obama tried to project unity. His supporters wanted a simple vote by acclamation where the entire hall of delegates would be asked to accept the nomination of Barrack Obama, and everyone could shout, "Yes!"

The actual nomination vote would come Wednesday, so the immediate concern was how Hillary Clinton would address the convention Tuesday night. Just how forcefully would she endorse Obama? A half-hearted pat on the back wouldn't do.

For San Francisco Mayor Gavin Newsom, it was a touchy subject. The healing will take time. "Let's not expect miracles," said Newsom, "This won't happen overnight." The mayor had been an early and committed Hillary supporter, but was now fully committed to getting Obama elected President. I asked Newsom what he thought Clinton should say to the delegates. "What she says matters greatly," Newsom told me. "A lot of words were exchanged, and it stung." But the Mayor said Clinton had to preach party unity and pledge an unequivocal endorsement to Obama. "Everybody needs to remind people what is at stake if we are not unified," Newsom said. "If she can point out and remind people what is at stake, she will have the greatest effect," Newsom said.

Others shared that sentiment. Marcia Harvey-Wright, a delegate from Michigan told me, "I am a Hillary delegate, but an Obama supporter now."

But well known Clinton surrogate Lanny Davis only fueled the controversy by saying the Obama campaign never truly vetted or considered Hillary for Vice-president. The political infighting threatened to divide the party at a critical time. A new CNN poll had Obama and McCain deadlocked at 47 percent each, with 27 percent of Clinton supporters threatening to vote for McCain, or not vote at all.

Needless to say, there was great angst and anticipation for Senator Clinton's speech. So, she hit the matter head on: "My friends it is time to take back the country we love. And whether you voted for me, or whether you voted for Barack, the time is now to unite as a single party, with a single purpose," and the crowd cheered wildly.

Clinton also appealed to a potentially significant group of her female supporters who were threatening to not vote in November at all. "We are on the same team, and none of us can afford to sit on the sidelines," said Clinton, "It's a fight for the future and it's a fight we must win together." All in all, the crowd loved it and Clinton seemed sincere. But reaction among delegates I spoke with was somewhat more mixed.

Molly Brennan from Berkeley, California was thrilled. Molly is president of the Cal Berkeley Democrats, and studies political science at the University of California. Being inside the convention hall is about the best education in that field she can get these days. "I think she made sure to say his (Obama's) name fifteen times, probably more than that," Brennan told me. Stating and restating the endorsement by Sen. Clinton was an effort to drive home the point she made. "I hope her supporters were convinced by that," said Brennan.

After the rally, one woman who asked not to be identified, told me gruffly, "I'll give him (Obama) my vote, but I won't give him any of my money!"

Karen Rubin, a photographer I met on the train home after the rally, was also a reluctant Obama convert. She was here from New York and was a big Clinton supporter. "I am resentful," Rubin told me, "I believe the election was stolen from her. I was in tears listening to her because to be frank, she's the better candidate." Rubin said she'll vote for Obama, but is not sure he can beat McCain. "I worry voters will choose experience over youth," Rubin said.

Clearly the line of the night belonged to Hillary Clinton who simply said, "Barack Obama is my candidate, and he must be our president." The crowd roared its approval and Clinton supporters, in general, seemed to get the message. Vera Hall of Baltimore told me, "I think Democrats were blessed to have two great choices."

On Wednesday, Bill Clinton also addressed the crowd, and his popularity with Democrats was still clear. He probably had the funniest line of the convention. He spoke of Hillary's very close and dramatic primary campaign against Senator Obama, saying it "generated so much heat, it increased global warming!"

The party also forged a compromise on how to take the nomination vote. There would be a partial roll call vote to honor Hillary Clinton and then Illinois would yield to New York. To the surprise and joy of many, it was Senator Clinton herself who took the microphone and asked the crowd to nominate Sen. Obama with "one voice, right here, right now, he is our candidate and he will be our President." The crowd roared its approval to nominate by acclamation and it was over!

It was one of the classiest moves I've ever seen in an often bitter political world. Delegate Robert Camacho of Walnut Creek, California saw it much the same way. Camacho, who is Latino, gay and was recently married, originally backed Clinton. He was truly touched by her motion for acclamation from the floor, knowing how hard it must have been. "First and foremost, I admire Senator Clinton," Camacho told me. "She's a human being. Just seeing her get behind the party. We know we lost. She's showing us how to unite."

It worked and the controversy evaporated. The party looked pretty unified as delegates readied to hear from Vice-presidential nominee Joe Biden and Presidential nominee, Barack Obama.

Part of the fun and intrigue of my job is finding people to interview for reaction to speeches, developments, controversies or historic moments just like this one. My training in journalism school taught me to not just interview the newsmakers, but also to interview the people affected by the news. Such was the case along the campaign trail this year. I talked to dozens and dozens of average Americans about their take on this historic campaign. I did the same at the conventions. There's no science to it. You just look around and walk up to people and say, "I'm a reporter, would you mind if I asked you a few questions for my story?" People almost always say yes and some of the "finds" you make are real jewels.

Here's a good case in point. On Wednesday night I was getting immediate reaction to the fact that Barack Obama had just been formally nominated.

As I was randomly going from person to person in the arena hallway, I approached an older black gentleman, whom I had pegged for a senior citizen. Figuring he'd seen a lot of history in his life, I asked him for his reaction. "I think this is a way for this nation to come to grips with its history, and save our souls," he said.

Now I found that comment interesting, so I asked him what he meant. "I was there in 1963 (for the 'March on Washington')," he said, "This sort of rounds out the circle." He told me his name was Nathaniel Jones of Cincinnati, Ohio and that he was a retired federal judge, who was appointed by President Jimmy Carter and served on the bench for twenty-five years.

Now I was really curious. When he marched in Washington with Dr. Martin Luther King, Jr., and thousands of others that hot August day, did he ever imagine an African-American candidate would be his party's nominee for President? "I never thought it would happen given what the polls were in 1963," Judge Jones told me.

He hoped the party can unify behind Obama, and leave the bruising primary battle with Senator Clinton behind. "I think too much media attention is focused on the disgruntled," said Jones, "There are winners and losers."

Judge Jones previously served as general counsel to the NAACP, a position once held by the late Supreme Court Justice Thurgood

Marshall. Like I said, you just never know what you might find as a reporter, when you simply introduce yourself to a total stranger.

One of the things I really enjoyed about Denver was riding the light rail system. Much like BART in the San Francisco Area or METRO in Washington, DC, you could get to lots of places without being stuck in your car, in a traffic jam. From my friends' house in Parker to the convention site took about 35 minutes by rail. In the morning, people were stoically going to work and keeping to themselves. But at night, it could be like a "party train," especially if some of the convention revelers had been drinking.

One of the funniest rides home was with a man named Calvin Taylor. Taylor was an extra large African-American man, who looked like he was a former college football or NFL lineman. He had a personality to match his hulking figure and he was holding court. Taylor was a McCain supporter and was advocating that McCain pick Condoleezza Rice for his Vice-President. With "Condi" on the ticket, the GOP could, in Taylor's words, "divide the black vote." Taylor, who was bellowing at the large crowd of Democratic Delegates, also said he was a NRA member and a conservative supporter of the war. None of this was menacing in any way, and he was so large no one would argue with him. He was just a jolly man, having fun with the fact that he was a Republican in a sea of Democrats. McCain will win in November, he extolled. "I love my Democratic friends," he said, "but I will be calling them on January 20 and say, 'I told you so.'" He was so big; the train seemed to shake when he laughed.

The stories of people at a convention run the gamut. They range from funny and touching to bittersweet, from triumph to tragedy. There are few stories more compelling than John McCain's heroic survival as a prisoner of war for over five torturous years.

In Denver we heard another story the night Joe Biden accepted his party's nomination for Vice-President; it was a night that almost never happened.

In 1972, a horrible car accident killed Biden's first wife and daughter, and severely injured his two sons. It happened just days after he was elected to the U.S. Senate. Biden nearly decided to not to take his seat in Congress. Biden's son Beau introduced him at the convention and said after the tragedy his father mused, "Delaware can get another Senator. My kids can't get another father."

Other Senators prevailed and Biden took the oath of office at his son's hospital bedside. Fast forward thirty-six years, Biden is remarried, and his boys are grown, with kids of their own. Beau is Delaware Attorney General and served in Iraq as a member of the National Guard. The Senator quoted his ninety-year-old mom, Jean, who was in the audience. After the accident she told him, "Joey, God sends no cross you cannot bear."

It has indeed been quite a journey for the senior Senator from Delaware, now the nominee for Vice-president.

The convention also provided a greater glimpse into Barack Obama's family. His wife Michelle addressed the delegates on opening night. At the end, their two girls, Malia, age 10, and Sasha, age 7, joined Michelle on stage. Barack was in Kansas City working on his acceptance speech, but joined his family via satellite on a giant TV screen in the Pepsi Center. He clearly enjoyed his wife's remarks and told the convention, "Now you know why I asked her out so many times, even though she said no. You want a persistent President!" Everybody laughed. Then his daughters spoke to him on the big TV: "Hi Daddy," "Daddy what city are you in?" and "I love you Daddy." It was spontaneous, charming and made for a warm convention memory.

Creating images like that is what political consultants dream of; an image can, conversely, cause a lot of sleepless nights when things go badly. You just never know what a perplexed little 7 year-old will say into a "live" microphone in front of thousands in the audience and millions of TV viewers at home but Sasha made Daddy's consultants proud!

Speaking of image creation, the whole concept of moving the convention next door to Mile High Stadium for Obama's acceptance speech was just that—image creation. It was a bold, but dangerous stroke of genius. What if it had rained, with tornados, as it had just four days earlier? It was a gamble, but it paid off.

The Mile High Stadium event was brilliant for another reason. Colorado was "in play" as one of the battleground states this year. While it often leaned Republican in Presidential races, this time Democrats had a chance. About half of the eighty-four thousand seats were reserved for delegates, dignitaries, press and other officials. The other forty thousand tickets were distributed to people in Colorado. In a toss-up race, that kind of goodwill can sway lots of undecided votes. It was a good tactical move.

I arrived at Mile High at 1:30 in the afternoon and was glad I did. It was utter chaos, at least outside. Getting in was a nightmare, but once in, things went smoothly. It was an endless sea of people, though, and provided an interesting perspective.

A football game here has the same size crowd, but there are 22 players and 7 referees on a field which is 100 yards long and 53 yards wide. That's a lot of action to focus on. By comparison, Barack Obama would be one man, standing on one small stage, with all eyes on him. This was a long way from having coffee in someone's living room in New Hampshire. If he wanted change, he got it. *This* was change!

"To all my fellow citizens of this great nation, with profound gratitude and great humility, I accept your nomination for the Presidency of the United States," said Obama, as the stadium erupted in cheers and many in the crowd chanted the now familiar campaign slogan, "Yes we can! Yes we can!" I have been to many stadiums for professional football and baseball games with capacity crowds and never felt anything this big, shake this much.

Figure 34. 84,000 attend Barack Obama's acceptance speech at Mile High Stadium, Denver, Colorado, August 28, 2008. (Mark Curtis)

"We are here because we love this country too much to let the next four years, look like the past eight," Obama said, and the crowd roared again. "Senator McCain likes to talk about judgment, but really, what does it say about your judgment when you think George Bush has been right more than 90 percent of the time?" Obama wondered, as many in the crowd laughed. These were good partisan punch lines, but the Republicans would return the favor in a week. It was classic American politics.

In between the wild cheers, Obama laid out an ambitious agenda if elected President. It included: tax credits to companies that create new jobs in America; a cap on capital gains tax breaks; tax cuts for 95 percent of working families; and an end to dependence on foreign oil in ten years.

"Now many of these programs will cost money," Obama conceded. While he talked about budget and program cuts to help finance his agenda, he did not mention tax increases or any further specifics on how to pay for it all.

I had a great vantage point. I was in one of the tunnels leading into the main level of the stadium, at about the 40-yard line marker for a football game. It was a straight-on view of Obama. There were two stairways leading up to the seating area, and I walked up those steps occasionally to take close up photos and videos of people waving flags and celebrating. As long as I did not block the stairs, the police let me do my work. It was exciting!

"It's time for us to change America and that's why I'm running for President of the United States," and the crowd went wild again. It was quite a show. The night ended with fanfare, music and fireworks. I videotaped the final ovation, which went on for six-minutes without letting up. The crowd was clearly pleased. Some told me the speech would silence those critics who thought Obama was not patriotic enough. "I thought it was just great. Very elegant," said Carolyn Molock-Shipp of Denver. "He spoke of things we all have in common. He's as American as you and I. He's an American." she said. "It was awesome! Great information. He gave us on a lot of his views," said Damon Morgan of Denver. "And he brought out more issues that need attention."

Still others in the crowd recalled that Obama's speech came on the 45th anniversary of Martin Luther King's "I Have a Dream Speech." Shirlea Neal of Denver reflected on that. "I just thought I'd never see the day," Neal told me, "I am so proud of him and am proud of my country, America!"

The promise of change—a continuing theme in this campaign was underscored again and again. "We can't turn back." Obama said, "America cannot turn back."

Chapter 12: St. Paul and the Republican National Convention:

Someone let the air out of Barack Obama's tires overnight.

Obama had gone to bed after one of the greatest outdoor political rallies in modern U.S. politics. Eighty-four thousand people had crammed into Mile High Stadium in Denver to watch Obama's stirring and colorful acceptance speech. Millions and millions more watched on television in their homes, setting all-time convention viewership records. Obama was red hot at midnight, but the bloom was off the rose by mid-morning. His momentum had been stalled.

"Breaking news from Dayton, Ohio!" shouted all the cable networks.

It was 8 a.m. in Denver, and word was rapidly spreading that John McCain had picked little-known Alaska Governor Sarah Palin to be his running mate. There had been speculation about this for a couple of hours. When I left Parker at 6:30 in the morning, Palin was all the talk on KOA-AM radio, the local news channel. Now I was at the Fox News Channel Bureau in Denver, and it was all "Palin, Palin, Palin."

I could find little excitement or even discussion anywhere in Denver about the Obama extravaganza at Mile High Stadium the night before. This was just stunning.

By coincidence, the only other person in the "green room" with me in Denver was none other than former White House advisor Karl Rove. Talk about a stroke of luck to get an early reaction from those is high places! "Well it sure shakes things up, doesn't it?" Rove said to me.

The choice of a woman by McCain was not surprising, but I thought he would pick Senator Kay Bailey Hutchison (R-TX), who had far more experience and name recognition than Palin.

"She didn't want it," Rove told me when I asked him about Hutchison. Rove and Hutchison are both longtime Texas politicos, so I assumed he would know.

We didn't have time to talk longer, as Rove needed to do his analysis for Fox News Channel after I had wrapped up my analysis for viewers back in the Bay Area. Still, it was one of those lucky moments as a reporter when you find yourself in the right place, at the right time.

Momentum is critical in politics. When something good happens in politics, you have to seize on it and run for daylight. Milk it for all it's worth. Bill Clinton demonstrated this in 1992, when he finished second in the New Hampshire primary and declared himself "the comeback kid!" This was a pretty gutsy move for a second-place finisher, but it made second place look like a win. The momentum from a poor showing in Iowa to a much better finish in New Hampshire was like stepping on the accelerator. Clinton "floored it" and made those who had written him off look foolish. The lesson this time was, you don't always control your own momentum. While Bill Clinton seized on his own bounce, Obama had no control over what John McCain did. From a tactical standpoint, McCain had just done the equivalent of "stealing home" in a baseball game.

Most of the delegates, dignitaries, officials and media were leaving Denver Friday, so gauging reaction at the airport was fascinating. Again, the buzz was all about Palin.

Obviously, Palin was still an unknown quantity. Democratic Party strategists like Bob Mulholland, of California, were quick to react. "We ought to have a Vice President who is ready to be President, rather than making a political decision, or one about gender," Mulholland told me, as we waited to check our bags at the airport. He believed the notion of McCain's trying to pick up some of Hillary Clinton's disgruntled women supporters was cynical, at best. Mulholland also tried to link Palin to GOP corruption scandals in Alaska involving Senator Ted Stevens and Representative. Don Young. "They are her friends," Mulholland said.

The problem was—that upon further examination—this did not appear to be true. Palin has already attacked many of those same Republicans. She rejected Stevens's pork-barrel "bridge to nowhere"; she recruited another Republican to take on Young in the Congressional primary; she ran against incumbent Republican Governor Frank Murkowski (who appointed his own daughter to the U.S. Senate in a blatant act of nepotism); and unseated Murkowski. That's why she had appeal as a maverick, an outsider and a reformer. This appeared to be John McCain's thinking, anyway.

The next stop on the campaign trail was St. Paul, Minnesota, site of the Republican National Convention, where Republicans were about to learn their own lesson in losing momentum.

It's a funny thing about political momentum. Sometimes you can manage and control it; other times it can be taken away by forces that have nothing to do with you. The latter is what happened to Barack Obama in Denver; now the same fate awaited Republicans as they arrived in Minnesota.

Hurricane Gustav was churning in the Gulf of Mexico and was threatening five coastal states, all of which were run by Republican Governors. The GOP convention would still open on Monday, but most formal events were cancelled. You just can't be clinking champagne glasses together in Minnesota, while Mother Nature is crashing homes together in Louisiana. "We are going to be standing ready to help our fellow man. We aren't Republicans or Democrats," said Lt. Governor Jeff Kottkamp. "Keep everyone who could be impacted by this storm in your thoughts and prayers." No one wanted a repeat of the botched local, state and federal response to Hurricane Katrina three years ago. President Bush and Vice-president Cheney cancelled their visits to the convention to monitor the storm from Washington. Many Republicans I spoke with breathed a sign of relief at that, given the unpopularity of both men.

The GOP convention staff quickly set up a Hurricane Information Center inside the Xcel Energy Convention Center. Large flat screen TVs were everywhere; phone lines and high-speed internet lines, too. Fortunately, the storm weakened and made landfall in a sparsely populated area of western Louisiana. It still caused death and damage, but that was minimal compared to the devastating Katrina.

By Tuesday, it was back to politics in St. Paul, both inside and outside the Xcel Center. The slate of Republican speakers was set to address the delegates, but at the same time there were large antiwar protests outside. "Troops out now! Troops out now!" shouted protesters and "Who's war? Their war! Who's war? Their war!" as they pointed to the GOP convention site.

Then there were counter protests by military families and veterans. It was getting pretty heated, as people argued over who was best able to battle terrorism overseas. Retired Army Lt. Colonel Joe Ripya helped organize the counter demonstration. "At 3 o'clock in the morning, when there's a crisis somewhere in the world, I want John McCain answering that phone and not somebody that has no experience at all and is going to have to turn around and run to get his Vice President to decide what to do," Lt. Colonel Ripya told me. The election fight was just heating up!

Other controversies erupted, too. Amid all the fanfare and excitement over Sarah Palin's selection to be the vice presidential candidate, word came that her seventeen year-old, unmarried daughter was pregnant.

"So much for the party of family values and abstinence," said one Democrat. But many of the Republicans I spoke with thought it wasn't a deal breaker for Palin's place on the ticket.

"I can't pass judgment on somebody else," said Nadine Gulit, a delegate from Washington State. "We all raise kids," Gulit told me, "but sooner or later they make their own decisions." Gulit gave the Palin family a lot of credit for supporting their daughter, who planned to marry her boyfriend and raise their baby.

I interviewed Gulit at Cossetta's Italian Market and Pizzeria. The place had the distinction of being one of the few restaurants immediately outside the convention checkpoint. That could be a blessing and a curse for business with traffic shut down; but the restaurant's owner wisely set up a big tent in the parking lot, with food, a couple of bartenders and live music, too. It became my makeshift newsroom at the end of the night. I could interview people after the convention let out, write stories and post video and photos on my blog via wireless Internet. It was a perfect mix with the cold beer and great hot pizza they served. CNN, Fox and all the networks had their fancy skyboxes with catered food, but I had Cossetta's. There was a certain romance to being a freelance reporter and political analyst. I loved this new media industry!

The convention was a farewell of sorts for the Bush family. While President Bush stayed at the White House to deal with Hurricane Gustav, he spoke to the convention via satellite on a giant screen TV. He endorsed his old rival John McCain and suggested Democrats were wrong to paint a McCain administration as a "third Bush term." The President said McCain had earned his "maverick" reputation on many occasions. "He's not afraid to tell you when he disagrees. Believe me I know," said President Bush, and the crowd roared with laughter.

Figure 35. President Bush addresses GOP National Convention via satellite, St. Paul, Minnesota, September 2, 2008. (Mark Curtis)

First Lady Laura Bush was in St. Paul and addressed the delegates in person. "I am proud that America's first female Vice President will be a Republican woman," said Mrs. Bush. "Women have always played an important role in our party," she added and noted that the current Secretaries of State, Labor and Education were women.

Others weren't so enthusiastic about Palin. Some Republicans told me they were concerned about her lack of foreign policy experience; while Democrats wondered whether she could really "step in" if McCain should die. All this led to lots of speculation on TV and radio talk shows, including suggestions that Palin had "no business running for national office with five kids, including an infant, at home." That drumbeat was pretty loud and relentless for days, and provided the backdrop for one of my most memorable convention moments.

When the elevator door opened on the third floor of the Xcel Energy Center, I got in, not knowing there was a firestorm inside. "There's a lot of sexism in the media," I heard a loud voice say. It was former Arkansas governor and presidential candidate Mike Huckabee.

"She's having to answer questions no man would ever have," said Huckabee to a radio reporter who had cornered him. Mike was mad! After venting, he praised Barack Obama, who had said on Monday that the candidates' children should be "off-limits."

"I think Barack Obama has shown a lot of class," said Huckabee very loudly and still visibly angry. The elevator door opened, and he stormed out with his aides in tow. Wow! You just never know what you'll run into at one of these conventions.

The public treatment of Palin became a predominant theme here, well before the Alaska Governor ever got to address the delegates. Former Hewlett-Packard CEO Carly Fiorina, a McCain backer, held a news conference with other female leaders to address the topic. "The Republican party will not stand by while Sarah Palin is subjected to sexist attacks," said Fiorina, "and indeed there has been a great deal of sexism unfortunately exhibited during Hillary Clinton's historic run for the Presidency."

Delegates felt very strongly about sexism, too, especially regarding questions concerning Palin's pregnant teenage daughter. "Nope. Family should not be brought up. If anything this may strengthen the ticket. It's something that people can identify with," said Joni Craighead, a delegate from Nebraska.

"Politics are a nasty business," said Susan Sandberg, a delegate from Stillwater, Minnesota. Sandberg was disgusted at the treatment of Palin and told me, "I would never run for public office."

Figure 36. Rep. Ron Paul (R-TX) ran a spirited campaign for President this year. He attended the Republican National Convention in St. Paul, Minnesota. September 3, 2008. (Mark Curtis)

Wednesday night, it was time for the convention—indeed for most of America—to finally meet Sarah Palin. It was serendipitous that we were in the Xcel Energy Center, where the Minnesota Wild hockey team plays. Hockey is huge in this state, as it is in Alaska. Sarah Palin's kids played hockey. This was a fitting place for her introduction to the nation.

"You know what they say the difference is between a hockey mom and a pit bull?" Palin asked the crowd, and then paused.

"Lipstick!" she said; and with that, the crowd burst into laughter. It was the line of the night from Sarah Palin, and it stole the show!

Palin impressed a lot of people with her story. She spoke of being a mom with five kids, adding that after twenty years of marriage her husband Todd "is still my guy." Her entree into politics had been via the PTA, she said, simply because she wanted to improve her kids' schools.

Palin had later run for city council in Wasilla, Alaska; then she became Wasilla's Mayor; and then she became Chairperson of the Alaska Oil and Gas Commission. She then challenged the incumbent Republican Governor of Alaska in 2006 and beat him. This lady was on a roll, and the Vice Presidential nomination came next. Delegates I spoke with were impressed.

"Any mother of five makes more executive decisions than Barack Obama," said Paula Campbell, a mom from Niceville, Florida, "I witnessed the first female Vice President of the United States tonight."

Mary Bowman, from Iowa, said, "I think it's the fact that she has no pretentions. She's a very grounded human being with a solid set of values, in addition to being very capable as an executive."

After Palin's speech, I ran into 26-year-old Jenniffer Rodriguez of Fremont, California, who was getting a text message from her mom. "She's a feisty one," the text said. Rodriguez was sold on Palin, just like her mom. "As a governor, she's a reformer," Rodriguez said, "She's a Washington outsider. She's an experienced executive who runs a state. That's what we need."

"I think she just inspires women," said Kymber Ebron-Phillips, of Oklahoma City. "The average female can have a family as well as a career. Juggle! That's what we do." Ebron-Phillips was African American and a Democrat. She was still undecided, but said she might vote for McCain-Palin.

What these women had in common was that they could relate to Palin. She was a mom; she was a wife; she had a job; she was a juggler! She cared about her family, neighbors and community. She came across as good and decent. She was likable.

Palin was certainly not a public speaker of Barack Obama's caliber; but what she lacked in eloquence, she more than made up for in sincerity. A lot of women I spoke with said they liked her because "She's just like me." They related and connected. She came across as authentic.

Palin mentioned her son who was going off to war in Iraq soon and her newborn baby with Down's syndrome. By now, of course, everyone knew about her pregnant teenage daughter. "Our family has the same ups and downs as any others," she said matter-of-factly, with no hint of complaint.

She also got a dig in at the national news media. "Here's a little news flash: I'm not going to Washington to serve their opinion. I am going to Washington to serve the great people of this country." The crowd roared its approval.

There were two people for whom I felt sorry after Palin's speech: Barack Obama and John McCain. Obama, because many Democrats were underestimating Palin, and that might be a mistake. I felt for McCain because he had to address the convention Thursday night, and Palin would be a tough act to follow.

After Barack Obama's glitzy acceptance speech in a Denver stadium, John McCain had his work cut out for him. McCain did not have Obama's eloquent, impassioned speaking skills, but he had little need for them. McCain's personal story was so gut wrenching, it didn't need embellishing. It was raw and unvarnished.

Aside from his military service, the Arizona Senator was perhaps best known for being passionate about wasteful government spending. He has tried to kill "pork barrel" spending in Washington and to eliminate federal budget "earmarks" for special projects in most Congressional districts, be they held by Democrats or Republicans. "I understand who I work for. I don't work for a special interest. I don't work for a party. I don't work for me. I work for you," McCain told the audience, which responded with loud applause.

Figure 37. Mark Curtis reports on John McCain's acceptance speech at the GOP Convention in St. Paul, Minnesota, Sept. 4, 2008. (MarkCurtisMedia.com)

McCain complimented Barack Obama on the historic and inspiring nature of his campaign. Then he took aim at Obama on a key issue: "I will leave taxes low and cut them where I can. My opponent will raise them," said McCain.

Another clear difference between Democrats and Republicans was on energy policy. "We will drill new wells offshore, and we will drill in Alaska. We'll build more nuclear power plants," McCain vowed.

Certainly the part of McCain's story almost everyone knows is his ordeal as a prisoner of war in Vietnam for more than five years. I always have mixed feelings when it is recounted. It is one of the most horrifying stories I ever heard; yet I never tire of hearing it. His resilience, character and fortitude to survive made a compelling case for McCain's leadership.

When the Vietnamese found out McCain's dad was an Admiral in the U.S. Navy, they offered him early release as a propaganda ploy. McCain refused, since the military honor code says prisoners should be released by seniority—according to the length of their incarceration. "I turned it down. A lot of prisoners had it much worse than I did," McCain told the convention. The enemy was infuriated by his refusal, so they beat and tortured him more.

Delegates I spoke with were moved by McCain's story. "I wept all through his speech," said Bonnie Triplett, of Kentucky. "He's everything our country's been needing and what we've been praying for," she told me.

"We know he has courage," said Charla Farnum, of Brooklyn, Iowa "We know he is able to make the difficult decisions. He's the kind of man we want to lead our country."

Dr. Prasanta Chandra, from New Jersey, said, "He has sympathy for ordinary people, because he suffered at the hands of evil people." Chandra added. "He (McCain) is very sincere. He says what he means; and he means what he says. He's a man of conviction."

McCain sprinkled his acceptance speech with references to Governor Sarah Palin, his vice presidential running mate. Truth be told, whenever McCain mentioned Palin's name, he got the loudest applause. "I can't wait to introduce her to Washington," said

McCain; and the building shook with laughter. Delegates were impressed by McCain's choice for his partner on the ticket. "The press and Democrats will pick on her," said John Triplett, of Kentucky, "and she'll run right over them!" That sounded like the kind of person McCain was looking for.

McCain told the convention he was ready to be President after twenty-four years in Congress, in addition to his years in the Navy. As he summed up his POW experience, McCain choked back tears. He recalled how his fellow prisoners urged him to survive— something he had finally admitted he could not do alone.

"I was never the same again. I wasn't my own man anymore. I was my country's," McCain said.

Chapter 13: The Fall Campaign & Election

I went everywhere I could this year and talked to just about anyone who would talk to me. I went to bars, pool halls, fine restaurants, dive diners, late-night coffee shops, small businesses, airports and every place else. In essence, I was trying to get "the pulse of America." Why were people supporting certain causes or candidates, and just what were their expectations, hopes and dreams for this Presidential election?

We now had a real horse race on our hands, and I was excited. There were two very competitive national tickets, each with its plusses and minuses. By all accounts, this could be a repeat of 2000 and 2004, when those elections were each decided by one single state. This was high political drama.

Watching the polls would prove fascinating. The day after the Republican National Convention, the Real Clear Politics composite poll was 46.6 percent for Obama-Biden, 44.0 for McCain-Palin. If you get a "bounce" from the convention or other big event, it usually isn't detectable for a few days. Sure enough, on September 8, the poll had flipped. It was now 48.3 percent for McCain and 45.4 for Obama. If this kept up, we'd all be biting our nails until Election Day.

There were four debates, but my application for credentials was turned down to all. No matter. I planned to watch them on TV and evaluate them from the comfort of my own couch. Besides, presidential debates are so canned and scripted they can hardly be called debates. They rarely affected past elections, either.

What did matter was the state of people's lives. I interviewed hundreds of people along the campaign trail for a sampling of their concerns.

James Apple, of Dallas, Texas, told me: "It's got to be the mortgage crisis going on right now. I think that something has to be done about all these people getting burned in foreclosures and losing their homes."

Helen Smits, of Connecticut, had a different—but potentially related—concern. "The terrible impact on the stock market," she said. "We're retired, and our nest egg has really shrunk. We need to get back to good economic times."

Employment issues came up a lot. Mark Felton, of Aurora, Colorado told me that his big concern was "Outsourcing, because of the fact that we are losing jobs. And we are losing our manufacturing, and it's absolutely necessary to bring back the economy of our country." He added, "The economy is a disaster right now and we need to get things back on track."

Certainly one of the new trends we saw in this primary season was young people coming out in droves to vote. By most estimates, we could expect a record youth turnout in November. Why? Education, for one thing. I interviewed Nadia Barkin, a seventeen-year-old high school student from Lakewood, Colorado. "The price of college as far as getting loans to pay for college is getting a little too expensive," Barkin said. "We are concerned about how expensive college is and how it's going to affect my family and its finances."

The common thread for all of these folks—the economy! It came up everywhere. When I spoke to people about issues such as the environment, energy, health care and immigration, the focus always seemed to be on the cost of those items.

One of the most telling interviews I conducted was with Representative Barbara Lee, a Democrat, who represents Oakland, California. You may recall that she was the only member of the U.S. Congress to vote against the war in Afghanistan. She was also a leading critic of the invasion of Iraq. Soon to be the head of the Congressional Black Caucus, she might be the most anti-war member of Congress.

During our five-minute interview on a show I host, "Comcast Newsmakers," Lee talked mostly about economic issues and her race for reelection. After we finished taping, we shook hands and said good-bye. Suddenly she stopped. "Oh, no!" she said. "I never got to talk about ending the war!" Now, my questions had all been pretty open-ended. When I asked about something as generic as her top issues if she was re-elected, she could have answered any way she wanted, including an anti-war message. The fact that she talked almost solely about the economy and related issues was very telling. Most voters brought up the economy in my interviews; very few ever mentioned the war.

To borrow Bill Clinton's mantra to his campaign aides again, "It's the economy, stupid!" Ronald Reagan knew the same lesson, though he put it more politely in 1980. "Ask yourself," said Reagan. "Are you better off than you were four years ago?"

The key to the 2008 Presidential election was—the economy! We found that out September 15 when brokerage giant Lehman Brothers collapsed and then other financial institutions folded, too. By no strange coincidence, the last day John McCain held the lead in the Real Clear Politics composite poll, was September 16, when it was McCain 46.3 percent to Obama 44.2 percent.

As the markets tumbled, so too did John McCain's poll numbers. On September 29, the Dow Jones Industrial Average experienced its largest one-day loss in history. It dropped 768 points. The next day the latest election poll read Obama 48.8 percent to McCain's 44 percent. The lead for Obama increased every day, as the economy worsened. Someday statistics professors will calculate and correlate the exact relationship between the economic data and the election polling data; but if you simply overlay graphs of the daily trends in both, the relationship looks quite apparent.

Were people blaming John McCain? Of course not. The souring economy certainly wasn't his fault; and besides there was plenty of blame to go around, both inside and outside of politics. Still,

McCain *was* hurt because he was a member of the party in power. Had there been a Democrat in the White House, Barack Obama could have encountered a similar fate. Economic downturns don't favor any political party, as witnessed by Jimmy Carter's defeat in 1980 and George H.W. Bush's loss in 1992. A recession was not a stable platform on which to stand when running for reelection.

The one thing I was grateful for at such a dire time was—comedians. With all the pain in our mutual pocket books, laughter helped a bit. Political comedian Will Durst was an old friend of mine from Milwaukee. We had done stand-up together thirty years ago at a dive named, "Jacks or Better!" Will was funny; I was not. That would explain why he is still doing comedy and I'm just delivering the news. We both wound up in San Francisco—and in our own way, wound up in politics. We were in a recession and Will made fun of it. "When everybody in America knows the name of the Secretary of the Treasury, that's not good," Durst said. And he wasn't done: "Line of the year courtesy of an anonymous Wall Street broker: 'This is worse than a divorce. I'm worth half what I was ... and I'm still married.'" I know, the economy wasn't funny, but sometimes people have to laugh!

Another way I tried to gauge public opinion was a bit more scientific. Throughout the course of the campaign year, I had people fill out surveys at various campaign rallies across the nation. I was studying for a Doctorate in Educational Leadership at St. Mary's College of California. My research focused on how effective communication skills can affect the perception of a person's leadership. I was fascinated by the fact that some political leaders could communicate quite well, while others struggled with their message and vision. My survey sample included 301 people in seven states. Here are some of my findings:

Forty-nine percent of John McCain's supporters ranked "experience" as the most important quality to communicate, compared to just 7 percent for Barack Obama supporters.

Twenty-three percent of Obama supporters said "empathy" was the most important communication message, compared to just 1 percent for McCain.

In ranking their candidates overall communication skills, 99 percent of Obama supporters rated him "Very Good" or "Good" on communication, versus 75 percent for McCain supporters.

In terms of overall public speaking skills, 66 percent of Obama supporters "strongly agreed" that effective public speaking was essential for a president to succeed, versus 48 percent among John McCain supporters.

It became very clear from my study that people considered communication skills to be an important attribute for leadership; and it was clear that something about Obama's message was resonating to a higher degree among Democratic supporters, when compared to McCain's message to his Republican supporters. I plan to do more in-depth research and analysis, but found these initial findings quite interesting.

One of the reasons I did the study was to help analyze the upcoming debates. The first debate on September 26 was supposed to be on foreign policy, but the nation was now in the midst of the economic meltdown on Wall Street and everywhere else. Congress was debating a $700 billion dollar bailout package, so the economy had to be discussed. Neither candidate would state how he would vote on the bill. In my opinion, Obama won empathy points by talking about how the economic crisis affected "ordinary Americans." He also said, "We've heard about Wall Street. Those of you on Main Street have been struggling for a while."

McCain scored points by talking about how the economy had been hurt by wasteful government spending and by all the special-interest budget earmarks he was trying to eliminate in Congress. "I didn't win Miss Congeniality in the U.S. Senate," McCain said, when he talked of blocking pork-barrel projects, especially those of fellow Republicans.

The second debate was probably the most anticipated because it featured the vice presidential nominees; and people still didn't know what to make of the folksy Governor of Alaska, Sarah Palin. Again, the economy was the major focus. Palin also might have scored some points with her Ross Perot-like philosophy that, as her parents said, "Don't live outside our means." Translation: A lot of people are frustrated that the government is bailing out Wall Street, while most families have to live within a tight budget. Biden was equally folksy at times, talking about middle-class families sitting around the dinner table, trying to decide what bills to pay and whether "Mary can go back to school next semester." Those were real issues that real people faced.

Palin, who some predicted would make many gaffes, really only had one. She referred to "the toxic mess on Main Street affecting Wall Street," but clearly meant it the other way around. Other than that (and the annoying mispronunciation of 'nucular' which George W. Bush and Jimmy Carter had both perfected), she did just fine.

One of Palin's best lines was correcting Biden on the offshore-oil-drilling chant. "It's drill, baby, drill!" she said. Whether you agree with the policy or not, it was refreshing to see a politician passionately defending a very controversial idea.

I thought Biden's most touching line came when he said, "I know what it's like to be a single parent," referring to the death of his first wife and daughter in a car wreck, leaving him with two small sons.

The third debate was in Nashville, Tennessee and focused heavily on the economy. The best question came, not from moderator Tom Brokaw, but from a woman in the audience. "How can we trust either of you with our money, when both parties got us into this crisis?"

She was right. Blaming either party alone was not accurate. Republicans had pushed for too much deregulation and too much deficit spending. Democrats had pushed for mortgage programs that put families into homes they simply could not afford, especially when their adjustable-interest rates ballooned.

"It's true," Obama conceded. "Nobody is completely innocent here." Obama was backed by former Fannie Mae CEO Franklin Raines, who was Bill Clinton's budget director. The Bush Administration was backed by many from Goldman Sachs, including the current Treasury Secretary, as well as by other Wall Street firms. Both institutions shared in the blame, too.

The lady's question also posed a real concern about both parties in Congress. If they didn't understand or foresee the economic problem, how could they possibly devise the solution? It was a $700-billion-dollar question, without a clear answer.

The best question actually came from Tom Brokaw in this town hall format, when he asked each candidate whom they might appoint Secretary of the Treasury.

"I like Meg Whitman," said John McCain of the E-Bay founder, "She knows how to create jobs." Obama countered that Berkshire Hathaway investment guru Warren Buffet was under his consideration. "Warren would be a pretty good choice," said Obama.

The final debate was October 16 at Hofstra University on Long Island, New York. It made me think even more about my research into how leaders communicate. Sometimes it's not just what they communicate verbally; it's their gestures or movements that speak volumes. McCain did well, but there were some answers when he seemed to stumble verbally or even to ramble a bit. The nonverbal language was even more interesting. Obama seemed much more relaxed and ready to respond. He focused on McCain while the Republican was talking. McCain, on the other hand, seemed uncomfortable. He blinked, fidgeted, smiled and grimaced often. He also looked away from Obama and seemed ill at ease at times. His agitation appeared to spill over into his actual debate performance. Perhaps the day's seven-hundred-point plunge on

Wall Street had deflated the confidence of McCain, who knew the economy was the number one issue.

McCain's best line of the night was: "Senator Obama, I'm not President Bush. If you wanted to run against President Bush, you should have run four years ago." McCain really needed to distance himself from the unpopular President, and this was pretty powerful.

Obama's best line of the night was: "Ninety-five percent of you out there will get a tax cut." Whether he can deliver on that is another story, but it was a pretty clear and memorable line that many voters will take to their polling places, if not to their banks. It had the simple elegance of something Ronald Reagan might have said.

With the debates over, there were twenty days left to campaign. There was a great deal of emphasis on battleground states, especially those that traditionally had voted Republican in presidential races, but where the GOP might now be vulnerable. The list included North Carolina, Virginia, Indiana and Nevada. Obama has promised to run aggressively in all fifty states, and this year I was seeing a huge trend I had never seen before: Large numbers of people were travelling from one state to another to campaign and canvass for their favorites. During the primary season, I found many Democrats and Republicans from California working the campaign offices and phone banks in Nevada. Now, in November it was happening again. Why? Well, a state like California was a sure bet in the Obama column. That had been clear for months. Since Nevada could go either way, many Californians took their time and energy to Nevada.

These migratory campaign workers included, Dean Elias, a professor I knew from St. Mary's College, and his friend Ellen Klutznick. The two spent a weekend in Reno and canvassed approximately seventy-five homes. "We were in despair about the state of Presidential leadership in the United States, desperate for a reason to have hope," said Elias.

"We were inspired to work to get Obama in the White House, no matter what," Klutznick said. "Since Nevada was a 'red' state we felt that it was a worthwhile challenge to try to get more Democratic votes and perhaps to turn the state 'blue.'"

The two found the Obama campaign in Nevada very organized, methodical and detailed. "We knocked on doors. We were given lists including only names of folks who the campaign had discovered were leaning towards Obama, or at least were open to discuss options," Elias said. "We visited an upscale neighborhood one day, a trailer park the next. "

They told me that most people welcomed them and didn't seem to mind that they had come from out of state to lobby for Obama. "I loved the woman who came to her door in her nightgown," Klutznick said. "Having been in bed all day, she congratulated us for doing what we were doing, even though we woke her up. I should only be so good-spirited."

The Obama strategy worked. Nevada was one of eight states that usually vote Republican in Presidential campaigns, but turned for Obama this election.

I spent Election Day in Southern California doing political analysis for Tribune Broadcasting, including KTLA Channel 5 in Los Angeles and KTXL-TV 40 in Sacramento.

The Democratic Party was holding its rally at the Century City Plaza-Hyatt Hotel, where a crowd estimated at ten thousand was gathered. When I arrived, a line wrapped all the way around the huge hotel and for blocks way. I asked a security guard, "Where's the press entrance?" and he said there was none. I knew I would never get in by waiting in line. I tried another security guard at a different entrance and "Bingo!" I was in. After descending several flights of stairs and making my way through the huge crowd, I showed my credentials at the door; and the guard said, "Go on in, but you're one of the last ones." Inside, it was packed shoulder to shoulder. It was crazy!

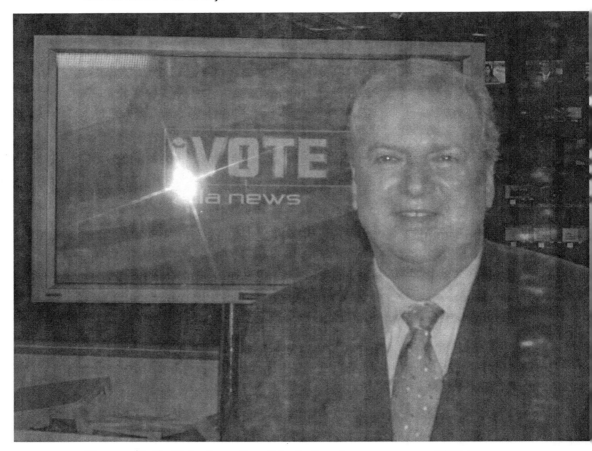

Figure 38. Political analyst Mark Curtis appears on KTLA-TV 5 in Los Angeles, CA on Election Day, 2008. Nov. 4, 2008. (Pavlos Rozis)

Just after 8 p.m. the polls closed in California. It took the news networks only a moment to declare California and its fifty-five electoral votes for Barack Obama. That was enough to put him over the top. He was President-elect of the United Sates, and this ballroom was bedlam. Amid all the cheering and hugging, I looked around and was struck by the number of people, particularly African-Americans, who were crying.

Andre Herndon, editor of the "Wave," in Los Angeles, was there with his two-year-old son, Marley. "I never thought I'd see a black President in my lifetime," Andre admitted. Herndon, who is 35, also explained his previous pessimism. "A lot of times, as an African-American, you feel like the deck is stacked against you. This is a complete shift," he said.

Two-year-old Marley seemed tired and not quite sure what to make of his surroundings as he wrapped his arms around his dad's neck. But Andre said he would someday teach his son the lessons of this night. "It seems now I can tell him you can achieve anything in this country," Herndon said.

Figure 39. Andre Herndon hugs his 2 year-old son Marley at Barack Obama's California victory rally. Los Angeles, California, November 4, 2008. (Mark Curtis)

While Obama did well with minority voters, he also held his own with white voters, winning 43 percent. In fact, that was slightly better than John Kerry's 41 percent in 2004, and Al Gore's 42 percent in 2000.

On CNN, former Education Secretary Bill Bennett rightly stated that there was too much press on potentially conflicted racial politics. "Some 'Bradley effect!' The country's grown up," Bennett said. "We have just achieved an incredible milestone that the world needs to recognize."

The "Bradley effect" is a phenomenon where white voters tell pollsters they are voting for a black candidate, even though they have no such intention, supposedly lying to avoid appearing racist. The term derives from the election in which former Los Angeles Mayor Tom Bradley, an African-American, lost his race for Governor of California in spite of having been well ahead in the polls. The inaccurate racial polling is now known as "the Bradley effect."

Many feared Obama would experience the Bradley effect, but he did not. That was good news to Stephanie Wilkinson. She stood crying in the back of the Hyatt Regency ballroom. Wilkinson, who is fifty, could barely speak to me. "I'm so choked up," she said. Wilkinson hoped Obama's election will heal racial divisions. She said, "I am thinking about my grandparents and ancestors. This means everything to me. He really did something. The fact that he had a black father and white mother means people had to listen to both sides."

CHAPTER 14: CONCLUSION

Oh what a ride it was! I often called it the "road trip of a lifetime," as if I would do it only once. I hope I can repeat it in future presidential campaigns. I saw much of America, and I liked what I saw. On Election Day, I was sad to see my journey come to an end.

John McCain, in my opinion, gave the classiest, most sincere concession speech I ever heard in all of the forty-four years I have witnessed them. "In a contest as long and difficult as this campaign has been, his [Obama's] success alone commands my respect for his ability and perseverance. But that he managed to do so by inspiring the hopes of so many millions of Americans, who had once wrongly believed that they had little at stake, or little influence in the election of an American president, is something I deeply admire and commend him for achieving. This is an historic election, and I recognize the special significance it has for African-Americans and for the special pride that must be theirs tonight. I've always believed that America offers opportunities to all who have the industry and will to seize it. Senator Obama believes that, too," McCain said from his campaign rally in Phoenix.

President-elect Obama was equally as eloquent in his victory speech from Chicago. "If there is anyone out there who still doubts that America is a place where all things are possible, who still wonders if the dream of our founders is alive in our time, who still questions the power of our democracy, tonight is your answer," he said, as the crowd cheered and applauded. "It's the answer spoken by young and old, rich and poor, Democrat and Republican, black, white, Latino, Asian, Native American, gay, straight, disabled and not disabled Americans, who sent a message to the world that we have never been a collection of red states and blue states. We are and always will be the United States of America." Hundreds of thousands in Chicago's Grant Park cheered wildly, and millions of others watched on TV across the nation.

The word "change" was used a lot this year. Barack Obama used it successfully as his message in the Iowa Caucuses, and then just about every other candidate started using some variation of "change" in their slogans, messages and campaign signs. It really was a year of change because—at the very least—we were going to get a completely new administration, regardless of which party won. But things changed in other ways, too.

The internet made a profound impact on the campaign in four ways: How campaigns communicated; how campaigns raised money; how the press covered the race; and how voters simply connected with one another.

The Obama campaign, more than all others, used technology to its advantage. It raised an estimated $750 million dollars, a lot of which came through ten- and twenty-dollar donations made online. Sure, it had major, well-heeled donors, too; but the number of "average Joes" who sent in twenty bucks was staggering. The internet simply made it quick and easy to donate.

Just as important, the campaigns used the internet to state their positions and rally the troops. My professor Dean Elias from St. Mary's College and his friend Ellen Klutznick decided to travel to Nevada to help campaign for Obama on a fall weekend. Like so many aspects of this campaign, they connected to a need by responding on the internet. "We'd given money, but wanted to do more," said Elias. "We emailed the Obama website, asking where the need was greatest, where they recommended we go. In response to our zip code, I imagine, they immediately responded: 'Reno.' Off we went."

It wasn't just Nevada. The internet was helping Obama organize and compete in other traditionally Republican states. In August, Indiana State Senator Errington told me her Republican state was up for grabs, and could go for Obama this year. "For the first time, a Democratic presidential campaign has regional offices all over the state," said Senator Errington. I thought she was way too optimistic.

Indiana had not voted for a Democratic President since 1964. I had traveled there this year and didn't think it would change. By November, Senator Errington had proved me wrong.

The internet also helped revolutionize the way we report and consume the news. From the top names in the mainstream media, to one-man blogging sites, it seemed everyone was online, sharing information, opinions, pictures and video. There were new and major players. Voters might use "YouTube" to watch videos of John McCain, rather than wait to watch them on CNN. Pollster Frank Luntz reported that, for the first time ever, the 18-year-old to 24-year-old age group used the internet as its primary source of news and information, instead of television, radio or newspapers. Obama used that to his advantage over McCain.

The mere fact that I had lost my own job in the mainstream media and was now out blogging and travelling the campaign trail as a freelancer was a testament to the power of the internet. Rather than to walk away in defeat, I had been encouraged by my friends to transition to the "new media" and to embrace it. Now my work can be found on YouTube, Twitter, Friendfeed, Facebook and my own website. Just "Google" Mark Curtis and politics, and you will find thousands of links to my work. It's staggering.

The internet also gave "voice to the voiceless" in new ways. On election night I received this posting on my Facebook page from Marc Martinez, a former co-worker at KTVU: "As I watched Barack's speech tonight with my three-year-old daughter asleep on my lap and my soon-to-be- nine-year-old son watching, I couldn't help imagining my parents back in 1960, with their three little children in the living room of their house in Baldwin Park, California, with 'Viva Kennedy' placards and posters, and wondering if this is perhaps exactly how they felt when they knew they were witnessing a watershed event. I wish I could ask them."

I asked Marc if I could post his reflections on my blog, and he said, "Of course." At the same time, I wondered whether any reporters ventured into his family's neighborhood for similar reaction back in 1960. I doubt it. The internet was bringing us new voices all the time.

The technology was helping me report the news in many ways. While I was at the Democrats' victory rally in Los Angeles, my sister Tierney was at the Obama rally at Grant Park in Chicago with friends. She was sending me text message updates on her phone for use in my blog. I asked her for some instant reflections during and after the Obama rally. She wrote back: "I was in Grant Park last night watching history unfold, and I have never felt more a part of America. Afterwards, like thousands of others, I walked up Michigan Avenue with people from every walk of life, color, size and shape, age, and economic status back to their daily lives. There was a good energy and enthusiasm, coupled with a sense of unity. There wasn't any rowdiness, arrogance, or violence, but rather a sense of peace."

This was gold for a "new media" operation on a shoestring budget. Tierney wasn't just my sister anymore. She was my "Chicago correspondent!" And, of course, once I finished my stories, they were almost immediately proofread by my editor, Shirley Ware, who lives in Plantation near Fort Lauderdale, Florida. The internet had changed the mass media landscape for good.

Another big change we witnessed this year was a record turnout among the nation's youngest voters. Whether it was apathy or ignorance, there had never been a big youth voter turnout in the years since the U.S. Constitution was amended, lowering the voting age from twenty-one to eighteen. Now things had changed. Some of it had to do with the way young people communicated with each other. A year ago, I never would have dreamed of having a Facebook page, or spending time watching videos on YouTube. "That's for kids," I would have scoffed. Today I am a daily user of both. Why? Because it's the way *many* people communicate these days, not just young people.

The youth vote formed a critical mass for Obama, and I often asked young voters why. Jenny Tsai was thirty, Asian-American, and worked for a corporation in Santa Monica. For her, the economic downturn and the wars in Iraq and Afghanistan weighed heavily this year. "I think, more than anything, I just wanted a change," Tsai said. "All the people in my age demographic felt the same way about Obama."

Some of the exit polling fleshed that out. People from age eighteen to twenty-nine voted almost exclusively for Obama. He took 72 percent of the youngest demographic, compared to 28 percent for John McCain. In fact, the only age group McCain won was people age 65 and older.

Obama communicated well with people via the internet. I received daily dispatches from his campaign and, on some days, multiple e-mails. He also got dialed into Bill and Hillary Clinton's e-mail list after she lost the nomination. The internet phase of Obama's campaign will serve as a case study. By comparison, the McCain campaign sent me just one e-mail in the final month. Republicans need to ramp up their high-tech pitches. They got out-hustled online.

It goes without saying that Obama's speaking style really appealed to young and, especially, to first-time voters. Critics worry Obama may turn out to be style over substance—a good speaker, but not a leader. We'll find out.

Until then, many of Obama's young voters remain optimistic. "It's exciting," Jenny Tsai told me. "There's a lot to look forward to."

Others, including Republicans, saw Obama's message as key to this campaign. When I had dinner with the late White House Press Secretary Tony Snow back in January, just weeks after the Iowa and New Hampshire contests, he said: "Barack Obama is the only one who 'gets it' in terms of hope and optimism." The message resonated with older voters, too. Bionca Gambill, age fifty-one, from Indiana, told me she was inspired by Obama's stirring speech at the Democratic Convention in 2004. "I've had an Obama bumper sticker on my car since July 4, 2007," Gambill said.

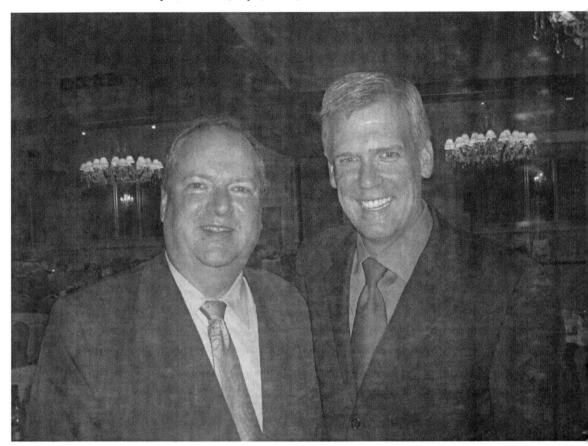

Figure 40. Political Analyst Mark Curtis and former White House Press Secretary Tony Snow, at Contra Costa USA. January 24, 2008. Concord, Califronia. Sadly, Tony passed away from cancer July 12, 2008. (Suzanne Schoenfeld)

This was an election that was watched overseas, perhaps more so than others in recent history. Foreigners were captivated, too. Mahvash Taqi was a 28-year-old from India, whom I interviewed at the Democratic Convention in Denver. She now lives in Washington, DC. Taqi can't vote because she is not a citizen although her application is in the pipeline. "I am supporting Obama," Taqi said, "and I came here to celebrate the unity."

As I've mentioned, the most common issue raised in my interviews with voters all over America this year was the economy. Most U.S. Presidential elections feature the economy as the top issue, and this one was no different. In one exit poll, 62 percent said the economy was the top issue. The Iraq War came in second at just 10 percent.Nowhere was that more evident than on Hollywood Boulevard in Los Angeles on Election Day. I spotted a young man panhandling with a cardboard sign. Gregory Klaeboe, age twenty-eight, was an unemployed tourism worker. I have crisscrossed the country with the candidates most of this year, but Klaeboe had the most unusual election-related sign I had seen: "Obama Ain't the Only One Who Wants Change!"

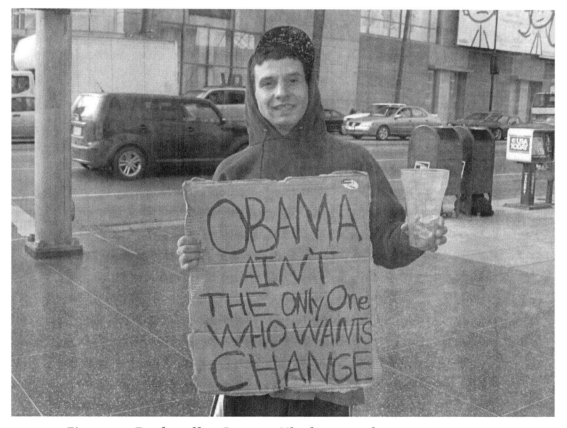

Figure 41. Panhandler Gregory Klaeboe says he wants "change" on Election Day, too. Hollywood, CA. November 4, 2008. (Mark Curtis)

Truth be told, Klaeboe's sign was more about panhandling, and less about an endorsement. Still, he would rather be back working in the tourist trade. "The jobs that I'm interested in are like promoting tourism at kiosks," Klaeboe said. "The less people go on vacation, the less money I make." Klaeboe worked as a "pedicab driver" in New York, which is a fancy way to say he drove a bicycle taxi. He was laid off in the economic downturn. Young people in Klaeboe's age demographic were the key to this year's election, voting almost 75 percent for Barack Obama. Klaeboe said, "I think that Obama has made ... young people to realize the importance of their vote. Klaeboe is hoping the economy bounces back soon and saw some mixed signals before leaving New York. "Yes, of course the tourism from Europe has gone up," he said. "But the tourism from within the U.S. has gone down," he added pessimistically. Indeed all Americans are waiting for the economy to bounce back. For most, the big question is not if, but when.

Another change this year was a shifting Hispanic vote. Latinos make up the fastest growing segment of the U.S. population and are the largest minority group. African-Americans voted in huge numbers for Obama, 96 percent to 4 percent for McCain, but that's no surprise. Democratic Presidential candidates usually win by that margin among black voters. The real surprise was the Hispanic vote, which went 66 percent for Obama to 34 percent for McCain. Republicans usually do much better with the Latino vote, with George W. Bush having received 45 percent of this key and growing group. The Latino demographic will remain a battleground for years to come. The last thing I want to address is future "change." I saw some things on the campaign trail this year that need fixing. Democrats should get rid of the super delegates. Having a system where party bosses and elected officials can swoop in and change the will of the people is dangerous and undemocratic. Remember, had enough super delegates sided with Hillary Clinton, she could have defeated Barack Obama even though he had won more primaries, more popular votes, and more of the delegates chosen directly by the people.

Republicans need reform, too. The "winner-take-all" primary system has to go. It flies in the face of the "one-man, one-vote" principle and is as undemocratic as the Democrats' Super Delegates. Take the Missouri primary, for example. John McCain finished with 33 percent of the vote; Mike Huckabee, 32 percent; and Mitt Romney, 29 percent. Despite how close they were, McCain won all 58 delegates. Huckabee and Romney went home empty-handed. The Republicans could have easily had a primary season as dramatic as the Clinton-Obama battle, but "winner-take-all" states meant McCain had the nomination sewn up by March 4 in Texas. Most states did have a proportional distribution of delegates, but twelve states held Republican primaries which were "winner-take-all."

The last reform I suggest is granting immigrant soldiers the right to vote. I will never forget standing in the shadows of Mount Rushmore interviewing Christina Townsend of Seattle, Washington. She was in the U.S. Army and had served in Iraq, but Christina was Filipino and not yet a U.S. citizen. She could fight and die for this country, but she could not vote. It just didn't seem fair. As with so many things in life, change takes time.

It was a historic election for many reasons, but it was also the continuation of a nation that was born out of hope and optimism and potential, despite all of our internal and external struggles. We've moved forward in many ways, but we always have a lot more to do. Our Founding Fathers created a solid foundation on which to build with the Declaration of Independence and the U.S. Constitution. Our nation continues to be a work in progress.

In 2008 "We the People," simply continued on our collective journey, "to form a more perfect Union."

Printed in the United States
221607BV00002B/2/P

"Nothing even comes close to *Shoot Out* in laying out both how the business really, *really* works and why it is a machine broken beyond repair. For one thing, it's written by two men with industry battle scars, sometimes self-inflicted . . . What makes *Shoot Out* more than a jeremiad, though, is the way Bart and Guber explain in detail *how* each dysfunction functions. A–."
—*Entertainment Weekly*

"Elegantly written and passionately argued, *Shoot Out* is a labor of love by two articulate, insightful, and seasoned insiders—an indispensable guide to anyone who aspires to navigate the challenging and often treacherous waters of contemporary Hollywood."
—Robert Rose, dean,
UCLA School of Theater, Film, and Television

"Bart and Guber are clearly committed to the value of a good script, and they write with real respect about directors who had the courage of their convictions when their careers were on the line. Plus, they are sincere in wanting to share what they know with aspiring filmmakers."
—*Premiere*

"Bart and Guber opine on every part of the filmmaking process and share insights, for example, on how best to deal with egomaniacal auteurs. They have plenty of juicy tidbits to share."
—*Movieline*

"*Shoot Out* spares no bullets in taking on Hollywood's favorite targets."
—Gil Cates, producer/director, and founding dean,
UCLA School of Theater, Film, and Television

"Writing in a direct, refreshing, and honest style, Bart and Guber offer an intimate view of the film industry and its unending economic, political, and artistic clashes. Fascinating illustrative anecdotes that range from the scary . . . to the charming . . . an informal, highly entertaining step-by-step survey of how all the parts of filmmaking fit together."
—*Publishers Weekly*

"What Bart and Guber clearly do enjoy is the art of the deal, the intrigue that permeates the corridors of power in Hollywood and the mechanics of how films are successfully put together and sold. Their enthusiasm, expertise and experience in these areas are what makes *Shoot Out* live up to its promise. [An] irresistible combination of juicy stories about the foibles of Hollywood moguls and stars spun out in Bart's silky smooth, compulsively readable style."
—*Newark Star-Ledger*

continued . . .

"*Shoot Out* is like the story of a film in Hollywood with villains and heroes, all behind the camera."   —Terry Semel, chairman and CEO, Yahoo!

"Fascinating . . . The real inside look into Hollywood and how films get made."   —Irwin Winkler, Winkler Films

"A must-read book for anyone interested in the movie business. Guber and Bart are the real deal, with great personal anecdotes that lead you through all aspects of moviemaking."   —Scott Sassa

"I've never had a shoot-out with either Peter Bart or Peter Guber. I'm too smart. Learn and laugh with them."
—Bernie Brillstein,
founding partner, Brillstein-Grey Entertainment,
and author of *Where Did I Go Right?*

"Their years in the industry give [Bart and Guber] the wherewithal to relate all kinds of interesting anecdotes about famous directors, screenwriters, studios, and other members of Hollywood film production society past and present. In some entertaining asides, Bart and Guber trade off giving short sidebars on famous personalities in the film industry. The result is an insider's view of how some of the most popular films in history were made and subsequently consumed by the public."   —*Library Journal*

"Tantalizing behind-the-scenes tidbits . . . Brisk, lively, and detailed, *Shoot Out* proves once again that there really is no business like show business."
—*BookPage*

"In *Shoot Out*, [Peter Bart and Peter Guber] have distilled the essence of movie magic to a single moment during a film's production—the shoot-out—when creative forces clash; a star walks off the set, a studio fires the director, the financial backers tighten the purse strings . . . [they've] packaged their best tales of Hollywood shoot-outs into an entertaining tutorial on how movies are made today . . . If you wonder why they don't make 'em like they used to (and whether they will again), you'll find the answer in *Shoot Out*."
—*The News-Press* (Ft. Myers, FL)

"Candid insight into why some movies become monster hits while others languish in developmental purgatory . . . the unflagging enthusiasm with which the authors share personal anecdotes and infamous Hollywood tales results in a surprisingly optimistic guide to surviving the perilous journey from the first draft to the final cut."   —*Contents Magazine*

"A skillful explanation of a high-stakes, high-pressure industry."
—*Book Magazine*

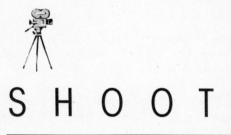

S H O O T   O U T

SURVIVING FAME

AND (MIS)FORTUNE

IN HOLLYWOOD

Peter Bart and

Peter Guber

A PERIGEE BOOK

A Perigee Book
Published by The Berkley Publishing Group
A division of Penguin Group (USA) Inc.
375 Hudson Street
New York, New York 10014

G. P. Putnam's Sons edition: May 2002
First Perigee trade paperback edition: June 2003

Perigee trade paperback edition ISBN: 0-399-52888-1

The Library of Congress has catalogued the G. P. Putnam's Son's edition as follows:

Bart, Peter.
    Shoot out : surviving fame and (mis)fortune in
Hollywood / Peter Bart and Peter Guber.
        p.   cm.
    Includes bibliographical references.
    ISBN 0-399-14808-6
    1. Motion picture industry—United States. 2. Motion
pictures—United States. I. Guber, Peter. II. Title.

PN1993.5.U6 B2977   2002
384'.8'0973—dc21   2001048193

Printed in the United States of America

10   9   8   7   6   5   4   3   2   1

Acknowledgments

In his introduction to *The Years with Ross*, James Thurber expressed surprise that "everyone I turned to for opinion and guidance without exception dropped everything and came running to my assistance." It turned out that Harold Ross, his longtime editor at *The New Yorker*, was revered as well as feared. Well, we cannot lay claim to a similar experience in this book. In fact, some people went running in the opposite direction when they learned of plans for this volume. The state of Hollywood at this moment is such that some industry leaders are less than eager to voice their true opinions. By contrast, other talented show business practitioners willingly stepped forward, not only for our course at UCLA but also in private conversation, both on and off the record. We wish to thank all those executives and filmmakers who gave of their time and wisdom.

PETER BART AND PETER GUBER

Special thanks also to those friends and mentors whose encouragement meant a lot to me in this period. They include William Goldman, Robert Evans, Art Cooper, Peter Gethers, John Duff, Kathy Robbins and, of course, my wife, Blackie, whose love, encouragement—and excellent insights—have always gotten me through the difficult times. If this were a movie, she'd deserve top billing. I also owe a debt to the editors and reporting staff of *Variety* who contributed so much to my knowledge, especially its principal editors Elizabeth Guider, Steven Gaydos, Timothy Gray and Todd Cunningham, and to my stalwart assistant, Bashirah Muttalib.

PETER BART

Virtually every event that shaped this book is the result of the inspiration, support and often leadership of many partners, colleagues and employees who have collaborated in this experience I call my life's work. My views stem from the combined energies and talent of authors, coaches and mentors far too numerous to mention. But if my career has been a lightning rod for opportunities, then the beacon is Lynda, my wife, who has supported me at my lowest and banged on me to keep me humble when I became full of myself. It's courageous to participate in supporting another's dream. To her I dedicate this effort.

PETER GUBER

Contents

SHOOT OUT

Roll Credits

The stakes have never been higher, nor the obstacles greater. Anyone setting out to create film, music, TV or any other product of our popular culture faces not only the intense competition of the marketplace, but also an intimidating landscape dominated by multinational corporate leviathans. The process of navigating these minefields requires both passion and strategic know-how, not only creative fervor but also consummate cool. The purpose of this book is to analyze this landscape and set forth these strategies.

The term "vision keeper" will crop up frequently in these pages. It is intended to describe those filmmakers, writers, musicians and random innovators whose imaginations galvanize those around them. What they see and think rallies others to their side and mobilizes the resources needed to bring that vision to reality. This book is not intended to present a stratagem on "how to" make movies, but "how come" movies get made and sometimes, frighteningly, why.

At any given time in human history, the vision keepers seemed as rare as an endangered species. Yet through the ages they've reappeared alternatively as shaman or storyteller, driven for whatever reason to plant their mark on the experience of the moment.

Only a generation ago, archeologists marveled over a special find, deep within a network of caves in a forest of oaks, three hundred miles south of Paris. On the wall of one cave there sprawled an elaborate depiction of what appeared to be a bison hunt. It consisted of a series of blurry images, as though its artist suffered from double vision, which was all the more intriguing since natural light could never have penetrated the depths of that cave. The vision keeper seemed to have designed his work as a sort of dynamic experience; as viewers carried the torch from one end of the painting to the other, passing it on to others, they sensed the bison running, the hunters pursuing, the blurred lines reinforcing the sense of movement.

What led this ancestral artist to create these images in the subterranean darkness? There was certainly no paycheck, no opportunity for residuals. On the other hand, there probably were no tribal naysayers either, no corporate arbiters to mandate a different approach, no demands to raise additional financial resources.

The shaman/storyteller survives today in many different and more sophisticated forms. Cyberspace has supplanted the walls of a cave as a means of conveying his vision, the cosmos becoming the ultimate repository of mankind's errant imaginings.

Bran Ferren, the former head of the Walt Disney Company's Imagineering think tank, observes that "[storytelling] comprises the core competency, not just of entertainment but also of education and commerce." The human brain, he goes on to suggest, is wired to observe and collate experience through story. We naturally convert everything into story, even information.

That indeed is one key reason why mankind has related with such intensity to literature, theater or movies. "Movies are the closest external representation of the prevailing storytelling that goes on inside our minds," writes Antonio Damasio, the prominent neurologist. "The brain naturally weaves wordless stories of what happens to an organism immersed in an environment."

To be sure, the fundamental alchemy of storytelling was forever changed by technology at the turn of this millennium. The new storyteller reemerged as a digital shaman, at once poet and engineer.

All this has inevitably created a new set of rules. Our mission in this book is to delineate and demystify those rules and, in doing so, we shall focus particularly on the art and craft of moviemaking. One reason is that the role of the vision keeper in film has undergone the most dramatic change, epitomizing the forces affecting every tributary of our pop culture. Further, our depth of experience is principally in filmmaking, and hence is our point of reference.

Throughout the book we shall frequently hark back to our collective odysseys spanning a period of three decades—cellular fragments of celluloid experience. We shall also summon up the "war stories" of others who've been immersed as creative and commercial participants in the process. Most of these other voices derive from guest appearances over the years at our courses, which were conducted at the School of Theater, Film and Television of the University of California in Los Angeles, and represent a unique broadband of key players in the Hollywood spectrum. On one level, therefore, the book provides an ongoing journal of their creative journeys. We thank all of them for their contributions to our understanding, and hence to this book.

1.

Eye of the Storm

Fellini once told me, "Robertino, remember always tell the truth." Now I understand he was lying to me.

ROBERTO BENIGNI

Peter Bart: Initiation

What have I got myself into?

I kept obsessing over that question throughout my first moments, indeed my first weeks, on my new studio job as vice-president of production at Paramount. Sure, there were obvious perks to gloat over. I drove to the studio in a new Mercedes, leased for me by my employer. It beat the sullen Chevy that the *New York Times* had supplied, a vehicle decorated with three bullet holes—a by-product of my coverage of race riots in Los Angeles and San Francisco. I had a sharp new office and a secretary, both milestones to a journalist whose accoutrements prior to this consisted of a gray metal desk and an insistently ringing phone. I also was the envy of my friends, many of whom were stunned to learn I'd become a studio executive. In their minds, I would now dine with stars, and women would throw themselves at me thanks to my exalted station. Several of my journalist friends were less congratulatory, to be sure. They told me I was selling out to Hollywood. They could not believe that I—that anyone—would voluntarily depart the hallowed halls of the *Times*, which was, to them, more a cathedral than a newspaper.

I had tried to explain myself to some of these friends but knew it was fruitless. I said I'd grown weary of writing about people who were doing things and that I wanted to try doing something myself. I explained that this would probably be a temporary gig. I would take copious notes for a book that would provide the ultimate insider's view on how a studio really functioned. I told friends that it was not about meeting girls (no one believed this) but rather that this, the year 1967, seemed a fascinating moment of transition in Hollywood history. Boldly innovative films were being made that could never have gotten through the old studio system, I told whoever would listen, and I wanted to be part of that process. The town seemed awash with bright young filmmakers—maybe I could actually lend a hand to some worthy ones.

Of course, no one really believed *any* of this—not my friends, not even my parents. To them, I was straying into dangerous territory, taking on a position for which I was ill prepared, also getting involved with people who "were not like me" and who ultimately would betray me.

They didn't put all that into so many words, but I could tell it from the wary glances, the nuances of our conversation. And frankly, during my initial days and weeks at the studio, I had come to the conclusion that they were probably right.

My new car and office notwithstanding, the reception accorded my immediate boss, Robert Evans, and me was not exactly sunny. To the established studio bureaucracy, we were intrusive outsiders whose tenure would be brief at best. We could be counted upon to make fools of ourselves and quickly fade into the night. As though to emphasize this attitude, Frank Caffey, an austere, silver-haired man who was operational head of the physical studio, casually informed me that the furniture in my office and in Evans' was all rented. There was no point in bringing in the "real stuff," he observed.

This made me curious where the "real stuff" resided. Since Caffey was not interested in responding to that question, I conned a studio art director into taking me to the remote building where sets were stored. One section of that building, I learned, housed office furniture to be allocated to filmmakers or new executives who'd moved onto the lot. The area was filled with mahogany desks, leather chairs, antique lamps, etc. This was the "real stuff," none of it destined for Evans or me. Why bother, since we were going to be gone in sixty seconds?

Caffey's hospitality was matched by that of other Paramount lifers. The head of business affairs was appropriately disdainful. The head of casting remained distanced. She kept a small dog in her office, which tried to pee on my shoe when I paid a courtesy call. At lunch I ate with the "commoners" in the commissary, rather than trying to penetrate the so-called executive dining room that adjoined it. Special tables in that room were reserved for the likes of John Wayne and Otto Preminger, the ferocious Teutonic director, and I had no desire to insinuate myself into that exclusive domain.

The frosty reception was to be expected, I learned. Working for a studio was like joining an elite club. Once your membership was assured, you could glide from one studio job to the next as the regimes changed. You still played golf at Hillcrest, ate dinner at Ma Maison and screened movies in your private theater at home.

Neither Evans nor I was a member of this circle. Evans was an actor who went on to found a clothing business with his brother, Charles, called Evan-Picone. He had then proceeded to use his winnings from the *schmatteh* trade to buy rights to a few novels and wedge his way into producing. He was Hollywood handsome and coveted a flashy lifestyle, but he had two traits that served him well in his new job. Endearingly modest by nature, he made no pretense to being the next Irving Thalberg, even though he once played Thalberg in one of his early acting gigs. Further, he was utterly lacking in vindictiveness, which set him apart from the rulers of other studios. Filmmakers and agents doing business with him realized that you couldn't get him mad nor could you get him mean.

The specifics of how Evans got his job are still the subject of speculation. But it appeared that Charles Bluhdorn, the erratic Austrian-born chief of Gulf + Western who had acquired Paramount when it was on the threshold of bankruptcy, had met Evans through a friend and taken an instant liking to him. A coarse, ill-mannered man who lived in a state of permanent belligerence, Bluhdorn admired Evans' style—and access to women. Had he hired an old-guard studio chief to run Paramount, that individual would surely have been scornful of Bluhdorn and unwilling to put up with his tyrannical ways. In Bluhdorn's mind, it would be far more satisfying to "discover" a new Thalberg—someone who would be at once aggressive, yet subservient. His fondness of Evans took on a father-son aspect; Bluhdorn made no bones about his disappointment in his own son, who was neither jaunty nor attractive. Evans, with all his panache, was the glamorous heir Bluhdorn had always wanted.

Evans and I had met through Abby Mann, a mutual friend who had won an Academy Award for his brilliant screenplay *Judgment at Nuremberg,* and the three of us frequently dined together. Though obviously quite different in attitudes and interests, we were all fascinated by the sweeping changes overtaking the entertainment industry, especially as they reflected the social unrest of the late 1960s. Each of us was witness to these transformations, but in unique ways.

After I survived a three-week stint covering the Watts riots and the subsequent racial upheaval in San Francisco, Evans sent me a huge tub of my favorite ice cream accompanied by a "get well" note. Soon he began sending an occasional book or script to Mann and me—properties he was thinking of acquiring. A three-way colloquy about the care and feeding of movie projects soon developed.

And there was a lot to talk about. Hollywood had embarked on a period of cosmic change. The big, glitzy studio movies that had succeeded in the past clearly weren't working anymore. Television had stolen the "habit" audience that for generations loyally greeted major studio releases. Also, the industry was being invaded by a brash new style of filmmakers—young men who refused to work under the old rules. They wanted to make personal, character-driven films and demanded the right to exercise greater control over how those films were written, cast and edited. The era of the old-style director who faithfully accepted his assignments from the studio production czar had vanished.

Having endured a financial battering, the studios were suddenly open to new ideas and new blood. A new day was dawning. Or was it?

When Evans asked me to join him at Paramount, I was at once excited and daunted. The *Times* had been good to me and I was freelancing pieces for prestigious magazines as well. Why not stay with what I knew? I asked myself. On the other hand, these were the 1960s, and every time you turned on the radio, some astonishing new album all but overwhelmed you. Every time you ventured into a movie theater, the film you saw changed the way you thought about movies: *Easy Rider, Midnight Cowboy, Tom Jones,* and *The Loneliness of the Long Distance Runner.* And then there was Vietnam, the Pill, and drugs. Nothing was as we remembered it only six months earlier. The ground was shifting under our feet.

In short, this was not a moment in history when one was tempted to stand pat. It was a moment to venture forth. Besides, despite all this decision-making angst, I realized how lucky I was. My big risk involved going to Paramount, not to Vietnam. What the hell was I ulcerating about?

Well, plenty, as it turned out. My initial months at Paramount were marked by periods of intense hazing. The "new boy" had to be made to feel like a clumsy newcomer. At the same time, the town's young agents seemed to welcome those very newcomers who were anathema to the studio lifers. They had young clients to showcase— bright young writers, directors and actors to whom the old-timers would not grant an audience.

Consistent with my fallback plan to write a book about the studio, I began keeping a careful log of all my meetings. Even as I recorded my impressions, however, I surprised myself by how favorably impressed I was by many of these filmmakers I was encountering. A few clearly felt they were God's gift to filmmaking. Egocentricity was rampant. Yet many of them had a damned good rap, and the shorts and student films they showed me reflected considerable promise.

Yet, even as I recorded my impressions of these meetings, I began to worry that I'd already lost my journalistic skepticism. Had life at a studio already obliterated my "bullshit detector"?

To a degree, it had. On the other hand, the youthful wannabe filmmakers I was encountering in that period included the likes of Francis Ford Coppola, George Lucas, Steven Spielberg, Peter Bogdanovich, Hal Ashby, William Friedkin—not exactly, as it turned out, an unpromising group. Rising to prominence in London, meanwhile, were Tony Richardson, Lindsay Anderson, Karel Reisz and Jack Clayton. No one has ever been able to explain why talent seems to come in waves, but a wave clearly was bursting on the scene in the late 1960s. And Evans and I started to make deals with them. Among the first crop of films to emerge were *Goodbye, Columbus; Medium Cool; Harold and Maude* and *Downhill Racer.* We were making plenty of mistakes along the way, but we were also finding our rhythm.

Before Evans and I could enjoy the first fruits of our labor, yet another form of hazing was to confront us—the impact of Bluhdorn's
bombs. Charlie Bluhdorn was not the sort of man who would hire a
new production team and simply turn things over to them. He had
his own ideas about what would make a successful movie, and he
was intent on implementing them. The results were devastating.

For one thing, Bluhdorn, as a European, venerated schmaltzy
Hollywood musicals and he was insistent on reviving this tired
genre. His flights of fancy resulted in some truly bizarre, hugely expensive turkeys such as *Paint Your Wagon* and *Darling Lili*. In *Paint
Your Wagon*, it was not enough simply to dust the cobwebs off this
Lerner and Loewe relic; Bluhdorn also assigned singing roles to Clint
Eastwood and Lee Marvin. The resulting movie was a fiasco. For
hours on end I underwent the daily torture of watching "dailies" on
Paint Your Wagon, looking on numbly as the two veteran, tone-deaf
actors lamely tried to give life to their ballads. The final film had to
be better than the dailies, I reasoned. But I was wrong.

Darling Lili was even more excruciating. The Mata Hari spy plot
was clunky, and the romance involving Julie Andrews and Rock
Hudson was unintentionally hilarious. Andrews was conducting herself with the righteous aplomb of the governess from *The Sound of
Music*, and it already was getting out that Hudson was not exactly
captivated by women in general, or by Andrews in particular.

The critical rejection of these cinematic anachronisms was blis-
tering, and Bluhdorn was not one to take ridicule gently. Even as he
flared at the press, however, he also was conjuring up some intriguing ways to bury the losses. First he tried to sell off a half-interest in
Darling Lili to an Italian hood named Michele Sindona, who was
later to die in jail. When that scam fell apart, he again sold the rights
to the film in return for $31.2 million in debentures in a company
called Commonwealth United, in which Bluhdorn had a major interest. Not surprisingly, the SEC ultimately closed in on this and

other Bluhdorn schemes. For a while it looked as though he might end up in jail, but that never became reality.

Yet a visit to Bluhdorn's office would always be interrupted by top-of-the-lung confrontations with attorneys or government investigators. He would simultaneously be conducting a negotiation for a film project, rebuffing an SEC attorney and trading millions of dollars in securities, all the while pacing his office like a caged animal.

Bluhdorn clearly was a man who courted danger, and hence was dangerous to be around. He seemed happiest when he was holding court at his estate in the Dominican Republic, regaling guests with stories even as scores of machine gun–toting guards patrolled the periphery of his property. No scheme was too exotic for his taste: He conducted raids on the most elite corporations and once tried to lure Fidel Castro into joining with him in establishing a worldwide sugar cartel.

I respected Bluhdorn's boldness but was repelled by his ethics and operating style. Not a deal could be made, however trivial, without him second-guessing details of the negotiation. He once yelled at me for spending too much money per page for new material—big bucks should go only to big manuscripts, he insisted. The "lean" properties I had tied up turned out to be *True Grit*, a novella that became the basis for John Wayne's final hit, and the sixty-page outline to *The Godfather*, written by Mario Puzo—the novel, when ultimately completed, became an international best-seller.

Given his nature, Bluhdorn not surprisingly attracted other players with proclivities similar to his own. He venerated Sidney Korshak, who came out of the Chicago Mafia crime scene and who was to become a fixture on the Paramount lot. Bluhdorn's relationship with Sindona became so tight that he actually sold a half-interest in the Paramount lot to a company controlled by the Italian (the deal ultimately fell through). Bluhdorn liked having strong-willed, temperamental people around him, but he also wanted his subordinates to take orders—a contradiction that led to many screaming arguments. In appointing a very smart but volatile twenty-nine-year-old Stanley Jaffe to become president of Paramount, he disregarded reports that Jaffe was emotionally unsuited for such a high-stress job. Even Bluhdorn was aghast when the high-strung Jaffe would argue with him with such fervor that blood would start streaming from his flaring nostrils.

Making movies is an emotional business, and given Bluhdorn's confrontational style, Paramount seemed like a company perpetually on the brink of a nervous breakdown. With the small size of the staff and its relative inexperience, alarming missteps were always being made, which added fuel to the chaotic atmosphere. During my first year, a movie started shooting in Spain, supposedly under Paramount's aegis, yet no one would admit to having green lit it and no paper trail could be discovered. The inquisition was a discomfiting one: Was it really possible that a movie with two major stars could just start shooting, sending us its bills, without anyone in our organization knowing about it?

As the "new boy," I was naturally a prime suspect. I even went so far as to search my phone records to see whether I'd inadvertently talked with the principals. Fortunately, my phone logs were clean. No one ever did find out who put his OK on the film in Spain, but it kept shooting and we kept paying the bills.

Meanwhile other problems were closing in on me. I had ardently advocated that Paramount finance a thriller called *Rosemary's Baby*, based on the novel by Ira Levin, and Evans had secured a commitment from the brilliant, if erratic, Roman Polanski to direct it. Here was a magical package—Polanski, Mia Farrow, an exotic best-seller. This was as far from *Paint Your Wagon* as you could get. But by the first week of principal photography, storm clouds were gathering. Without confiding in anyone, Polanski had concluded that the only way to elicit a passionate performance from Farrow was literally to break her down, relentlessly demanding take after take, sometimes shooting more than thirty takes. Alternately tearful and defiant, Farrow would endlessly recite her lines under the hot lights, only to hear the Polish filmmaker say, "one more time, Mia."

A pro, Mia Farrow did not complain about this treatment, but her then husband felt differently. Frank Sinatra was not one to stand passively on the sidelines. Sinatra always made it clear on his own films that he would do a limit of two takes on any scene. If these didn't work out, that was the director's problem. The same rule should pertain to his bride, Sinatra reasoned.

Toward the end of the second week on *Rosemary's Baby*, a representative of Sinatra appeared unannounced in my reception room. My secretary, thoroughly intimidated, burst into my office and blurted, "Sinatra's sent one of his goons—what will I do?" I asked her to usher him in. He did not bother taking a seat. His message was brief and to the point. Ol' Blue Eyes, he said, wanted a two-take limit for his wife and I had been selected to carry the message. When I asked why I'd been so honored, not Evans, the emissary replied, "'Cause you were a reporter and you know how to listen. Evans don't hear so good." Were Polanski not to heed this warning, he added, I would be held responsible. Indeed, my "health" might suffer a serious setback.

I never delivered the message to Polanski. Sinatra was clearly way out of line. Besides, I knew the little Pole, a monumentally stubborn man, would never alter his modus operandi, even under threat.

Driving home that night, however, I reviewed the chain of events. Sinatra was threatening me. The Mafia was closing in on the studio. The Feds were closing in on Charlie Bluhdorn. For this I left a good reporting career?

My gloom was compounded by the publication of a long article in *Life* magazine, which eviscerated Bob Evans. The young studio chief, said *Life*, "has no credentials, has never even produced a film, doesn't know that much about movies, so why should he be boss of Paramount? He's entirely too rich, too young, too lucky. If there's anything Hollywood wants out of Robert Evans, it's to see him fail." The article was accompanied by a rather lurid Alfred Eisenstaedt photo of "the playboy peacock of Paramount" splayed atop the mink spread that covered his massive bed, talking on the phone, a breakfast tray to one side, a pile of unread scripts on the other.

Even the normally ebullient Evans felt mortally wounded. What had seemed like a dream job was taking on nightmarish proportions. The golden opportunity suddenly was becoming a giant trap. The town was turning on him. Maybe even Bluhdorn would lose hope.

Evans was in a funk. He had just completed renovating a new home in Beverly Hills, for which the studio had constructed a handsome screening room, and now he took refuge there, steering clear of the studio. Friends such as Warren Beatty and Jack Nicholson phoned him, trying to summon up appropriate words of encouragement, but they sensed Evans' confidence was ebbing.

We all knew what was needed to turn things around. He needed a movie that would put lines around the block.

That movie magically appeared, and it was called *Love Story*. It was an unlikely blockbuster, but its impact was instantaneous. It legitimized the new regime. For once and for all, it put a stop to Bluhdorn's own erratic deal making. It announced a new day at Paramount, opening the way for *The Godfather* and the other hits that were imminently to follow.

From the outset, *Love Story* was to be a curious venture. The transparently manipulative original screenplay was the work of Erich Segal, a young classics professor at Yale. It was basically a version of the classic doomed-young-lovers tale, but Segal had infused it with a certain megamaniacal passion. Several studios had already turned it down before it came to Paramount. Nonetheless, I felt it could fill a void in the marketplace. There were a lot of swaggering, tough-talking, 1960s protest movies out there, but there were no films that offered anything resembling old-fashioned sentiment. Evans read the script and agreed. Neither of us understood, however, that we were in for a chaotic ride.

It was one thing to buy a script, but another to assemble a director and cast. No one wanted to direct *Love Story*. Further, a long string of young stars ranging from Michael Douglas to Jon Voight to Keith Carradine not only passed on the role—they openly disdained it. I began to feel foolish even talking to agents about it.

Finally there was a bite. Larry Peerce, a bright young filmmaker who had scored with an independent film called *One Potato, Two Potato*, stepped forward and said he'd tackle *Love Story*. Peerce had "heat." Perhaps we could go back to our leading men with him in tow. And then there was a young actress named Ali MacGraw, who desperately wanted to play the female lead. Her limitations as an actress were on vivid display in screen tests, but Peerce agreed she had a special "look" and intensity. After some more turndowns, a soap opera star named Ryan O'Neal, who had just completed a five-year stint on *Peyton Place*, was signed to play the lead, Oliver Barrett. Though the team of MacGraw and O'Neal was hardly box office magic, this was a viable cast and the budget, after all, was barely more than $1 million.

As Peerce studied the script, however, he became increasingly troubled by the thinness of its characters. His proposed solution: Add some weight to Oliver Barrett by making him a returning Vietnam veteran. The nightmare of the war, added to his bride's deadly illness, would surely add poignancy to the film. As Peerce further explained his changes, though, the war seemed to confuse the narrative. It was becoming a movie about post-Vietnam stress rather than doomed lovers.

I was delegated the job of saying "bye-bye" to Larry Peerce. I knew it was the right move to shelve him, provided, that is, I could find someone else to step in. Luckily, along came Arthur Hiller. A diminutive Canadian, Hiller liked to keep working, like studio directors of old. He had just completed shooting a Neil Simon comedy for Paramount called *The Out of Towners* and there was a gap before he'd start yet another Simon effusion, *Plaza Suite*. Hiller was less than avid about *Love Story*, but Phil Gersh, his agent, talked him into it. A deal was made and *Love Story* was a "go."

Except Ali MacGraw didn't like the idea of Arthur Hiller as director. The young actress, it seems, was a bit of a snob. She wanted to be consulted about the choice of a director, and Arthur Hiller was not her choice. Evans was apoplectic. To him, MacGraw was an obstreperous flower child who didn't know her place. Reluctantly, he agreed to fly her to California to secretly view an early cut of Hiller's *The Out of Towners*. Fearful that Hiller would learn of this "audition" for an unknown actress, Evans decided to show the movie in his screening room at home. No one would be present except for him and MacGraw.

The actress flew to Los Angeles the next day. After two hours together, however, MacGraw was too intrigued by "the playboy peacock of Paramount" to see any movie. They had a late lunch, Evans asked her into his screening room, but she jumped instead into his pool with all her clothes on. They were not to remain on for long.

It was several years before MacGraw left Evans' company.

A couple of months after the swimming pool incident, *Love Story* started shooting, but there was certainly no special aura surrounding this project. Hiller had made it clear he had no enthusiasm for Ryan O'Neal and also was worried about MacGraw's limited talents. His purpose in shooting the film seemed more about filling out his schedule than creating a hit.

But then movies are all about surprise, and *Love Story* seemed to create its own mythology. I had talked to Erich Segal about turning his script into a novella, and he had performed his task expertly. By the time the movie was released, his novel had leaped to the number one spot on the best-seller lists. After Segal concluded a teary interview on the *Today* show, there was not a copy available at any major bookstore. The proverbial lines around the block materialized promptly with the film's opening. The audience was young, hip and, most surprisingly, insistent on seeing the movie again and again. This was not just a date movie; it was a serial date movie.

Puzzled, during the movie's first week I set out to determine for myself what motivated these devotees. After a few minutes of interviewing, the answer was clear. *Love Story* had become a sort of cinematic aphrodisiac. A kid would take his date to the film, they would cry together, commiserate about the tragedy, then they would go to bed, as though to celebrate their survival. Hence each night the lines seemed to grow longer as the boys kept pressing their luck.

For Charlie Bluhdorn, the impact of Paramount's first blockbuster was immediate. He was almost giddy with joy, and also greedy. Riding in his limousine on a cold, rainy New York night, he passed one long line on Third Avenue and noticed the theater manager observing the action. Bluhdorn could not contain himself; he leaped from his car, charged up to the startled manager and screamed, "Don't just stand there, you fool, raise your fucking prices!"

The success of *Love Story* vastly lifted my spirits and those of Evans. This was certainly not a great movie—not even a particularly good one—but it worked, igniting that extraordinary alchemy that can exist between a movie and its audience. It was a reminder of the unique power of the filmmaker, indeed of the studio chief as well— the power to manipulate the moods and styles of the pop culture.

Miraculously I had survived my initiation into the movie business. Though I felt I'd aged a few years, friends assured me there were no visible signs. Each day's events were so roilsome that I had fallen into the habit of regularly popping sleeping pills—any kind would do. My nervous system had attuned itself to press conferences and race riots, but still found it difficult to adapt to the noise level of a film studio.

It was as though I had somehow plugged into another energy source. Each day presented a new parade of chaotic adventures and misadventures: A film needed a new ending. An actor could not cope with the bullying of his director. A screenwriter refused to make mandated script changes. A novelist would sell the rights to his work only if certain fears were allayed. And though there were the usual Hollywood characters to cope with—agents with their private agendas, stars with their narcissistic obsessions—there were also some provocative and forceful new voices to be heard. There was Tom Stoppard wrestling with his first screenplay, Truman Capote striving for a comeback, Francis Coppola struggling for some artistic breathing room, Warren Beatty searching for a new persona. Sure, along with all this came petty politics and exasperating exercises in egomania. This was, after all, a movie studio, but one whose landscape suddenly encompassed some truly first-rate minds.

I had hoped, going in, that I might have the opportunity to have just these sorts of encounters—that somehow, in some small way, I might take a modest stab at replenishing filmdom's tired talent pool. And that was what now seemed to be happening. It was more than exciting. It was indeed an adrenaline rush.

But one night I wandered home, dead tired, and found myself leafing through the journal I had been keeping—notes that I would some day turn into my "definitive" book about life at a studio. I was riveted as I relived these day-by-day experiences—encounters with Mafioso and managers, with the Roman Polanskis and the Sidney Korshaks. I'd even noted down one conversation with Korshak, the ever-somber attorney who had started out serving Al Capone and ended up mentoring stars and studio chiefs. "Peter," he said, "do you know what's the best insurance policy—one that guarantees continued breathing?" I thought this an odd question, but I asked for his answer. "It's silence," he intoned. He said it as though he had just imparted great wisdom, and in a sense he had. This was, after all, advice emanating from someone who was arguably the industry's most talented "fixer."

I decided it was advice worth taking. I would stay at Paramount, but I would shred my notes.

Peter Guber: Initiation

In 1968 I had little interest in movies and less in the film business. So when I put "Peter Guber," on the sign-up sheets for career interviews at New York University Graduate School of Business, where I was pursuing an MBA degree, I was not particularly aggressive in taking a follow-up meeting with Columbia Pictures. I had earlier met with the corporation as part of a cattle call recruiting session. I'd already received my B.A. and completed a Juris Doctor degree as well as a master's in law. The possibility of being drafted for Vietnam was still at the forefront of my consciousness; my wife, Lynda, was pregnant with our first daughter. The all-consuming reality was that I was in hock with student loans to the tune of $19,000, which in today's terms would be a small ransom. I had neither the time nor the money to go to movies. When not studying or working, I was worrying.

All of the other corporations that had initially interviewed me had me careening around the country to meet their top brass from Battle Creek, Michigan, to Wall Street. While my academic credentials were certainly in order, my mindset was one of total confusion. I didn't want to practice law, yet a law firm might likely be my best choice. But I recoiled particularly at seeing beds at the law firm's offices. The recruiting partners referred to them as employee benefits so new attorneys working late into the night wouldn't have to travel home. That was not compelling; I already had a bed and a home.

So when I was asked back for a third lunch interview at Columbia Pictures, at 711 Fifth Avenue, it seemed innocuous enough to accept. The president even sent his car and driver to fetch me from the grad school library.

And so it began. They wooed me and ultimately Sy Malamed, the CFO, and Stanley Schneider, the president, invited me to California where they were going to place their one annual recruit. That was their protocol, one "biz school tool" a year placed somewhere in the world. This year it was for the West Coast. For a young fellow who grew up in the East, California was the magical place you saw on television on New Year's Day where everyone was in T-shirts with tans and beers.

I stayed at the Beverly Hills Hotel, and between meetings I drove incessantly up and down Wilshire Boulevard. Where did the poor people live? Where was the equivalent of my East Twelfth Street and Second Avenue apartment?

After my return to reality in New York, I got the call to come up to corporate headquarters for a final conversation. I had pretty much made up my mind to pursue situations other than Columbia, which were closer to home. I hadn't a clue what I would do at Columbia, so the worst it would be was one more free lunch.

But this was different. Leo Jaffe, the CEO, and Stanley Schneider did all the talking. It was as if they had filled in the empty spaces and all I had to do is drop the ballot in the box. As the drama of the meeting began to unfold, I realized that this was my first shoot out. I started out cool and collected, expressing my appreciation for their interest. Then I poured out my fears: never being able to pay off my student loans, having spent all that time and effort to take and pass the New York bar, the uncertainty of moving my family to California. Finally, I had no interest in being in any corporate legal department. That certainly would do it. My intention was now clear. I hesitated for just a millisecond, taking in all the grandeur of corporate America in these Fifth Avenue offices. In that single pause, they drew and fired a fusillade directly at me. They would pay for my family to move all of our belongings to California. Columbia would put me on full salary while I took whatever time deemed necessary to study and pass the California bar. Furthermore, they would provide a special one-year living allowance to assure that my family would be comfortably settled. They would also pay off my student loan in full. Further, if I were unhappy after the year, they would move me back to New York at their cost. Oh yes, they pegged my starting salary at better than twice any of my other offers.

I literally reached across the table and said, "I'm in." They'd made me the offer I could not refuse. After a lot of hand clasping, I was eager to get to my family and tell them of our future. As I made it to the door, I suddenly turned about to ask what in the world I would do three thousand miles from here where I knew nobody. Was I headed to legal affairs? Stanley replied, "You will work in the creative area at the studio." I smiled as I walked seventy-plus blocks back to the library. I forgot about the limo waiting for me on Fifth Avenue. I was on my way to Hollywood.

Columbia Pictures was actually located in Hollywood, unlike MGM, Universal or Fox. The small studio at 1438 N. Gower Street had a five-story administration building and no back lot. Its most famous resident had been Harry Cohn, Columbia's legendary founder. Many of his cohorts were still in residency and even though Cohn had long since passed, they would lower their voice a decibel whenever mentioning him. I'd been assigned to the creative packaging area, whatever that meant, to move about the studio for a two-year stint.

Columbia had recently survived a fierce takeover bid and the old guard had reestablished its hold. Yet life at the studio was like living in the eye of a hurricane. All appeared calm in spite of the political maelstrom.

At Columbia, yet another battle was raging for the hearts and minds of the faithful. On one side were Abe Schneider, the chairman, and Leo Jaffe and Stanley Schneider. Aligned against them was a group focused around the Geritol king, Mattie Rosenhaus, who held an enormous block of stock as well as important board seats. The television operation, led by Jerry Hyams was the moneymaker for the company with big series like *I Dream of Jeannie*, while the theatrical division was wallowing in red ink. Columbia's stock had fallen from a high of forty-plus dollars to the teens.

John Van Eyssen, the chief of the London operation, had been widely criticized for being out of step with the young moviegoing public, yet it was this English operation that had given so much history to the company—David Lean's *The Bridge on the River Kwai* and *Lawrence of Arabia*, Stanley Kubrick's *Dr. Strangelove* and Fred Zinnemann's *A Man for All Seasons*.

Mike Frankovich, the past European production chief, had come home to Hollywood to run the studio but had just departed to form his own independent company with Columbia. He was, in 1968, still overseeing his last project, *Oliver!*, which went on to win Best Picture Oscar that next year.

In 1967 Bob Weitman had taken over the helm of Columbia. An ex-MGM bigwig, he was long on story—his own—and short on real creative talent. Well into his sixties, he tended to lean on Jonnie Taps, one of Harry Cohn's old cronies and king of the musical department, and Billy Gordon, another Cohn crony. Chief among their talents was political savvy. You didn't want to run afoul of them.

The one bright spot at the studio was also a source of political consternation for many inside the tent. Abe Schneider's eldest son,

Stanley, was president of the studio and his second son, Bert, had fashioned a successful career in television and now was given virtual autonomy in the theatrical area. This separate production pod outside the normal scrutiny of the studio brass threw its first grenade into the tent with a low-budget production called *Easy Rider*. This explosive hit mesmerized all in the Columbia fold. Indeed, it signaled the youth movement in Hollywood. Bert, Bob Rafelson and Steve Blauner had given Columbia a collective boot in the pants. Suddenly if you were young, you were in.

Despite my youth, I still realized I'd be window dressing unless I cut out some distinct territory or role. The executive bloodletting consumed everyone's attention. The company released more top executives that first year than pictures. The place was rife with fear.

Eight short weeks after I was ensconced at the studio, I overheard a rumor. An employee was chortling over the imminent demise of several executives. It baffled me why one would take such glee at his colleague's ill fortune. But as I was to learn and experience in Hollywood, it's not so much your own success that is relished, but more your friends' failures. Nevertheless, I then overheard that I was to be let go in a new wave of cost cutting. The rumormonger told whoever would listen that "it was nothing personal—just the bean counters doing their jobs."

My throat closed up, and a wave of anxiety swept through me. I felt helpless and fell into analysis paralysis, pondering every nuance of the rumors.

There was a ritual in the building that whenever someone was to lose his job a little furniture wagon would appear mysteriously at that office one day before the ax fell, as if to take inventory prior to notification. I waited with bated breath.

I could stand it no longer and a day later called Leo Jaffe in New York and blurted out, "Why, why, why?" And he admonished, "What! If you're going to listen and act on rumor in this business, you will fail. I'm a lot older than you, and I've had many crises, most of which have never happened."

Still, the late 1960s was a volatile and dangerous time. Revenue streams for all the studios had been centered on the theatrical release of motion pictures. It was a far simpler business than it is now. Revenue from international release accounted for little more than 20 percent of a film's financial performance. Thus decisions on what films to make were motivated largely by American sensibilities. Yes, there was a Bronson and an Eastwood who generated business out of what was then called "foreign." But the executives and filmmakers wanted to see their films being boffo in Baltimore. The big films had platform releases and some like *Funny Girl* in 1968 went hard ticket (i.e., reserved seat engagements) before going wide.

New technology had not yet presented its onslaught. The Moviola was still in vogue as an editing tool; no one even dreamed of Avids. Becoming relevant in the late 1960s, in addition to being young, meant hanging your hat on something new. A challenger had to have a different set of tools to propel himself forward. The incumbents were determined to defend their turf against all comers. They had the hubris to believe that no assault on their authority could succeed.

In the fall of 1968, two events occurred that shaped my reality. For theatrical movies after their initial exploitation in theaters, the only additional revenue stream was possibly a network showing followed by a television syndication package. Now many companies were experimenting with technologies to capture, store and play back images on television. The Japanese, led by Sony and Panasonic, were betting on magnetic tape. Frank Stanton of Volkswagen fame bet on Cartrivision, a cartridge-based magnetic tape system. RCA promoted Laservision, which had the images imbedded on platters like record albums. CBS, through Peter Goldmark, was basing its hopes on Electronic Video Recording (EVR). Only the Japanese were deploying both a record and playback system. The others could use only prerecorded material.

As each new discovery came down the pipe, I became the self-styled guru on the virtues and drawbacks of each technology, as well as the herald for a new era in which the public owned its own feature library. Leo Jaffe fielded complaints from his own executives and competitors who argued about letting a junior employee publicly support technology that would result in an erosion of theatrical revenues and would cannibalize the current releasing protocols. It seemed outrageous that studios would even consider long-term licensing of their product to companies to build their own video libraries.

In fact, Columbia eventually did just that. Though it was clearly in a position to leverage its great content capacity to build a new business, it let others do it on their back for a pittance—to wit the RCA-Columbia joint venture. This mortgaging of the future was a bad habit that would plague studios for some time. But for me this became my jackpot. I rode the new technology bandwagon to the top of the studio. Wooed by other companies, and having created exposure in the media, I leveraged technospeak into a top spot in the studio hierarchy.

Jerry Tokofsky, who was one of Columbia's young "smart" guys, was my first supervisor, and his initial advice was wise: Keep the tongue still and ears wide open. He had more moves than Magic Johnson. One of his moves in my first months at Columbia was a doozy and nearly wrecked my career before launch. Jerry was the object of desire of Paramount Pictures. He had become friendly with Sidney Korshak, who was the consigliere to that company, a relationship that culminated in an offer to join Paramount. Jerry felt it was an unusual opportunity. He was at the end of his Columbia deal and was in the process of angling for a new contract. Jerry thought that if the rumor got out that another studio was after him, his stock at Columbia would soar—a hairy scheme tried often by many, and with mixed results. He was asked to come to New York to meet with the Paramount brass and commanded, "Pack your bag; you're coming with me." The pretense was some movie project being hatched in Gotham. I should never have gone. My ego and curiosity got the best of me and suddenly I found myself careening around the Big Apple in a limo. Tokofsky met with some of the Paramount folks and apparently told them he'd come aboard. Out of the blue, MGM now suddenly offered Jerry a top position at the company. Wallowing in attraction and loving it, Jerry decided to explore the MGM offer and meet with Frank Rosenfelt, then their general council. Yet the press announcement had already been framed regarding the Paramount position. Columbia knew nothing of either MGM or Paramount.

Young as I was, I knew this was not a winning scenario. I could envision no soft landing. Sure enough, Jerry took it in the ear and some other places as well. He scuttled what ought to have been a terrific studio career. Though he was to be out of Columbia, he managed to get Stanley Schneider's pledge to hold me harmless.

But the Tokofsky incident reminded me that careers are fragile, that the appearance of disloyalty can shoot down even the most promising future. Given this volatile environment, however, how could anyone afford to be risk averse? That indeed was the anomaly.

Columbia couldn't escape its own history. It was suffocating in relationships with old timers such as Stanley Kramer whose early hits included *Guess Who's Coming to Dinner*. Kramer dined out on this film for years. Though out of sync with the public, he was in vogue with the senior corporate management. Yet flops like *Bless the Beasts and Children* helped derail the studio's future.

Jack Warner, the legendary co-founder of Warner Bros., was in his late seventies when he decided to make the Broadway musical *1776* into a film at Columbia. Leo Jaffe made the initial deal, though most of the production team resisted it. After a long development process,

Leo, under siege, decided at the last moment that we should abandon ship. Suddenly, I was selected to give the order. "Peter, you never wanted to do this film, so go over to Jack Warner's office and give him the news that we're passing," said Jaffe in an early-morning phone call from New York. This was not an appealing chore. Warner's reputation preceded him. He was tough, and you never crossed him. Everyone assured me he was now a toothless tiger. It was easy for them to say. I had to go over and confront him with the bad news. His office was different from all other studio executives. It was filled with autographed pictures not of the star of the moment but of Douglas MacArthur, President Franklin Roosevelt, Winston Churchill, Babe Ruth and other legendary illuminati. He was having a haircut as I was ushered in. Greeting me with, "What's up kid," he swiveled around to have a look at his visitor. Then, raising his finger, he glared and said, "Don't you dare." I didn't. I offered a few salutations and raced back to my studio digs. Within a very few minutes, Leo called for an update. After I hemmed and hawed for a few moments, Jaffe simply said, "Well, if you didn't pass, I guess we're doing it." The film was made; it failed miserably and put yet another nail in the studio's coffin.

Then there was Ray Stark. In his fifties, he was the epitome of the big-time producer. Well into production with Barbra Streisand's first film, *Funny Girl*, he was charming, energetic and disarmingly dangerous. He came to occupy a unique position of studio consigliere. He steered careers—and sent them careening when it suited his purpose. He maintained his perch no matter who occupied the top executive post. He had become the de facto studio chief. He reviewed all projects that even his competitors had with the studio. "What did Ray think?" That was the question asked on every key discussion that seemed to go on in those early years. I decided right then that the *perception* of power was power.

Columbia was sinking fast into dire straits. Could the management hold off the wolves? The current films certainly weren't doing the job. "Cut the Overhead" was a story that needed no synopsis. It was black comedy with a host of villains and even more victims. When the creative community perceives that a studio is on life support, it becomes the last stop for potential projects and makes every deal harder to close.

Finally, mercifully, it came to an end. Columbia owed the banks nearly a quarter of a billion, a staggering sum at that time given the company's balance sheet. Yet had Columbia owed less, it would have been easier for the banks to liquidate. Instead, through the brilliant banking efforts of Herbert Allen, Jr., a deal was struck whereby the financial institutions were held off, and an infusion of fresh capital was provided to the beleaguered studio. There was a cost; there always is. The current movie management had to be replaced. Alan Hirschfield, who had captained several enterprises backed by Allen, was inserted as corporate president. Leo stayed but was largely a figurehead. Stanley Schneider and Van Eyssen lost their heads. A whole new regime was installed. Ray Stark called me to his office and said, "Keep your mouth shut; you're in." Quietly Stark brought in his new management team. As head of the studio, I would report to the new president of Columbia, and Stark now asked that I meet him.

"When?" I asked.

"Now," he said, "He's driving over here."

"Who?"

"David Begelman will run the whole film company from here on out."

When David paid this first visit, I was awed by his charm. This ex-agent was very smooth. Clearly, he was sizing me up. Could he expect my loyalty? Would I do his bidding? Would I add to his image? My fate seemed uncertain at best. Then he barked, "Where the hell is the toilet in this place?" I pointed; he trotted off; I was in. Anyone having to ask that question was going to need me for a while. Stark had his man on the inside, and Begelman had broken free from the shadow of his better known partner, Freddie Fields, co-founder of the power-house Creative Management Agency (CMA) talent agency. It would be his show now. There would be new fireworks, but they would be his fireworks. And here I was his production chief, still just thirty years old but already the survivor of a parade of regimes. One after another, a succession of executives had either been fired or had, like Jerry Tokofsky, simply self-destructed. It seemed a childlike game of "all fall down," and I was the last man standing.

I had never thought of myself as a corporate survivor. I had a tendency to speak my mind. I was rambunctious. I was habitually unaccepting of conventional wisdom. In short, I was the sort of person who would get into trouble in a big corporation.

But my period of initiation had ended, and here I was. What I most wanted now was some semblance of stability. Times were difficult enough without the incessant political disruptions. Columbia needed a time of peace, and so did I.

It was not to be. David Begelman, with all his "cool," had his own demons to battle. Working together, we would package a promising program of pictures at the studio, but new scandals were to break and Begelman would face possible jail time for petty theft.

The lesson I was fast learning was not one that I'd anticipated. After all, my professional education had created a fairly logical mindset. But what I now had to accept was not just that my life was bound to movies, but rather that my life was a movie.

All right. Then I was determined to build, at least, a plausible plot. And, I hope, one with a great third act!

2.

The Holy Grail

Seventy-five percent of the ideas people try
to sell me are no good, so if I turn them down,
that makes me right 75 percent of the time.

HARRY COHN

When interviewing legendary director Billy Wilder for his book *Conversations with Wilder,* Cameron Crowe couldn't resist the obvious question. "Were you ever nervous the day before starting a new film?" asked Crowe, himself a director (*Jerry Maguire*).

The venerable Wilder quickly snapped, "No." Then he agonized for a beat and added, "I was only nervous when confronted with an empty page. One with nothing on it."

The empty page—everyone's terror. Not only does the writer fear the empty page, but also the director, the producer, the financier—everyone associated with film. For no matter what dazzling cyber-shots the director may have in his head, no matter what hot financing schemes the producer may conjure up, absolutely nothing happens until words start filling that empty page.

Yes, words. Old-fashioned verbiage. With all the talk and techno-dazzle, someone has to sit down and frame an idea. Perhaps even fashion a story. Mold a character. Create dialogue.

That's how it all begins. The arcane process of shaping that pivotal idea.

The basic vision for a motion picture can take many forms. It can start as a play, a novel, a script, an article or even a poem. It can start as an epiphany—a bolt from the blue that overtakes the vision keeper, indeed changes his life. But then that vision must be communicated. It must be set down. Someone has to fill that empty page.

But let's get back to that epiphany. Before the green lights start flashing, before the screenwriter starts crafting his dialogue, someone must mobilize support for the Big Idea. The frantic scramble to come up with that key vision—i.e., the Holy Grail—is unlike any other phenomenon in show business, combining elements of a gold rush and a celebrity auction.

For evidence, sit across the desk from a literary agent who controls a super-hot, once-in-a-lifetime best-seller and listen to the frantic pleas from prospective bidders, the offers of bribes and favors. Or spend a few moments with a newsmaker, someone who inadvertently has captured the media moment, and monitor the offers as they cascade in from around the world as everyone vies for his life story. Whether its Lindbergh or Lewinsky, that nanosecond of instant celebrity is like blood in a shark pool.

And, of course, it's all illusory. For every best-seller that has been turned into a big hit, such as *The Godfather* or *Gone With the Wind*, there are ten cases such as *Primary Colors, Jonathan Livingston Seagull* or *The Bonfire of the Vanities* where the work simply didn't translate. For every true-life hit such as *Erin Brockovich*, there have been scores of true-life debacles. That's because most of the bidders have no idea what they're looking for, or why. They are competing feverishly in the marketplace of ideas without a clear understanding either of the market or of the ideas.

The vast majority of those competing are guided by one motivation: commerce. They are throwing money at projects that will attract the interest of stars and studios and filmmakers. They are both heat seekers and bottom feeders because the properties they are targeting usually represent the lowest common denominator of prospective material.

Yet also in the marketplace are those who are looking for a different kind of Holy Grail—a story that moves or inspires them, one that might translate into a movie of quality.

In short, the search for the Holy Grail brings out the best and the worst in everyone. It evidences the energy and the zeal that's generated by the dream of having that one, great megahit. It also casts an unforgiving spotlight on the sheer exploitive nature of the business, the hunger to capitalize on celebrity. The marketplace reflects at once the loftiest of ideals and the grossest mendacity.

And who are these fervid bidders? They represent a vast blur of industry veterans and neophytes, of battle-hardened producers and starry-eyed dilettantes who've decided to dabble in something glamorous. A major studio can make what it considers an intelligent offer to buy movie rights to a novel only to discover that it is bidding against someone it never heard of. This is because material that is "hot" inevitably leaks out from the normal channels. There are many possible sources for these leaks—an assistant who's been bribed to make that one extra photocopy, an obscure subagent specializing in foreign rights who's been persuaded to share his or her copy, etc. These leaks are especially irksome to the buttoned-up pros who like to think they control the marketplace.

Bob Bookman, an agent for Creative Artists Agency (CAA) in Los Angeles who wheels and deals each month with many best-sellers, likes to control leaks so that he can use the "hot" new property as his own ammunition. When he strides into his Wednesday morning meeting of his motion picture staff, he wants to give his colleagues "information that they can trade, barter or use for their own or the agency's benefit." Translated, that means that exclusive access to a hot new book might persuade a top director to sign with his agency or might help an existing client to rope in a major star. It's doubly frustrating when Bookman has put his ducks in a row and has elicited an offer for the basic material only to find that an "outsider," someone who didn't figure in his game plan, comes forward with a huge offer that effectively takes the property out of his control.

"It's easy to sell a book or hot screenplay for a lot of money," he points out. Bookman's goal "is not necessarily to squeeze the last dollar out of a sale, because oftentimes when you sell it for the most money, you're not selling it to the person whose going to make the best film. Which means in the long term my client's best interests are not served."

It's all about control and perception. Agents across the landscape attempt to control the access to material, thus heightening the illusion of heated competition. The idea that everybody wants to get it but few have the access makes it even more valuable. The idea of having to wait for it builds anticipation, escalating its value to yet another level. So Bookman is "stirring up this thing, and we don't tell anyone until the last minute who's going to get it." He creates the perception not so much that he is trying to sell it but that everyone's trying to buy it.

Breakthrough ideas in show business, as in any field, can come in many different shapes and forms besides a best-selling book. In Hollywood, inspiration has often stemmed from adversity. In 1934 Walt Disney got so angry that competitors were stealing away his best animators by offering them work in longer formats that he resolved to produce his first full-length animated feature, *Snow White and the Seven Dwarfs*, which marked the birth of the Disney empire.

The Godfather came to life in the form of an outline for a novel because a writer named Mario Puzo realized there was no way he was going to feed himself or his family by turning out more of the stylized literary novels he'd been writing. The rich family saga he devised represented to him a crass descent into commercial fiction, but to millions of readers the work represented a fresh and fascinating family chronicle.

All of which points up the question: What defines the perfect movie idea?

It's a legitimate, if complex, question. It's incredible how many truly *bad* ideas are put forward even by "old pros" in the business. By "bad," we mean concepts that are intrinsically self-defeating. They may be stories that are simply impossible to shoot without bankrupting a studio because of their scope or period. Or they may be stories that are so numbingly downbeat that they would scare off any audience. (One finely written screenplay about the Black Death epidemic of the fourteenth century made the rounds of the studios for more than a decade without getting picked up.) Or they may be static theater pieces that defy "being opened up" or convoluted novels that have little in the way of plot, or they may consist of an article or articles dealing with real-life people who would clearly never be willing to sign away their life stories.

Sometimes a misbegotten subject is recycled over and over again, with the same disappointing results. F. Scott Fitzgerald's superb novel *The Great Gatsby* has been made into an unsatisfying movie four times. It's also been crafted into an opera and a play. Each time, however, the same basic, if mundane problems defied the dramaturges: There's really no story there, and Gatsby is more a metaphor than a character.

On rare occasions a project comes to life through a simple misunderstanding. In his early years as a director, Peter Bogdanovich revered Orson Welles, hanging on his every word. As with many vision keepers, Welles' words were often not easy to follow. On one occasion Welles went on a kick about the writings of Henry James, citing particularly his novella *Daisy Miller* as especially evocative. To most people in attendance, the great filmmaker was simply discoursing on literature, but to Bogdanovich, Welles was sending him a personal message. The young filmmaker had just ended his marriage to Polly Platt and, having begun an affair with actress Cybill Shepherd, was searching for a seminal project for her. That project would be *Daisy Miller,* he concluded—that was what his idol, Orson Welles had advised him.

The film was, of course, a failure, and Welles later confided to friends that he did not, in fact, intend to send Bogdanovich any such signal. In any case, the misunderstanding represented a significant setback for a young directing career.

Of course, some seemingly "impossible" subjects may defy the odds and find their way successfully into film. Try pitching a period movie about the porn business to a studio and you'd likely get laughed off the lot, yet *Boogie Nights* created a career for Paul Thomas Anderson. Try pitching a $200 million period disaster movie about the sinking of an ocean liner—an idea that seemingly had already been done—and you might be asked to surrender your studio office and secretary. Yet *Titanic* broke box office records.

None of which proves anything, to be sure. The passions of a hot filmmaker, or of a bankable star, will often melt the resistance of any studio bureaucrat. Having said that, certain imperatives nonetheless prevail when it comes to the selection of properties for motion pictures or television. There is, to begin with, the question of novelty. Novelty moves mountains, everyone agrees, but what is novelty? The enduring truism holds that there are only seven basic stories—

everything is a variation on these. Indeed, the brains of those executives at networks and studios are wired to the past, not to the present. They may insist they're looking for that watershed idea, but in fact they are groping somehow to connect that idea to some past success. Hence the shorthand used at company discussion always links new ideas to old, such as "it's *The Fugitive* meets *Fatal Attraction*." Because our associative subconscious is always probing for the familiar, the trick for the vision keeper is to turn the familiar into the unique, to establish novelty without surrendering the comfort of certainty.

One can merely run down the list of all-time box office winners to find examples of this phenomenon. In its time, *Jaws* represented a brilliant breakthrough idea, a high-class terror story that played upon serious Freudian demons. Movies as diverse as *The Exorcist, Revenge of the Nerds, Home Alone* and *The Sixth Sense* also seemed to burrow their way into the public consciousness to become cult movies, yet remained within familiar genres and themes.

The potential for unique casting also fortifies the illusion of novelty. *Rain Man* was first considered as a movie for television, but its two primary roles (played by Dustin Hoffman and Tom Cruise) were so enticing to actors that it was upgraded into an expensive superstar studio movie. The easiest, albeit most obvious, way to lure a star is to offer him a chance to play a blind man (*Scent of a Woman* with Al Pacino), a cripple (Tom Cruise in *Born on the Fourth of July*) or an idiot savant (Dustin Hoffman in *Rain Man*).

Stories that capture the zeitgeist also are enticing. *Easy Rider*, hardly a great movie, was an oddly perfect fit for its time. So was *The Graduate*. At a moment in history when young audiences were aching to experience a good head trip, what better vehicle than *2001: A Space Odyssey* to fulfill that fantasy?

Of course, almost every wannabe producer insists that he's perfectly in tune with the moment. Few are, and exacerbating their problem is the inevitable time lapse between the idea and the actual "green light." Stanley Kubrick's stultifying *Eyes Wide Shut* would have been far more pertinent had he made it when he first pondered the idea a generation earlier. The film Kubrick had in mind was small and darkly portentous. Ultimately *Eyes Wide Shut* became a glitzy Tom Cruise–Nicole Kidman vehicle.

As producer Denise Di Novi puts it, it's important to strike "when one still has the goose bumps," but many can testify that's a tough objective to achieve. Wendy Finerman's goose bumps all but ossified in the tortuous road to bring *Forrest Gump* to the screen. Warner Bros. bought it and financed its development before decreeing that it was "too risky." Columbia had a look only to come to the same conclusion. The project finally took root at Paramount, armed then with a world-class director in Robert Zemeckis, and Tom Hanks, the biggest star on the scene. The project still endured a series of near-death experiences, most relating to the budget and shooting schedule. Upon release, of course, *Gump* was universally proclaimed a surefire winner.

Lynda Obst experienced goose bumps upon reading a magazine article called "Crisis in the Hot Zone." Surely a successful thriller could be fashioned around the desperate struggle to ward off a deadly epidemic. Alas, Warners hit upon the same notion with its project called *Outbreak* and was quicker to the starting line, thus dooming the Obst venture.

Sometimes the path to victory takes an unexpected twist. Suzanne de Passe, who graduated from Berry Gordy's Motown school of hard knocks, put down $50,000 of her own money to option Larry McMurtry's novel *Lonesome Dove*. Regarding herself more an entertainment entrepreneur than a conventional producer, de Passe didn't flinch at the gamble but soon discovered that she faced two serious challenges. First, McMurtry insisted that his novels become theatrical features. His earlier work, *The Last Picture Show*, had been a surprise hit in 1971. Most of the studios had already looked at *Dove* and had passed—a reality that had been kept from McMurtry.

The author finally set aside his bias, and to good effect. *Lonesome Dove* went on to become a phenomenal success as an multi-hour movie for television with the backing of Robert Halmi. It pulled a 35 share, vastly bigger than anyone anticipated.

The pursuit of the Holy Grail reaches its level of greatest hysteria on those rare occasions when it's clear that ownership of the property effectively guarantees a green light. Money no longer is the issue in these cases. Celebrity and ambition now take center stage.

A classic example is *Jurassic Park*, the novel by the prolific Michael Crichton. At the time of its publication, Crichton was hardly a babe in the woods, having written several best-sellers and directed six motion pictures. Crichton and his agent, CAA's Bob Bookman, wanted big bucks but they also wanted a clear path to production. Having hatched his vivid and cinematic tribe of dinosaurs, Crichton was ready for a big play.

While any number of producers stood ready in the wings, willing and able to make the pilgrimage to Crichton's office in Santa Monica to make their pitch, Bookman had his sights on yet another CAA client, Steven Spielberg. There was already a link between Crichton and Spielberg, growing out of an abandoned Crichton film script called *ER* set in an emergency room. No one wanted to shoot *ER* as a movie, but Spielberg and his colleagues came up with the masterstroke of refashioning it as a television series. Now Spielberg came forth with an even more exciting scheme: He would buy *Jurassic Park*, direct it and see that it got made at Universal, where Spielberg had his long-standing deal. Such a proposition could create income for Crichton from ancillary revenues far beyond his normal up-front fees. Spielberg plus dinosaurs meant huge paperback sales, theme park rides, income from merchandising and even bigger guarantees for his next book. This was no longer a simple rights deal; it was a superstar deal.

From Spielberg's standpoint, a commitment to shoot a commercial film such as *Jurassic Park* would strengthen his ties at Universal. The busy filmmaker was also contemplating a far riskier project that he wanted the studio to support, *Schindler's List*. The script had long been in the works under the aegis of Spielberg's friend, Martin Scorsese. Mindful of Spielberg's obsessive interest in the Holocaust, Scorsese had traded *Schindler's List* to his friend in return for the thriller, *Cape Fear*, which Scorsese felt would restore his own credentials as a commercial filmmaker after several misfires.

The ubiquitous Bookman, who covets complex schemes, was also at the center of the bidding on *The Horse Whisperer* by Nicholas Evans. Here was that rare situation where an incomplete novel by a neophyte author so captured the imagination of Hollywood players that his agent was able to auction it as though it were a Michael Crichton dinosaur book. Bookman was literally under siege by buyers waving large sums of money, and he did everything he could to fan the flames. This was the book of the decade, according to the well-orchestrated CAA campaign.

Having created the frenzy, Bookman decided on a simple plan to exploit it. Five top filmmakers *would* be given the chance to get on the phone with Evans to explain why they wanted the property. The price had already been set at $3 million. Now it would be a question of the pitch, not the price. None of the would-be purchasers knew the full list of rivals, but all flinched when they heard one was Robert Redford. Redford's presence as a producer would certainly carry weight. If he also agreed to star, they knew that might be the ultimate persuader.

Redford, in fact, went a step farther. He promised Evans he would also direct the film and, with that, the writer succumbed and so did Redford's rivals. All his competitors could offer was money and passion. Redford provided celebrity and the momentum for a surefire green light.

The presence of celebrity also figures importantly in the more confined market of cable movies where novelty is as critical an element. Channels such as HBO and Showtime and even Lifetime have spent heavily on projects with star involvement, not only in acting roles but also behind the camera, as in the case of HBO's lavish *Band of Brothers*, which Tom Hanks co-produced. Having steadily eroded the conventional networks' market share, the cablers felt that star power helped them get there.

Not uncommonly, the Holy Grail may materialize from obscurity, not celebrity. *Rocky* could not have had more humble roots. At the time, Sylvester Stallone represented the sort of fringe player whom experienced producers avoid assiduously—a wannabe actor who decided to write a role with which to make himself a star. The project was brought to Irwin Winkler, a former William Morris agent, by his right-hand man, Gene Kirkwood, himself a struggling actor. Winkler had mixed feelings about both the script and Stallone, but decided to try to squeeze it through his deal at United Artists (UA), which gave him the right to select a "put" picture (one that UA was mandated to release), provided it cost no more than $1.5 million—a tiny amount even in the early 1970s. The producer realized the project could be set up at other studios with "name" casting, but Stallone drew his line in the sand—no role, no *Rocky*. Finally Winkler found himself in the position of mortgaging his house to cover any overages. Winkler ended up with a billion-dollar franchise yielding a bundle of sequels. Paradoxically, not much later he purchased *The Right Stuff*, a best-selling book by Tom Wolfe, built star casting around it and ended up with an unsuccessful movie.

Veteran producers such as Winkler understand that, whether their projects are celebrated or obscure, their ultimate success in levitating them will boil down to an accident of history or a war of attrition. David Brown pitched *War of the Worlds* to Barry Diller when he first took over at Paramount in the 1970s. He waited twenty years, until 1998, for his idea to come to fruition in the form of *Deep Impact* on which Brown shared producing credit with Steven Spielberg and others. A resolute man, Brown has been optioning and reoptioning two of his favorite classic American novels for more than two decades, John O'Hara's *Appointment in Samarra* and the John Dos Passos epic *U.S.A.* He's convinced that he will ultimately prevail with them as well.

In 1999, *Variety* examined the fifty top-grossing pictures of the previous year to determine which sources generated the most material and found that twenty of the fifty films stemmed from original scripts. These were scripts developed by the studios or by filmmakers under contract to the studios or those written on "spec"—that is, writers working on their own in the hope of auctioning off their finished work. The remaining thirty films were culled from novels, plays or TV series or were recycled from previous films.

With production and marketing costs soaring, the risk-averse studios are desperate to remake properties that ostensibly have built-in awareness—hence, Steven Spielberg's interest in *The Mask of Zorro*, which had hooked him as a kid and which had been made into several films and TV shows over the years. Sony fixated on *Godzilla* for the same reason—presumably the Japanese market, which had seen twenty-two previous Godzilla films, would especially welcome a remake. Twentieth Century Fox in 1998 was even willing to gamble on a comedic version of *Dr. Dolittle* starring Eddie Murphy, despite the fact that its musical rendition a generation earlier had been a disaster. Given Hollywood's ever-increasing recognition of the overseas market as a source of materials, the remake fever also extended to European properties. *You've Got Mail*, the Tom Hanks vehicle, represented a dusting-off of the Ernst Lubitsch 1940 classic, *The Shop Around the Corner*.

But if recycled material represents the safest bets for studio executives new ideas have paradoxically produced the biggest box office winners. Three of the top five grossing films of 1998 came from writers who walked into a producer's office and pitched an original story—*Saving Private Ryan*, *Armageddon* and *The Waterboy*—movies that together grossed over $3 billion worldwide. In the case of *Armageddon*, it was Jonathan Hensleigh, a young writer who had worked with Michael Bay on an action film called *The Rock*, who triggered the project. Hensleigh told Bay the basic narrative and the two then marched in to see Joe Roth, chief of the Walt Disney studio. They instantly launched the $150 million venture. Their decisiveness was fortunate: At least three other writers were also pitching asteroid-hits-the-earth stories to other studios at the same time.

If movies based on pitches were bringing in big bucks, so were original screenplays—that is, scripts written on spec by writers willing to gamble their energies. In crafting *There's Something About Mary*, the Farrelly brothers, Peter and Bobby, completely rewrote a script written a decade earlier that had been mired in "development hell." Their film proved to be a huge international hit, grossing close to $1 billion. On the other hand, Warner Bros. felt far more secure in remaking the fourth iteration of the *Lethal Weapon* franchise, even though it cost some $150 million to produce and the studio had to give away almost half of the gross receipts in order to reassemble the cast and director.

Another supposedly safe bet, remakes of TV series, has proven equally dicey. *The Avengers* from Warner Bros., based on a 1960s vintage series, was a complete bomb. Twentieth Century Fox, on the other hand, had a modest winner with *The X-Files*—one of the very few instances of a movie based on a current, ongoing TV series.

Many thought Sony was out of its mind to lavish nearly $100 million to recycle *Charlie's Angels*, a series seemingly forgotten by most young filmgoers. Yet the film rolled up box office records and became renowned as one of the hottest "chick flicks" of the decade.

The results of the *Variety* survey seemed to reinforce screenwriter William Goldman's oft-quoted conclusion that, in Hollywood, "Nobody knows anything." Fresh ideas proved the most difficult to get off the ground, yet they produced the biggest returns by far. Remakes and sequels proved the easiest to get made, yet resulted in the most expensive and riskiest ventures.

Indeed, if the process of levitating a project seems daunting to the outsider, it can be even more discouraging to a development executive working within the system. From a cursory glance, the development lists of most studios would confirm one's worst imaginings about the system. Most of the stories being hatched seem humdrum and derivative at best. Many projects appear to be odd couplings of old movies. Two actual examples culled from studio developments charts: "Wrecked": *Clueless* meets *Alive;* and "Sentimental Maniacs": *Moonstruck* meets *The Big Chill*. Entries in a studio development chart include a title and a one-sentence summary, called a "log-line," then the names of the writer and other elements that may be attached. Hence " 'Dog Eat Dog': A young woman hires her dog trainer to reprogram her pampered boyfriend," or "When gorgeous bimbos turn up at their bachelor pad, two buddies discover that their visitors are actually aliens bent on obtaining DNA-laden sperm samples." These hardly sound like the basis for an auspicious film. Indeed, both died in development hell.

Given the fact that more than 80 percent of the projects put into development at studios never see the light of day, producers are all the more eager to find that "special" project that generates its own momentum—a process that can be both time and capital intensive.

A producer will not succeed easily in getting a studio to acquire an expensive project for him unless he belongs to the small circle of highly credentialed filmmakers such as Jerry Bruckheimer or Brian Grazer. Moreover, a hot script or novel may command well over $1 million in asking price.

That's why most producers cannot go it alone but rather must surround themselves with productive, knowledgeable associates and backers who can help them reach their objectives.

Manning the front lines in the hunt for that Big Idea are trackers, readers and random story spies who help ferret out the basic material, which is in the hands of literary agents, foreign rights operatives, publishers and other outposts along the literary trail. The original sixty-page outline to *The Godfather* was discovered by a "tracker" who came upon the material on an editor's desk. Trackers, who tend to be aggressive, feral types, occupy a curious niche in New York's literary fraternity. Their job is to come up with the goods, not to evaluate, synopsize or estimate their worth. A reader will write a synopsis; a tracker will find the treasured manuscript. Operating on the same principal as a heat-seeking missile, a tracker knows how to zero in on a property that's generating excitement. He might have overheard an editor enthusing about it in a bar, or perhaps he heard that a bidding war was shaping up for the overseas rights. Upon occasion, a tracker is suckered in by clever operators who create the illusion of "heat" where none, in fact, exists. The literary marketplace is a hotbed of orchestrated disinformation; all it takes is one shrewdly planted rumor, or a blind item in a gossip column, to get all the town's trackers vibrating with excitement.

Building an entourage is not an inexpensive exercise. A full-time tracker may cost $70,000 a year and a tracking service may cost $25,000. A good reader may add $40,000 to the overhead. Add to that the cost of wining and dining the town's leading literary agents and an occasional foreign rights operative who negotiates overseas sales of novels, not to mention the other fringe players in town who may have random intelligence to impart.

Then come the agents and lawyers. Every step in the process toward securing the Holy Grail encounters legal speed bumps. It's mandatory to have a clear chain of title to the basic material. Not infrequently, previous owners may come out of the woodwork once it looks like a project is moving forward. If the material is based on a real-life story, new sets of hazards appear. Multiple lawsuits followed the release of *Boys Don't Cry*, an independent picture based on a true story set in Falls City, Nebraska. A former girlfriend of Teena Brandon, the protagonist in the film, who claimed that the filmmakers never secured the rights to her story, filed one legal challenge. The script for *The Insider* moved forward even though Jeffrey Wigand, whose story was the focus of the film, was legally barred from cooperating because of a confidentiality clause.

Since lawyers have rendered themselves ubiquitous, producers have managed to work out a variety of arrangements to compensate them. Some lawyers are willing to take a 5-percent cut of a producer's earnings instead of charging on an hourly basis. Most lawyers, however, not only demand an hourly fee, but also insist on additional compensation to help negotiate foreign presales or other ancillary income streams.

While lawyers are a given, the role of agents in the process is more complex. The agent is your friend: He's tipping you off to a terrific screenplay. He's confiding that a major star he represents is desperate to do a love story and he just happens to know just the right piece. He's alerting you that the important studio executive to whom you've just submitted a manuscript is on his way out, converting his executive deal into a producing deal, and he intends to buy the particular property out from under you.

The agent may also be your enemy. He's demanding an absurd price for a client. He's lying to you that his client hates a script you submitted, when in fact he never showed it to him—he just happens to hate his client's manager who will use the project to get a producing credit.

Literary agents—those representing novelists, playwrights or screenwriters—tend to be more benign than their compadres on the talent side. For one thing, they usually have a simpler game plan: They want to sell a property or the services of a writer. They don't have to worry about assembling a cosmic package. They also tend to be better educated; they may even have read the hot manuscript they just slipped you, not just the "coverage."

To be sure, the key concern of the agent is to "move the goods," not find the Holy Grail. His focus is to connect the right property or idea with the right buyer. The precise nature of that connection may take many different forms. In some cases, it may take the form of an auction. In others, it may simply involve dispatching a writer to the office of a producer or studio executive to pitch his project. Sometimes he may be pitching a one-liner; sometimes a meticulously mapped-out story. And, as every agent can testify, the sale may stem not so much from the actual quality of the idea as the theatricality of the storytelling.

The art of the pitch has achieved mythic proportions in Hollywood, where the spending of enormous sums of money may be prompted by a half-hour meeting. There are legends of pitchmanship—a sort of informal Hall of Fame of pitchmanship.

The person generally regarded as the King of the Pitch in Hollywood is neither a full-time producer nor an agent. He is an actor—in fact, a star. But unlike most stars, he has thoroughly done his homework. Indeed, Warren Beatty has mastered not only the dealmaking side of the entertainment industry but also the strategy of setting up new projects. His close friends like Jack Nicholson and producer Robert Evans call him "the pro." If you find yourself in business with Beatty, they testify, you'd better come armed.

Beatty's credentials cover many areas of the business. His acting credits range from *Splendor in the Grass* to *Town and Country*. His work as a producer and director encompass such varied fare as *Reds*, *Dick Tracy* and *Bulworth*. In Hollywood, however, Beatty's mythic status stems from his brilliance at manipulation and salesmanship rather than from his creative prowess. Beatty never has to demand "show me the money." He can sense its proximity and pick up its scent. As one former studio chief put it, "Warren can pick you clean, and do it with elegance."

He instinctively understands that the art of the pitch involves a lot more than simply walking into an executive's office and spinning a story. One has to persuade a buyer that he desperately needs a project, thus magically transforming a buyer's market into a seller's market—something few others do as well.

Beatty has been good at this game for a very long time. In the early 1970s, he decided that there was no reason to pitch one project at a time when he could, with a little finesse, set up two at once. In this instance, the first boasted a remarkable cluster of talents. Beatty would star along with Jack Nicholson and they would be directed by the estimable Mike Nichols, who was still taking bows for his work on *The Graduate* and *Who's Afraid of Virginia Woolf?* To clinch things, Beatty also threw in musical superstar Paul Simon, newly liberated from the golden team of Simon and Garfunkel, to compose the score. Writing the screenplay would be Carole Eastman, who had won an Oscar for *Five Easy Pieces*.

The catch was that no studio could acquire rights to this mesmerizing package titled *The Fortune*, without also committing to a second film that Beatty had also conjured up. The combination of the two would involve a huge investment, one that could easily sink a studio if both movies failed—or even if one proved to be a failure and the other a so-so success.

Columbia Pictures, then headed by David Begelman, was selected to be the first target for this twin package. Begelman was a cagey, tough-minded man, but Beatty knew that he was also an ex-agent who often got carried away by his own appetites. If he was "played" the right way, "I want it" could be transformed into "I must have it." Begelman's voracious style ultimately would lead to an involvement in a nasty check-kiting scheme, which almost landed him in prison, but at Columbia in this period, he still commanded wide respect among his peers.

Begelman made it very clear to his production staff at Columbia that he wanted to make a deal with Beatty come hell or high water. He wanted *The Fortune*. His support troops diligently set about to cover the two screenplays, and their report reflected youthful self-confidence. *The Fortune*, the reader's synopsis asserted, would be a runaway hit, perhaps a blockbuster. The second project, dealing with a Beverly Hills hairdresser and entitled *Shampoo*, had little going for it, they said. The reader's comment asserted that no one would care about the misadventures of a priapic hairdresser.

Begelman read their summaries, shrugged them off and then closed a deal for the two films, the first of which, *The Fortune*, proved to be a box office disaster. *Shampoo*, which many on his staff had so ardently dismissed, became a major hit.

Beatty went on to many other colorful and enriching exploits. In 1998, he set about to make the political comedy *Bulworth*, focusing his pitch this time on an old friend, Barry Diller. According to Warren Beatty, Diller committed to make *Bulworth* but resigned from Fox shortly thereafter. Diller himself adamantly denies having made such a commitment and indeed the other executives who succeeded him also demurred, saying they had no idea how the film got greenlighted. Indeed, given *Bulworth*'s political message, one that was guaranteed to infuriate the archconservative Rupert Murdoch, who owned the studio, no one wanted to be remotely associated with its forward progress.

But Beatty was determined to get his film made, irrespective of who tried to get in his way. He succeeded in doing so, though no one at Fox ever admitted to giving him the go-ahead. Top executives at Fox report that when Rupert Murdoch finally got to see *Bulworth*, he hated it, finding its liberal-leaning message to be infuriating.

Warren Beatty doesn't like to admit that he's a master pitchman. Even when prodded, he's reluctant to share his ground rules. He insists he's simply a filmmaker who occasionally gets passionate about his projects and finds ways of getting them made.

Nonetheless, anyone studying the tactics of Hollywood's skilled pitchmen can identify certain common talents and tactics. For one thing, they are superbly informed about the marketplace; they understand which studios at any given time are in desperate need of product and hence vulnerable to attack. They also have mastered the landscape of prospective buyers. They know which executives are the best listeners and which have the clout within their hierarchies to get a project approved.

In Hollywood, attention spans vary from executive to executive. Some can tolerate detailed presentations, others start twitching after three or four minutes and few mask their tolerance level. One studio executive had a thoroughly distracting apparatus consisting of an aluminum pole at the top of which perched a little wooden woodpecker-like creature. When someone started his verbal pitch, he would prod the woodpecker on his downward course, and it would peck away at the pole each step of the way. It took precisely three minutes for the bird to reach the bottom and that was the span of time allowed the person pitching his script. This process was made all the more demanding because the woodpecker made a distinct hammering noise as its beak banged against the pole as it headed downward, presenting a further challenge to the storyteller's concentration.

Inevitably, some Hollywood pitchmen are better raconteurs than others. Bob Kosberg, who has sold a myriad of pitches and produced thirteen films during his twenty-year career, tends to spin his yarns like the classic after-dinner banquet speaker, replete with clever asides building up to the inevitable payoff. Usually his objective is to obtain studio money to hire a writer and then develop his story. Some stories "tell" more excitingly than they read. Alan Gasmer, a literary agent at the William Morris Agency, acknowledges that, from time to time, he has advised clients with finished scripts to set them aside and pitch their stories as though they were as yet unformed. If the executive likes the pitch, but advances some suggestions, as is often the case (studio executives like to demonstrate their creative prowess), the writer can then go back to his material, make the necessary changes and submit it as though he had just churned it out. Needless to say, an appropriate period of time is allowed so as not to give away the process.

No matter how many artifices and tactical flourishes are introduced, however, inevitably words have to be put onto paper, scripts have to be written and judgments made. It all comes down to the word, which is where we started. Irrespective of the money or passion that has been lavished on a project or how much deft salesmanship is invested in launching it, the words have to be on the page. They have to be arrayed imposingly and, just as important, someone must be forced to read them.

And that, of course, is where the process ultimately bogs down. Every producer, director or studio executive can recite countless war stories about groundbreaking ideas that were translated into mediocre screenplays, or about elegantly crafted screenplays that were misunderstood and misread by other producers, directors or studio executives.

The punishing paradox of show business is that, with all the digital wizardry and morphing magic, the core of the process still focuses on some stressed-out individual sitting down quietly and turning pages. Someone has to write something and someone else has to read something. And the art of reading is just as imperiled as that of writing.

Catch a Hollywood decision maker in a relaxed moment, and he or she will readily admit their dread of reading. Stand outside the production offices of a studio on a typical Friday night, and you'll see one functionary after another plodding wearily toward his BMW or Mercedes, toting a bag full of what's called "weekend reading." Inside will be between ten and fifteen screenplays or, more rarely, manuscripts that have been carefully screened and apportioned. In most cases, other studio eyes have already viewed this material, ordered it covered (or synopsized), then deemed it acceptable for wider distribution. Indeed many of the executives assigned to read these scripts over the weekend will, instead, peruse their "cheat sheets"— i.e., the synopses, which conclude with a brief analysis of the characters, quality of the dialogue, etc. Appended will be a critique: "pass," "recommended" or even "strongly recommended." Not surprisingly, these documents are highly seductive for executives who would rather be playing golf or tennis or who simply lack the patience to read.

The coverage, to be sure, is notoriously inaccurate. Most of the truly memorable movies to come out of Hollywood received dreadful coverage. Projects as diverse as *Batman* and *The Godfather* were dismissed in reader reports. More important, in reducing the material to bare-bones summaries, the projects are stripped of color and texture. All that survives are naked narratives.

As inadequate as studio coverage may be, some studio apparatchiks take the process even farther. One prominent, famously dyslexic producer instructed his assistants to prepare synopses in the form of comic strips, replete with little dialogue-packed balloons. One studio chief sat with an aide for at least half an hour each day and listened as plot summaries were described to him—all in the interest of avoiding that terrifying confrontation with the page.

There are exceptions to this rule, of course. Some Hollywood decision makers conscientiously read the material preselected for them, but their reading habits vary markedly. Director Gil Cates won't start reading a script unless he knows he has the time to complete it. Reading in bits and pieces shortchanges the material, he feels: "No phone calls, no meetings—it's time to read." Others admit to start-and-stop habits, often while watching a sports event on television. And most concede they never penetrate beyond the twenty-page mark if they are not pulled in.

Of course, the material that reaches this level already has earned an elite status. A chief of production normally takes home only the final shooting script of a studio production or perhaps a script submitted on behalf of a major star or top director. During their halcyon years as co-heads of Warner Bros., Bob Daly and Terry Semel often did not even read a script at this stage, studying instead the casts, budgets and recommendations of their senior staff. The directors of some pricey Warner Bros. films insisted that they could tell from the questions asked of them in "green-light meetings" that their scripts had not yet been read.

In view of the cavalier treatment accorded their carefully crafted screenplays, veterans of the filmmaking scene often refer reverently to the "movie god." They understand that, for a project to move forward into production and to emerge unscathed, a beneficent nod from the movie god was mandatory.

Or put in a less spiritual context, it's the luck of the draw.

And often that's what it comes down to: luck. What else could account for the fact that what's anathema at one place becomes the Holy Grail at another? A classic example was *Lenny*, the biopic of

Lenny Bruce, which producer Marvin Worth spent years promoting. Worth's prime studio link was to Columbia, whose management coveted such family fare as *Oliver!* and *Butterflies Are Free*. To Columbia, at that time, *Lenny* was abhorrent in terms of both language and politics. It languished in development hell until Worth had an epiphany. Dustin Hoffman was at the top of his game and on the lookout for challenging parts. *Lenny* was just the ticket. It was raunchy and controversial, and a damn good role. Under Worth's prodding, Dustin himself pitched the project to David Picker, then UA's president. *Lenny* was as exciting to Picker as it had been appalling to Columbia. Worth extracted the project from Columbia to its new home at UA with Dustin attached to star.

So in the end, the quest for the Holy Grail comes down to the issue of commitment. Involvement with a film property is not a trial engagement; it's a marriage, even if it's a marriage of convenience. The project may be more an exercise of self-aggrandizement than a spiritual adventure, but it is a marriage nonetheless, which will challenge one's emotional as well as financial resources.

Those setting forth on that journey must therefore ask themselves some hard questions: Do the values inherent in a given project truly merit the sacrifice of time and energy? Does it express something of importance or convey a message of value to society?

Or does it come down to this: Is it such irresistible fun that one simply cannot resist the temptation? Amidst all the self-important pronouncements, there is surely nothing wrong with simple forthright entertainment. Giving the world a good laugh is its own just reward.

To the shaman storyteller, great entertainment is itself the Holy Grail.

CUT TO: Peter Bart on *The Godfather*

Of all the films I've worked on, by far the most difficult to get off the ground was *The Godfather*. Every time the project seemed to be gaining traction, some new obstacle would present itself.

The Godfather's problems were exacerbated by one pivotal dilemma: The project had two separate but distinct lives at Paramount, each in its own way traumatic.

Its initial life was low profile and unobtrusive. Mario Puzo, a portly writer of singularly unsuccessful books, submitted several chapters of a new novel to me. Though the sixty-odd pages contained several completed chapters, they also encompassed a step outline delineating some dramatic scenes to give the reader a sense of scope and context. Puzo had gone through this exercise for a very important reason. He desperately needed money to feed his fast-growing family; his obscure literary works such as *The Fortunate Pilgrim* weren't paying the bills. Perhaps Hollywood would beckon; after all, Mafia stories had always commanded good prices for authors.

Paramount did not represent the ideal market for this work. The studio had recently suffered through the stillborn release of a Mafia movie called *The Brotherhood* starring Kirk Douglas—an experience which persuaded the company's marketing mavens that Mafia movies, like Westerns, were a thing of the past. Nonetheless Puzo's plot was clearly riveting, the characters well drawn. As vice president for production, I intended to acquire an option on the project and my boss, Robert Evans, agreed. Besides, a mere $8,000 was at stake, hardly a big investment even for Paramount, which was going through lean times. Evans also indulged my unlikely choice of a director to steer the project through development. I had known Francis Ford Coppola since his days as a UCLA film student. Even though his directing credits had by no means established him as a major filmmaker (his most recent film, based on the musical *Finian's Rainbow*, was slammed by the critics), I greatly respected his talent as a writer, not to mention his keen intelligence. I also understood his reluctance to tackle a conventional genre movie, which he feared *The Godfather* could become.

As we continued to debate the novel, however, Coppola began to talk expansively of another kind of movie entirely—a broad-canvass family saga that would chronicle several Italian-American generations. The movie marinating in his imagination was not about crime, but rather about dynasty. More important, it was about the American experience, as seen through an especially unique, and violent, prism.

No one in Hollywood, not even at Paramount, paid much attention as Coppola, Puzo and I toiled away at *The Godfather*. This was another offbeat project destined for development hell, it was assumed.

A funny thing happened on the way to extinction, however. Puzo's completed novel became a best-seller; indeed, it was a literary phenomenon in terms of worldwide acceptance.

On one level, this was great news. Instantly the script that would never get made became the hottest property in town. Every Paramount executive at every level, from the guy who booked the theaters to Charles Bluhdorn, the chairman of the parent company, Gulf + Western, had brilliant notions about who should star, who should direct, and how the script should be structured. Why go with a relatively obscure filmmaker like Coppola, they demanded, when superstar directors would salivate to take on *The Godfather*? Besides, Coppola had made the mistake of confiding he wanted Marlon Brando for the lead and a no-name young actor named Al Pacino to play his prodigal son. Brando was regarded as an irascible "has-been"— his latest film, *Burn!*, was a disaster—and Paramount executives dismissed Pacino as "that Italian dwarf."

Foolishly, I thought I could combat this corporate cacophony, but I was woefully wrong. Suddenly it seemed as though everyone in the company, from the youthful president, Stanley Jaffe, to the head of distribution, Frank Yablans, to the studio chief, Bob Evans, was dispatching copies of our long-protected script to favored directors and stars. My colleagues had conveniently forgotten that we had deals with Coppola and Puzo and that I had even signed Al Ruddy to be the producer. The more I protested, the more I was ignored. This was clearly the blockbuster of the decade, everyone felt. If you don't believe it, just look at the best-seller list.

I surrendered. In a company where everyone was an instant genius, there was no hope of imposing order. I would simply wait it out. That was the only prudent course.

And then an amazing thing happened. To the surprise of all the instant geniuses, everyone started turning down *The Godfather*. Franklin Schaffner, who won plaudits for *Patton* and *Papillon*, felt the book glamorized the Mafia. It was downright immoral. His view was seconded by the likes of Richard Brooks, Costa-Gavras, Arthur Penn and others. The only major filmmaker who seemed vaguely interested was Sam Peckinpah, but with his particular approach the story's body count would have encompassed half of North America. Stars were backing away in droves, too. The role of the Godfather was too passive and that of his son, too conventional.

Just as quickly as the excitement of my colleagues had arisen, it faded. No one showed up at meetings to discuss *The Godfather*. The project that had belonged to everyone was now sliding back into my court by default. My strategic surrender had turned out to be the correct stratagem.

But could the project be resurrected in its original form? I wondered. Though pissed by the behavior of the studio, Coppola was willing to come on board once again. He had even invested time in a rewrite. Pacino had committed to another film, *The Gang That Couldn't Shoot Straight* at MGM, but he was pried loose with a few

well-placed phone calls. Brando's career was still cold; he signed on
for Screen Actors Guild (SAG) scale and a piece of the gross—a deal
that was later renegotiated wherein Brando surrendered his points in
return for a mere $100,000.

The Godfather was ready to roll at last. The studio's expectations
were not high. After all, how could a movie that every major filmmaker had turned down possibly succeed?

A year later, the answer emerged: It can succeed if it happens to
be one of the great movies of all time, regardless of who turned it
down.

CUT TO: Peter Guber on *A Chorus Line*

If ever there was a "sure thing" in the way of film properties, *A Chorus Line* was it. It was a huge hit on Broadway. Virtually every film
company wanted the rights. It seemed like a dream role for a star.

But it turned out to be anything but a "sure thing." In fact, it was
a study in frustration.

My own history with it dated back to its opening night off Broadway. There was such a demand for tickets that Marvin Hamlisch, the
composer, actually set up a folding chair for me in the aisle. I was
desperate to buy the rights for Columbia, but after a week of arguments, it was clear I was getting no support from my corporate colleagues. Universal finally offered $5.5 million and won the bidding
war. In acquiring the show, however, Universal also had to agree to a
long list of conditions, one of which mandated that no film be made
until after the Broadway production had run its course. That could
be years.

By the time the run ended ten years later, Universal had cooled
on the idea. By then, however, I was head of Polygram and saw a

chance to step into the breach. Ned Tanen, Universal's production chief, liked the show; he wanted co-financing for what would be an expensive movie. The key to reviving interest in *A Chorus Line*, it was clear, lay in finding star casting. The notion of just shooting the stage musical straight on did not have much appeal to most directors.

We thought we had a better idea anyway. Why not team John Travolta and Mikhail Baryshnikov? Travolta had shown his talents in *Saturday Night Fever* and *Grease*. Baryshnikov rose to fame in the Kirov Ballet. If one of the other male roles could be expanded, the show could be transformed into a contest of sorts between male top-liners. This was a risky gambit involving major tinkering with a celebrated property. But with masterful execution, the rewards could be spectacular.

The two agreed to do the project. Universal was keen to co-finance it. But a new problem loomed: The German partners in Polygram didn't like the numbers. Polygram's film charter imposed a budgetary lid on film projects, and *A Chorus Line* with its stars exceeded that limit. I argued fervently that this was shortsighted. Some $7 million was now invested in the project, and it would be much more responsible to make the film rather than write off such a huge sum. The conundrum was that we'd actually lose less if the film was made.

The Germans were adamant. An order was an order. I was frustrated. How could a company get into the movie business yet have no appreciation for what would clearly become movie magic?

Inevitably, the project fell apart, and Polygram wrote off its investment. Some years later a movie of *A Chorus Line* was made under the direction of Richard Attenborough. Instead of star dancers, Attenborough built his film around Michael Douglas, portraying the director of the show. It didn't work. Didn't even come close.

Success is more attitude than aptitude. I had surrendered too easily but recognize that past failures are navigational stakes for future success.

3.

The Mapmakers

I never thought I had more brains than a
writer has. But I always thought that his
brains belonged to me, because I knew how
to use them.

MONROE STAHR IN
F. SCOTT FITZGERALD'S
THE LAST TYCOON

In 1971, Waldo Salt was the hottest writer in Hollywood.
Savvy and blunt-spoken, Salt had survived the dark days
of the blacklist and was widely acclaimed for his brilliant screenplay
of *Midnight Cowboy*, the Oscar-winning film of 1969. Irwin Winkler,
a producer with no lack of street smarts himself, was delighted when
Salt agreed to write a far more lighthearted film, *The Gang That
Couldn't Shoot Straight*, based on a popular Jimmy Breslin novel.
Salt's name would give the project some momentum at MGM,
which was a troubled studio at the time.

When he turned in his first draft, Salt reiterated his enthusiasm
for the project but also confided his modus operandi. It was his practice, Salt explained, to create two versions of his first draft. There
was a "real" draft; then there was a draft submitted to the studio,

which would be missing several key fragments. The purpose of this exercise was very pragmatic, he related. "These so-called studio executives need something to keep them busy," the veteran writer said. "So I remove a page here, a snippet of dialogue there—things that throw scenes out of whack. Then the geniuses come to me with their story notes. 'Maybe this scene needs a little clarification, this piece of dialogue seems truncated,' they will advise. And I dig out the pages that I'd taken out and turn them in and everyone's happy." The studio may be puzzled by these oversights, but their esteem for the writer rises even further because he proved open to their superb suggestions.

Salt's methodology had served him well and continued to do so with *Gang*. Salt's little game, which has been adopted by other writers in one form or another, points up the basic attitude of screenwriters toward the conditions of their craft. Writers feel unappreciated, and understandably so. In the movie business, unlike the theater, writers are hired and fired at will. A writer may find that Holy Grail of a property and use it to craft a masterful film script that attracts stars and a star director, yet not be invited on the set during production. He usually doesn't even see the film until its release. Worse still, many directors demand "a film by" credit, thus implying that they created the script as well as shooting it.

When a potential writers' strike looms, as in 2001, these tensions come to a head. The writers demanded not only higher residuals, but also heightened respect. They wanted to be welcome on the set and at dailies and even at premieres of their films. Like frantic squirrels, the networks and studios, meanwhile, stash away a year's supply of scripts. Directors are off shooting and actors acting, so theoretically there's no need for a writer to backstop the work. Besides most filmmakers, not to mention ordinary filmgoers, feel they know how to write and can summon up dialogue as needed.

"Everyone in this business believes he understands storytelling," observes Becky Johnston, who wrote the screenplay for *Seven Years in Tibet.* "That's one thing they have in common."

While most writers share a persecution complex (that's surely one trait that drove them to write), in corporate Hollywood the syndrome has basis in reality. The writer is at once lionized and scorned. He is treated like the lord of the manor, yet required to eat at the servants' table. He may sell a spec script for $5 million, then have trouble getting his agent on the phone.

His is, in short, a crazy-making trade, yet one that offers astonishing rewards. A writer who's mastered TV writing can reinvent himself as a writer-producer with an income of $10 million–plus a year. His equivalent on the movie side can generate more than $1 million from a script assignment and, when summoned for an urgent production rewrite, he may pull down up to $250,000 a week.

In rare cases, the writer can even build a cocoon of seeming invincibility. At his peak, turning out films such as *Network* and *The Hospital,* Paddy Chayefsky controlled his own destiny, exercising ultimate influence over the choice of director and cast as well as the final edit. Michael Crichton, who himself directed six films before withdrawing to the status of novelist, also auditions his directors and, when he decides to adapt his own novels, turns a deaf ear to dreaded studio script notes. He simply dispatches his first draft and walks away, surrendering the right to have further input.

From a business standpoint, the mania to employ the "hot" writer of the moment has proven to be marginally self-destructive. In film as well as TV, the costs involved in the development process have become so excessive as to defeat risk taking. Some film projects build up $5 million to $7 million in script costs as they plod through a succession of drafts. Ultimately, their accrued costs run so high they must be molded into star vehicles to justify their existence. It's no surprise that the average studio film in the year 2000 cost $54.8 million to produce with another $27.3 million going for just domestic advertising and prints, according to the Motion Picture Association of America (MPAA), with story costs having become an increasingly significant contributor.

At the other end of the spectrum however, neophyte writers find it ever harder to break into the system. A generation ago, the studios and top agencies boasted of their ability to identify new talent. Today a new writer who sends a "cold submission" say, to CAA, gets a form letter back stating that it won't be covered unless he has an agent; the reason CAA received the material in the first place usually was because the writer was looking for an agent. On a rare occasion, a "new" writer like Alan Ball may strike pay dirt with an *American Beauty* or Andrew Niccol with *The Truman Show*. Both had to wander through a maze of rejection letters before getting a fair reading, however.

The most urgent dilemma facing writers in the pop arts, however, does not relate so much to status or money, but rather to the sort of material they must create. There's no misreading the signals: Hollywood, by and large, wants "safe" commercial fare. It wants projects that travel across boundaries, that entice overseas audiences, hence scripts not burdened with nuance. It wants "concept" action movies like *The Matrix* and gross-out comedy like *There's Something About Mary*. Most of all, it wants grist for its special effects wizards—a *Grinch* or a *Godzilla*. More often than not, clever dialogue doesn't factor. In fact, it's essentially irrelevant.

After her first couple of years on the job, watching several of her more ambitious dramas fail, Amy Pascal, president of Columbia Pictures, shifted her focus to making sequels to such special effects bonanzas as *Jumanji* and *Men in Black*. Projects such as these, she reasoned, can become hits with all their imperfections. "In the case of serious drama," she argued, "all the elements had to achieve a level of perfection before attracting an audience. The movie had to be a 'ten.'" All that was a euphemistic way of saying, why make risky movies if you can get away with schlock? Or, as William Goldman once wrote, "Remember, movies began as entertainment for illiterates."

Given all this, the care and feeding of writers has become a sophisticated art form. The process of recruiting a writer, of motivating him to deliver his best, and of nurturing his neuroses without surrendering to them, can surely tax the talent of even the most resourceful producer or studio functionary. When it all comes together, the satisfaction is bountiful, both financially and artistically. When it unravels, however, the anger and recrimination can be daunting.

Paradoxically, though most writers feel like "outsiders" to the filmmaking process, there's not a moment when the writer's presence is not felt. Most projects begin with a writer who has created an original screenplay, a novel, a play or at least an original idea. Even a high-concept megafilm such as *Armageddon* was triggered when a writer named Jonathan Hensleigh scrawled a note to himself. Why not remake *Hellfighters*, the old John Wayne movie about a man who extinguished oil fire blazes? Except in the new version the hero would be dispatched to extinguish an asteroid hurtling toward earth.

Once a first draft screenplay has been written, other writers— sometimes as many as thirty-five as in *The Flintstones*—are brought in to reshape it. It's become increasingly commonplace to bring in writers even during the actual shoot to deliver a final on-set dialogue polish. When a picture is "in the can," the studio often turns to yet another writer to enhance the final product, perhaps to prepare a voice-over narration, or to create a new scene that may bridge a clumsy transition.

There are those rare exceptions that have become folklore. When Billy Hayes escaped from his incarceration in Turkey in the mid 1970s, the story of his travails was widely publicized. Its subject matter wasn't the most favored fare for Hollywood—overzealous authorities hunting down youthful drug offenders. But the press coverage fascinated a young screenwriter named Oliver Stone who had yet to get anything produced or even sold. His writing samples revealed grit and reality—an ideal match to Hayes' story. A deal with Columbia was struck and this high-strung neophyte plunged into his first draft, having resisted preparing any outline or treatment. Lists of names were already being made by executives for the "real" writer to come aboard after the first draft had been submitted. At the same time, the continuing press reports about Hayes interested Alan Parker, a young English filmmaker whom the studio auditioned. Parker himself had no studio credits, but his modest English film, *Bugsy Malone*, provided ample evidence of his talent. He had a passion for this project but was not happy that a first draft was already underway by a stubborn and uncredentialed writer. Parker fancied himself to be a writer but realized that first on board would invariably have the first position credit on the film. Equally important, a first draft that misses badly undermines the momentum on a project.

Parker waited. He had no choice. Besides, the several prospective Hollywood writers suggested by the studio wanted no part of this project.

When the first draft was delivered, Parker read it and reacted quickly with the sort of call that warms any producer's heart. "It's perfect. No one can change a word," he said. And Columbia, itself impressed, gave the green light. *Midnight Express* was launched, and Oliver Stone, the first-time screenwriter, went on to win the Academy Award.

But most writers, not as talented or as lucky as Stone, still complain about their niche roles. "I'm now typecast as the 'lighten-up-the-ingenue' specialist," said one well-paid scenarist. "If the woman's role is playing flat, I'm supposed to give her a bit of swagger. That's what I do for a living."

While the script is the center of gravity, the final product may reflect the input of several writers. Was it Barry Morrow or Ronald Bass who was truly responsible for the script of *Rain Man*, which won the Academy Award for both of these writers? When there are two or more writers who work successively on a script, it's really hard to tell whom to honor. (In fact, it's the Writers Guild that determines ultimate screen credits, and it does so independent of what the studio, network, producer or director might feel.)

The process of auditioning potential screenwriters entails focusing on ideas rather than pitching skills. Jeffrey Berg, chairman of International Creative Management (ICM), correctly points out that "many great writers just don't give good meeting." Still others, who are skilled storytellers, warily say as little as possible at these auditions, mindful of the fact that some filmmakers are notorious for swiping writers' ideas without hiring the writers themselves. Celebrity writers feel confident that they can land a writing job just by gracing a director with their company, offering vague compliments about his work and indicating enthusiasm for the basic material under discussion.

When Truman Capote sought the screenwriting assignment on *The Great Gatsby*, he charmed the director, Jack Clayton; the studio chief, Robert Evans, and the producer, David Merrick. No one, however, asked any questions about his approach. Capote, after all, was a star in his own right. It seemed untoward to toss out questions such as, "What are you going to do about the third act?"

As things turned out, Capote did not have any answers anyway. He turned in a script that represented a mere retyping of the F. Scott Fitzgerald novel, with dialogue and stage directions presented in screenplay format.

The studio read it and gulped. There followed vague threats of a lawsuit and unpleasant comments that Truman Capote had been typing, not writing. But ultimately he received most of his pay and another writer was hired—one subjected to an intensive interview.

To a director who sees himself as a sort of maestro, conducting a vast orchestra of diverse talents, each of these players fills a specialized role in his grand scheme, while it's his responsibility to keep the overall vision. "There's something seductive about being summoned to do rewrites," acknowledges Paul Attanasio, a former film critic for the *Washington Post* who has done his share, in addition to getting screenplay credit for *Quiz Show, Donnie Brasco* and *Disclosure.* "You come in as the heroic gunslinger. The trouble is, the whole exercise is basically ridiculous. You do a dialogue polish, but dialogue isn't just flavoring. It's an organic part of the script that grows out of the characters. If you change the dialogue, you're also changing the characters, so the idea of a dialogue polish per se is silly. The rewrite process trivializes what writers really do."

Yet top writers such as Attanasio get rich off their body-and-fender work. While the great novelists of the prewar era, such as F. Scott Fitzgerald or William Faulkner, earned slender rations from their brief forays to Hollywood, today's assembly line writers make $2 million to $3 million a year.

But few derive creative satisfaction from what they do. "There are so many writers on films today that their characters rarely have a unique voice," observes one high-paid body-and-fender man who covets his anonymity. "This is ultimately tough on the actor who must deliver stale lines and on the director who thinks he's making his movie better."

The multiple-writer syndrome also prompts battles over final credits—disputes that end up in the lap of arbitration committees created by the Writers Guild. Faced with a myriad of drafts and conflicting claims, the arbiters tend to rule for the humble, long-forgotten soul who slaved over the first draft and who created the characters and situations to begin with.

On the face of it, this would seem a reasonable solution, but problems arise when the shooting script bears little resemblance to the original story, when the so-called rewrite man has essentially given birth to a new movie. This occurs not only with serious films, but even with popcorn epics like *Godzilla*. In that instance, two young writers, Ted Elliott and Terry Rossio, built their techno-thriller around a clash between two monsters, Godzilla and his flying, fire-breathing adversary, the Gryphon. When Roland Emmerich and Dean Devlin became involved, they veered off on a different course. Having just made the global blockbuster *Independence Day*, they had the cachet to persuade the studio to eliminate the Gryphon, thus making Godzilla himself the heavy, which proved to be a tactical error. Elliott and Rossio ended up with "story by" credit and they, like the Gryphon, were banished from the project while Devlin and Emmerich got screenplay credit.

Often, the rewrite man, rather than fighting for credit, welcomes his anonymity. It's just a job, after all; they'd prefer to hang their hats on their more estimable work. When the celebrated William Goldman takes on "quick jobs," not only does he prefer to do so without credit but also, as he puts it, "I make a point of never reading anything I've written." When Robert Benton, Academy Award–winning writer was brought aboard *Gorillas in the Mist* by producer Arne Glimcher, to rewrite Anna Hamilton Phelan, Benton also disavowed any screen credit. Though he styled himself a filmmaker, not a writer for hire, he was enough of a realist to understand the difference between screen credit and bank credit. In other words, he got paid for his labors.

On the Warren Beatty film *Bulworth*, on the other hand, two skilled rewrite men, James Toback and Aaron Sorkin, felt slighted when the credit-hungry star awarded himself the final writing credit along with a writer named Jeremy Pikser. Tobak insisted he'd turned in a seventy-seven-page first draft to Beatty and that a lot of his original material ended up in the final version, but in deference to the star, a longtime friend, he didn't pursue his claim with the Writers Guild.

Among all the rewrite men, Robert Towne tends to instill the most confidence. In the 1970s, considered the best script paramedic in the business, he accepted only those assignments on films that seemed certain to be made. These were the projects that offered him the greatest satisfaction and the fattest paycheck. When Columbia acquired *The New Centurions*, the best-seller by Joseph Wambaugh, producer Irwin Winkler was able to attract George C. Scott hot off of his *Patton* Oscar-winning performance. The studio embraced the project—until it received the first draft of the script. This was clearly a package in search of a story. Towne was brought in and the script soon came to life. Even the moody George C. Scott embraced Towne in a wrestler's hug when he read the draft. Towne remained on the picture through much of the production and was paid handsomely for his babysitting. Today, Towne's mantle has been assumed by William Goldman.

Other prominent writers have been more vocal about credits. Barry Levinson, the gifted writer-director, threatened to withdraw as a member of the Writers Guild in 1997 after David Mamet was denied sole writing credit on the political satire *Wag the Dog*. Before Levinson committed to direct the project, Hilary Henkin had written an adaptation of Larry Beinhart's novel entitled *American Hero*. Levinson then brought in Mamet who, he insists, wrote every line of dialogue in the movie. Consistent with its practice of favoring the original writer, the Guild arbitration committee awarded Henkin the first position credit. Henkin wasn't embarrassed by the situation. She claimed she made an important contribution to structure and dialogue and hence deserved what she asked for—shared credit. Levinson, however, was furious but, in the end, he lost.

No writer has a more unpredictable record on credits than Michael Crichton, the novel-writing superstar. On *Rising Sun*, a Crichton novel, there were heated creative differences between Crichton and director Philip Kaufman while Crichton was writing the adaptation. Crichton was fired and vowed he'd never let that happen again. When his next novel, *Disclosure*, was sold, the contract mandated Crichton's approval of producer and director. Milos Forman was approved as director and immediately offered Crichton the opportunity to write the screenplay even though Crichton made it clear this was not required. About a hundred pages into it, creative differences arose, but because Crichton was the producer now, Forman exited the project. The next filmmaker to win Crichton's approval was Barry Levinson, who said he wanted to hire Paul Attanasio to write. Crichton happily agreed. Because Crichton was the producer, there was a mandatory credit arbitration, and even though no one but Milos Forman had seen the partial draft that Crichton had written, the Writers Guild awarded him shared screenplay credit. Crichton felt that was simply not fair to Attanasio and took the unusual step of removing his own name from the film.

Given the ever-mounting intrigues surrounding the development process, studio executives and producers alike thread their way cautiously through the complex maze. Their focused objective is to nurture screenplays that will attract the high-profile creative elements needed to move their projects forward. Their pervasive fear is that they'll run through so many drafts that the creative community will regard their project as "troubled." Their concern is justified.

In the 1960s and 1970s, it was extremely rare for a project to be locked in development hell for more than a few months. The studio hierarchs wanted to shoot films, not develop them. The studio-initiated, high-concept projects of the 1980s and 1990s—such as *Beverly Hills Cop* or *Top Gun*—however, triggered a new mind-set. Suddenly studio chiefs regarded multiple drafts as a badge of honor, exhibiting meticulous preparation and creativity. *Runaway Bride* was in development at Paramount for a decade, yet its shooting script wasn't any more inventive than its first draft—probably less so.

To the studio development bureaucrats, the preparation of "script notes" on each successive draft came to represent a favorite indoor sport. Scanning the contents of these "script notes," one quickly realizes why writers rebel against them. There are nonstop references to "character arcs," plus abundant comparison to other films, as though to suggest that key story points be insistently lifted from them. The notes are all about style, not content; they obsess about structure but never passion. The writer thus finds himself in a delicate political position. His every instinct tells him to follow the advice of Joe Eszterhas, the iconoclastic writer of *Basic Instinct*. "Your only option with script notes is either to shred them or burn them," he advised. Nonetheless, the writer knows who writes his check. Future employment opportunities might be blown away, or he might be shoved aside to make way for a replacement part.

From the standpoint of the filmmaker, firing the writer is often an expeditious route. The studio always likes the idea of a "fresh point of view," and directors, an insecure lot, share that impulse. Further, the process of interviewing new writers is a cost-effective way of tapping into new ideas. Most writers will readily read someone else's script if they feel a paycheck is in the offing. If properly flattered, they'll also volunteer what they feel is wrong and what steps can remedy these flaws. It's like a free visit to the doctor.

But it can also be profoundly confusing. Many a producer has watched the enthusiasm of his director evaporate as writer after writer delivers his script criticisms. A prospective writer inevitably will magnify the script problems; that's how he justifies an extensive rewrite. The greater the problems, the bigger the payday.

However, a seasoned studio executive like Walter Parkes, the co-chief of production at DreamWorks SKG, himself a writer, will not make a deal until a new writer has delivered a detailed, three-act breakdown of the project. It may take hours of meetings to lay it all out, but Parkes wants to hear each twist and turn before writing the check.

Confident veterans relish this painful procedure. "Television gives you invaluable experience in tackling this process," points out director Mike Newell. "You're doing shows on short turnarounds, so you get used to spreading out your scripts on the floor of the office and actually cutting and pasting right then and there."

Increasingly filmmakers are bestowing upon themselves the additional responsibilities of producer and writer and thus prefer to direct only their own screenplays. This is especially true of some of Hollywood's newer directing stars, such as Alexander Payne (*Election*), who writes with a partner, or David O. Russell (*Three Kings*). If the filmmaker in question began his career as a writer—Woody Allen being the classic example—the results may prove felicitous. Those directors who decided they were also writers after their careers were launched, often stumbled in the process. Roland Joffé's initial film, *The Killing Fields*, was well received, but as Joffé focused on his new self-assigned role as writer-director, what seemed like a promising career began to yield the likes of *The Scarlet Letter*.

The late H. N. Swanson, a fabled agent of the 1950s and 1960s, once said, "You can't put in what God left out. Accept your poor choice and cut your loss. Make it a learning process and set a new course with a new writer rather than find yourself in analysis paralysis." Swanson, to be sure, represented writers who were always ready to move in for a quick rewrite.

The script is always under constant assault. Network standards and practices, bureaucrats, development executives, actors and even the media all profess to have the magic answer.

What all this means for the writer is time—extraordinary outlays of time. And through it all, he must also sustain his own point of view, or at least a semblance of it.

It is bone-rattling work. In the end many writers simply abandon films and move on to the presumably greener pastures in television. Others such as Paddy Chayefsky (*Hospital, Network*) of old, try to construct a more protected environment within the system.

Among today's crop of screenwriters, perhaps Ron Bass has gone to the greatest lengths in this regard. Bass' obsession with screenwriting was so intense that, as a young show business attorney, he would set his alarm clock for 3 A.M. so that he could carve out a second workday for his writing. As he became successful enough to quit law, he built his own self-contained scriptwriting organization—a "hit team" of seven writers and researchers who worked with him on all his screenplays. At any given time, he toiled on three or four different projects, each involving a couple of co-workers to do research or edit or even embellish. Grinding out hits like *My Best Friend's Wedding, Sleeping with the Enemy* or *Dangerous Minds*, Bass and his entourage managed to earn as much as $10 million a year through this mechanism. "I don't like downtime between projects," says the strong-willed Bass. "This is what I do for a living."

Besides his high price, Bass injected other stern conditions in his deals, the most important mandating that he could not be rewritten without his consent. Some accommodations have been made, to be sure. Julia Roberts wanted to rewrite her toast at the end of *My Best Friend's Wedding* because she had trouble saying Bass' lines; the writer readily agreed. When summoned to a studio meeting, Bass usually arrives with two or three aides, who will diligently take notes on whatever is being said—a procedure that intimidates those who stand ready to tamper with his plots (Bass denies this is a stratagem).

The ultimate irritant for Bass or any other established writer is to turn in a screenplay only to learn that his director insists on a credit like "a film by Woody Allen" or "a Woody Allen film." To be sure, Allen is among the few who deserve a credit of that sort, if anyone does, since he customarily writes his films as well as directing and also often starring. They are truly Woody Allen films. Writers become mutinous, however, when neophyte filmmakers who pay little attention to script development join the select company who demand the so-called possessory credit.

Some filmmakers resist this temptation. Kevin Smith, who has written and directed four feature films including *Dogma*, never takes "film by" credit, arguing that filmmaking is "the most collaborative art form." No one person makes a movie, he insists. Another young director, Michael Bay (*Armageddon*, *Pearl Harbor*), refutes this argument, on the grounds that a director is the one who puts his butt on the line, devoting perhaps four or five years of his life to a project.

In 1966, the Writers Guild hammered out an agreement with the Association of Motion Picture and Television Producers providing that "film by" credits be limited to directors who actually wrote their own films. When the Directors Guild threatened a strike, the writers relented with the understanding that "film by" credits would be accorded only directors such as Frank Capra or David Lean who had built up a "distinguished body of work." That understanding soon faded before a credit-grabbing onslaught of young directors. Darren Aronofsky took a "film by" credit on only his second film, *Requiem for a Dream*, claiming that "a director's involvement is a lot more significant than a writer's." Like Michael Bay, he contends that he lives with his movie for three or more years while a writer may put in six months. Of course, this conveniently ignores the many writers who spend several years writing and rewriting a script, with little if any guarantee of compensation.

The credits issue has added a further note of creative tension to the already uneasy working relationship between writers and directors. Writers feel used and abused. "I can't get it out of my mind that, while I write the script and invent the characters, I need an invitation to visit the set," says David Self, a gifted writer who, before hitting thirty, established himself with movies such as *Thirteen Days*. Inevitably, writers like Self resolve this by trying to become directors themselves—a transition that is never easy to make. In the days of the studio system, most new directors came from the theater; others were former film editors or assistant directors. In recent years, however, more and more directors start as writers—witness Cameron Crowe, Oliver Stone or Anthony Minghella. "I can't imagine wanting to write a film and not to direct it," Minghella declares.

The lure is obvious. Directing entails the ultimate power. It also releases the writer from what is arguably an anachronistic ritual. It is, after all, a study in frustration to write a script without knowing who will direct it, who will play the key roles, etc. It is akin to laying a foundation without knowing what will go on top of it.

A script, one may argue, is merely a blueprint. But as a writer becomes more skilled at his craft, he understandably grows weary of executing blueprints that will be torn apart. Hence, the writer's dream is to function as Mike Leigh does. The director of *Secrets & Lies*, his sixteenth film, Leigh believes the only way to "discover" a film is by making it. To trigger the process, he writes a brief document that outlines the story schedule and key locations. Once he assembles his financing and his actors, only then, during extended rehearsals, does he hammer out how each character will interact with the others.

Leigh's outline for *Topsy-Turvy*, for example, began as follows:

What was it like for a group of Japanese men, women and children to come to London in 1885, and to appear daily in a "real" Japanese Village at an exhibition in Knightsbridge?

Legend has it that at the same time, a recently acquired ancient Japanese sword crashed from the library wall of W. S. Gilbert, the successful dramatist, just as he was struggling with the subject matter for his next collaboration with Sir Arthur Sullivan, the composer.

Did this accident really inspire their most celebrated comic opera, that nonsensical soufflé, *The Mikado*? Or was Gilbert merely adroitly tapping into the craze for Japanese arts and crafts that was then at its height, less than twenty years after the Meiji had opened up Japan to the West?

And if the Knightsbridge experience was strange for those Japanese folk, must it not have been even stranger for those of them who soon found themselves at the Savoy Theatre in the Strand, teaching Gilbert's actors and actresses authentic Japanese deportment, makeup and fan technique?

And what was Gilbert's relationship with the girl they nicknamed "Miss Sixpence Please," because those were the only two English words she knew? (She sold tea at the exhibition.)

What, indeed, was Gilbert's relationship with his wife, Lucy? She was fourteen years his junior, and they never had children. Yet why were they forever throwing extravagant children's parties? And what went on in the room at Gilbert's house he called the Flirtorium, where he tutored young actresses?

Winging it Mike Leigh–style, of course, is anathema to studios. Studios demand a carefully worked out screenplay that can be boarded and budgeted and reviewed by all the appropriate departments. Some also want detailed storyboards of complex action scenes and special effects sequences. Their aim is to take the surprise out of filmmaking. The Mike Leighs of the world thrive on surprise. Studios want to limit deviations from the script. Mike Leigh and his brethren would insist that the art of filmmaking lies in deviation.

And the screenwriter is caught in the middle of this shoot out. He senses that what he is doing, indeed what he's paid to do, is more often than not a waste of time, but it's what makes the system run. It is often pointless, but it's what the boss wants, whether he's the studio chief, a cable hierarch, network mogul or director.

To escape this ritual, some writers have shifted their focus to spec scripts rather than taking a succession of writing assignments. In doing so, the writer basically gambles that his story will evoke a bidding frenzy from the studios, and he will thus be richly rewarded for his gamble.

By the early 1990s, the spec script market seemed to be turning into a well-oiled machine, spawning its own mythological heroes.

One was a young UCLA Film School graduate named Shane Black who racked up a $1.75 million deal on a script called *The Last Boy Scout*, then hit a $4 million jackpot with *The Long Kiss Goodnight*, a violent action drama. There was also Joe Eszterhas, a burly former *Rolling Stone* journalist, who scored an amazing $7.5 million double jackpot with a script entitled *Foreplay* and a short outline called *One Night Stand*.

None of these provided the basis for an even marginally successful film, to be sure, but nonetheless literary agents soon mobilized a sort of spec script assembly line. Two agents at the William Morris office, Alan Gasmer and Rob Carlson, were perhaps the most proficient. Writers would come to their office, pitch their ideas and hope to get the green light to write them. If the script fulfilled their expectations, Gasmer and Carlson would issue a sort of red alert to the studios. A "hot" script—every script they offered was "hot," of course—would be distributed at 5 P.M. Wednesday. Bids would be accepted starting at 10 A.M. Friday. The tight deadline was designed to arouse a sense of urgency. The agents understood that if the studios were rushed into a quick decision, and were motivated by fear that a rival was making the deal, they'd be more prone to action. If there were time for deliberation—even a weekend—the lottery-like excitement would be vitiated.

The scheme worked perfectly for a year or so, and other literary agents joined in enthusiastically. Soon some studios became almost entirely dependent on their spec acquisitions; they even got to like the sudden trend. The bidding wars were costly, of course, but on the other hand executives were no longer tied to the tedium of development hell. They were dealing with finished scripts; some even had important elements attached, which made their job easier.

And then the bubble burst. The bidding wars, it seemed, were more exciting than the scripts that fomented them. Despite their high prices, many of the spec scripts were discarded. Those that were produced proved disappointing. As quickly as it had developed, the spec script market simply disintegrated. Gasmer and Carlson dismantled their assembly line and moved on to other activities within the agency. The heroes of the movement, however, had more difficulty adjusting. Shane Black developed writer's block and hasn't been heard from as a writer in a while. Joe Eszterhas, after finding no buyers for several "hot" scripts and firing several agents, wrote *American Rhapsody*, a book that became a best-seller. As though to underscore his change of pace, he even packed up his family and moved from Malibu to Cleveland.

For a brief moment in time, writers actually felt they'd beat the system. Some even had the paychecks to prove it. Their triumph proved evanescent.

They should have known better.

CUT TO: Peter Bart on *Red Dawn*

It never ceases to amaze me how greatly a project can be transformed in shape and substance once a studio has acquired it. All too often, the changes are not for the better. A classic example was "Ten Soldiers," a script written by a young Texan named Kevin Reynolds. Reynolds wrote a touching, quite original antiwar story vaguely reminiscent of *Lord of the Flies*. By the time MGM was done with it in 1984, Reynolds' project had become a jingoistic saber-rattling war movie called *Red Dawn*. This transformation was not exactly pleasing to me, since I was the one who fostered Reynolds' script at the studio.

The script was set in the near future when a combined Russian and Cuban force invade the southwestern United States. Ten high school students managed to escape the attack, taking refuge in the hills surrounding their small town. At first, their impromptu guerrilla unit seems like a lark as they harass the invaders, but the story darkens into a cautionary tale about the brutalization of the innocent.

The idea seemed to resonate in the early 1980s when the Cold War still was a hot-button issue. I bought the script with the plan of making it into a relatively low-budget movie. Reynolds himself had just completed directing a movie called *Fandango* for Steven Spielberg's unit at Universal, and he seemed a likely candidate to direct "Ten Soldiers."

But the president of MGM, Frank Yablans, had a better idea. Why make a *Lord of the Flies* sort of movie, he argued, when the same script could be turned into a *Rambo*-like story? He even had the right man for the job—a tough-talking, gun-toting writer-director named John Milius, who was best known for such films as *Conan the Barbarian* and *Dillinger*. When Yablans' proposal was challenged, he registered righteous indignation. "Milius will shoot Reynolds' script," he flared. "He'll just give it a little more energy. After all, *First Blood* grossed a lot more than fucking *Lord of the Flies*."

He gave it energy, all right. Milius exponentially increased the firepower of the battles, as well as their body count. Yablans even offered up General Alexander Haig as an adviser on the film—Haig had recently become a member of the MGM board of directors. Now even Milius was worried about the course of his project. "This was once a movie about the futility of war," he observed. "I don't think Haig and Yablans quite see it that way."

Red Dawn turned out to be a rather arch and inept war movie. If its message was fuzzy, so was its following. Haig liked it; Reynolds didn't. I voted with Reynolds.

4.

The Alchemists

*A poet needs a pen, a painter a brush and a
filmmaker an army.*

ORSON WELLES

When word leaked out that Steven Spielberg had opted
to direct *Saving Private Ryan*, some Hollywood insiders reacted with surprise. The script had been read and passed on by a number of other filmmakers as well as by two studios. World War II was hardly an "in" subject with today's teens. Moreover, the basic story seemed dangerously one-note. Once the mission to "save" Private Ryan had been accomplished, the narrative lost direction and the dialogue became stilted. Even those in Spielberg's inner circle expressed concern. While the director's fertile imagination was always vividly on display during the actual filming of his movies, incessantly conjuring up new angles and random bits to "cook" a scene, his strength did not lie in solving script problems. Writers who worked for him commented on the frequent oversimplicity, even naiveté, of his suggestions: Stories from Spielberg always seemed to

come down to the good guy against the bad guy or the good team against the bad team. "Steven's not strong on nuance," observed one writer who had labored with the director on a script.

What most people didn't know about *Saving Private Ryan* however, was that Steven Spielberg had a brilliant core idea that would so galvanize the audience during the first twenty minutes that it would render the film unforgettable. For Spielberg, the key lay in capturing the nightmare reality of Omaha Beach. Though he had storyboarded *Jurassic Park*, he resisted doing so on his war film, fearing it would cast a rigid structure over the chaos. He'd been enamored of Robert Capa's combat photographs of the D-Day invasion, indeed, had obsessed over them. He'd also viewed countless war documentaries, studying how, in real combat, you can count each piece of dirt that flies into the air after an explosion while in contemporary action films an explosion had become a sort of colorful, stylized eruption—almost glamorous in its effect. Spielberg wanted grit, not glamour. He and his aides basically deconstructed their Panavision cameras, stripping the lenses of coating, altering the shutter openings, fixing blood packs to handheld cameras and increasing their ability to vibrate. The result was a riveting, unglamorized D-Day, not a slick, action movie. The script's third-act limitations no longer seemed to matter.

Most of the world's top film directors, if pressed, will admit that, unlike Steven Spielberg, they don't really like directing. They relish the overall process, to be sure. They like hammering the script into shape, enjoy casting their actors and thrive on the creative tensions of the editing room.

It's what happens on the set that they don't particularly covet. Roberto Benigni admits he doesn't sleep at night, and he hears voices demanding, "What are you doing?" Mike Newell finds himself desperately searching for ways to create a sense of spontaneity, knowing that movie spontaneity must be rehearsed and preordained. Peter Weir habitually listens to music, turning it louder and louder when he's troubled, and finds himself wishing he could "cram his trailer full of Gauguins and van Goghs and all the great art in history" to stir his imagination.

Shooting a movie is as much a study in desperation as it is in inspiration. But more desperation because the pressure is too intense, the time frame too short, the financial risk too great and the egos too fragile. Indisputably, the director is the captain of his ship, but, irrespective of everyone's best intentions, the ship habitually heads into uncharted waters.

Were a corporate human resources guru allowed on the set of a movie, he would call it "a flawed work environment." He would be right, but he wouldn't know what to do about it.

The primary reason for this dysfunction is lack of communication. A group of mostly strangers has been assembled, often in an inhospitable location, and asked to work in harmony under demanding circumstances. The shooting days are limited, the budget closely monitored, the cast quarrelsome. Each individual is guarding his turf, feeling this is his only line of defense against the absolute monarch of the production, the director.

In an environment of semi-paranoid, noncommunicative turf guarders, the director more often than not also feels he's on alien ground. He may have previously worked with a few key members of his crew—the cinematographers, the assistant director—but most are unknowns. He's probably rehearsed the principal members of his cast for a week or two, but he also knows their behavior is unpredictable once he yells, "Action." Most of all, he realizes that he must display a command presence—a difficult role for the standard introvert or passive-aggressive.

Directors usually aren't very good communicators, hence their disciples often feel rudderless and unappreciated. Visit a movie set and you'll usually hear the bit actors or grips complaining that "we're just drifting along; there's no leadership."

Ask a filmmaker what he's thinking about on the set, and he'll either say something self-effacing like, "Just trying to stay alive," or something self-important like, "I'm trying to transform the commonplace into art."

In fact, his mind will probably be roaming over a cluttered landscape of demands and issues. And he surely won't have all the answers.

If he's prepping a scene, he's wondering, first and foremost, where to put the camera. Should he block out the scene, let his actors rehearse their lines, then place his cameras to accommodate their movements, or should he choreograph his actors to accommodate his camera movements? Should he use a handheld camera to stay in close to his actors, as Steven Soderbergh is prone to do, or should his camera be stationary? Barry Levinson likes to use two cameras, the second camera capturing unexpected angles, while Steven Spielberg favors one camera, to ensure that he captures the actor's true eye line.

Even as he sets up his cameras and lights his scene, the director is trying to establish his point of view. Spielberg feels every scene has its own "theme," which he wishes to reinforce. Curtis Hanson calls it "a visual key," which is played out as the actors rehearse the scene. It's the filmmaker's job to structure the scene; once it starts, the scene belongs to the actors. And many directors instinctively resist this loss of control.

Alfred Hitchcock, who admitted his disdain for actors, would instruct his cast on the minutiae of their performance, often delivering line readings. Spielberg will avoid talking too much to actors, mindful of the fact that each actor has his own instincts about performance, and that a director, within reason, shouldn't impose his own instincts on an actor's. Indeed, some directors, such as Clint Eastwood or Oliver Stone, will encourage improvisation. Mike Leigh basically wants his actors to fall so completely into their roles that they effectively create the script.

During these rehearsals, some directors will stand back and study their actors; others will become so involved they almost become part of the scene, while still others utilize all manner of video viewfinders so that they can see what the camera sees. James Cameron, among others, champions this procedure.

Once the cameras roll, the filmmaker may seem alternatively frantic, ecstatic or merely quietly assuaged. A combination of desperation and fatalism governs his behavior. To the crew, his demeanor may seem eccentric, even disoriented. The crew will busy itself to create a new setup, moving lights and equipment, laying down dolly track, and rearranging backdrops. The director, meanwhile, is hoping desperately that, out of twelve hours of shooting, he may elicit two minutes of wonderful film. Those two minutes are the target of his quest; the rest of the material is simply time wasted. "You look for the inspiration," says Spielberg. "You look for all the mojos."

"Film directors are terrible people," observes one veteran studio executive. "But I haven't decided whether they start out that way or that's what the process does to them."

Some directors, especially the young ones, actually enjoy the angst. Alexander Payne, whose credits include *Election*, feels he does his best work against the biggest obstacles. "Directors shouldn't get everything they want," he observes. "I find I'm sharpest when I have to compromise, to 'make do' with an attenuated scene or and inadequate location."

His more senior colleagues would argue with him. They feel it's their mandate to hold out for the highest budget, the most opulent sets, the longest possible shooting schedule—and also to demand the most from their actors. These demands, along with those of the cast and crew, create the aura of tension, even panic, on a movie set. It's also why veteran filmmakers come to equate conflict with success. Visit a serene set, they will testify, and you know the film will probably be a yawn. Visit one where the principals are embattled and everything appears to be on the verge of chaos, and the artistic rewards will be bountiful. *Jaws* and *The Godfather* were unhappy, if not utterly miserable, sets. Their directors arrived on location each morning fearful that they would be summarily fired before the day's work was completed. Yet Steven Spielberg and Francis Ford Coppola survived, and their films were cinematic milestones.

All this explains why producers and studio chiefs ulcerate endlessly over the choice of a director for any given project. They wrestle with such practical questions as: Who's hot? Who's available? Who's affordable? Who will attract the necessary financing?

Then come the intangibles: Whose talents will mesh with the material? Who will deliver the movie on budget? Finally, and most intangible of all, who will be a comfortable creative partner? That is, if having a "creative partner" is even in the cards.

It is axiomatic that the best director for any given movie will probably not be the most congenial partner. From the standpoint of sheer commerce, for example, the tough old-time director Howard Hawks surely would stand high on the list of anyone's all-time wish list. Here was a filmmaker who not only turned out hits, but also did it in every genre from *Scarface* to *Bringing Up Baby* and *Sergeant York* to *To Have and Have Not* to *Gentlemen Prefer Blondes* and Westerns, such as *Red River*. More important, as film critic Todd McCarthy reminds us in his incisive biography, Hawks felt an urgent need to make "audience movies." "He wanted to make good films with big stars that bring in a lot of money," McCarthy wrote. "For Hawks there was something wrong with a picture if it didn't go over with the public. Unlike John Ford, his drawer was not full of difficult, uncommercial, socially conscious scripts that he thought perhaps he would be allowed to make if he would play ball with the studios."

All this was pleasing to Hawks' producers. The trade-off was that they had to cope with a standoffish, cold-eyed, manipulative patrician who insisted on doing things his way. Anyone who gave him an argument would be frozen with a look of total disdain.

More often than not, working successfully with a world-class filmmaker inevitably means simply getting out of his way. The producer who finds himself in business with a James Cameron or a George Lucas has effectively reeled in a two-hundred-pound marlin. He should feel very proud. But he also should be prepared to run for cover.

Paradoxically, the studio may not even be on his side during the fishing expedition. Though studios always pay lip service to big-name directors, they also become nervous when confronted with their actual presence. A classic case involved *Gorillas in the Mist*, a project that attracted the interest of both Cameron and Oliver Stone, two talented but immensely egocentric filmmakers.

Warner Bros. was in final discussions with Michael Apted, a middling English director whose best feature credit was *Coal Miner's Daughter*, but was already fretful about the heavy expenditures on the project's development. It had suffered severe overruns on its last gorilla flick: a Tarzan film titled *Greystoke*. There was also a TV mini-series on the same subject in development, which was making everyone nervous. The studio was thrilled that the material now elicited interest from world-class alchemists, but at the same time it knew it would undoubtedly mean a much more expensive picture. Yet no one could refuse a Jim Cameron meeting, which took place at his sprawling Mullholland Drive home atop the city. Introduced by Gail Anne Hurd, his producer and then wife, Cameron set forth his vision for the movie. His affable manner and soft-spoken approach masked a steely resolve—

one that had become renowned in the industry. He knew exactly what he wanted this film to be. On the other hand, here was someone who was not going to engage in a creative shoot out. This might have been an audition all right, but it was Cameron auditioning everyone else.

At the end of the meeting, everyone seemed to believe that Cameron was coming aboard. Almost as an afterthought, however he'd warned that he was not immediately available but could start in five or six months. Hearing that, the attitudes of the Warner Bros. executives changed noticeably. Twenty-five yards from Cameron's door the producers were congratulating themselves, but the two studio executives at the meeting had already made up their minds not to wait—not for Cameron nor for Oliver Stone. While acknowledging Cameron's greatness, they nonetheless hoped greatness could find Apted.

Cameron may have said all the right words but he also represented a risk, and his request for a five-month wait provided a convenient out. The movie was Apted's. Cameron turned his attention instead to *Titanic*, which produced record box office results, but also realized every studio's worst fears in terms of excess.

A director whose style resembled that of Cameron in a previous generation was Richard Brooks, best known for *In Cold Blood*. Anyone entering into a deal with Brooks quickly learned the rules of the game. He was the boss. Everyone else was irrelevant.

When Brooks signed on to do a project called *$ (Dollars)* at Columbia, Bob Weitman, the top studio executive at the time, naively expected that when Brooks completed his screenplay he would routinely turn it in to the studio. That was wrong. Brooks curtly let it be known that he had no intention of letting his script fall into the hands of what he called "the little people." His idea of creative collaboration was to summon the top studio exec to his incredibly disheveled office, hand him two or three pages of script at a time to read, provided, upon reading them, he promptly turned them back to him.

When it came to budgeting his film, Brooks was similarly un-
forthcoming. John Veitch, Columbia's head of physical production,
got only the most basic information—the shooting schedule, locations and names of the cast. When it ultimately came time for that
green light to flash, a call was placed to the corporate chief, Leo
Jaffe, in New York. Veitch wanted to express his concern about the
budget, but Jaffe didn't want to talk about either script or budget.
"Can he make his release date?" was his only question. Once learning that this seemed likely, that was all that was needed. "Let's bite
the bullet; I want the picture," he snapped.

$ (*Dollars*), which starred Goldie Hawn and Warren Beatty, turned
out to be a flop. Brooks' next film at Columbia, made under the same
ground rules, ironically was called *Bite the Bullet*. Again the studio financed it, but with not much better results.

So much tension surrounds the filmmaker because few understand what he really does and what should be expected of him.
In corporate America, virtually everyone, from chairman to office
boy, is given a precise job description. Yet no one has ever devised
a job description for a director and, indeed, no two directors do
things alike. Further, directors function differently from country to
country.

In most parts of Europe, especially in France, a director sees himself as the true author, or auteur, of a movie. In many cases, he may
also have written the screenplay. But even if a professional screenwriter has crafted it, the French filmmaker feels that the ideas and
images put on the screen embody his unique vision. He has final cut;
he even owns the copyright. No one questions his creative judgments, certainly not the producer. For the distributor, the decision-
making process is simple: He can either release it or turn it down,
but he can't tamper.

In the heyday of François Truffaut and Jean-Luc Godard in France
and of Federico Fellini and Michelangelo Antonioni in Italy, their

unique vision probably would not have flourished in a less autocratic environment.

When the Hollywood studio system came of age in the 1920s, by contrast, the presumption was that the director was little more than a hired hand. He was given a script by a producer who said, "Shoot it." By the time studios reached their zenith in the late 1930s, some filmmakers such as Alfred Hitchcock, John Ford and William Wyler had achieved sufficient stature that producers and studio chiefs took pains to caress their egos and applaud their casting ideas, but it was still customary for powerful producers such as Hal Wallis or David O. Selznick to supervise the cut and for studio chiefs to preview it and make still further changes. It was, after all, the studio's film.

The balance of power began to shift in the late 1960s and early 1970s when several developments conspired to give directors more clout. The studios had lost both their influence and their financial strength as a result of TV's fierce onslaught. A new generation of filmmakers, led by Spielberg, Lucas and Coppola, were making their mark, all influenced by Europe's auteurs and eager to build their own power base. With the star system fading, directors suddenly found themselves the center of the universe and, hence, demanding European-type credits. Instead of the normal "directed by" credit, it became "a film by."

Even as the blockbuster mentality took hold in the 1980s and more commercially oriented directors came into their own, more directors demanded and received final cut. Avid young filmmakers emerged from music videos or commercials to direct movies, all of them insisting on final cut and auteur-style credits. The problem was that they weren't schooled as auteurs and displayed scant understanding of the intricacies of the process. Many seemed hopelessly lost at the script stage and reduced to total confusion in the editing room.

Thus Hollywood has come to find itself in an awkward dilemma. The director is god, but few are willing to line up for worship. Indeed, many of the industry's most powerful writers are in open rebellion against the so-called "possessory" credit. "I wrote a play called *A Few Good Men* and then a screenplay for the movie entitled *A Few Good Men*, yet the credit on the movie read, 'a Rob Reiner Film,'" observes Aaron Sorkin, a gifted writer who, partly out of impatience with this system, turned away from screenplays to TV series such as *The West Wing*.

Faced with this dilemma, the fraternity of studio executives, producers and agents in Hollywood has found itself playing ego games with the directing community. A director might be assured that it's his show—the final word is his and he has a contract to prove it. At the same time, everyone stands prepared to compensate for a filmmaker's perceived frailties. A director, renowned as a good "shooter" but as a functional illiterate when it comes to the script, would meet with the writer, but that writer gets the message that he'd better take further marching orders from the studio or the producer. It's not unusual for a producer to hire yet another writer behind his director's back (the guilds representing both writers and directors officially frown on this practice). Similarly, a filmmaker who is famously indecisive in the cutting room will find himself backed up by another editing team introduced into the process by the studio.

It's a high-risk game, and open warfare now and then breaks out between the director and the "suits." Final control may still rest contractually in the director's hands should he wish to exercise it. But, the task of building a career has become so complex that those directors who have anything resembling a survival instinct know it's a good idea to keep the studio on their side.

Filmmakers during the era of studio supremacy may have generated four or five movies a year, turning out occasional turkeys, but all the while honing their craft. Today a director may go four or five years between films, confronting a succession of delays, all the while feeling a growing pressure to prove himself. Either he's waiting for a writer to finish that next draft or he's on hold until his star becomes available. By the time all this is resolved, a key location may have become impractical, forcing still further delays.

Sometimes, too, a director may find himself caught in corporate politics—witness what happened to one world-class filmmaker when he undertook making a film for Tristar, owned by Sony, a Japanese company, about sumo wrestling, a favorite Japanese pastime.

The Czech-born Milos Forman was the ultimate alchemist. His extraordinary gift was apparent from the moment he shot his first American film, *Taking Off*. Hits such as *One Flew Over the Cuckoo's Nest* and *Amadeus* only confirmed his promise. His choice of subjects, however, was as quirky as his talent. Now suddenly, he was keen on doing a comedy about the art of sumo. It wasn't clear why a Czech would fixate on sumo, but many never understood why he'd decided to shoot the 1960s hit musical *Hair*, either. Nonetheless, Tristar could hardly contain its excitement over the fact that Milos Forman was doing the film. Because of the subject matter, the movie would have to be shot substantially in Japan, but this seemed not to be a concern. The parent company had no creative control over its films, but surely the senior Japanese could help in arranging contacts for Forman and in clearing locations. The key would be Norio Ohga, the chairman of Sony in Japan, a brilliant and complex individual. While he was very much the protégé of Akio Morita, the founder of Sony, he was less conservative and more Westernized.

A conference call with Ohga about Forman's mission set all this in motion. Ohga was told that a comedy about sumo wrestling was in the works, and that the director hoped that Ohga could introduce him to the head of the sumo federation. Ohga didn't reply, but uttered a quick guttural sound that seemed to be the start of a further question. It proved instead to be an answer, which no one understood at the time. When told that a script would soon be dispatched to him, he responded with something less than enthusiasm.

Ultimately a dinner was set up in Tokyo involving Forman, studio execs and their corporate hosts at one of the most expensive restaurant in Tokyo—the sort of place where the washroom attendant expects a fifty-dollar tip for a towel. Ohga was polite but distant. Following the ritual toasts, he leaned over to his executives and declared, "We are not making this film." It was not so much an advisory as a corporate command. The boss had spoken and his word was not subject to negotiation. A world-renowned filmmaker had come halfway around the world to meet him with the expectation that he would help him get his film made. Ohga's strategy: Listen to the director's ideas; accord him every courtesy; let no one lose face; then firmly, but politely, say no. After all, sumo was a virtual religion in Japan. A company such as Sony could not risk rattling the cage of the sumo establishment.

Milos Forman, of course, did not give a damn about anyone losing face. He was understandably furious. He felt Sony had betrayed him. He tried other approaches to the vaunted sumo federation, but they simply ignored him as though he were a pesky insect. Ultimately he got paid for not making the movie.

Though a career in directing increasingly resembles a high-wire act, filmmakers are well compensated as risk takers. Director deals have become as rich and as complex as those of superstars. Agents for top-rung directors demand as much as $10 million in up-front fees for their clients. Relative newcomers with one hit under their belt routinely ask $3 million. These salaries are augmented by hefty percentages of the gross receipts. Steven Spielberg's formula climbs to a fifty-fifty split once a movie has recouped its initial negative cost. Filmmakers also demand a substantial slice of other revenue streams—video, merchandising, pay TV, etc.—and further augment their deals, in some cases, by negotiating co-producer credit, thus invading the producer's cut of salaries and points. And some directors have been known to insist on still further fees for contributing to the script.

Based on an actual film, a typical deal for a middle-to-high-rung director will run something like this: A basic fee of $5 million against 5 percent of the first dollar gross receipts (i.e., the director gets a piece of every dollar paid into the theater box office). In addition, the director receives a $4,000 per week nonaccountable expense allowance. He'll also receive six round-trip first-class airline tickets to and from the location, a full-sized rental car, an additional car and driver on location, a first-class trailer and a personal assistant.

Besides all this, a series of bonuses will kick in if the movie reaches the status of a hit. His percentage of the gross will escalate from 5 to 7.5 percent at such point that the movie grosses $125 million, and to 9.5 percent when it hits the $150 million mark. In addition, the director is paid another $250,000 when the U.S. box office gross equals twice the final negative cost of the picture, an additional $250,000 when the film hits $100 million; $500,000 at $150 million; and $500,000 at $200 million. The director is thus doubly covered in the eventuality that the movie's box office performance takes off.

Finally, the director is accorded approvals over virtually every element of the film, including the crew department heads, composer, casting director, all locations, the production lab, the head of special effects, the credits, the final mix, the initial trailer and even down to which members of the press are allowed on the set. Rights of consultation also extend to the ad campaign and the theatrical release pattern within the United States.

Do directors deserve all this? In the Darwinian world of movies, anyone deserves whatever he can get. Since every other part of the studio filmmaking equation has the effect of driving up costs, why should directors abstain? Their rationalizations are persuasive. "Look, when I work on a film, it becomes my film," argues Michael Bay. "I'm out there in the vanguard, working with the writer. I may be in preproduction for a year, then shooting for six months, then in postproduction for another year. It's my ass that's on the line."

It's the director who will assemble the cast, attract the stars, bully and cajole the actors into saying their lines in take after take. It's the director who may come up with the special vision that will transmogrify the ordinary into the exceptional. The script of *American Beauty* was sharp and literate, but it was the young theater director, Sam Mendes who found a way to elevate the material and skew the performances into a truly memorable cinematic experience.

Yet it's also the very same director who can mess up royally, who can trash a fine script and embarrass gifted actors. Nora Ephron thought she was shaping a sharp black comedy in *Lucky Numbers* with a "can't miss" cast headed by John Travolta. No one went to see it. Rob Reiner thought he'd re-created *When Harry Met Sally* when he started work on a movie called *The Story of Us* with Michelle Pfeiffer and Bruce Willis. The film was utterly lifeless.

A "name" director is no guarantee of success. The same Ridley Scott who delivered *Thelma & Louise* and *Gladiator* also directed a turkey called *White Squall*. Sydney Pollack, the edgy maverick who directed *Tootsie*, was also responsible for that stodgy anachronism, *Random Hearts*.

Star athletes like Tiger Woods may have winning streaks, but few directors seem to. Quentin Tarantino will leap from *Pulp Fiction* to *Jackie Brown*, Cameron Crowe from *Jerry Maguire* to *Almost Famous*. Indeed many savvy stars prefer to work with a filmmaker coming off a flop because he will likely be more open to an exchange of ideas. A filmmaker coming off a megahit, lionized by critics, may fight for his every idea and for every frame of film. Given the right of final cut, he will surely win those fights.

From the studio's point of view, and even that of the producer, final cut has become anathema. Many directors tend to fall in love with every scene, resulting in painfully overlong movies. No one would second-guess David Lean for insisting on his three-hour and forty-two-minute cut on *Lawrence of Arabia*, an epic saga that cast a spell over its audience. But when Oliver Stone sent forth his three-hour biopic of Richard Nixon, audiences all but boycotted the film. Perhaps the ultimate example of directorial self-indulgence was Martin Brest's turgid film starring Brad Pitt, *Meet Joe Black*. Brest's film, a remake *of Death Takes a Holiday*, earned the epithet around Universal of "Meet Joe Slack" grinding on for three hours and one second of protracted close-ups and lugubrious exchanges about mortality. Surprisingly, Casey Silver, Brest's long-term friend and the studio chief at Universal, was totally supportive of Brest's cut.

It was about 7 P.M. when one newspaper editor received a phone call from Casey Silver. His voice carried a certain urgency. The director's cut of *Meet Joe Black* had just been completed, Silver said, and he was very excited. "I'd like to show the film to you," he continued, "but I'd like you to see it alone in my private screening room. Then tell me how you feel about it."

It was unusual, but not unprecedented, for a studio chief to extend this sort of invitation. Usually, however, there's a hidden agenda. Perhaps there was a disagreement among executives at the studio and an outside opinion was being sought. In the case of *The Truman Show*, for example, the studio and producer Scott Rudin were quarreling over whether to take the film to the Cannes Film Festival. Most often, however, invitations of this sort were given when a studio chief, or one of his associates, was convinced that the film in question would be a spectacular hit, perhaps a sleeper, and wanted to marshal support in the press.

Silver is a serious, almost grave man and so his invitation was to be taken seriously. There was, of course, the usual draconian condition from Silver: "If you like the film, you can tell anyone you want about it. If you disagree with me and dislike the film, I would appreciate it if you kept that view to yourself. Can you live with that?"

"OK by me," the editor replied. He actually was curious about the movie. He had seen *Midnight Run*, one of Brest's earlier films, which showed great promise but also showed him to be a self-indulgent filmmaker. But after all, Brad Pitt, an important young star, had cast his lot with Brest, so he must have something going for him.

The editor drove out to the studio and, per the promise, he was the only person in the screening room. Three hours later, he was numb. Also a bit angry. The movie he had seen was astonishingly dull. He felt as though his sensibilities had taken a pounding. He decided to head home, have a drink and then decide what he would say to Casey Silver in the morning.

Silver had something else in mind as he materialized suddenly in the doorway of the screening room. "What did you think?" he asked.

The editor never expected there'd be an instant confrontation. "I must tell you honestly, Casey, I just hated this movie. Hated it."

"Well, you're wrong. You know that. I mean, I respect your opinion, but you're dead wrong."

"And I respect yours," he mumbled. "I have just one word of friendly advice. There's a wonderful editor named Billy Weber. He worked with Marty Brest on his last film. If I were in your shoes, I would call Billy and beg him to take an hour out of this movie. At two hours it has a chance. I know you don't want to hear that . . ."

"An hour! You've got to be kidding."

"Look Casey, we made a deal. I will live by it. No one will know I saw this movie. Except my wife, perhaps. I have to explain to her why I'm so grumpy."

Casey Silver managed a pained smile. "Look, thanks," he offered. "I appreciate your taking the time."

The editor never learned precisely why he had been asked to see the movie under these circumstances—whether a controversy was raging within the studio and Casey was looking for outside support or what. *Meet Joe Black* was released to a dim reception, and, not long thereafter, Casey Silver was also released as production chief at Universal.

Often the atmosphere surrounding the deal-making process colors the creative relationships during the shoot itself. If the negotiation is contentious, the filmmaker may feel that he'll always be at odds with producer, and that he must thus go it alone during the production process. The nature of the creative collaboration on a film reveals itself early in the game during meetings with the writer or during discussions about budget and location.

The collaborative or noncollaborative nature of these meetings reflects the insecurity of the filmmaker as well as his attitude toward his colleagues. Given the frenzy commonly associated with each of the three principal stages of the filmmaking process, a productive creative collaboration can greatly help all sides.

In preproduction, the director often is stretched thin among his responsibilities for choosing his cast and crew, working with the writer, selecting locations, hammering out a production schedule and preparing his shot list. Filmmakers vary widely in their attitudes toward these tasks. Some, like Frank Darabont (*The Shawshank Redemption*), insist on meticulous preparation; they want to lock in their script prior to shooting. Others, like Oliver Stone, thrive on chaos. "I don't worship the script as a sacred thing," he declares. "Sometimes I just get rid of it and improvise on the set. It has to be spontaneous. It has to be felt."

Again, some directors not only work side by side with the writer, but also go so far as to storyboard their scenes. Curtis Hanson (*L.A. Confidential*) finds this process constricting. "I visualize the scenes and setups while I'm scripting each scene," he says. To Anthony Minghella, directing is simply an extension of the writing process. "You write on paper, then you swap that instrument for a camera and continue to write. You keep writing all the way through the filmmaking process."

Francis Ford Coppola, a longtime technophile took all this a step further. Before he started principal photography on *Bram Stoker's*

Dracula, he told startled studio bosses that he'd actually had what he called "a pre-preview" and obtained the relevant audience response that would form the basis for final script changes. "This is the actual reaction to the movie, so I know what to do because now I know how I can take thirty pages out of the movie," he said. "I've been on this show for three or four weeks, but like always, I look at it as an experiment that is going to teach me something. I fooled around with every way to rehearse a film, or 'pre-see' it before you've actually made it. This came about through my relationship with Akio Morita of Sony. When he showed me some electronic imaging Mavica cameras, immediately I saw the application to my pre-previews. The way I used to do it, actors would read my script, and record it like a radio show with some selected music, pre-dubbed effects. That took several weeks to edit. I then played it to an audience and made changes in the script. Then with this new technology I dumped the whole audio onto three-quarter-inch tape, and with the Mavica system, took hundreds and hundreds of images from symbolist paintings, which I then integrated. Then I showed it to a group and got their reactions. I did all this within the first six weeks I was on the film." Coppola even offered a copy to the studio toppers and said, "Here, go look at it." As Coppola put it, "I've always wanted the radar that lets you see a film before you make it so you can really do a good job."

For filmmakers, the entire preproduction process involves a network of partnerships with writer, producer, cinematographer and principal cast. Often the chemistry between director and stars overrides all others, and the closeness of their bond provides a cone of silence, warding off the input of outsiders. Such was the case between Barry Levinson and Warren Beatty on *Bugsy*. Similar alliances included such formidable players as Sydney Pollack and Robert Redford or Howard Hawks and John Wayne.

On the other hand, a director and producer may also develop the sort of symbiotic relationship that permits one effectively to cover for the other—Alan Pakula and Robert Mulligan (*To Kill a Mockingbird*) had that sort of mutual trust. Sam Spiegel and David Lean had an intuitive bond, which strengthened their hand through several complicated productions.

During the shoot itself, a producer can play a pivotal role for his movie by maintaining a crucial "overview." While the director and crew become absorbed in day-to-day, scene-by-scene problems, it's the producer who must keep his eye on such an overriding issue as whether the key emotion of the film is being delivered. Will this be a thriller without thrills or a comedy without laughs?

Sometimes the producer, too, loses perspective. David O. Selznick achieved a sort of filmic immortality in producing *Gone With the Wind*, but his enthusiasms on some of his other films were utterly misguided. During the shoot of a dreadful movie called *The Garden of Allah*, Selznick rhapsodized to his director: "This script is poetry. I want to hear every syllable on the sound track, every consonant, every vowel." Selznick got what he wanted, but it only further guaranteed the movie's disastrous failure.

Filmmakers enter a whole new world in postproduction. Suddenly the pressure is off—or at least a new sort of pressure takes its place. The nattering hordes demanding instant answers have scattered to other productions. There are no more actors to placate. The director's universe comes down to his editor and his composer, unless there also are special effects wizards lurking about working on their magical morphs. A casting mistake can be all but obliterated by editing out scenes, revoicing or even shooting new material. Stanley Kubrick in *Eyes Wide Shut* was not above substituting a new actress after his film was complete, shooting new scenes for her. "I call my editor my second brain," Robert Zemeckis explains. "The madness, the insanity of shooting is over. When you wrap, it instantly funnels down to just you, your editor and your film and you don't have to worry whether it's rainy out there or the sun is coming up."

Some directors bask in their own work, culling through their footage for months before delivering an edited version. Francis Ford Coppola fondled and caressed each frame of *The Conversation* for well over a year before finally zeroing in on a playable cut.

Such a luxury is not available for directors of so-called "event" movies, which almost always have preordained release dates. On *JFK*, Oliver Stone had a four-month window to complete his long, complex film. He thus set up four editing teams in adjacent rooms, moving relentlessly from one to the other. If things weren't working right in one room, he'd shift around his editing personnel. As Stone notes, "There's a natural flow to editing as there is to writing and we were playing with time—present, past and future—so it was an exercise in totally disassociative editing."

Once the director delivers his cut to the studio, yet another process is triggered. Regardless of the film's running time, the studio nearly always argues that the film be further tightened. If the director has final cut, this debate itself becomes a lot shorter, but even here the studio customarily advocates previews or screenings before focus groups. The studio hopes it will elicit data from the test screenings to bolster its case for further edits. In some cases, these audience screenings prove helpful to everyone's cause. When the apocalyptic movie *Deep Impact* was first screened for the heads of its two financing entities, DreamWorks and Paramount, all the various executives, including Steven Spielberg, deemed the film to be in excellent shape. Shortly thereafter, however, a test screening before a live audience proved disastrous with many walking out before the end. The film was reedited, a new voice-over narration added and a new scene was shot with Morgan Freeman, who played the president. Further, the subplot involving two teenage lovers was sharply curtailed. The new version tested positively, and the movie became a box office hit. "This sort of thing can be a very humbling experience," recalls Walter Parkes, the co-chief of production at DreamWorks. "You easily forget that no one is as smart as 500 civilians sitting in a theater."

Yet another flashpoint for postproduction debate surrounds the issue of ratings. Once a director completes his cut, it is dispatched to a ratings board set up by the Motion Picture Association of America, a self-regulatory body that dispenses its G, PG, PG-13, R or NC-17 ratings. The studios customarily wince at an R, which restricts a film's potential audience, requiring that filmgoers under the age of 17 be accompanied by an adult.

Inevitably, filmmakers tend to be skeptical about the entire ratings process. Some display a high degree of gamesmanship in negotiating with the ratings board. In one case, for example, a director submitted a cut containing some sixteen mentions of "fuck" in the dialogue. When his film was slapped with an NC-17, he cut the "fucks" down to two and resubmitted his movie. It received an R. In making these concessions, the director felt he had managed to divert attention from two sexually explicit scenes, which he was eager to protect. The "fucks" were a mere bargaining ploy.

Even as the completed cut survives these hurdles, yet another obstacle awaits: music. Though many filmmakers are decisive during the editing process, their resolve crumbles when they confront the score. Clint Eastwood, an especially disciplined filmmaker, admits he lives in dread of that moment when a composer delivers what he calls "a sweeping score" that all but overwhelms the movie. He is not alone. Filmmakers throw out roughly one-third of all film scores, demanding either an entirely new approach or a new composer. The composers in turn feel that directors are congenitally incapable of describing the sort of "sound" they are seeking, and hence are impossible to satisfy. On *Il Postino*, Michael Radford recalls sitting with his renowned Italian composer, Ennio Morricone, as he played the proposed theme on his piano. The music was grand, but Radford was beside himself, finally blurting, "I'd like the music for this movie to be more . . . discreet." His renowned composer stared at him for a moment, then responded, "I do not do 'discreet' music," and he promptly walked off the picture.

When magic strikes, and the music perfectly complements the film, the results can be extraordinary. James Cameron, an especially opinionated filmmaker, recalls instructing James Horner that he didn't want "a conventional" period score for *Titanic*. "I don't want to hear a big violin section," he intoned.

Horner seemed surprised: "No violins?" he repeated. "Find another way to be emotional," Cameron urged. This is the sort of vague advisory that drives composers up the wall. In this case, Horner got it perfectly. When he finally sat down with his director to play the three main themes, Cameron recalls, "I literally cried. I knew I was there."

Given the highly emotional atmosphere surrounding the entire filmmaking process, inevitably there are times when a chasm opens up between the director on the one side and the studio or producer on the other. When this occurs, most often it is the producer who gets the ax.

Dismissal of the director during the actual production of a film brings with it some formidable risks. Since most major productions have co-financing partners, there's always the possibility that one of these entities will withdraw its backing. There's also the star to consider: Will he back the action or will he, too, withdraw? The process of finding a replacement for the director can also pose a dilemma. The new director must be prepared to start quickly and not succumb to the temptation to tinker with the screenplay. Many projects have become hopelessly bogged down when the new person at the helm brought in a new writer and one delay after another ensued.

More often than not, a studio opts to stay with the original film-maker, irrespective of the problems involved, thus avoiding the potential bad publicity, not to mention other ramifications. When James Cameron was going vastly over budget on *Titanic*, the rage felt by production executives at Twentieth Century Fox was indescribable. Not only had Cameron deceived the studio on the budget, but also he was uniformly discourteous in fielding inquiries about the progress of the film. Yet Fox was in a dilemma: As recklessly as Cameron seemed to be behaving, it was his show. He wrote it; he cast it; the movie somehow lived in his head. Who else could carry this filmic leviathan forward without losing its dramatic tension? In the end, Fox executives decided to play out their gamble—perhaps the richest in movie history. Their patience, or temerity, paid off handsomely.

The bottom line is this: Studios are owned by corporate hierarchs. Men and women of this ilk don't like taking risks, but they don't want the word to filter out in the creative community that they are bullies, that they don't respect their filmmaking brethren.

Moreover, there's always the chance that the movie will surprise them and that what seemed like a total loser will emerge an Oscar-winning embellishment to their career.

That, after all, is what keeps everyone going—the feeling that a wonderful surprise might be just around the corner, that what seemed like schlock may turn out to be art, or at least inspired commerce. Hollywood has always lived from one astonishing accident to the next. No one, it's true, really does know anything.

CUT TO: Peter Bart on Walt Disney

When I got to Hollywood in the late 1960s, I quickly realized that an entire generation of stars and moguls seemed poised to pass from the scene. It was a moment of historic transition. These were seminal figures in the entertainment industry—men whose presence could never be replicated. At the time I was a reporter with the *New York Times*, a newspaper that carries great clout around the world. I decided to use the access that the *Times* provided me to meet as many of these old-timers as I could. I knew that some of my requests for meetings would be scorned. A few of the old moguls were fabled for their gruffness—Jack Warner and Walt Disney, for example. Nonetheless, I decided to give it a try.

Within the next six months I lunched with Samuel Goldwyn and David O. Selznick, the two old mavericks of the independent scene. I visited with Warner and Disney, with Hitchcock and Billy Wilder, with William Holden and Richard Burton. I asked them how they viewed the changes sweeping their industry and inquired about their view of the future. As predicted, their responses varied widely. Selznick was remote and dismissive. His later years as a producer had been disappointing, and he clearly was a bitter man. Goldwyn, by contrast, was effusive and eager to talk. He reminisced about *The Best Years of Our Lives*, then added, "That was a long time ago. We've passed lot of water since then." A fabled malapropist, Goldwyn's eyes twinkled. "I just threw that in in case you needed a new Goldwynism to take back to your newspaper." Jack Warner seemed confused by everything happening at his studio and in the movie business. He'd clearly lost touch. Burton was, by contrast, superbly informed and articulate about the state of the pop arts while William Holden was distanced and tragically ravaged by alcoholism.

Of all the moguls, I'd expected the least from Disney. And indeed when I first encountered him over lunch at the studio commissary, he seemed a bit suspicious. As we talked, however, it became clear that, among the "founders," he was the most engaged in the art and craft of movies, especially animation. Indeed, he was incapable of discussing a project, new or old, without growing animated himself. Old Walt was especially thrilled by his new theme park, by the possibility of extending that vision to other cities and other countries and of translating some of its precepts to the design of model communities. Sure, Walt was crusty and cranky, but he was also a true visionary and relished sharing his ideas with others.

Old Walt was often accused of running his company as though it were a neighborhood candy store. He seemed to sense the encroaching shadow of Michael Eisner's mega-corporatism. Clearly Walt himself was not a creature of business, which he readily acknowledged. Once when we were having lunch, I asked him a question that had business overtones. He started to respond, then paused and said, "Before answering, I'd like to ask my Jew to come over and help me on this one." He motioned toward a man sitting two tables away at the commissary who probably was his chief financial officer, but I tried to tell him that we didn't need him. I didn't want him turning and saying, "Oh, Jew, please come over here," so I quickly changed the subject back to theme parks. Mind you, I didn't feel this behavior reflected any glint of anti-Semitism; this was simply the blunt way old Walt talked. In his flat midwestern accent, it didn't sound like a pejorative, just a job description.

Later, he even showed me around his theme park, explaining its intimate inner workings. I'd taken my seven-year-old daughter along, but Walt, true to legend, did not seem comfortable with her. He asked if one of his aides could look after her while we made our way around the park, and I readily consented. Theme parks were really for adults, not children, he seemed to be saying, and the child in him was clearly never going to perish.

Not long thereafter Walt died, and his company became exactly the sort of global corporate behemoth in which he never could have survived. He was, first and foremost, a creator, not a corporatist, who seemed eager to share his ideas with the world, not merely to find ways of profiting from them.

CUT TO: Peter Guber on John Huston

In 1974 John Huston, that vision keeper extraordinaire, was prepping *The Man Who Would Be King* in Marrakech, Morocco. Huston had written the script himself based on the classic Kipling yarn, and it had sufficient weight to attract Sean Connery and Michael Caine. Huston, a truly gifted storyteller, had written a brilliant script. But I fretted that the downbeat ending would scare off some of its potential audience.

Of course, it was one thing to reach these conclusions but another to persuade Huston, the old master, that I was right and he was wrong. But I was young and immensely confident about my powers of persuasion. So, despite the advice of my skeptical colleagues, I decided to get on a plane for Marrakech and make my case in person.

Throughout the interminable plane ride from Los Angeles to Morocco, I relentlessly rehearsed my lines with every nuance and gesture. My traveling companion, John Veitch, the studio's chief of physical production, listened stoically. A tough ex-Marine, Veitch had fought battles of this sort with many other filmmakers, and he knew the score. "You gotta do what you gotta do," was all the encouragement he offered.

Feeling like a mini-mogul, I was in such a lather by the time I checked into the grand hotel, La Mamounia, that I summoned everyone to a meeting even as my bags were still making their way to my room. Veitch and John Foreman, one of the producers, led several others to the back of the lobby. As we were awaiting Huston's arrival, we all watched as a tall man in a white suit slowly made his way across the crowded open courtyard that fronted the lobby. I was already intoning my message to the assembled and well-paid minions when Sean Connery, looking very much in his James Bond mode, walked directly up to me. He poked his finger into my chest and said sternly, "Now what's all this shit about not shooting the ending we want?" I was so intimidated by this unexpected confrontation, all I could manage by way of response was, "No, I just came by to wish you luck."

Connery, always the consummate professional, clearly decided not to fire another bullet between my eyes. "Come, son, you'll buy me a drink to celebrate," he said as he guided me toward the lobby bar.

The lesson was in the pain. Leading with ego brings only a quicker surrender. The great success of the film bore out Huston's vision and enhanced a number of careers. In a creative collaborative process, I learned, you don't get caught up in winning. Be curious rather than critical. Ask high-quality questions that provoke reflection and further inquiry. Do not create a fortress mentality. Surrender the addiction to total control; it's an illusion.

5.

The Illuminati

God makes stars. It's up to producers to
find them.

SAMUEL GOLDWYN

Over the years, one director after another has nurtured the dream of rehabilitating Marlon Brando. The recent decades of Brando's film career have consisted of a series of train wrecks. His choice of vehicles suggested a path of self-destruction, exacerbated by his record of bad behavior on set after set. Brando seemed to relish the process of torturing his would-be saviors, constantly prodding his directors and publicly defying them at crucial moments. Even on *The Godfather*, Brando's finest moment in the opinion of the director and the producer, he arrived totally unprepared, having not pondered his approach to his role. It was not until the third or fourth week of production, after he had "hung" with some real-life Mafia dons and learned to emulate their mannerisms, that his performance began to take shape.

On the 2001 caper film *The Score*, Frank Oz decided he, too, would "rediscover" Brando, who this time would portray an aging master thief. The studio tried to discourage the idea. Brando was in his seventies, he was fat and he was trouble. But Oz, who had first made a name for himself directing *Little Shop of Horrors*, was determined. Michael Douglas originally had been set to head the cast, but now, instead, he signed Robert De Niro and Edward Norton—and the presence of Brando would give his movie a certain luster.

The first five weeks of the shoot were going smoothly until Brando arrived in Montreal to begin his star turn. He was, as predicted, both grumpy and enormously rotund—so fat, in fact, that the cameraman had to give serious thought as to how to shoot him. The legendary star made it clear from the first moment that he had no intention of doing what he was told. He took to addressing Frank Oz as "Miss Piggy," a crude reference to the fact that Oz got his start directing Jim Henson TV segments and was instrumental in creating the Miss Piggy character. Oz hoped that De Niro, the consummate pro, would serve as a calming influence, but it was not to be. With each passing scene, Brando became more defiant. Finally he simply took refuge in his dressing room and refused to report for his next scene, announcing that he hated his wardrobe.

David Zelon, Mandalay's man on the set, made the obligatory calls to his superiors, then—with airline ticket in hand—marched into Brando's dressing room and laid down the law. Brando would put on his clothes and do his scene. If not, he could catch the next plane to California. The production company still owed him $4 million, and he had only ten working days left. He could either do the work or get sued. Ah, the color of money! Brando sighed and slowly started getting dressed for his scene. Oz had indeed "rediscovered" Brando but had paid the predictable price.

■

First, a reality check: Stars are a pain in the butt. It is a lot more satisfying to make a movie, a play, a TV show or, for that matter, even a commercial without them. There's no giant ego to appease. There's no entourage of sycophants to placate. There are no eleventh-hour script changes to accommodate. There are no last-minute demands for a bigger trailer or a larger jet. The budget is lower. The schedule is tighter. The producer's share of the profits is greater. Besides which, it's easy to make a case that stars are an expensive anachronism.

A glance at the big surprise hits of the last few years shows that many, if not most, did not owe their success to the star system. *Titanic* did not open to big business because of Leonardo DiCaprio who was not yet a star. Similarly, *Good Will Hunting* made stars of Matt Damon and Ben Affleck. Such diverse megahits as *Jurassic Park, Bean, The Full Monty, Shakespeare in Love, The Blair Witch Project* or *Four Weddings and a Funeral* were not star-driven movies. No one argues that *The Sixth Sense* grossed $600 million around the world because of Bruce Willis.

By contrast, consider the major flops that had star casting: Could Harrison Ford save *Random Hearts*? Did Kevin Costner deliver for *The Postman*? Could Sean Connery pull anyone into *The Avengers* or John Travolta in *Lucky Numbers*? Even traditional action stars like Arnold Schwarzenegger and Sylvester Stallone have watched their batting averages tumble. Their presence in a shoot-'em-up no longer guarantees giant audiences around the world.

When Hollywood's studio system was at its apex, it was possible to make a strong case for star casting. Stars were under contract to the studios. Because of that, their salaries were affordable. Further, the studios stood firmly behind their contract players, wielding their advertising and publicity clout to build their following from picture to picture. They could take idiosyncratic actors like Humphrey Bogart, Spencer Tracy, Jimmy Stewart and Katharine Hepburn and orchestrate a vast public acceptance of them.

But that was a long time ago. The studios no longer have actors, directors and writers under contract. In fact, they're becoming more like banks or distribution companies, and less like traditional studios.

In view of all this, the smartest strategy is to avoid star casting, right? Wrong. The awful truth is that there are some solid reasons why stars are still around—indeed, why they're grabbing a bigger piece of the pie than ever. The top stars command specific and tangible market worth around the world. The presence of a Tom Hanks or Tom Cruise in a cast will elicit multimillion-dollar advances from exhibitors or TV networks in Spain or Germany or Japan. Their precise "valuation" may rise or fall based on recent hits or flops or on the genre of film (Jim Carrey is worth less in a drama than a comedy, Bruce Willis more in an action film), but their names nonetheless guarantee financing. Star-driven movies are booked into prime theaters at the best times of year—summer or the Thanksgiving-to-Christmas corridor. They play the biggest auditoriums at the megaplex, not the closets. Further, distributors spend big bucks on marketing star-driven movies. The producer doesn't have to battle for a decent opening campaign.

Besides which, star-driven movies often turn out better. One reason stars become stars to begin with is that they are super talented and charismatic. *Saving Private Ryan* was a better movie because Tom Hanks was its star. Tom Cruise played only a small role in *Magnolia*, but his brief turn elevated the whole picture. Going back a few years, what would *Casablanca* have been without Bogart and Ingrid Bergman?

And that's really the nub of it. One can array all sorts of intelligent business and aesthetic arguments against the star system, but they ultimately crumble before one overriding reality: Movies are about stars. Show business is and always has been about *star power*. Stars have an aura, a presence that lures audiences. Combine the right star with the right role, and you have a megahit.

Persuade a studio executive to level with you, and he'll admit that the most feared movies are those costing between $20 million and $30 million and having no stars. They can vanish so quickly one can almost hear the film cans clanking shut at megaplexes all over the world. As far as the studios are concerned, stars aren't employees anymore. They are franchises, ultimately earning as much as $50 million a film, depending on their share of the gross receipts and, of course, on the success of their latest movie.

The way most movies are constructed, the star can make a huge profit from a film before the studio has even recouped. Given the principle of first dollar gross, the financial risk of starring in a movie is really no risk at all.

The power of a star on the set is tantamount to that of a potentate. His every command is promptly met. If he doesn't feel like working that day, he won't. He can sleep late, then order his chef to prepare a lavish breakfast. If the director gives a stage direction that the star disdains, he will usually simply not do it, or he'll leave the set and sulk.

Every top star is renowned, and feared, for his own idiosyncratic method of defying authority. Dustin Hoffman may start nitpicking over virtually every script point, insisting on protracted sidebar creative colloquies with his director. Gene Hackman relentlessly prods his directors, as though measuring their macho. And, of course, some of the more passive-aggressive stars take another route entirely—they simply refuse to come out of their trailers or dressing rooms.

Yet star-driven films, despite their cost and attendant headaches, tend to be the path of least resistance. That is, provided the basic material can attract one. An intimate "four-wall" story or a project with distinctly "arty" overtones may not call for star casting. A multi-character ensemble piece may not embrace weighty-enough roles to attract a major talent. Very few stars will agree to cut their salaries to play a supporting role in a film—Bruce Willis is one of the few who has consistently done so.

Indeed, a project will likely not attract star casting unless it has a substantial budget to encompass star salaries of between $15 million and $25 million; it has a director with major credentials (few stars will take a shot with a newcomer); it has a major distributor (top stars do not like to have their representatives burrow through the accountings of regional distributors to recoup their gross percentages); finally, it has a solid script and, even more important, an intriguing lead character.

An actor's evaluation of a role is, of course, a subject of ongoing frustration to producers and directors alike. Stars throughout history have consistently displayed a schizoid attitude toward their choice of roles. On the one hand, they realize that their fame derives from playing a certain type—Jim Carrey as *Ace Ventura*, for example. But while Jim Carrey in a ribald comedy is a "sure thing," Carrey, like all actors, resents being typecast. Given his druthers, he'd prefer to play a disturbed, unfunny character like Andy Kaufman in *Man on the Moon* or a downbeat psychotic in *The Cable Guy*. These movies may fail at the box office but they serve as a miracle cure for an actor's ailing ego.

And it has always been thus. Stars like Bogart or Clark Gable during Hollywood's golden era were regularly on suspension for turning down roles they regarded as typecasting. When Charlie Chaplin formed United Artists in 1919, together with Mary Pickford, Douglas Fairbanks and D. W. Griffith, he immediately used his new "muscle" to foster a weary melodrama, *A Woman of Paris*. It tanked. Though such behavior often turned out to be self-destructive, that didn't prevent stars from replicating Chaplin's actions. When Paul Newman was at his peak in the 1960s, he plunged into a series of "message" films that all but destroyed his career—*WUSA*, for example. Steve McQueen helped set up the First Artists Company in the

1970s and promptly decided he'd do a movie based on the Ibsen play *Enemy of the People*. After *Titanic* propelled Leonardo DiCaprio to stardom, he turned down a series of interesting roles in movies, such as *The Talented Mr. Ripley*, to accept a rather pedestrian part in *The Beach*. Few actors, in short, exhibit much of an ability to view a project in its totality, and instead respond to a particular role or idea that showcases their ability to emote. Sometimes they get away with it. Al Pacino did well as a blind man in *Scent of a Woman* and Dustin Hoffman scored as Tom Cruise's idiot savant brother in *Rain Man*.

Few stars have demonstrated the consistent intelligence in selecting scripts as that exercised by Tom Hanks. In mid career he hit the wall playing the white-bread good guy in such bland movies as *Turner & Hooch*. Skeletal and poignant in *Philadelphia*, Hanks suddenly vaulted from one star turn to another—*Forrest Gump, Saving Private Ryan, The Green Mile, Cast Away*—emerging not only as Hollywood's wealthiest star, but also sharing with Jack Nicholson that rare double designation as both superstar and character actor.

Nicholson's own longevity testifies to his talent on the screen and his sixth sense about where the audience is going. In the 1960s it was *Easy Rider*, enshrining the antiestablishment film. Again he struck in the 1970s with *The Last Detail*, an off-the-road road film. Then with *Carnal Knowledge*, he explored sexual politics, extending it in the 1980s in John Updike's *The Witches of Eastwick*. Changing gears, he morphed into a comic villain everyone could love as the Joker in *Batman*. He struck in the 1990s with the curmudgeonly *As Good as It Gets*. He clearly understands the Jack Nicholson business and where it fits.

While Jack Nicholson and Tom Hanks have proven to be both shrewd and decisive, other superstars are ambiguous in their responses to material. A firm offer may elicit not so much a "yes" as a "yes . . . if." The list of "ifs" can be daunting—if a certain actress plays a leading role, if a certain director can be signed or, most common of all, if "improvements" can be made to the script. It's rare that these "improvements" are spelled out—that would make things too easy. It's just that the material needs them.

A classic example: the reteaming of Kevin Costner and Oliver Stone in *Beyond Borders*. They seemed a perfect pairing—Costner and Stone, both as talented as they are headstrong. They'd worked together on *JFK* and had seemed comfortable with each other's excesses. The idea of Mandalay, the independent company, was to reteam them in a $79 million–plus project about daring volunteer doctors who venture into the world's trouble spots. Costner had had his hits, like *Dances With Wolves*, and his flops like *The Postman* as well as controversial projects like *Waterworld*. But he was a gutsy performer who would shoot in locations like Cambodia, Africa and Eastern Europe, which this film required. His stubbornness equaled his gutsiness, however. When Stone finished his first draft of *Beyond Borders*, he gave it to Costner with the following stipulation: If you want to do this film, commit to the script in its present form, tell me what changes you want to make and I will deal with them. Costner dutifully read it and liked it. He agreed to do the picture, provided that Stone make additional changes first, before he'd close his deal. Not surprisingly, Stone went crazy. He would not agree to be "auditioned." The messages flashed back and forth via agents. A shoot out was underway. Who would blink first?

Finally, a summit meeting was arranged. Costner agreed to the date, then postponed it, claiming he'd forgotten it was his birthday. When the meeting finally took place, Stone was ninety minutes late, leaving Costner simmering. Ultimately the actor stormed out of the meeting, claiming Stone had given no weight to his script suggestions. As the negotiations continued, problems multiplied. Catherine Zeta-Jones, who had committed to play Costner's love interest—a subplot Costner wanted enhanced—suddenly withdrew from the project. Her reason was more sympathetic: She was pregnant with her and Michael Douglas' first child. But the domestic distributor of the film required superstar casting. With Zeta-Jones' withdrawal, Costner was all the more crucial.

Getting all the elements correctly positioned is always a juggling act. Differing schedules for actors, location availability, weather, script completion, all create their own imperatives. So when Zeta-Jones withdrew, each of the other variables so neatly ordered came undone. Would Costner take another film? Who should replace the female lead? There had to be star balance above the line, since the love story was central. Julia Roberts was interested, said her agent. She wanted to read the script. Was it a waste of time? She was well beyond the financial profile not only in her direct cost, $20 million, but also in her backend participation. When her first dollar gross was combined with those of Stone and Costner, there was no air left in the package. Studios, unlike independents such as Mandalay, have more room to combine multiple pre-break gross players because they are the distributors and can recoup with their distribution fees, a luxury the indies don't enjoy. Mandalay began to fashion a byzantine strategy predicated on the assumption that Costner and Stone would accept their gross participations being reduced to accommodate Roberts, and that she would reduce her asking price and participation percentage to join them. The theory was that the movie god would bless the undertaking with bountiful box office returns so that less would ultimately become more.

Each of the actors proved reluctant to embrace this logic, however. Sure this is a film that has social and political weight, one that would be good for their careers, but the agents really want the money. Reducing a star's price for whatever good and valid reason, they argued, represents a crack in the wall that they have so carefully erected. There being no secrets in Hollywood, the next film studio that wanted Julia Roberts would haul out the price she got paid on this last epic and hurl it back at the zookeeper.

So now what? Hope springs eternal that if she reads it, and meets with the director, a solution may be found. Agents and managers all assume that when the studio says there is no more money, not one cent or point left, they are always lying. She read; they waited. The financiers threatened to move on. Finally, she said yes but not now. Stone and Costner said move on. The producers sensed that each time you wait it rattles everyone's cage. Too many rattles and the animals in the cage get crazed.

Gwyneth Paltrow would be wonderful. A year earlier at the mere mention of her name, she would have been in makeup, but now she was having difficulty making up her mind. Oscar intervened with *Shakespeare in Love*. Meanwhile Costner still hadn't seen a revised script and Stone was on a location jaunt to Asia and Eastern Europe. All the while, money kept pouring from Mandalay's coffers in a continuing attempt to prime the pump. Meg Ryan read it and was in, sort of. She was also in the tabloids as her marriage to Dennis Quaid was on the rocks. Stone had scheduled a meeting with her, but now she was hiding out in London to stay out of the media glare stemming from her new involvement with Russell Crowe. Exasperated, Oliver Stone decided Meg Ryan was a bad idea. Angelina Jolie, who had just won an Academy Award for *Girl, Interrupted*, was in London—interested, available. She was about to begin *Lara Croft: Tomb Raider* for Paramount and would be available three months later. Would Costner go with her, and would he wait? There were lots of moving parts to keep oiled. She agreed, he agreed, Stone agreed, but still no final script.

Suddenly the fortunes of *Beyond Borders* began to change. The writer-director and his star had quietly begun to work together on the script. Angry rhetoric had given way to creative collaboration. Costner never formally withdrew his conditions; everyone simply decided to get down to work. A December 2000 start date loomed, the other roles were cast, the financing was locked in place and the cameras were ready to roll. *Beyond Borders*, with all its nightmares, was becoming a reality.

Just weeks before the anticipated start of principal photography, Costner announced through the media that he was squeezing in another film before the start date of *Borders*. This was a dangerous gambit as the impending writers' and actors' strikes meant that *Borders* would be imperiled if it had to be pushed back. Angered, Stone said, "I'll find someone else to star in the movie." A flurry of negotiations was quickly initiated to substitute Ralph Fiennes for Costner. He was not as big a star, but he could get the picture made. The shoot, however, would still have to be delayed for financial adjustments. Finally, Stone now threw in the towel. The project was put on hold awaiting new chemistry.

But sometimes the movie god has a way of shining down at the moment of highest distress. Angelina Jolie's *Tomb Raider* was hurtling toward a third-of-a-billion-dollar global box office. Her glitter, combined with a now-trimmed Oliver Stone script, attracted top directors, including Martin (*The Mask of Zorro*, *Golden Eye*) Campbell, who now came on board. Suddenly the project was percolating yet again.

Impatient with the capricious behavior of the illuminati, some studios periodically have experimented with combinations of lesser stars hoping to create that magic "want to see" alchemy. *Steel Magnolias* from producer Ray Stark combined "almost-star" casting consisting of Dolly Parton, Shirley MacLaine, Daryl Hannah and Olympia Dukakis, all coming off shining career moments. Stark finished off his casting with an upstart named Julia Roberts. This was a case of something old, something new, all creating big box office bucks.

Going back in Hollywood lore, there were *The Dirty Dozen* or

The Wild Bunch or *The Magnificent Seven* and a mega attempt with Joseph E. Levine's *A Bridge Too Far*. It even worked well where the cast consisted of a bunch of old geezers in *Space Cowboys*.

The most inspired mixing and matching of stars and wannabe stars over the years stemmed as often from inadvertencies and accidents of timing as from shrewd strategizing. In short, someone was at the right place at the right time. A classic example is *48 HRS.*, which producer Larry Gordon had been desperately attempting to levitate at Paramount in 1981. The colorful Mississippi native had personally paid a writer to develop his idea about the oddball relationship between a cop and a convict, but for years he had been unable to achieve the right casting. He'd elicited a commitment from Clint Eastwood several years earlier, but the actor changed his mind. Gordon had actually had a go from United Artists at one point to pair Stallone and Hackman, but the project got canceled when the regime at UA changed. Gordon next signed Burt Reynolds and Richard Pryor, but that fell apart when the comedian unexpectedly demanded the top billing. Now the persistent producer found himself in the office of Michael Eisner, president of Paramount at the time, pitching his tired project yet again. And he wasn't getting anywhere.

Gordon was almost relieved when Eisner, an often-stubborn man, interrupted their meeting to accept a call from Jeffrey Berg, the president of ICM. Suddenly Eisner was in the middle of a heated argument about one of Berg's top clients, Nick Nolte, with whom Paramount had a pay-or-play deal. Since the studio had not been able to come up with a mutually acceptable project to trigger the deal, Berg wanted his star to be paid off. Eisner was demanding an extension. Even as they argued, Larry Gordon saw his instant of opportunity. When Eisner hung up, Gordon explained the purpose of his meeting. He was there to present Eisner with the ideal Nick Nolte project. "What's it about?" Eisner demanded. Gordon rattled off the brief story line. "Can you have it in theaters by December seventh?" Eisner asked. "A piece of cake." Gordon responded, adding that he had a bright young director named Walter Hill standing by.

It was not until he was outside Eisner's office that Gordon realized the subject of a co-star had never been mentioned. Given his narrow time frame, he had to act fast. He had switched the role to that of a black actor when he went after Richard Pryor, so now he plunged ahead, offering the role to Gregory Hines, then to Bill Cosby. The rejections kept rolling in. Desperate, Gordon demanded new ideas from his casting people. "How about that funny black kid on *Saturday Night Live?*" someone suggested. Gordon took the next plane to New York to court Eddie Murphy, who was admittedly shocked by the sudden attention. He readily accepted the role. The film was a huge hit.

"That's the genius of casting," Gordon reflects.

Certainly, the most orthodox route for landing a star is through an agent. The system is supposed to work like this: A call is made to the agent in question. A script is delivered. If it is judged to be a contender, it is passed on to the actor and a decision is duly rendered.

It rarely happens that way. Most agents who represent top stars decline even to discuss a project, no less read it, unless a firm offer is placed on the table. This means that a studio, or some other responsible financing source, has to certify that, say, Tom Cruise will be paid $20 million against 20 percent of the gross if he and his representatives read and respond positively to the project. To elicit an offer of that magnitude from a studio is no small task. It means the studio itself has to cover the script and judge it favorably. If an independent producer wants to make a firm offer and avoid the bureaucratic hassle, the agent may demand that the full salary be deposited into an escrow account at a bank. Again, it's no small order to raise several million dollars and let it sit in a bank in the hope that someone will cozy up to a script.

Agents have their own agendas that must be appeased. There are past favors to pay off, past slights to avenge. If an agent knows that the producer fee, too, will be commissioned, that's an enticement. Then, if another actor or director already is involved in the project—a talent the agent would like to sign—he is more tempted to look favorably upon the deliberations.

At times, the scenarios can become complex. Bruce Willis greeted the outline for *Armageddon* with interest because his agent, Arnold Rifkin, saw it as a way out of his client's immediate dilemma. Willis had started shooting an independent film called *Broadway Brawler* but, after four weeks, had become convinced that the project would be a disaster. In desperation, Willis offered to compensate the producer for his costs provided he could escape the embarrassment. It was Rifkin's hope that Joe Roth, the shrewd production chief at the Walt Disney Studio, would bail Willis out—giving him an $18 million loan as "escape money" for starring in *Armageddon*. In return Willis would agree to do two more films to be designated later. Roth agreed to the deal, Rifkin committed Willis to *Armageddon* and the project promptly rolled forward. The "back-up" project turned out to be the megahit *The Sixth Sense*.

Some stars also are vulnerable to pitches that sync up with their own ideological bents, religious beliefs or other predilections. Hence John Travolta, as a fervid Scientologist, was lured into starring in *Battlefield Earth*, a project based on a sci-fi novel written by L. Ron Hubbard, founder of that religious group.

A dramatic financial offer will surely galvanize a star's attention. Jim Carrey became a lot more interested in *Cable Guy* after he learned he would be the first major star to be paid $20 million. No one is immune to the dollar sign but the top illuminati can get it from many places, so the writing has to be on the page as well as on the checks.

But does the star truly spell the difference between success and failure? Right on the heels of the success of *Bram Stoker's Dracula*,

the same team of James Hart and Francis Coppola set out to repli-
cate it with their version of *Mary Shelley's Frankenstein*. This time
Kenneth Branaugh would play the role of the doctor as well as direct. Though a talented actor, he wasn't considered to be a star in the
firmament of Hollywood, so a big star was needed to play the monster. The studio's choice was De Niro, an actor everyone thought
would make all the difference. De Niro gave a hair-raising performance, but the film failed nonetheless. No one at the studio took
credit for casting De Niro.

Some top stars who have become money machines seek to embark on directing careers as a means of flexing their artistic muscles—
Mel Gibson among them. They're flattered if a producer offers them
a script to direct, even if he then adds, "Of course, if you also want to
play the lead, that would be all right, too."

The star's zookeeper groans over these submissions, to be sure.
He wants his client to keep working as an actor and generating the
big bucks. The decision to direct a film may entail a two-year commitment, during which time a Mel Gibson could have taken on four
or five acting roles. This potential $100 million earnings gap does not
come as thrilling news to the agent, or to the agency chief to whom
he reports.

Once a star is committed to a project, the biggest challenge is
how to sustain that commitment. The annals of filmmaking are rife
with horror stories of stars pulling out of projects at the eleventh
hour, often for reasons no one, including the star, could ever explain.
Often the problem stems, not from the project in question, but
rather circumstances surrounding a previous one. One factor in the
withdrawal of Harrison Ford, surely one of the most reliable and
steadfast of movie stars, from *Traffic* was his alarm over the abject
failure of a romantic movie called *Random Hearts*. Ford's new agents,
United Talent Agency (UTA), felt that an action picture along the
lines of *Air Force One* would be a smarter bet. "A movie star under-

stands that he is as much a 'brand' as he is an 'actor,'" observes Arnold Rifkin, one-time president of the William Morris Agency. "Projects must be sequenced to protect the brand."

To be sure, Harrison Ford didn't exactly glide into *Air Force One*. Armyan Bernstein, a savvy writer-producer who runs Beacon Productions, one of the industry's most successful independent companies, originally offered the role to Kevin Costner. Costner liked the script and signed on—with one proviso. He had just finished an arduous shoot on *Waterworld* and also was going through a divorce. "I want a year off," Costner advised, urging Bernstein to wait for him. "Don't worry—the time will fly by." Bernstein didn't think so. He approached Harrison Ford, who also liked the script and agreed to do it with one condition: He also wanted Bernstein to wait a year while he indulged in some "sequencing"—he was interested in doing a romantic lark called *Six Days Seven Nights*, at Disney for director Ivan Reitman. "I had a company to run," Bernstein later explained. "I didn't want to be on hold." He approached Joe Roth, production chief at Disney, and explained his dilemma, and Roth soon came back to him with a solution. *Air Force One* would be moved ahead of the Ivan Reitman movie, but again there was a condition: Disney would get the foreign rights to *Air Force One*. In the end, Bernstein got his movie going without the year's wait, Disney realized a financial bonanza from its foreign rights and Harrison Ford had his sequencing rearranged.

When stars are unhappy about something, they rarely sit down for an earnest conference. Most often, they simply vaporize. Robert Redford has long been known by producers to be the king of nonconfrontation. If he's unhappy about a project, he'll simply disappear and not answer his phone. John Travolta also is renowned for disappearing acts. Fresh from such successes as *Broken Arrow* and *Get Shorty*, Travolta decided to take on a more adventuresome project, committing to star in a movie called *The Double*. His salary: $17 million. His director: Roman Polanski, renowned for edgy thrillers like *Rosemary's Baby*. A perfectionist who makes great demands of his actors, Polanski represented a sharp contrast to the more conventional Hollywood directors with whom Travolta had been working. Nonetheless, the star's enthusiasm seemed high. He even ordered his $200,000 made-to-order trailer shipped to the Paris location to ensure his creature comforts and also made plans to transport his personal entourage, which ranged from trainers to cooks and assorted hangers-on.

Then events started to misfire. A meeting only three days before the start of principal photography between the star and the director did not go well. According to Polanski, Travolta read portions of the script in a dull monotone. There was a fleeting discussion about Scientology, the organization to which Travolta is fiercely loyal. Polanski may or may not have used the word "cult" in describing the group, depending on which version one wishes to believe. In any case, Travolta simply got on his plane and disappeared.

The late Steve McQueen, a vastly different personality than Travolta, was capable of equally mercurial disappearing acts.

In prepping a film called *Islands in the Stream*, based on a novel by Ernest Hemingway, producers were stunned when McQueen, then the biggest star in the world, suddenly bolted. In read-throughs of the script, McQueen had been displaying nervousness over some of his more challenging dramatic scenes involving his relationship with his family. "I can't say those lines," he complained, "I'll do it with a look." One day he phoned the director, Franklin Schaffner, and blurted, "I'm out." His replacement: George C. Scott, who was then at the top of his game, following his Oscar-winning role playing General George S. Patton in the film also directed by Schaffner.

A cranky, brooding man who had a habitual drinking problem, Scott had both talent and "problem" written all over him. One of the first problems related to location. *Islands* is set in the Bahamas during World War II. Shooting the film somewhere in the Caribbean was an obvious option—and a delightful one—but people who'd worked with Scott warned that he was distinctly uneasy around black people. "He's a Southern guy," one associate warned. "If he starts hitting the bars after a day's shooting, you've got to expect some brawls and a few arrests." The prospect of bailing out the brawling star did not appeal to Schaffner so he opted for another location: Kauai. Few blacks lived on that Hawaiian island. Even the bars were quiet and friendly, relative to those in the Caribbean. The costs to shoot in Hawaii were about the same, though the unions were stronger and less negotiable.

All things considered, the decision was made to go to Kauai, and it turned out to be a prudent one. Scott got thoroughly swackered many nights, but there were no bars for him to invade. Ironically, the biggest problem posed by the Hawaiian location proved to be the lack of extras. Since the story took place in the Caribbean, black "natives" were needed to dress the set, but the tiny local population could not meet the needs. In the end, additional extras were flown in from other islands.

Still, no matter how many precautions a filmmaker may take, or how many perks one may supply, the hard reality is that the star may still bolt, and often the reason is impossible to identify. It might relate to panic—an actor suddenly sensing he's not right for the part. It might relate to discomfort with a co-star, or it might relate to some personal problem, such as a fight with a spouse or a bout with drugs.

Usually the producer and director will never really learn the key cause for the defection, the news often coming in the form of a phone call or e-mail from the star's agent, citing "creative differences"—one of the most daunting and widely used euphemisms in show business. The press often reports these "creative differences," the implication being that the principals had engaged in a profound debate about the dramatic and aesthetic implications of the material and, after pondering questions of structure and verisimilitude, parted ways. In truth, the principals probably just melted into the night to avoid confrontation.

Under such circumstances, the most important task facing the producer is to keep his ship afloat. No veteran producer, irrespective of his protestations, ever starts a movie without having a mental checklist of backup actors and directors. Speed is of the essence. The key elements must be held together, momentum must be sustained, the studio or other financing entity must be held in place. Whatever happens, the producer must announce to everyone who will listen that, thanks to these developments, his project actually has been enhanced, not damaged.

Occasionally, this is actually the case. When Burt Reynolds pulled out of *Terms of Endearment*, the filmmakers turned instead to Jack Nicholson, who transformed it into an unforgettable movie. Indeed, from today's perspective, it's all but impossible even to imagine the picture with Reynolds.

Prodding Nicholson into *Terms of Endearment* was relatively painless, since it was accomplished with the enthusiastic support of the director, James Brooks, as well as co-star Shirley MacLaine. This sort of consensus is rare in the movie business. A more common scenario is that the replacement of a star triggers a domino effect. The new star insists on script changes, which upset the director or send the co-star into tantrums. "He is stealing my best scenes," is the most common complaint. Effecting a smooth transition of this sort requires heightened skills of diplomacy—skills beyond the ken of many producers.

But if negotiating a star's exit from a movie is a delicate operation, negotiating his entry can be vastly more demanding. A movie star deal has become an art form unto itself, one that involves the talents of agents, lawyers, tax advisers, managers, overseas distributors and, of course, the customary bevy of studio functionaries.

Under the old studio system, star salaries were pre-negotiated. A Spencer Tracy or Cary Grant was under contract to a studio for a number of films over a period of years, with the understanding that an upward adjustment might be in the cards if one of the films became a stratospheric hit. In the late 1950s, stars like James Stewart and Charlton Heston decided to take a chance on a new type of deal—one that called for reduced compensation up front but a piece of the back end in the form of net participation. Times were lean in the movie business because of the advent of television, and the studios wanted stars to share some of the risk.

Over the course of a generation, these "share the risk" deals evolved grotesquely into "no risk" deals. A top star in the category of Tom Cruise or Harrison Ford now demands as much as $25 million in up-front payment against 20 percent of the gross receipts. His deal may also call for a major participation in another significant revenue steam: home video. Studios originally carved out an 80 percent slice of this income pie, limiting profit participants to share in the remaining 20 percent. In recent years, however, this 80/20 split has broken down, so that stars now dip into the lion's share of video, which has become all the more important given the runaway growth of DVDs worldwide. Besides video, stars also take income from merchandising, music and other ancillary revenues. A prototypical deal for a middle-to-upper-range star might read something like this: His fee could total $15 million against 5 percent to 10 percent of the gross from first dollar, which might escalate to 15 percent of the gross when the film crosses the $120 million mark in box office gross and 17 percent when it hits $150 million. In addition, the star could receive an additional $1.5 million when the movie grosses $75 million in the U.S. or $100 million worldwide; another $1.5 million at $125 million U.S. or $175 million worldwide and yet another $500,000 when the movie first breaks even in terms of its overall production and marketing costs. Finally, if the actor wins an Oscar for best actor, another $750,000 bonus could kick in.

In addition to all this, the star often receives a weekly nonaccountable expense allowance of $15,000 per week. He also could be provided with a jet aircraft at a cost not to exceed $2,000 per hour for fuel and maintenance, plus $1,000 a day for two pilots and $250 a day for their accommodation. Aside from the plane, the star is guaranteed a full-sized Mercedes Benz, a first-class trailer, two personal assistants, a separate makeup trailer, a dialogue coach, bodyguards, a personal chef, a personal trainer, plus free hotel rooms for visiting friends. The star also is accorded approvals over the still photographer, plus wardrobe and makeup assistants and hair stylists.

What all this means is that a star's payday from one picture is assured, and if it works there can be the windfall of $50 to $75 million in profits. Jim Carrey realized this kind of result with *The Grinch*.

Studios are understandably nettled by deals like these because they enable stars in some cases to earn more than the studio. To forestall this possibility, studio lawyers try to invoke all sorts of "safeguards." There are substantial distribution fees. There are provisions for overhead on offices, advertising, etc. Complex formulas also are introduced governing the levels of gross participation at different moments of a movie's life. On *Rain Man*, for example, the stakes of the two stars, Tom Cruise and Dustin Hoffman, bounced up and down from as little as 10 percent of the gross to as high as 50 percent, depending on the flow of box office receipts.

Given the complexity of these deals, some negotiations take as long as a year to complete. A few star lawyers deliberately prolong the culmination of the deal-making process until the start date of the film looms, since a studio's bargaining position melts away as it continues to pump money into sets, crew and location expenses. The lawyer's fees from these movie star deals have escalated to the point where the town's top lawyers sustain an exotic standard of living on a level with their prize clients. "The process has become so laborious that, by the time you finally nail down the basic terms, you tend to look the other way when it comes to negotiating a perk package," acknowledges the business affairs chief of one major studio. Star perks are the goodies that go beyond paying the illuminati their price. They constitute tribute. Perhaps a tribute to the stupidity of the business.

The movies need stars and the stars need movies, but to sustain the financial weight of star casting, a film must be geared to the widest possible audience. It must offer a story accessible to the global market—no subtle character conflicts in the plot, no shadings of irony in the dialogue. Considered purely as "content," the word favored by the multinationals, the only way a superstar vehicle can justify its cost is if it's predesigned to tap into all revenue streams, especially overseas television and video. Revenue from American box office may constitute less than 30 percent of the overall totals.

Theoretically it should be possible to tailor-make projects that meet these criteria, but surely the odds are heavily against it—witness the fact that more and more superstar vehicles fail to satisfy on any level, critical or financial. The superstars, wary about protecting their franchises, are taking ever fewer risks, much to the relief of their handlers. Why abandon the status quo, when the results are so bountiful? The answer, of course, is that they're bountiful only for the superstars. For moviegoers around the world, the system isn't working, nor is it working for the multinational companies that own the relatively unprofitable dream factories. The public wants better movies, or they'll stop buying tickets—a phenomenon that's already evident in declining theater admissions. It's no surprise that the multinationals, by and large, want to get out of the volatile movie business—that is, if they can find a buyer.

To be sure, the illuminati are happy. But it's getting lonely out there.

CUT TO: Peter Guber on James Stewart

The act of moving into my very own office at a movie studio was a tremendous boost to the ego. The realization that no one really wanted to hear my opinion about anything brought me quickly back to earth. As a young movie executive, I felt that I had special insights into everything—scripts, casting, editing. I also felt that it was vitally important that the old guys running things take note of my youthful perspective. I soon realized that they didn't see things that way. The old guys believed they alone had the answers and that it was a necessary evil to have young people around, provided they weren't taken seriously.

In the late 1960s when I was a novice at Columbia, I loved watching dailies with the senior executives, none of whom ever asked my opinion or even, for that matter, acknowledged my presence. One day I missed the dailies but learned they'd be running again in early evening. Since I was working late anyway, I ventured into the darkened theater just as the dailies were beginning. The theater was empty except for the silhouette of a man sitting toward the front. The first film to come up was *Fools' Parade*, a rather conventional James Stewart vehicle, which seemed something of an instant anachronism when it was released. A close-up of Stewart appeared on the screen, then the figure at the front of the room turned and said, "C-c-c-could you please run that again?" It was Jimmy Stewart himself, and I was in awe. I moved to the control board and asked the projectionist to re-run the last takes. Stewart had been fitted for a prosthetic eye in this film and wanted to study how it looked close-up. After the film ran again, he got up from his seat, strolled to the rear where I was seated, paused over me and said, "Well. . . ?" It was the nicest thing anyone had ever said to me. Jimmy Stewart, the legend, was actually asking my opinion of his scene. Or so it seemed.

"Wonderful, simply wonderful," was all I could utter.

"Thank you," said the movie star, as he proceeded to the exit. I felt a tingle of delight. The geezers who ran the studio didn't solicit my views, but at least the stars were interested.

I was too distracted to continue watching dailies. As I exited the theater, I heard Jimmy Stewart's voice through the open door of the projection booth. Moving to the door, I saw Stewart chatting with the projectionist and with another man who was cleaning the area. "So the eye didn't bother you?" Stewart was asking them. The projectionist shook his head. The cleaning guy said, "Thing looked just fine to me." Satisfied, the star turned, walked by me and headed back to his dressing room. I felt totally deflated. Jimmy Stewart wanted everyone's opinion, not just mine. In fact, he seemed most interested in the reaction of the cleaning guy. So much for my sudden influence.

To make matters worse, Bob Weitman, Columbia's production chief, referred to the prosthetic eye at a staff meeting the next morning. "I talked to Jimmy Stewart last night and told him he had to replace that goddamn eye," Weitman said. "And Jimmy says, 'I kind of like it and, what's more, one of your own executives told me he liked it, too.'" Weitman glowered at his assembled minions. "I'd like to know who was the son of a bitch who said that to Jimmy. I mean, no one is to speak to the stars except for the head of production, and that happens to be me."

I sat on my hands. In fact, the entire room was silent. I vowed never again to utter a word about the dailies to anyone, unless specifically ordered to. Fortunately, Weitman never learned that I was the guilty party.

Some years later I ran into Stewart on a plane headed for Hawaii. I introduced myself and mentioned the incident. He chuckled and said he remembered. Weitman had indeed called him about the eye, he recalled. Moreover, Stewart had been worried that he would get some young apprentice fired because of his remarks. I told him I had survived—if barely. But I also had learned a lesson. "Which one is that?" Stewart asked. "To keep my mouth shut," I replied. "No, son," he said. "Ideas won't work unless you speak up."

6.

The Zookeepers

You're no one in Hollywood unless someone
wants you dead.

BERNIE BRILLSTEIN

F Scott Fitzgerald reminded us "the rich are different
from you and I," and the same could even more appropriately be said about agents.

They may look like normal people. At times, they even talk like
normal people. But they're agents; no one can survive in the world
of show business without assimilating that fact.

Proximity to power and talent is the wellspring of agenting. Consider for a moment the entertainment food chain from the flash of
inspiration through the perspiration of production. Show business is
set up with a string of intermediaries to coddle and caress talent
through the process. There are agents for authors when one acquires
literary rights, others keyed to the emotional ricochets of actors, still
others who look after composers and cinematographers. There are
even agents for the sale of international rights for completed films.

So it's altogether necessary to have a fundamental grasp of the peculiarities of the relationships that exist between these individuals and their clients. Without a command of the argot of the agent, the shoot outs between the combatants become a massacre, and more often than not, friendly fire will take down a promising project.

Agents dwell in their own sociopathic cocoon. They dedicate themselves to the proposition that perception is reality. If an actor is perceived as being a star, his agent must command a star deal, regardless of whether his last film was an abysmal failure. Witness John Travolta off *Battlefield Earth* and *Lucky Numbers*, both of whose domestic box office grosses equaled little more than their combined catering bill. On his next planned effort, *Domestic Disturbances*, neither his agent at William Morris, Fred Westheimer, nor his manager, Jonathan Krane, would hear of any reduction in his fee—or theirs for that matter. All the perks, planes, trailers and trainers would have to be maintained even with a little bump here and there to "keep Johnny happy." Neither of these two messengers would want to deliver the dour message to Travolta that his failures might mean he'd command less.

Similarly when a literary work is perceived as having "heat," it better fetch a stellar price whether or not anyone really covets it. Irving "Swifty" Lazar, who was as brash as he was short, represented the likes of Bogart, Hemingway and Capote, but never caught the heat—he created it. When he pitched the film rights to *Hand Carved Coffins*, with a million-dollar price tag, Lazar was disturbed that Paramount passed. A week later he was back on the phone, absentmindedly pitching the identical project but at a still higher price. Reminded of the earlier conversation, Lazar shot back, "Don't you realize it's improved with age?"

Over the years, agents' self-perception has changed significantly, as has the way they are viewed in the industry. The "ten-percenter," as *Variety* labels agents, of a generation ago was a creature of show business. He was drawn to entertainers as a moth to flame but was content to remain anonymous while his client took center stage. He was a man who represented artists, who molded their careers. "William Morris, Jr., insists that his agency is not concerned with the tawdry aspects of commerce," wrote E. J. Kahn, Jr., about the son of the founder of the century-old William Morris Agency. "'We practice in the humanities,' he prefers to say."

The agent of old prided himself on the closeness of his relationships. Lew Wasserman, who co-founded the giant MCA talent agency, mediated divorce settlements for superstar clients like Myrna Loy, when she split with her first husband, Arthur Hornblow, Jr. When Mae West's pet chimp developed stomach cramps while they were traveling in Europe, she called upon her agent, Johnny Hyde of the William Morris office, to find a suitable veterinarian.

If an agent is perceived to be a power player, his calls will quickly be returned and his access to other power players will be assured, irrespective of his shifting client list.

What zookeepers do is quite simple: They represent their client's interests—and today's agent has no illusions about art. He is a businessman, an unabashed deal maker. It's as likely he graduated from the Harvard Business School as the William Morris mailroom. He dedicates himself to his own self-aggrandizement even over that of his client. The William Morris credo of anonymity and the MCA mantra of client-above-all are gone. The birth of such agencies as the original CMA headed by Freddie Fields (later to become ICM) and the eruption of the Creative Artists Agency (CAA) from the bowels of the William Morris office marked the beginning of a new epoch.

Variety and the *Hollywood Reporter,* as well as the *New York Times* and *Los Angeles Times* with their expanded entertainment coverage, constitute an integral part of the way an agent communicates both in and out of his own agency. They provide leverage for his career as well as a place to assuage his ego. Prospective clients peruse such papers, weighing their own moves. Perception creates reality. Cultivating the reporters covering the entertainment beat has become an obsession for talent representatives. In recent years, it has spread to managers and even attorneys in the battle to sign clients and create the image of being the consummate power broker.

Agents view themselves more as warriors than facilitators. "I see Hollywood as the Wild West for Jews," says Gavin Polone, a tough-minded young agent turned manager. "I see myself as the guy protecting the townsfolk, my clients, from the greedy landowners, in this case the studio or network executives. . . . My goal is to erode my opponent's self-confidence, to make him doubt whatever leverage he thinks he has. Experience has taught me that unless my gun jams or I am ambushed, these tactics will usually leave my rivals lying in the dusty street."

Some Hollywood players disdain these attitudes: They miss the gentlemen-agents of a previous era. They admit agents today spend too much time trying to hustle new clients, often at the expense of their existing ones. Some top agents acknowledge half their time is spent in the "hunt." Before the 1980s, there was an unwritten "code" among agents: One didn't try to steal a client from a competitor unless it became clear that that particular client was looking for a change. Behind-the-back maneuvering was frowned upon.

In the 1960s the Chasin Park Citron agency was the prototypical gentleman's agency. Its client list included Charlton Heston, James Stewart and Ross Hunter. The three reps formed their agency after the Justice Department forced Lew Wasserman to disgorge his talent agency, MCA, since he had chosen to focus on the production business. The Chasin agency was tough but true to its word. Its favorite tactic was forcing a producer to negotiate with himself. When George Kennedy was offered the starring role in one of Ross Hunter's films for Columbia Pictures, *Lost Horizon*, George Chasin wouldn't set the bar. The tall, silver-haired agent said, "Make me an offer." After hearing that offer, he'd say, "That's not good enough; you'll have to do better." What was better? Back to the drawing board. If it went on too long, Chasin would say, without a trace of anger, "We'll catch you next time."

On occasion, the former chairman of William Morris, Abe Lastfogel, would bluster that being an agent was "the single greatest training for understanding what the business was all about—namely talent." He regarded it as his religious duty to guard against its unfair exploitation.

Today, Lastfogel would find intense competition from that busy tribe of professionals known as talent managers who are increasingly upstaging agents. Indeed a surreptitious warfare has broken out between agents and managers—one that has greatly complicated the way business is transacted in Hollywood.

The traditional role of the manager was that of career counselor and mentor. He worked for fewer than a handful of clients, often just one. He plotted out career strategy while the agent negotiated the deals and sifted through submissions.

Things aren't that simple anymore. Today's managers are part of a coterie of individuals who feed from the client's bowl. Some clients assert that it seems like the other way around. With the establishment of entities like Brillstein Grey Entertainment, which is at once a mammoth production company as well as a management firm, the manager has reemerged as the employer of his own clients. Brillstein Grey produces movies as well as TV shows and, at one time or another, was itself in partnership with the major distribution companies. To be sure, it also conscientiously represented the interests of its clients, but the complexity of these interrelationships has inevitably triggered the occasional conflict-of-interest suit.

These tensions are further exacerbated by the manager's insistence on inserting himself into the production package. In addition to the 5 to 15 percent he collects from his client, he may elicit a generous production fee and a back-end piece of the action. The network or studio anxious to secure the talent may readily add this fee to the budget of the production, and if the originating producer doesn't carefully structure his deal, he will end up bearing a good portion of this greenmail.

Some managers, like Chuck Binder, who looks after Sharon Stone, simply put their fee into the budget. The studio just figures it into the above-the-line cost for the actress.

All this makes the agent crazy. To begin with, Screen Actors Guild rules forbid him from producing. This deprives him of ego satisfaction as well as remuneration. It also places him in the uncomfortable position of having to collect his 10 percent from his clients rather than being able to boast that "the studio will take care of me." A great selling point for managers is being able to tout, "You don't pay for me."

The big talent agencies find themselves in the position of spending millions of dollars on "support troops" for clients. Aides scout for material and cover books and scripts submitted for client consideration. Both William Morris and ICM have extensive international literary operations and as such they have access to critical information on forthcoming literary properties.

Managers, not surprisingly, refute all this. "We're the ones who log the long hours with the client," says Bernie Brillstein, a veteran manager who once represented virtually all the talent on *Saturday Night Live*. "Besides, when's the last time you saw an agent in the clubs or theaters scouting new talent? That's what I do."

The brilliant, if mercurial, Michael Ovitz argues that both agents and management companies are essentially anachronistic as presently structured. In building his Artists Management Group (AMG), Ovitz created a company that theoretically not only represents clients in a management capacity, but can also develop, produce and even co-finance movies and television shows, perhaps ultimately distributing them as well. Ovitz' critics, and they are legion, claim his company will never become financially viable. His TV subsidiary underwrote six pilots for the major networks in its first year. None stuck, meaning he was stuck with the deficits. Wallowing in a sea of red ink, he shuttered his TV dream in the summer of 2001. His adventure once again demonstrated that having the talent relationship doesn't necessarily mean it can be turned into profits. This lesson could have been learned from one of his predecessors, Freddie Fields, who created a talent-rich escape vehicle called First Artists. The artists he assembled at the top of their game included Barbra Streisand, Steve McQueen, Sidney Poitier, Dustin Hoffman and Paul Newman. The films they produced failed, and the company folded.

Most acknowledge that Ovitz, Ron Meyer and Bill Haber reinvented the talent agency business when they founded CAA. The son of a liquor salesman, Ovitz had an instinctual grasp of the dynamics of the talent business. As a young agent at tradition-bound William Morris, he also understood why that agency was falling behind. Starting with zero capital, he set out to build a new company that would redefine the talent representation business.

A smallish man with a doughy, unmemorable face and a quiet, insistent voice, Ovitz was extraordinarily persuasive and fueled by monomaniacal ambition. "Mike instinctively knew how to play on clients' insecurities but at the same time tease their ambitions," observes a long-term colleague. When zeroing in on a potential director client, for example, he would not merely ask, "What are you doing next?" or "What's on your slate?" Rather, he would stare at the filmmaker portentously and inquire, "What is your biggest dream? I need to know so I can make it come true."

"He reminded me to focus, not on what the studios wanted me to do, but what I wanted to do," acknowledges Martin Scorsese about his encounters with Ovitz.

Ovitz built his new agency around an almost paramilitary code of conduct. Individual agents never represented a client alone, but rather worked in teams. This was ostensibly to ensure a depth of representation, but it also filled an important survival precept that clients did not develop a fealty to a specific agent, who could opt for another agency, but rather to CAA as a whole, and particularly to Ovitz.

A steely discipline pervaded CAA that governed dealings with clients, deal making in general and even attire. Serving as a CAA agent was not just a job; it was a calling, and one was remunerated accordingly. A sharp young agent who performed to his potential could find himself pulling down more than $1 million a year before he reached thirty. In the same vein, however, a CAA agent was expected to negotiate not just a good deal for a client, but the best deal ever.

There also was a dark side of CAA. Some clients who were wooed away from CAA by rival agencies claimed Ovitz and company would make veiled threats about future career problems if a director defected. The implication was that no CAA star would ever agree to appear in his films.

Then, too, there was the question of ego. As Ovitz' wealth and power grew, so did his sense of self. "I understand I am the single most powerful force in the entertainment industry," he told one journalist, without insisting that it was off the record. It was ego that drove Ovitz to abandon agenting for more prestigious roles, first as a possible president of Universal (a post he was offered but rejected when the company declared his demands exorbitant) and then as president of the Walt Disney Company (a job he held for only a year). It was not enough for Ovitz to be a "super-agent," as the press took to calling him. He also aspired to be a corporate hierarch. It was after his relationship with Michael Eisner, the volatile head of the Disney empire, imploded that Ovitz returned to the business of talent representation, this time as a manager. And, once again, he set about to realign the rules according to his own grand design.

The question of whether his stratagems will now reshape the entire talent representation business has powerful implications for all concerned. He is despised by some of his former legions at CAA for what they felt was a sneak attack at the foundation of their business.

The simmering resentments boiled over as one agency client after another migrated to Ovitz' new firm. In some cases, their CAA agents accompanied them. Robin Williams took the leap, for example, and so did Mike Menchel, his primary agent. CAA's youthful president, Richard Lovett, promptly convened an emergency session to declare a state of war as Hollywood looked on in shock. Not escaping the community's notice was the quasi-Freudian tenor of the conflict. Ovitz had trained Lovett and all his colleagues. They were, in a sense, his children. Indeed, they still paid him rent, since Ovitz owned a principal share of the rather grandiose I. M. Pei–designed building, not to mention the many works of art hanging in the hallways.

A superb spinmeister, Ovitz took pains to explain his side of the clash to heads of other agencies and power players. "If some CAA clients like Michael Crichton or Barry Levinson want my company to manage their careers," he argued, "that doesn't mean that they won't also need agents." He was careful to distribute his management clients among the other agencies, such as ICM and William Morris. If Ovitz was going to go to war, he was going to be sure that the conflict would be confined to one front, namely CAA.

Given the complex egos of the agency and management businesses, filmmakers and producers must thread their way cautiously through this minefield of talent representation. A major star may be represented by a manager, agent and attorney, all of whom have their own agendas. Hence producers must find a way to incentivize all these representatives, without antagonizing any. In some cases, this may mean sharing a producing credit with a manager, as well as doing some fancy footwork to keep a manager out of a studio negotiation. It may also mean tossing some additional business at the attorney to help ensure his loyalty. Some attorneys become remarkably more

cooperative on co-financed films where there is a chance to negotiate lucrative international agreements.

Yet it's all too easy to get whipsawed by these competing players.
Some attorneys systematically renegotiate all the deals previously
made for clients by their agents. The studios are aware of this legal-
istic featherbedding, but they fear blowing the deal. Faced with this
alien landscape, the deal-making process can advance only through a
series of creative accommodations, else artists and projects alike get
chewed up by the very machinery that's designed to serve them.

All too often, agencies seem superbly constructed to maximize
the income of their clients, and hence their own agency commissions,
and yet they are monstrously obstructive to the deal-making process.
The "Big Four," as they are unaffectionately referred to (William Morris Agency, Creative Artists Agency, International Creative Management and United Talent Agency), together with several specialized
agencies with considerable clout—such as Endeavor or Writers and
Artists Agency—operate in vastly different styles.

ICM is composed of an alliance of boutiques built around strong
personalities. From its inception, mega agents of the past, such as
Sue Mengers, with client lists that included Streisand, Peter Bogdanovich and Ryan O'Neal, reigned in a fiercely entrepreneurial
fashion. Today veteran agent Ed Limato represents the likes of Mel
Gibson and Michelle Pfeiffer, and studios know one deals with him
alone. Presiding over the agency is Jeffrey Berg, a cool, aloof man
who defends this autonomous approach. Not only is it more effi-
cient, he argues, but it's also more consistent with the personalities
of the agency business. Berg was stung in the year 2000, however,
when one of his autonomous agents, Jim Wiatt, defected to the
William Morris agency with a string of clients that included Eddie
Murphy, Tim Allen, Billy Crystal and Rob Reiner. Wiatt had served
as president of the agency. Berg shrugged off the incident as one

more example of the vicissitudes of an entrepreneurial business. Indeed, he shortly recruited a key William Morris agent, John Burnham, head of that agency's motion picture department, whose clients included Woody Allen and Diane Keaton. It is, after all, a game of tit for tat.

In moving to William Morris, Wiatt assumed the stewardship of a far more staid institution that believed in collaborative agenting. Burly, but soft-spoken, Wiatt had begun his professional life working for Democratic political candidates, but he swiftly adapted to the William Morris ethic. Hence a producer doing business with the Morris office likely would face a team of agents, somewhat in the style of CAA.

Despite the constant raiding, there have been many instances of enduring relationships between agent and client. Leonard Hirshan of William Morris handled Clint Eastwood when he was a kid starring in Italian-made Westerns and nurtured his growth into a major actor-auteur. (Hirshan ultimately left the Morris office to head Clint's company.) Jack Nicholson has remained loyal to Sandy Bresler, an independent agent, since the days when he was making low-budget gangster films in the Philippines, this despite constant assaults by big-time agents to steer him away. Similarly, Warren Beatty remained loyal to Stan Kamen of the Morris office until Kamen's death. Mindful of Beatty's business savvy, however, rumors persisted that the star paid his agent less than the standard 10 percent commission, if he paid any commission at all. Arguably the benefit Kamen got from this association was the prestige of representing Beatty, which in turn attracted other full-paying clients.

In working assiduously to position their clients in important projects, agencies assign specific agents to look after each studio. Competition rages among agents to get their clients in the faces of decision makers as the projects unfold. Hence finding oneself with a film in development at Paramount, one will inevitably intercept agents who will be making inquiries about specific roles. The big agencies also have their own business affairs specialists and attorneys who will weigh in on the deal.

Still, the hazards of dealing with the major agencies and their conflicting agendas are manifold. A producer who wants Russell Crowe for his film will have to accommodate the fact that Crowe has just hit it big in back-to-back pictures like *The Insider* and *Gladiator*, hence his agent will be looking for a big jump in his price. Crowe's demands leaped from $3 million to $12 million after *Gladiator* and that doesn't take into consideration his back-end participation. His agent will inevitably be worried that, if he doesn't make a "score," it will constitute an invitation for a rival agency to court him. The producer is thus caught between a possessive agent and the studio, which is outraged at the leap in asking price. Zookeepers are keenly aware that their clients' time at the top may be short-lived. Witness what happened to Jennifer Beals after *Flashdance* or Brad Davis after *Midnight Express*.

Agents and managers tend to be a risk-averse bunch. At any given moment, top stars and directors confront a dizzying array of choices. Literally everything is thrown at them—scripts, books, plays and pitches—and an artist can understandably get numb to the possibilities. While some agents will take a strong stand on a project, many others, fearing the possibility of getting second-guessed, will simply equivocate or opt for the biggest deal or "safest" package—i.e., one with a big-name director and a known co-star.

Complicating the picture is that the richest offers often come not from the studios or mainstream studio producers, but from freewheeling independents who often advance the biggest offers but for the chanciest projects.

Given the wide range of players, intelligence-gathering is the key to success for agents seeking to navigate this obstacle course. The more you know, the stronger your hand.

"Information is power," says Bryan Lourd, a managing director at

CAA who represents the likes of Brad Pitt and Robert De Niro and who presides over a company with nearly 450 agents and support personnel. He exults, "CAA has the best agency infrastructure for gathering and disseminating information." Thus if a writer represented by CAA crafts a "hot" script, other CAA agents representing directors and actors quickly learn about that property and, if interested, see to it that the property gets channeled their way. Indeed some writer clients complain that this process places them at a competitive disadvantage, since they're effectively denied access to an open market. Lourd refutes this, arguing that just because a CAA client may see that script or book first, it doesn't mean the writer client will necessarily be denied a bidding situation.

In a remarkably high number of instances, the process of connecting a piece of material to a star revolves around a stroke of blind luck. *Saving Private Ryan* is a classic example. The script represented a collaboration between Mark Gordon, a producer with a deal at Twentieth Century Fox, and Robert Rodat, a young writer whose only credits were in light Disney family films like *Fly Away Home*. Gordon's home studio, Fox, rejected the idea of a World War II movie out of hand. In contrast, Don Granger, a production executive at Paramount, liked the notion and lobbied to get the further development funded. Both Gordon and Rodat were fretful, however, because two far more high profile projects dealing with World War II were also in preparation at other studios and each had a star attached—Bruce Willis and Arnold Schwarzenegger respectively. Suddenly World War II had been rediscovered in spades, and Gordon and Rodat were going to get buried. Adding to their fears, Paramount had offered their script to director Rob Cohen, who liked it but lacked the "heft" to get an expensive war movie mobilized without the involvement of a major star.

In desperation, Gordon dispatched the Rodat script to a friend at CAA named Caryn Sage—that rare agent who always does her

homework. Within a week, Sage came back to him with two mes-
sages: First, she liked the script. Second, she described it to her boss,
Richard Lovett, who in turn decided to slip it to his biggest client,
Tom Hanks.

What Sage did not tell Gordon was that an important CAA
client, Steven Spielberg, was scheduled to come in the next day for
his annual pilgrimage to discuss material. Though Spielberg had
been faithful with his visitations, he also knew that his agents had
yet to come up with a single project he wanted to direct. All the
films he had made came from direct submissions to his own company or through other channels. Seated amid a group of some thirty
avid agents, however, Sage decided to pitch *Saving Private Ryan* describing the plot in a few succinct sentences. The filmmaker, polite
by nature, seemed impressed; it was not clear how impressed.

During the next couple of days Spielberg also heard about the
script from another source—Tom Hanks. The two were neighbors and
close friends and often compared notes on material. Hanks had read
Ryan and liked it. Suddenly Paramount got a phone call from Richard
Lovett. Spielberg and Hanks were willing to commit to *Saving Private
Ryan* he reported, provided DreamWorks, which was Spielberg's company, could be squeezed into the equation as an equal partner.

Paramount's key executives, Sherry Lansing and Jonathan Dol-
gen, were incredulous at first. Mindful of how difficult it was to elicit
commitments from two superstars, they had to be persuaded that
the call was not an elaborate hoax. Mark Gordon and Robert Rodat
were even more dumbfounded. All they had done was to dispatch a
script to a willing agent, and from that simple act a $60 million
movie was now rolling down the tracks.

Deluged with unsolicited submissions, most talent agents, unlike
Sage, don't even read coverage, much less the full material. Indeed,
they are not by nature readers. It's the deal that starts the energy
pumping, not turning pages of a script. It's the task of the producer

to be relentless and persuasive and to find the right agent to whom to argue his case. The bad news is that if he gets turned down by one ten-percenter at an important agency, it's tantamount to getting rejected by all the agents at that agency because they all talk incessantly to one another.

Is it possible to circumvent the agency system? Only if one's personal contacts and financial resources are superb. If a producer has a close friend at a studio who is willing to put his material in front of a desirable star or producer, that, too, represents a viable course. Some producers, to be sure, specialize in currying the favor of specific stars and uniformly take that person-to-person route. Elie Samaha, the Italian-born producer, deployed the money made from his dry cleaning business to open clubs in Hollywood, which in turn attracted a number of stars. A macho-looking wheeler-dealer, Samaha's lifestyle was attractive to male performers: pretty girls, a never-ending party and lots of action. Before long, Samaha developed a formula for luring actor friends into movies. He would ask them, "Show me that piece of material that you've always wanted to make but that studios turned down." In fact, almost every star has such a script in his drawer, and usually it's been set aside for a good reason. A case in point is *Battlefield Earth*, which John Travolta had long wanted to do as a film. A turgid sci-fi epic written by Scientology founder L. Ron Hubbard, the piece resonated with Travolta, a devoted Scientologist. The actor simply could not understand why no one else had responded to it.

Throwing his own resources into the fray and raising tens of millions off Travolta's name from overseas subdistributors, Samaha stitched together his $70 million science-fiction movie, which opened to disastrous reviews ("The worst movie of the decade," said the *New York Times*) and also to dismal box office results. Sure, Samaha had nailed his star project, but he also had hatched a spectacular turkey.

Samaha has managed to mount several other film projects through his strategy of focusing on "labors of love," but the jury is still out on the results. His very presence in the business, however, serves as a vivid reminder that there are no hard-and-fast rules for success. Indeed, in show business, there are no hard rules for anything. The entertainment industry has always been a magnet for iconoclasts and rule breakers—those who are attracted instinctively to the offbeat, the unique. The possibility always exists that some powerful agent or studio chief or filmmaker or even some star will simply fall in love with a pitch, a story or a book and see it through to its fruition, whatever the personal toll.

That, in itself, is enough to keep most wannabes in the hunt—the possibility that there's a kindred spirit out there who will rise to their challenge. It's a long shot, but it's enough.

All things considered, the role of the zookeeper is a deliciously ambiguous one. Tune in an awards show and you hear one performer after another sing the praises of his agent for getting him the right parts and rescuing him from depression, not to mention saving his marriage. Chances are that at the same moment the very same performer is shopping for a new agent—he may even be having some opportunistic conversations at parties after the show. His old agent knows the drill. Once a star finds himself in the limelight, it is axiomatic that he will shed his former representatives and former friends as he ascends into the lustrous new world of greater celebrity. Thus a Brendan Fraser will suddenly emerge as a client of CAA. At the same time, a Sylvester Stallone, who's on the downward curve, will switch three times in one year from one agent to another (at last report, he had moved yet again from William Morris to ICM). For these former agents, the options are clear: find new clients, make some hot new deals. There's no standing still in the world of zookeepers.

All the while, the agent knows he remains, now and forever, the favorite whipping boy. Just as the ills of career failure are blamed on him, so are the ills of the industry. Ten years ago, even the august Lew Wasserman launched into a tirade against the behavior of talent agencies. Addressing a board meeting of the Motion Picture Association of America, Wasserman zeroed in on the decision of Columbia Pictures to succumb to an agent's demand to pay Jim Carrey a $20 million up-front salary to star in *The Cable Guy*. Breaking the $20 million barrier, Wasserman charged, was a signal of corporate carelessness that would lead to the demise of the studios. But he saved his toughest criticism for the agent who managed to escalate his client's fee from $12 to $20 million in one masterstroke. No greater proof could ever be found that agents were killing the industry, Wasserman intoned.

His fellow company heads looked on, startled. Here was the one-time master agent, turning on his own. And why? For making a good deal!

Wasserman has since retired, assuming the role of elder statesman. Reminded of this attack not long ago, he sighed and responded with a wry smile. "The thing about agents is that they're still a wonderful target."

Members of the zookeeping tribe would heartily agree.

CUT TO: Peter Bart on Butch Cassidy

When I first came to Paramount, the place was a shadow of what a studio should be. The support systems were in disarray. There was still any number of talented people there, but there was no chemistry. People weren't working together. So one weekend I was going through my pile of scripts, and I started reading a Western. Now, I don't particularly like Westerns. Even by the late 1960s, the Western seemed like a genre that had run its course. But as I turned the pages of this script I realized this wasn't an ordinary Western. This was brilliantly stylized writing. I called a couple of my colleagues, telling them of my enthusiasm and imploring them to read it. They gave me sort of that "sure, kid" response. Understandably so. I was the new boy on the block, a journalist who had just crashed the gates of "the club" without realizing what the club was all about.

When I got to work Monday, I realized that I alone had read it. I made some phone calls to try to learn its status. The piece had been read at other studios over the weekend and there was keen interest. There was also interest from stars, but I couldn't pin down exactly who. Beatty was one rumor. Maybe even Brando. But the agent wouldn't tell me anything firm. Clearly he was carefully orchestrating all this but had no intention of giving away this theme. I asked him how much it would cost to take the script off the market, and I could sense his disdain. In his eyes, I could never mobilize the gonzo offer needed to win this battle. Frantic, I lobbied members of the Paramount team: I had a terrific Western in my clutches. There might even be star casting.

It was clear to me that no one wanted to support my initiative, so I decided to take the leap. On my own, without authorization, I offered $200,000 for an outright buy of *Butch Cassidy and the Sundance Kid*. If I was going down in flames, I might as well go big time. Surprised, the agent said he would take my offer under consideration, but he called back late that afternoon to say Twentieth Century Fox had topped my offer by $150,000. And that Redford and Newman had indeed committed, with George Roy Hill to direct. The whole thing had been beautifully orchestrated. The big players at Fox had worked in sync all weekend while I was thrashing around in the dark. I envied their teamwork. They had a real studio while we were a bunch of people bumping into each other. I understood then, more than ever, that we'd have to get our act together. I wanted to feel functional, not frustrated. There was a daunting job ahead of us.

The Golden Rule

Where the money is, so will the jackals gather.

RAYMOND CHANDLER

As movie mavens go, Joe Roth is a friendly family man who avoids industry functions and disdains studio politics. In the year 2000 as his contract at Disney was winding down, Roth realized he had an opportunity to change his life. He remembered Yogi Berra's admonition, "When you come to a fork in the road, take it." Roth had spent most of the previous fifteen years working for three of the most demanding bosses in the entertainment industry: Rupert Murdoch, Barry Diller and Michael Eisner. He'd run up a solid record as president of the Disney Studio but the prospect of dealing with Disney intrigues for several more years was unappealing. In his younger years, Roth had worked as an independent producer and had even directed a couple of films. He'd relished his autonomy in those days. At the same time, Joe Roth had been around long enough to understand the nuances of Hollywood's Golden

Rule: He who has the gold, makes the rules. That much was very clear to him. With that truism in mind, Roth decided to try for the best of both worlds. With the help of a talented attorney named Skip Brittenham, he put together a well-financed new company that had the resources to create a slate of eight to ten movies a year. The funding came primarily from so-called "end users"—mostly TV networks around the world that were willing to pre-buy movies to assure an ongoing access to top product. Such stars as Julia Roberts, Bruce Willis and Adam Sandler in turn promised Roth that they would deliver a specified number of projects to his new company. Roberts even agreed to start off her commitment by starring in a film Roth himself would direct.

Feeling that he had met the mandates of the Golden Rule, Joe Roth thus started his new life at Revolution Studios, as he named his new entity. He would be free to make his pictures. He would also be free to set his rules. And, with a little luck, he would contrive to keep his overhead low and beat the major companies at their own game. He knew it was a difficult game at best.

Indeed, in the fall of the year 2000, as Hollywood's writers and actors were marshaling their contract demands and making noise about a possible strike, a shrill cry of anguish arose from the inner sanctums of the major entertainment companies. How dare you demand bigger paychecks and fatter residuals, the moguls chorused. Don't you realize this is a lousy business? Don't you understand we barely make any money even under present conditions?

The writers and actors guilds quickly registered their disbelief over these protestations. If show business is a nonprofit industry, they asked, why do global companies like News Corp. and Vivendi spend billions to buy movie studios? Why does Disney acquire the ABC Network and why won't General Electric sell its interest in NBC? The Rupert Murdochs and Jean-Marie Messiers invited themselves to the party—no one coerced them.

The entertainment economy, as it's come to be called, has always been a volatile affair, but it's become even more so under the influence of the sprawling multinationals. Their sheer financial heft has triggered inflationary spirals in the talent market. With the cost of producing and marketing a Hollywood motion picture soaring in the 1990s, each time a studio steps up to the table to release and market its film, it's risking $100 million–plus. Again, as the salary demands of the Tom Cruises and the Harrison Fords climbed from $15 million to $20 million and then $25 million, the moguls not only have ponied up these sums but actually fought for the right to do so.

The end result of this profligacy is that few movies or TV films turn a profit from their initial releases or their first seasons on the air. But while companies may complain about these losses, they're also building up incredible inventories (or "libraries," as the analysts like to call them) that generate millions from ancillary revenue streams. Hence the economics of the multinationals are hardly as dire as they want you to believe.

The great debate about bank credit versus screen credit colors almost every negotiation within the industry. On one side sits the money; on the other, the talent. Each wants more—more perks, more profits. "Show me the money," screeched Jerry Maguire's client. No four words could better characterize the struggle to find it, keep it and showcase it. Money is the barometer of power and prestige. In Hollywood you don't get what's fair; you get what you're able to negotiate. Sometimes the talent will get even more than they negotiated. On *Lethal Weapon 3*, the heads of Warner Bros. decided that the fabulous back-end gross participations might not be sufficient to lock the deal, so they gave the creative group an "attaboy," in the form of a surprise jackpot. Each of the collaborators, including Mel Gibson and director Richard Donner, got a new Land Rover.

Flash back eighty years from 2000 to 1919. A renegade band of filmmakers had decided they'd had enough. They said they were sick of corporate domination. They were artists and, as such, didn't like being bossed around by "suits." They wanted to focus on their art, not the bottom line. Besides, they said, it was about time someone thought about the needs of the filmgoer and protected him from "threatening combinations and trusts that would force upon him mediocre productions and machine-made entertainment."

Those pronouncements, made in 1919, reflected the sentiments of Charlie Chaplin, Mary Pickford, D. W. Griffith and Douglas Fairbanks, who decided to break free from the major studios to form their own independent company. Their new venture, United Artists, represented a mini revolution in Hollywood. For the first time, filmmakers were seizing control of their own work. Or, as one reigning studio chief put it, "The lunatics just took over the asylum."

Their revolution was short-lived. Artists rarely make good managers, and Chaplin and company were no exception. They fought with one another, became distracted by divorces and random scandals and had trouble deciding how to use their new freedom. They ended up hiring management types to run their company—men who quickly turned into the bureaucrats they'd been fleeing.

The saga of United Artists reminds us how history keeps repeating itself, even in the ever-volatile motion picture industry. Time and again, Hollywood has reinvented itself along the lines of a classic oligopoly, with power focused in the hands of a few corporate players, only to splinter when times turned bad, then coalesce yet again. By the 1930s, for example, the so-called Big Five dominated the landscape, producing and distributing their films worldwide. They also owned sprawling theater chains to exhibit their product. The charter members of this tight little club were Warner Bros., Paramount, Twentieth Century Fox, RKO and Loew's, which owned MGM. (Universal, Columbia and UA fed into this mechanism but couldn't match the heft and bargaining muscle of the Big Five.) By the millennium, hegemony over the marketplace had shifted to globe-spanning multinational corporations such as Rupert Murdoch's News Corp. (Fox), Viacom (Paramount), Vivendi (Universal), Sony (Columbia) and AOL/Time Warner (Warner Bros.) augmented by Walt Disney, which now encompassed the ABC Network among other holdings.

Along the way some major companies faded into peripheral players, such as MGM (now combined with UA) while others, like DreamWorks, were striving to join the elite circle. But all the while, a vivid panoply of so-called "independents" were busily percolating along the margins of the industry, gaining strength as the majors periodically faded into disarray, then fighting for survival when the tentacles of the studios tightened over the marketplace. Whatever their economic condition, it was the so-called "indies" that infused the movie business with artistic verve.

The precise role of these indies has never been defined because, from the beginning, they've appeared and reappeared in a bewildering array of shapes and structures. The Samuel Goldwyns and David O. Selznicks were self-financed indies in the 1930s and 1940s, even though they were solidly aligned with the establishment and made glossy Hollywood movies. Still their modus operandi was idiosyncratically noncorporate, and it was not until Selznick ran vastly over budget on *Gone With the Wind* that he had to surrender distribution and some controls to the dreaded MGM monolith.

Further blurring the line, by the year 2000 a series of well-funded indies appeared on the scene, prompted in part by the growing demand of overseas "end users" (i.e., TV networks and theater circuits) for Hollywood films. These newcomers, too, were solidly funded companies, such as Revolution, headed by Joe Roth; Spyglass Entertainment, headed by Roger Birnbaum, who worked for Roth at Fox and Disney; and Bel Air Entertainment, run by Steve Reuther, a one-time William Morris agent.

At the same time, a dizzying array of small, more artistically venturesome independents also were setting up a beachhead. They took their inspiration from pioneering singular filmmakers, such as John Cassavetes or John Sayles, or genre filmmakers fostering gay, Hispanic or black cinema or merely so-called "credit card" filmmakers—those who appropriated their parents' credit cards, shot their films on the run and prayed for deliverance at Sundance or Slamdance.

Independent film thus encompasses a wide spectrum of sensibilities but a common denominator of economics. Indies make their films with their own money, or at least with money they control, rather than relying on corporate funds. While they still interface with the realities of the marketplace, they do so in the context of their own vision. As film critic Emanuel Levy put it, they are unified only in their disunity—in short, by their own "eclectic aestheticism." Hence, Levy titled his book exploring independent film *Cinema of Outsiders*.

When the "outsiders" become insiders, of course, the waters become muddier. Harvey and Bob Weinstein built Miramax through the acquisition of subtitled foreign films such as *Belle de Jour* or, subsequently, a distinctive English product such as *The Crying Game*. Their savvy in the international sector was so respected that for a time they became unofficial arbiters on what films would or would not cross borders. While they retained their creative autonomy after their sale to Disney, their success with more expensive films like *The English Patient* and *Shakespeare in Love* prompted a shift into a different scale of projects like *All the Pretty Horses* in partnership with Sony or the $130 million *Gangs of New York* starring Leonardo DiCaprio and Cameron Diaz, in concert with foreign partners and Touchstone. Miramax insisted it was still making independent films, but clearly an inflationary spiral had carried it into a different orbit.

Even as Miramax was steadfastly moving upmarket, another wing of the company, headed by Bob Weinstein, was forging ahead with an entirely different game plan, further blurring the Miramax image. While Harvey enjoyed projects like *Chocolat*, an Oscar nominee in 2001, Bob busily cultivated such fare as *Scary Movie* and *Spy Kids*. Even as Harvey took aim on the cerebral market, Bob had his eye on the gut. If Bob's sights were lower, so were his marketing costs. While some long-term Miramax employees felt whipsawed, working for a totally schizy company, competitors, too, were thrown off. Whenever this redoubtable indie seemed boxed in in one market, it consistently managed to break out in another.

As Miramax continued to diversify its product, studios like Paramount and Warner Bros., enticed by Miramax's sporadic success in the art market, decided to institute their own classics divisions, thus joining the established Sony Classics in this arena. These moves in turn triggered grave concern among indie filmmakers. What qualified studio executives to decide on the viability of independent cinema? they demanded. What did studios know about marketing quirky indie films?

Indeed, by dipping their toes into the independent scene, the studios exhibited a certain ambivalence about their own basic strategy. The majors had shown growing reluctance about deviating in any way from the most basic pretested commercial fare. "There's no margin of error anymore," said Tom Rothman, Fox's president of production. "Your movies have to be excellent. Good isn't enough." They have to be excellent, but also excellently commercial, most studio chiefs would add. Sequels and special effects extravaganzas are the order of the day. Adult drama has been all but condemned to the scrap heap. To the studios, the failure of "issue" pictures such as *The Insider* or *Thirteen Days* reinforced the single-mindedness of their mission. The studio assembly lines would be focused on big, brassy star vehicles that would play around the world and would generate ancillary revenue streams through video, pay TV and merchandising.

Given the studios' focus on big-budget extravaganzas, it would clearly be up to the indies to fill out the filmmaking spectrum—to create more personal, character-driven films that reflected the filmmaker's special vision. And if the studios wanted to hedge their bets by becoming minority investors, so much the better, provided they didn't suffocate the process along the way.

"What it comes down to is this," said Joe Roth. "The bigger the parent companies get, the less meaningful the film divisions will become and the less impact they will have. Independents will be the only ones who will be making movies they're passionate about. The others will make 'product.'"

Given this divide, indie filmmakers face a growing temptation to straddle the two worlds, when possible, playing one against the other. One gifted practitioner at this gamesmanship is Steven Soderbergh, whose first film, *sex, lies, and videotape*, became a classic indie success story. The Louisiana-born Soderbergh had tried to crack the Hollywood club as a young man, but he couldn't land an entry position nor get anyone to read his screenplays. He settled for a job holding up cue cards on a talk show. Returning home, he finally landed a gig shooting concert footage for Yes, the rock group, which led to a video. Impressed with his work, a home video company, RCA/Columbia, put up the modest financing for a film that became *sex, lies, and videotape*, which was accepted at Sundance. Again, no one paid any attention to the twenty-six-year-old filmmaker at the festival until *Daily Variety* published a glowing review of his film. Suddenly he was the indie director of the moment, his film going on to win the Palme d'Or at Cannes.

Declaring dryly that "it's all downhill from here," Soderbergh decided to stay in the dicey confines of the indie world, but his next three films—*Kafka*, *King of the Hill* and *The Underneath*—failed to generate excitement. *Schizopolis* and *The Limey* were even more stylized and cerebral. When Universal offered him *Out of Sight*, which was a chance to work with a big budget and a major star in George Clooney, Soderbergh succumbed. The film was greeted with excellent reviews, but Universal's decision to jam it into its summer schedule as a last-minute replacement crippled its box office potential.

With *Erin Brockovich*, Soderbergh solidified his credentials as a commercial filmmaker. Its success persuaded Fox to finance his next effort, *Traffic*, an expensive, complexly plotted movie about the drug trade. Given his indie roots, Soderbergh agreed to defer a substantial portion of his salary, thus enticing his then-star, Harrison Ford, to follow his example. But Ford grew nervous about the subject matter and his new agents at United Talent Agency reinforced his doubts. Ultimately Ford bowed out, and so did Fox, only to be replaced by a semi-independent, USA Films, a subsidiary of Barry Diller's TV mini-conglomerate. Michael Douglas then committed to the starring role, thus attracting overseas funding, and *Traffic* got the green light at $55 million. This was a budgetary figure far beyond the customary indie lid, but Soderbergh got to make the film he wanted, a dense narrative set in nearly 100 different locations, which won him an Oscar as well as running up excellent box office results.

If Soderbergh, like the Weinstein brothers, successfully inhabited that twilight zone between the studios and the indie world, few others manage to do so. To most, the two remain worlds apart. It would be hard to imagine the team of Merchant and Ivory, for example, laboring within the confines of, say, Warner Bros. That was a lesson learned early by the gregarious, hard-driving, Bombay-born Ismail Merchant, who assumed he could take Hollywood by storm. Armed with an MBA from New York University, Merchant had shot a fourteen-minute short called *The Creation of Women* and dispatched a press release announcing his impending arrival in Tinseltown. To his surprise, no newspaper picked up his release and no studio granted him an interview. Merchant sold classified ads for the *Los Angeles Times* while formulating a new plan to jump-start his film career.

In concert with director James Ivory, Merchant ultimately went on to produce a long series of rather mannered films ranging from *Shakespeare Wallah* and *Howard's End* to *Savages* and *Jefferson in Paris*. Even when they misfired, their films were uniformly cultured, sometimes dogmatically so. They were also a tribute to Merchant's entrepreneurial zeal and Ivory's filmic discipline.

The longevity and fecundity of the Merchant-Ivory team harks back to the indie titans of old, which managed to sustain their fragile enterprises even at a time when the studio system was predominant. David O. Selznick built a thriving indie in partnership with John Hay Whitney, the socialite-millionaire, despite fierce opposition from the majors. Selznick had made himself a lightning rod by marrying the daughter of Louis B. Mayer, the czar of MGM. A control freak, Mayer was determined to keep his son-in-law in his employ. When Mayer learned of Selznick's determination to start an independent company, he went so far as to call a meeting of all studio chiefs, insisting that none agree to ever distribute Selznick's films. Independent companies, he warned, would undermine the absolute power of the majors. An expert intimidator, Mayer succeeded in his mission, thus forcing Selznick, also defiant by nature, to go to work as an executive at RKO. It would be years before his dream of establishing his own label became a reality.

As an indie, Selznick himself became almost as tyrannical as Mayer in his treatment of talent. He wrote exhaustive memos to his writers and directors, often arguing arcane issues. His choice of projects, too, was often bizarre. *The Garden of Allah*, a casbah romance starring Marlene Dietrich and Charles Boyer, was a notorious flop. When Selznick committed to back *Little Lord Fauntleroy*, Ben Hecht, then a top screenwriter, wrote, "The trouble with you, David, is that you did all your reading before you were twelve." Another top writer, Nunnally Johnson, turned down a deal with Selznick because "an assignment from you consists of three months of work and three more of recuperation."

Selznick's stubborn backing of *Gone With the Wind* elevated him to legendary status as a producer, yet the project was all but thrust on him through the combined efforts of his story editor, Kay Brown, and his partner, John Hay Whitney, both of whom had read the book first and instructed Selznick that if he didn't buy it, they would do so without him. Once the film got rolling, Selznick intruded himself into every detail of the production and also helped propel it massively over its skinny $2.5 million budget. Unable to cover his overages, Selznick finally was driven to the one action he most dreaded—asking his father-in-law for help. Ever the sharp deal maker, Mayer covered the added budgetary costs in return for distribution rights plus half Selznick's share of the profits.

Another mythic figure in the indie world of that period, Samuel Goldwyn, matched Selznick in stubbornness as well as in promulgating his own mythology. When the *Saturday Evening Post* wrote a glowing profile describing "the Goldwyn touch," William Wyler, a top director who often worked with Goldwyn, blew his top. "I don't recall Goldwyn contributing anything other than buying good material and talent," he said. "It's all his attempt to make a name for himself as an artist, but as far as being creative, he's a zero."

Goldwyn nonetheless had a genius for involving himself with the right projects at the right time, spanning the likes of *Wuthering Heights, The Little Foxes, The Secret Life of Walter Mitty, Guys and Dolls* and, of course, *The Best Years of Our Lives*, which not only won him his first Oscar but also grossed almost $10 million in its first year—remarkable by the standards of the 1940s.

Goldwyn's pursuit of talent was frenzied if not maniacal. Though he himself mangled the language, he admired good writing and hired the likes of Robert Sherwood and Lillian Hellman. He even launched a campaign to sign George Bernard Shaw, the elusive playwright who was notably contemptuous of Hollywood. According to A. Scott Berg, Goldwyn's biographer, Shaw once wrote to Goldwyn that no one in Hollywood had any "more notion of telling a story than a blind puppy has of composing a symphony." Their lengthy correspondence resulted in Shaw agreeing to sell screen rights to his plays providing Goldwyn would pay Shaw 10 percent of the gross plus give him final cut—demands that were revolutionary in that epoch but probably would have received serious consideration today.

Goldwyn worshiped at the altar of celebrity, throwing lavish parties at his home as often as four times a week, courting the likes of Ronald Colman and Gary Cooper, at one point even signing the son of President Franklin D. Roosevelt to a deal working for his company with no specific responsibilities. Goldwyn even tried to hire Irving Thalberg away from MGM.

But unlike Selznick, Goldwyn had the security of an ongoing distribution deal with United Artists through much of his career, creating, however, a state of permanent warfare with its executives, undermining one regime after another at UA. He finally wore down his opponents, annexing their facilities and renaming it the Samuel Goldwyn Studio. While establishing his own mini-major, however, he still had to scramble for financing and distribution. While *Gone With the Wind* came early in Selznick's career (he was only thirty-seven), *The Best Years of Our Lives* came late in Goldwyn's.

Hence, while Selznick spent much of his professional life trying to top himself, Goldwyn managed a strong third act. In his book, Scott Berg quotes a dialogue between Garson Kanin, the playwright, and William Wyler, who directed *The Best Years of Our Lives*. Wyler explains that one of the great reasons for Goldwyn's success was that "he convinced himself he's never wrong. He's a god. Not a bad thing to be, especially if you live on earth." To which Kanin replied, "What makes you think he lives on earth?"

Among contemporary filmmakers, the closest to Goldwyn and Selznick are Joe Roth and Harvey Weinstein, both of them occupying a space and income bracket that bears no relation to the realities of the indie world. In the indie arena, filmmaking is still a hand-to-mouth affair, devoid of lavish dinner parties or glitzy premieres. The process of getting the film made is the ultimate high. Out there with his crew and actors, setting up the shots, shaping the performances, telling the story—that represents a filmmaker's moment in the sun.

Getting there, however, is sheer agony. There are no shortcuts to raising money, no banks to call and no philanthropists like John Hay Whitney to summon up. It is a business of one-buck-at-a-time baby steps. Pete Shaner, a determined Annapolis graduate who flew for the Navy before fixating on film, describes his search for investors: "I call up the girl who sat behind me in eleventh grade and who is now an ophthalmologist in Florida. I call my sister's high school boyfriend who I never met but I've heard is now a stockbroker. I hope that friends will tell other friends. When I finished my first film, *Lover's Knot*, and it started to bring in some money, I was already raising money for my next movie, *Nicolas*. I'd tell them, 'I will send you a profit check on *Lover's Knot*, unless, that is, you wish to roll it over and make even more money on another movie called *Nicolas*.'"

One of the people Shaner hit on was Randy Simon, a freewheeling young dealer in classic cars. Simon admits he "always wanted to be a producer because producers have an interesting lifestyle, meet cute girls and make lots of money. So far I've accomplished two of those three." Simon, in short, has managed to raise money for his productions but has yet to make a profit from his producing and fund-raising activities.

Simon connected with an attorney named Jack Schwartzman who had lots of friends in the business. Schwartzman offered to develop scripts with some young writers and, if any worked out, he would help get them funded, with Shaner's script part of the deal. By the time Shaner turned it in, however, Schwartzman had died unexpectedly. It now fell to Shaner and Simon to raise the $100,000 budgeted to make the film, shooting it on Super 16. Further analysis of the figures showed that a more realistic budget would be $260,000.

"Once you raise your first $100,000," says Simon, "you call everybody back and say, 'Listen, I hate to do this to you but if you don't put in another 20 percent we're not going to be able to put the movie together and you'll lose your first money.'" Another Simon-Shaner rule-of-thumb: Los Angeles may be where most movies get made, but it's the worst place to raise money. "In LA everyone's eyes glaze over when you say you're making a movie," says Shaner. "If you call someone in, say, Pennsylvania, they light up and say, 'How can I get involved?'"

Though Simon acknowledges that it's theoretically easier to twist the arms of backers if there's a distribution deal in hand, "It's a chicken and egg situation," he says. "It's also much easier to set up distribution once the financing is in hand. And you can make a far better deal."

This works fine for a filmmaker like Shaner. "I see myself like a sort of master carpenter, building a table. When the work is finished, I'll bring it to market and see if I can find a buyer." *Lover's Knot* ultimately got a brief theatrical release window but has run frequently on cable TV outlets like Lifetime and Encore.

Mindful of the risks involved, Shaner and Simon will accept no more than $5,000 from any single backer. "Within that limit it's sort of disposable income for them, but beyond that it gets serious," says Shaner. "Besides, I don't want to lose too many friends." Shaner sets up a limited liability company, as opposed to a limited partnership, for his films, so that it resembles a real estate deal, minus the actual real estate. The first money that comes in pays off deferments, including creative talent—that is, salaries talent agreed to delay until financial returns started to flow. The second block of funds goes to investors to the tune of 125 percent of their original investment. "After the investors get their 125 percent, I declare us in profit," he says. "Any further funds are split fifty-fifty between the producers and investors."

Ideally, indie producers would like to emulate the majors in raising money from overseas TV networks and distributors, but this is no easy task, given the absence of stars. "You run into these foreign sales types and you tell them who's in your movie, and they roll their eyes," says Simon. "Or they'll look at your lead actor, who's not exactly Bruce Willis, and say, 'OK, he's worth $150,000 in Spain and $650,000 in Germany,' and you think, OK, maybe they're right. Maybe that's all I've got."

In trying to nail down their casts, indie producers find themselves dealing with the diciest of all documents, a letter of intent, which declares that an actor has committed to play a particular role in a film. Theoretically such a document should be useful to a producer in raising money or obtaining distribution, but it doesn't always work out that way. As several lawsuits have demonstrated, these documents are difficult to enforce. Valerie Breiman, who has directed two indie films, recalls obtaining such a letter of intent from a TV actress that helped raise $500,000 from German television alone. Realizing her power, the actress promptly demanded approval over her male lead, coming up with a list of actors who either would never do an indie movie or would never work with her. Fortunately, the empathetic Germans left their money in the film, which finally got made with another cast.

To Breiman, the cast of an indie film cannot be evaluated by foreign presales alone but also, as she puts it, "by their level of cool." Audiences for indie films want "cool" actors, she points out. Famke Janssen and Jon Favreau, who co-starred in her film, *Love and Sex*, meet her definition of "cool," and indeed, *Variety*'s critic, Todd McCarthy, praised their "winning performances," adding that it's an "ultra mainstream indie"—the ultimate compliment to a low-budget film.

In negotiating with cast members, indie producers again play by different rules than do the studios. It isn't a question of asking an agent for a quote and paying that price. An indie producer ideally wants to pay nothing or at least no more than SAG scale. Some money can be deferred. Perhaps the actor will accept a piece of the profits. The ideal actor for an indie is one who needs a role but doesn't need the money. Perhaps he's a TV star who wants exposure in a feature, or one who feels he's been typecast and wants to showcase himself in a new persona.

The same bargaining principle applies to everything else connected with an indie feature, from the lab to the trailer to the music. Everything is a negotiation from ground zero. On *Nicolas*, Pete Shaner paid each of his twenty-five crew members a flat fee of $100 a day, except for his union cameraman, who settled for a fee far below his normal rate. On *Lover's Knot*, he even used a newly developed high-definition digital video camera, the HD24P, originally created by Sony for George Lucas. That yielded substantial savings in film stock and processing costs.

In an environment where everyone is hustling everyone else, certain compromises must inevitably be made. The indie filmmaker becomes accustomed to the fact that a lot of people are looking over his shoulder. "Creative freedom is something of a fantasy," says Valerie Breiman. "I realize people feel they have no control when they're in the studio world, but I've never been in that world and as long as I'm playing with someone else's money, I'm always going to have some very bright, wonderful people or some major league assholes trying to tell me what to do. It's always an ensemble situation. That's the nature of filmmaking, irrespective of the budget or backing."

Creative control is a hot-button issue especially for those niche players aiming their work initially at minority markets. Doug McHenry put down $50,000 to sign several groups to pay-or-play deals for his film *Krush Groove*. He was bailed out at the eleventh hour by Warner Bros., which agreed to a skimpy distribution deal. McHenry went on to make *New Jack City*, which combined action and gangster subplots to broaden the appeal beyond the niche market. Though he covets conventional distribution channels, he is constantly alert to the intrusion of corporate sensibilities that might conventionalize his films.

Another major, Columbia, came to the rescue of Robert Rodriguez who had completed a $7,000 16-mm film called *El Mariachi*. The then twenty-four-year-old Austin, Texas, filmmaker had shot the film in two weeks in a Mexican border town with nonsync sound. The studio blew it up to 35 mm, cleared up the sound track and staked Rodriguez to a career.

Some indie filmmakers have found themselves sandbagged on issues of final control even when they thought they were firmly in the driver's seat. In 1969, Haskell Wexler directed a provocative film for Paramount called *Medium Cool*, set against the chaotic background of the Democratic National Convention. Mindful of his controversial subject matter, Wexler constructed the film as a negative pickup deal. This meant that he would come up with the funds to produce the picture, and when he turned in his finished product, Paramount would give him $600,000. Though this arrangement granted him a high degree of autonomy, Wexler, a gifted cinematographer by trade, was highly collaborative with the studio. He showed executives an early cut of his film, which contained a great deal of frontal nudity—the privates of Robert Forster, his leading man, were out there in plain view as he playfully chased a girl around his apartment. Wexler agreed to remove the nudity and, in turn, studio executives were completely supportive of his effort. At the eleventh hour, however, a major problem loomed. A top executive of Paramount in New York also turned out to be the chairman of the Democratic Party's finance committee, and he was up in arms when he saw the final cut. To his biased eye, this was a full-scale attack on his party and he demanded that the studio abandon its release. Wexler was in shock; so were executives at the studio, who had admired his work. Finally the issue was presented to Charles Bluhdorn, chairman of Paramount's parent company, Gulf + Western. Often unpredictable in times of crisis, Bluhdorn in this case took the high road. Pointing to his European origins, he reminded his colleagues that censorship ran counter to the American tradition. "This is something I thought I left behind me in Europe," Bluhdorn railed.

In the end, Paramount released *Medium Cool*, which generated solid reviews and built its own cult audience.

When it comes to final control, ironically, the indies that exercise the most clout are those self-financed entities that have locked-in deals at studios. Though their distributors may press for changes (they may want cuts to facilitate a PG-13 rather than an R, for example), the producing companies call their own shots.

Two prominent members of this fraternity are Imagine Films, founded by director Ron Howard and producer Brian Grazer, and Castle Rock Entertainment, founded by Rob Reiner, with a few producing partners. Imagine and Castle Rock have both been around for fifteen years, yet their fortunes have veered sharply. Castle Rock began with a bang only to subside into a series of whimpers; Imagine's beginnings were somewhat unpromising, but it later became a major force in the industry.

At the outset, Castle Rock could do no wrong. Its initial cluster of film releases included *Stand by Me* and *When Harry Met Sally*. As its first TV entry, Castle Rock came forward with a comedy that no one in the broadcast industry would champion. *Seinfeld* would have no lasting power, most wrongly predicted.

Castle Rock drew its financing from a variety of sources and distributed its films first through Sony, then Warner Bros. Despite its astonishing beginnings, the company quickly hit a series of speed bumps. Rob Reiner, who seemed to have the director's equivalent of perfect pitch, suddenly was fostering clunkers like *The Story of Us* and *Ghosts of Mississippi*. The very expensive Russell Crowe–Meg Ryan movie, *Proof of Life*, tanked. And the company could come up with no promising TV fare to follow up *Seinfeld*.

Imagine, too, was identified with some surprise hits early on—*Splash* and *Cocoon*—but, like Castle Rock, couldn't sustain it. Succumbing to the Wall Street fever of the mid 1980s, Grazer and Howard were persuaded to become a public company, one that would assume the mantle of a diversified entertainment conglomerate. Once transformed into "suits," rather than filmmakers, both partners, however, seemed distracted. Suddenly Imagine was releasing flops like *Cry-Baby*, *Sgt. Bilko* and *The Chamber*. "A frantic neurosis seemed to take over our company," Grazer recalls. In 1993, he and Howard decided to bid Wall Street farewell, going into hock to finance a $23.4 million buyout of what was once their own company. Having gone public at $8 a share in 1986, they now took the company private at $9 a share, which didn't exactly make their investors happy. Nonetheless, within a couple of years they seemed to hit their stride again. Imagine's parade of hits included *The Nutty Professor* and *Dr. Suess' How the Grinch Stole Christmas*. There were even some respectable forays into television. Working within the overall framework of Universal for film and Disney for TV, Imagine managed to preserve its autonomy and shape its own destiny.

Of all the mega-independents, none has attracted more attention and second-guessing than DreamWorks, the brainchild of Steven Spielberg, David Geffen and Jeffrey Katzenberg. It has never become clear precisely what motivated the so-called Dream Team to embark on their venture—perhaps a combination of megalomania and boredom. Having just departed a long and bountiful tenure at Disney, Katzenberg needed a job. Geffen had made a billion dollars in the music business and was restless for new challenges. Spielberg seemed caught up in the idea of building his own studio facility and transforming himself into a sort of neo-Thalbergian mogul.

They had little trouble raising the funding from a combination of banks, Internet tycoons and overseas sources but, ironically, could not propel themselves to instant success as Castle Rock and Imagine had. Progress on the television and music fronts was spotty. Initial film releases like *The Peacemaker* and *Deep Impact* seemed utterly conventional. Even Spielberg, who'd been counted on to devise a blockbuster of *Jurassic Park* proportions for his new venture, delivered instead the thoroughly respectable but commercially disappointing *Amistad*.

Again, the Dream Team managed to create an entity that afforded them total autonomy, yet one that also seemed derivative of the major studios in terms of style and output. DreamWorks was even gripped by the same internal political intrigues that afflicted the majors. None of its executives assumed formal titles (a symbolic effort to discourage bureaucracy), but with some 1,300 employees on board, its decision-making machinery was cumbersome. Outside producers and agents struggled to figure out how to thread through the layers to reach Spielberg.

Spielberg's dream of building a studio at Playa Vista, California, was scuttled, and by its third year, rumors began to circulate that the Dream Team had wearied of their own invention. While denials came hot and heavy, it was not until the release of *American Beauty* that Hollywood began to believe them. *American Beauty* seemed to reflect all the ideals of an indie company: Its thrust seemed boldly uncommercial—an adult drama with satiric overtones directed by a first-time filmmaker. Its success was extraordinary, rolling up a domestic gross of $130.1 million and winning eight Academy Awards. And it changed DreamWorks forever. Suddenly the company seemed to gather new energy with such mainstream films as *Gladi-*

ator, What Lies Beneath and *Chicken Run*. Even *Almost Famous*, its money loser of summer 2000, was greatly admired and became a cult favorite.

In summer 2001, DreamWorks unfurled its ultimate surprise hit, the witty animated feature, *Shrek*. The success of *Shrek*, which soared past the $200 million mark in less than six weeks, represented a double-barreled vindication for Jeffery Katzenberg. Several scenes in the film parodied the Walt Disney company and Disneyland, which represented a somewhat churlish message from Katzenberg, whose exit from Disney had been stormy—he sued his former boss, Michael Eisner, for back bonuses, coming away with a judgment totaling some $250 million. In addition *Shrek* all but buried Disney's own animated summer picture, *Atlantis: The Lost Empire*, thus drilling a large hole into Disney's long-standing domination of the summer animation market.

With it all, however, DreamWorks' self-image seemed caught irrevocably between that of an indie and a mini-major. In some ways, they were more "major" than the "majors." Its three hierarchs clearly thought of themselves as mainstream players. They were wealthy moguls whose lives were built around their corporate jets and other billionaire perks. Their style of micromanaging was so driven and intense that many executives at the "conventional" studios admitted they were loath to do business with them. Even as DreamWorks sought to move its distribution deal away from Universal in 2001, the working executives at other studios actively lobbied against closing a deal with DreamWorks, arguing that life was too short to put up with their demands.

As a result of all this, DreamWorks seemed a Hollywood anomaly. As an economic model, it made little sense. It was a pure play movie company, emerging at a time when Wall Street frowned upon companies that focused only on movies. On a practical level, however, DreamWorks was nothing short of a home run, creating brilliant movies and forging a program in animation that left even the Disney powerhouse panting. Yet DreamWorks, like Imagine and Castle Rock, was bent on creating star vehicles aimed at the worldwide audience. Like the majors, many of its films were so expensive as to eliminate the remote possibility of recoupment from domestic box office alone. They were all caught up in essentially the same values, and the same inflationary pressures. They were part of the establishment, not of the world of Sundance. If anything, their product would squeeze out indie releases from the megaplexes, preempting screens that normally might go to true indie fare.

And that indeed was what was happening to an alarming degree.

At the beginning of the new millennium the market for art house or independent films was declining year to year by between 5 percent and 10 percent, depending on the criteria of measurement. Now and then a specific indie movie would break from the pack and stir up box office excitement. *The Blair Witch Project* of 1998 was certainly the flashiest of this crop, though its sequel fell on its face. *Crouching Tiger, Hidden Dragon* was another surprise hit, especially since it carried subtitles. But both were rare exceptions. In the view of Harvey Weinstein, there were so many indie features competing for playdates that they'd become caught up in a sort of Darwinian cycle of self-destructiveness. At the same time, the multiplexes were allotting their screens not to indie films but to the Hollywood hit of the moment. Movies aimed at niche markets could not count on playdates.

And finally it boiled down to the product itself: Not enough indie films were generating word-of-mouth enthusiasm. This was especially frustrating for filmmakers at a time when the exponential growth of the Internet was providing an ideal new networking platform. Self-anointed on-line critics could quickly spread the word about a groundbreaking new movie—a phenomenon that certainly

gave a boost to *Blair Witch*. But by and large, these on-line aficionados were obsessing about films from the majors, not the indies; they
were blabbing endlessly about the hidden meanings of *The Matrix*,
not the subtle nuances of *The House of Mirth*. Clearly, the sheer promotional noise level of the wannabe blockbusters was all but drowning out the soft murmurs of the art house entries.

In short, filmmakers who dedicated themselves to the "cinema of
outsiders" were feeling even more outside than ever.

Paradoxically, those players who were the least discouraged—
indeed they were newly invigorated—were true outsiders: namely, foreign media mavens who increasingly were fascinated by Hollywood's
alien landscape. Now, more than ever, American movies held pre-
dominance in the world marketplace. European filmmakers, whether
in France, Germany or Italy, consistently demonstrated their inabil-
ity to create films that crossed boundaries even in Europe—forget
playing in the U.S. And since Europe now reflected an ever-growing
appetite for filmgoing, a financial opportunity clearly presented itself.

European filmmakers long ago tried their hand in Hollywood with
occasionally felicitous results. Stars like Clint Eastwood or Charles
Bronson, who early on were more popular across the ocean than in
the States, were shrewdly packaged by Euro producers like Dino De
Laurentiis and presented to the U.S. studios for distribution. When
they ventured beyond these tried-and-true formulas, however, the
results were disastrous.

It was Arnon Milchan, an Israeli-born businessman, who took the
precept a step further with New Regency Productions, building a
sturdy co-financing relationship with Warner Bros. that resulted in
such films as *Pretty Woman, L.A. Confidential, Natural Born Killers*
and *JFK*. The relationship had a tit-for-tat quality to it. The studio
would alert New Regency, Milchan's company, to promising properties. In return, New Regency would take some dicey projects off the

studio's hands, putting up as much as 60 percent of the cost. Much to Milchan's delight, some of the projects that Warners considered scary, like *Free Willy*, turned out to be immensely profitable.

The cozy partnership ultimately was undone by mutual suspicion. Milchan felt the studio was favoring other production entities; Warner Bros. in turn, was uneasy that New Regency was getting the better part of too many deals. When New Regency finally marched off to Twentieth Century Fox, Warner Bros. launched other entities loosely modeled after it—one in concert with Village Roadshow, an Australian producer-distributor, and a second in concert with Canal Plus, the French pay-TV conglomerate.

And other studios soon were emulating the model. Disney helped set up Spyglass and donated *The Sixth Sense* as its first film— an embarrassingly generous gesture. Mandalay set itself down at Paramount. All these and similar entities were essentially dependent on overseas funding. The projects they put together embraced plots and casts that would appeal to an international audience though the movies themselves would be distinctly American. It was hoped that the payoff would be emphatically international.

The financial model of these companies was essentially built around the following structure: Roughly 60 to 70 percent of the budget would be raised from advances on licensing agreements covering foreign territories, with the bulk of the money coming from France, the U.K., Germany, Italy, Spain, Japan and Australia. Typically, the Australian investor would acquire all rights in his territory, encompassing theatrical release, video, TV, cable, etc. The remainder of the budget would come from a U.S. distributor, which would also obtain all U.S. rights. The U.S. distributor would charge a beneficent distribution fee—say 12.5 percent. After it recouped its costs for prints and advertising plus its distribution fee, the indie company would then become the major profit participant. Under ideal circumstances, the movie already would have benefited from the distributor's output deals so the break-even point would not be too difficult to reach. But the real bonanza would be overseas, where the indie acted, in effect, as its own distributor, relying on a network of subdistributors. If the deals were executed correctly, the results in these foreign territories would not be cross-collateralized. Hence if the film did well in Italy but badly in Spain, it would not have to sacrifice any of the moneys from Italy to make Spain whole.

For the filmmaker, the emergence of companies such as Mandalay, New Regency, Beacon and Mutual opened up a vast new array of options for getting projects off the ground. On the surface, of course, the easiest road was still conventional studio financing. A studio's decision to back a film brought with it all the attendant advantages. Its infrastructure could service the filmmaker's needs for budgeting the film, scouting locations and building sets, plus furnishing marketing and distribution expertise. It was up to the studio to worry about completion bonds or cast insurance. Further, the studio's various output deals supplied a financial underpinning for the project. Hence from the moment of a film's release, a network of revenue streams kick in.

But studios are run by committee and require a plethora of bureaucrats to agree on every detail from budget, script and cast to marketing strategy and distributing patterns. The movie gods must smile on the filmmaker to prevent his project from being relegated to development hell.

Then, too, once a studio has closed a deal, it may then summon up its own financing partners as well as its marketing affiliates. A filmmaker may find himself in business with a group of studio-selected German financiers, for example, with their own casting suggestions. He may even find himself consigned to a satellite production company, such as New Regency, where he will confront yet another set of creative and marketing experts. And there's no guarantee that his contingent compensation won't be affected by deals with these new financing partners. On the marketing side, a representative of Mc-Donald's or Hasbro toys may suddenly materialize to declare that there's too much sex or violence in the script or that scenes must be added to augment their merchandising efforts.

Life has never been simple for a filmmaker working in a studio environment, but in recent years this relationship has become even more of a mixed blessing. As a result, an increasing number of film-makers are opting for the middle ground of the "new indies"—a marriage of studio funding with that of another entity. Such high-profile films as *Gangs of New York* or *Ali*, for example, received their funding from a three-way combination of studio, independent and foreign presales. In the case of *Gangs*, roughly one-third of the funding came from Miramax, plus two-thirds from European-based Initial Entertainment Group. From the filmmaker's perspective, one financier can be played off against the other. No one entity has bought the power to force significant changes in script or cast. On the other hand, such alliances are volatile by nature. The involvement of an Initial or, indeed, even a Miramax, is dependent on the ability of those players themselves to lay off certain foreign territories in return for advances. The presence of stars and a star director is vital to facilitate presales, and this talent and their representatives are keenly aware of their muscle with the attendant potential for shifting power from financier to star.

The filmmaker who chooses to steer this entrepreneurial course inevitably takes on the mantle of part-time banker. He must be prepared, for example, to deal with that curious instrument known as the completion bond. The moneymen will not advance needed funds unless they're persuaded that, whatever happens, they will get a movie for their money. A completion bond thus serves as a sort of insurance policy that a film will emerge from the creative cauldron. The cost of such a bond is roughly 10 percent of the budget. This is no small amount, especially since bonding companies demand that a 10 percent contingency be written into the budget. What all this does, of course, is to vastly diminish the money that can actually be spent on production. Where the producer once thought he had $50 million to spend, for example, that sum suddenly has melted to $45 million. It's not uncommon for some financiers also to demand screen credit plus a producing fee, which may cut into spending money even further.

If sufficiently concerned, a bond company may actually take over the direct production of the movie, firing the director and moving into the producer's chair. Or, as in the Paramount/Miramax remake of *Four Feathers* in 2001, assume control of the project but keep the director on, making it clear that the bank is sternly looking over his shoulder.

When a filmmaker is guiding a project co-financed by two major studios, no completion bond is required since the studios self-finance completion. Such was the case on *Titanic*, whose cost doubled to more than $200 million between the time the first draft was budgeted and the final film was in the can. Twentieth Century Fox persuaded Paramount to share the torment and was tormented even more when the movie turned out to be one of history's highest grossers. Paramount relished its share all the more since it put up only 35 percent of the budget.

In the case of Mandalay, a key to its initial viability was a commitment from Sony to make a substantial equity investment in the company, to guarantee distribution of its "put" pictures (those films Sony was mandated to release) and to provide a generous domestic guarantee covering prints and advertising. This meant that Sony subsidiaries had the rights to distribute in cable TV, video, etc., under negotiated distribution fees. Mandalay, meanwhile, negotiated "caps" on what the studio could spend on P & A (prints and advertising) since its films were cross-collaterized in the U.S. Sony could thus balance losses of one picture against wins on another, and also look to TV, video and other merchandising revenues to recover possible losses.

The domestic distributor is also well protected under Mandalay-type deals, while the indie could look to its foreign subdistributors to make their big bucks—that is, if the movies performed well abroad. Each sub was entitled to recoup his advance, and then collect distribution fees of between 20 and 30 percent. Once these output deals were made in the major territories, a company like Mandalay could sell off rights to remaining territories at Cannes, Mifed in Milan or the American Film Market in Los Angeles.

Having cemented its deal structure, first with Sony and then with Paramount, Mandalay not surprisingly focused on films that would perform well, especially overseas. *Seven Years in Tibet*, starring Brad Pitt, was such a project. Directed by Jean-Jacques Annaud, an internationally known filmmaker, *Seven Years* was filmed in Argentina, Tibet, British Columbia and Austria—a global "look" which kept investors happy.

In committing to *Seven Years*, Mandalay hoped that a truly international film would carry some of its other projects that were distinctly American, such as *I Know What You Did Last Summer*. Ironically, subdistributors who did Mandalay a favor by picking up the little domestic film were amply rewarded: *Summer* grossed worldwide revenues of $238 million. *Seven Years*, by contrast, generated U.S. revenues of $80 million and international revenues of more than $170 million.

■

What all this comes down to, from the perspective of the vision keeper, is that there is more than one way to pry the gold loose from its ever-zealous caretakers, but the complexities of raising money have grown ever more intricate. And often, when the money finally comes together, there are too many masters to serve and the money available for actual production is far less than anticipated. Finally, the proliferation of funding sources has not resulted in a diversity of product. As competition has intensified, the people making the calls have grown ever more conservative.

Inevitably, the driving force behind too many major international movies is the deal, not a filmmaker's passion. Too many films are being green lit because the numbers add up, even though the story elements don't. Pragmatism has always been a factor in the filmmaking process; lately it has become the key to the process.

Yet there are, as always, exceptions to the rule. An iconoclastic British company called Working Title—itself a whimsical name—has succeeded since 1985 in stitching together co-financing deals for an eclectic slate of films that reflect both passion and pragmatism. They have ranged from such immensely successful, if idiosyncratic, commercial hits as *Four Weddings and a Funeral* and *Bean* to even more offbeat entries like Joel and Ethan Coen's *O Brother, Where Art Thou?* and Stephen Daldry's *Billy Elliot*. By the end of 2001, six of Working Title's pictures had managed to gross more than $100 million worldwide, with three grossing more than $200 million (*Notting Hill* at $363 million, *Four Weddings and a Funeral* at $246 million and *Bean* at $237 million).

There have been flops along the way, to be sure. *The Man Who Cried* disappeared without a trace. But given their low overhead, their cautious budgeting and their shrewd choice of subject matter, the two young Brits who run Working Title, Eric Fellner and Tim Bevan, have managed to produce a steady array of interesting films without surrendering their creative autonomy. Fellner and Bevan have structured and restructured their boutique so that they, not the giant companies with whom they do business, control their fate.

This process has entailed a high degree of persistence and deal-making savvy. When their initial backer, the European-based Polygram, was acquired by Universal, Fellner and Bevan were wary about placing their fate solely in the hands of an American studio. Instead they brought Canal Plus into the equation, with the French-based pay-TV company contributing between $50 and $100 million a year to Working Title's overhead and production budget. Under this five-year arrangement, Working Title retains the right to green light its own films up to a budget of $25 million. Canal Plus controls TV rights across Continental Europe and also theatrical and video rights in France on every other project, with Universal holding rights on the alternate films. To ensure its continued eclecticism, Working Title also insisted on establishing a low-budget division that would produce art films on budgets of less than $5 million.

Given their ability to navigate the tricky waters of international finance as well as marshaling the loyalty of top filmmakers, Fellner and Bevan have defied the cynicism of some of their rivals. In so doing, the jaunty young filmmakers have effectively invented their own version of the Golden Rule, reminding the film community that good films, as well as good schemes, can also bring in the gold.

CUT TO: Peter Guber on Steve Ross

For me, what first seemed like the opportunity of a lifetime was morphing into a nightmare. I knew it the moment I entered the Rockefeller Center conference room in New York City. Across the table sat Arthur Liman, famed attorney hot off his Iran-Contra/Oliver North prosecution. During this meeting he would be on the phone almost constantly with Steve Ross, the Warner Bros. wizard behind the curtain. Liman was flanked by Bob Daly and Terry Semel, Warner's co-CEOs and a gaggle of their underlings. My partner, Jon Peters, together with Walter Yetnikoff, chairman of CBS Records, and attorneys of varying ranks representing Sony all felt the pressure in that room. I had just signed a deal whereby I was to become chairman of Columbia Pictures Entertainment, which had just been bought by Sony.

Guber-Peters had earlier in the year inked a long-term extension of its existing production agreement with Warners, having just released *Batman, Gorillas in the Mist, Rain Man,* and *Tango & Cash.* Clearly, on the face of it, we had no legal right to leave or negotiate an arrangement with anyone else. We had, less than a year earlier, pursued the purchase of MGM from Kirk Kerkorian and, after concluding an arrangement in principle, Warners agreed to let us out of the remainder of our agreement. When, at the eleventh hour, we concluded that the MGM cupboard was bare and that we couldn't make it work, Warners led us to believe in conversations, before signing their extension, that if such an opportunity arose again, they would be equally willing to let us pursue it. Steve Ross may have been willing, but he was going to extract whatever he could from this deal.

There would be no going back to Warners if this Sony deal fell through. Our complete *Batman* franchise and all of our considerable development were at risk. Ross was relentless and even those on his side were afraid to stand in his line of fire, even if they felt what was coming down wasn't particularly fair.

In business, you don't get what's fair. You get what you negotiate. As Jack Nicholson's character in *The Last Detail* said, "Fair's only a point of view." Fortunately the Sony brass showed steely resolve. They made a succession of proposals duly conveyed to Ross by Liman. As it became even more complicated, I pondered the worth of it all. Was I worth it? Was anyone? Clearly not. But the conversation kept moving along, and we felt the vise tightening. Sony cobbled together a complicated deal, which featured the swap of assets including the Columbia House Record Club and the physical studio. Warners desperately wanted to get the Burbank studio lot back, which it shared with Columbia. That, oddly enough, was a deal in which I had been instrumental twenty years earlier while at Columbia.

To my great relief, Warners accepted. We got out, and Ross got his pounds and pounds of flesh. But the whole experience only served to remind me that I was just another corporate asset, to be traded and manipulated—there was nothing personal.

Of course, I realized that the extraordinary terms of the deal would become known to my industry colleagues, despite the pledges of nondisclosure. It would become a cross I would have to bear for a long time. Besides committing to generous salaries and perks, Sony also had had to swap an astonishing amount—some $200 million in assets—to liberate us from our former employers. It was their choice; no one forced the Japanese to agree to Steve Ross' demands. But at the same time, it meant that I was taking on an added burden to my new job.

The Sony job would be a great adventure, I sensed, but a turbulent one from the start.

CUT TO: Peter Bart on Hal Ashby

So often on a movie you see the elements coming together, and you tell yourself, This is going to be a winner. Something for posterity. But that wasn't the case on *Harold and Maude*. If anything, the portents were all dire.

Hal Ashby was just starting his career. He had done one film, *The Landlord*, which was OK. Just OK. He'd been very reluctant to commit to direct *Harold and Maude*. It scared him. When he finally said yes, he showed up with Cat Stevens, of all people, to present his approach. The way they saw the story, it was almost a musical. And Cat would do the music. Cat was wild looking, even by the standards of the day. He was unkempt. He also was inarticulate.

They wanted to use some of his existing songs—they were great, bizarre pieces. And he would write new ones as needed. Bud Cort would play Harold, and Ruth Gordon would be Maude. And, of course, they would be lovers. The script was superbly inventive—Colin Higgins, who wrote it, was a pool cleaner at the time. So here was a script by a pool cleaner that would be turned into a semimusical.

But this was 1971. You could take a shot on a project like that for less than $2 million. And this was definitely a shot. Ashby was smoking a lot on the set, and we're not talking Lucky Strikes. The show was lagging behind schedule. At one point I flew to San Francisco where they were shooting and handed Hal a one-way ticket back to L.A. I told him that if he kept on getting stoned and losing days, he might as well use the ticket 'cause he wasn't going to stay on the movie.

Anyway, he was on schedule from that point on. And then one day it was done and a few of us, including Hal and Colin Higgins, took it to preview in a little theater in Palo Alto. The theater was filled with Stanford students. I sat there, watching the film for the first time with an audience, and I couldn't believe what I saw. The movie, with all of its odd moments and stray tunes, came together brilliantly. It was a completely realized piece of filmmaking. At the end, more than half the audience got to its feet and applauded. I'd never seen that at a preview. I literally shook with excitement, then hugged Hal, who was in shock. The kids in the audience followed us outside and wanted to talk about the movie. They wouldn't quit.

The advertising people at Paramount had no idea what to do with the movie, however. They opened it at Christmastime with a tombstone ad. Nobody came. The movie died.

I was in shock. Here was a perfect oddball movie. The preview audience had loved it. How could it simply perish?

Harold and Maude had an amazing afterlife, of course. It kept coming back. Some theaters kept showing it for years. People still talk about it today.

In its own small way, *Harold and Maude*—this odd little movie about death—achieved its own immortality. But it should have been a hit at the outset. I still wince when I remember seeing those empty seats on opening day.

8.

The Crucible

No matter how much you rehearsed it and
how good it was in rehearsal, it doesn't mean
shit when you're out there.

OLIVER STONE

It had been billed as a rock 'n' roll dance movie, but the
behind-the-scenes production intrigues, starting in 1979,
were downright operatic. Midway through *Flashdance*, its many mas-
terminds couldn't seem to agree on anything except that the movie
wasn't working. The acting was ragged, the dancing clumsy. No one
except the director, Adrian Lyne, liked the female lead, an unknown
out of Yale named Jennifer Beals. Now, faced with the climactic dance
number, the production seemed immobilized. Beals couldn't bring it
off, but who could?

Flashdance had been ill starred from the outset. Lynda Obst, a
fiercely determined young executive and former journalist, had originally pitched her project to Casablanca Record and Films, an independent company, and had elicited some funding to develop a script
by a first-time writer named Tom Hedley. The multicharacter story

was inspired by the Toronto dance club scene and made up in energy what it lacked in focus. When Casablanca was sold, the producers dutifully pitched *Flashdance* to Universal and then to Paramount before finally getting a bite. Joe Eszterhas, a feisty former *Rolling Stone* writer, was brought in to create a single lead from the mélange of characters. Then Katharine Reback was hired to sharpen the dialogue and, as the project developed, more and more producers also were added to the mix. Jerry Bruckheimer joined the party. Next came Don Simpson, who floated down on his golden parachute from his job as Paramount's chief of production. They joined Obst and her bosses from Casablanca, Peter Guber and Jon Peters. A Guber-Peters favorite, Georgio Moroder, was brought in to write several songs and Phil Ramone was added as music supervisor. The choice of Adrian Lyne, a young Brit, to direct *Flashdance* was not a popular one at the studio, and his casting choices provoked still further discord.

Lyne had directed one film, *Foxes*, which had proved a commercial failure. Thus Paramount insiders were surprised that *Flashdance* finally got a green light, attributing the decision more to staff changes at the studio than to the merits of the production. Now as the climactic dance scene approached, the second-guessing was rampant. Studio executives had been especially critical of earlier dailies featuring errant street dancers rolling and twisting on the soundstage. In their view, the dances weren't working, the love scenes weren't playing, and dismay surrounded the set.

Jennifer Beals' dancing wasn't ready for prime time, and the director was keenly aware of it. A talented dance double named Marine Jahan already had been used in several scenes, and now a professional acrobat was added to the mix to perform some stunts. The theatrical floor spins still defied execution, however, and yet another double was brought in, this time a young man in a wig who was ordered to shave his legs. He also was instructed to shave his mustache but refused. His brilliant spins quickly quieted his critics. Indeed, the four performances, stitched together, proved a brilliant tour de force, especially when the Oscar-winning song, "What a Feeling," was added to the sound track.

Watching the footage, Lyne and his veteran editor, Bud Smith, sensed they had a winner, but the badmouthing at the studio persisted. The word on *Flashdance* was that it was hodgepodge and the two men who ran the studio, Barry Diller and Michael Eisner, bought into it. Even after seeing the final cut, they decided to sell half of Paramount's interest in the film. They then had to eat crow through the long summer as the film went on to gross almost $95 million in the U.S. and 14 million albums flew off the shelves. The project was a blockbuster, and Lyne had "oh what a feeling."

The *Flashdance* experience is far from unique. Have a drink or two with any production veteran, and inevitably he'll start telling his war stories—harrowing tales of movies that went awry, directors who cursed and stars who walked. Time and again, however, shoots that seemed nightmarish resulted in brilliant movies while conversely, those movies with "happy" sets turned out to be turkeys—a perverse axiom of filmmaking.

Perverse it is, but usually true. History's great movies, as stated earlier, almost always stemmed from productions that were racked by fear and loathing—directors fired, stars in full rebellion, funds running out. The director of *Gone With the Wind*, Victor Fleming, had a nervous breakdown in mid-production. Francis Ford Coppola was considered dead meat on *The Godfather* after the second week. Yet productions on which everyone got along famously, where stars and filmmakers seemed joined at the hip, usually ended up as singular bores.

One obvious reason is simply this: There is something intrinsically crazy-making about life in the crucible of a movie production once the cameras start rolling. Everyone feels the pressure. The shooting days are limited, the budget closely monitored, the crew possibly inexperienced, the cast quarrelsome and the intrigues predictable. Perhaps someone's role has been diminished because the director or the writer, or both, have played favorites—a girlfriend is often involved. Perhaps the crew disdains the accommodations or the food. Whatever the irritants, they take on cosmic implications once a company is working eighteen-hour days and shooting nights and once the star or star director becomes temperamental.

To be sure, most of these problems should have been anticipated before the start of principal photography, but they rarely are. The last few weeks before the shoot are usually consumed by unexpected crises. The star has demanded a last-minute rewrite, or a primary location must be changed to get the budget back into line. Usually by the time the company actually starts shooting, they look at one another in stunned disbelief, incredulous that all obstacles have finally been removed, that they're really there, at last.

As a result, they are unprepared when circumstances turn against them—when the script isn't finished on time or a cloud suddenly surrounds the basic rights to the material or a star becomes tempestuous or a key performer becomes ill or even dies in the middle of the shoot. It's always amazing to see battle-hardened production veterans lose their cool when their world suddenly collapses around them. And, perversely, everything that can possibly go wrong in the middle of a production usually does. Such is the will of the movie god.

The crucible of filmmaking has changed radically since the days of the studio system, and not always for the better. In the 1930s and 1940s, the studios were, literally, paramount. The producer, taking his mandate from the studio production chief, ran the show. The director was a hired hand who would contribute ideas on casting and editing, but definitely did not have the final say. Such top directors as William Wyler or Alfred Hitchcock carried great clout, but they were nonetheless employees. In Hollywood today, on the other hand, usually the director is king. It's his "weight" that gets the green light and hence the production moves at his command.

The implications of this power shift are formidable, giving rise to a sort of creative tyranny that encourages self-indulgence rather than order. What was once an open, if often contentious, dialogue among director, producer, studio and star has become instead a one-man show. Again, this can be constructive if that one man is a master of his craft—a Howard Hawks or a David Lean. If he is a raw alumnus of music videos or commercials, however, the results can be disastrous.

In the heyday of the studios, a rigid chain of command prevailed that governed budget, schedule, location, etc. When a project showed signs of drifting out of control, the "suits" descended on the set like a swarm of locusts. The prospect of replacing the creative elements was real. Today, the multinational corporations that own the studios may be just as dogmatic about the numbers, but they are oddly inept in implementing their dicta. Their emissaries usually have little if any experience in filmmaking. More often than not, a studio's efforts to rein in a project are rebuffed by the director or star. The so-called producer may often turn out to be the star's manager whose job is to "protect" the talent, not the movie.

One unlikely advantage of the old studio system was that it was essentially undercapitalized. When a studio chief like Jack Warner screamed that he couldn't afford a star's demands, he was often telling the truth. When a representative of Rupert Murdoch's News Corp., which owns Fox, or of Sumner Redstone's Viacom, which owns Paramount, makes a similar declaration, no one believes him. Everyone realizes that the resources of those corporations are massive, that they can afford anyone or anything—if they so choose. Another key distinction: The old-time studio chiefs loved movies. Movies were their only business, and they lavished money on the stars in their pantheon. Today's corporations, however, have persuaded themselves that filmmaking is at best a marginal business. They indulge their movie divisions only because they need "product" to nurture their global distribution apparatus as well as their ancillary businesses such as theme parks, music and TV. Movies have become a necessary evil, not a glamorous necessity, which inevitably translates into a sort of nasty, adversarial management style.

The people who ran the old studios did not brood over management style. They hadn't matriculated at the Harvard Business School. No one had even heard of an MBA. Yet, paradoxically, a Thalberg and his minions or still later, a Dore Schary or Hal Wallis, actually "managed" the filmmaking process far more skillfully than the MBA-laden executives of today's studios do. While creative shoot outs still raged with regularity, their resolution was swifter and more decisive. Moreover, there were fewer projects with built-in self-destruct mechanisms than exist today. Movies still ran into trouble once they started shooting, but their problems were not so blatantly obvious that a professional would scratch his head, wondering why such a project ever elicited a green light.

In fact, production nightmares customarily have never been that hard to predict. A producer or production manager with a sharp eye can usually sense the danger zones and deftly steer around them. Unless, that is, they are of such magnitude that they simply overwhelm the process.

The most common, and most obvious, danger zone relates to budget. Though every studio and financing entity has its budgeting executives, it is remarkable how many movies nonetheless move into production armed with utterly bogus numbers. The reasons are several: Studio executives may be so enamored of the package that they simply don't want to know the truth. Many films that call for unusual locations—shooting on water, for instance, like *Jaws* or *Waterworld*—do not make sufficient allowance for bad weather and other difficult conditions. Then, too, some filmmakers simply lie about the numbers and get away with it.

Surely Hollywood's most infamous case of budgetary miscalculation occurred with the 1980 disaster called *Heaven's Gate*. Michael Cimino was a very bright and manipulative young filmmaker who'd achieved some success with his first movie, *Thunderbolt and Lightfoot*, and had just completed a far more ambitious project, the Vietnam war film *The Deer Hunter*. Though no one had seen the finished film, Cimino had succeeded in building up a worshipful buzz. It was, rumor had it, the best movie of its kind since *The Best Years of Our Lives*, and Cimino was very simply, the next superstar filmmaker. If you didn't believe it, ask him.

Armed with the then most respected agent in town, Stan Kamen of William Morris, Cimino decided to set forth with his next project before the release of *The Deer Hunter*, whose box office results would be hard to predict. Kamen agreed that the most prudent course would be to strike quickly, taking advantage of the buzz.

With this in mind, Kamen made the rounds to three or four companies with the first draft script and budget for Cimino's next film, a Western called "The Johnson County War." It was Cimino's intention to revise the script once his postproduction duties on *The Deer Hunter* had been completed, but, declared Kamen, "the story is there." "It's going to be a classic Western and Cimino will shoot it in sixty-nine days on a budget of less than $10 million." The budget was available for anyone to scrutinize, and Joann Carelli, Cimino's occasional girlfriend who had been the line producer on *The Deer Hunter*, was available to respond to questions.

Script and budget were duly analyzed. The script was thin and sloppily written, but it was, of course, a first draft. More troublesome, however, was the budget. In the opinions of production executives at the various studios, the $10 million total seemed wildly optimistic for a Western and the budget appallingly slipshod in its details. Period costumes, props and even livestock were underbudgeted. The schedule contained too many exteriors, with not sufficient interiors to allow for cover in case of bad weather. There were too many horses and too few extras. Even the estimate for music was half what it should have been. Warning signals emerged from the budgeting gurus at every studio to which the project was submitted: Stay away from this one, they advised.

Most important, senior executives were skeptical about the schedule itself. Cimino hadn't worked that much, but he already was exhibiting an erratic streak. *The Deer Hunter* had exceeded both its budget and its schedule, and the shoot had been a troubled one.

Asked about these reservations, Carelli was as abrupt as she was immovable. There might be a few shortfalls in the budget, she said snippily, but Cimino was a resourceful filmmaker and he would deal with them. Cimino himself was unavailable for detailed discussions because of the pressures of meeting his release dates.

Given all this, old pros around town were surprised to learn that United Artists had decided to go ahead with "The Johnson County War," now retitled *Heaven's Gate*. There were worries about the budget, to be sure, but the company wanted Cimino's next project. Indeed UA's top production executives, Danton Rissner and Steven Bach, seemed downright macho about their decision, suggesting that their rivals at other companies were faint of heart. (Years later, Bach wrote a fine book, *Final Cut*, explaining the background of the debacle and readily acknowledging his culpability. Rissner sustained a mild heart attack soon after making the green light decision and was not involved with the project thereafter.)

Heaven's Gate was in dire straits even before it started production. Despite his promises, Cimino had never solved the script problems. Though the budget had doubled to $20 million, it still seemed insufficient because his appetite for grander scenes and a more expensive cast had expanded. By the time Cimino delivered his first cut, *Heaven's Gate* was crossing the $40 million mark. Adding to the alarm was the fact that his cut timed out at more than five hours. By the time the film was honed down to releasable length, the battles surrounding the film had become mythic. The reviews reflected the full nature of the debacle. As Vincent Canby wrote in the *New York Times,* "*Heaven's Gate* fails so completely that you might suspect Mr. Cimino sold his soul to the Devil to obtain the success of *The Deer Hunter* and the Devil has just come around to collect. . . . Mr. Cimino has written his own screenplay whose awfulness has been considerably inflated by the director's wholly unwarranted respect for it." He concluded: "*Heaven's Gate* is something quite rare in movies these days—an unqualified disaster."

The disaster of *Heaven's Gate* not only decimated the regime at United Artists but dealt a death blow to the company as a whole, despite its distinguished past. But to industry insiders, the biggest surprise about *Heaven's Gate* was that it was a surprise at all. There were abundant warning signs from the moment of submission—the drastically underestimated numbers, the absurd schedule, the rampant ego of the filmmaker. This was clearly a disaster ready to happen. And it did.

If there was a secondary lesson to *Heaven's Gate*, it was this: Never start a movie with an unfinished script or one that will supposedly be "fixed" during the course of the shoot. Yet the annals of filmmaking reflect a steady pattern of such incidents, many ironically stemming from mistakes of packaging. In 1998, Harrison Ford and Brad Pitt agreed to co-star in a film called *The Devil's Own*, conditioned on approval of a director. The stars delivered a list of "acceptable" directors, but by the time Alan Pakula had finally agreed to helm the project, start dates loomed. The film began shooting without an approved script, and during many days the actors simply sat around the set, chatting, while writers desperately struggled to craft their lines—a costly indulgence.

The Pursuit of D. B. Cooper in 1981 provides an even more extreme example. The idea of shooting a film about the enigmatic figure who hijacked a 727 and disappeared with a bundle of cash was so seductive to directors, actors and backers that the film literally seemed to levitate itself despite the absence of a coherent script. Treat Williams and Robert Duvall were cast as the leads, with John Frankenheimer directing. But there was nothing to shoot. Despite his distinguished track record, Frankenheimer was admittedly having drinking problems at the time. A veteran TV director named Buzz Kulik replaced him in mid-schedule. He in turn was supplanted by Roger Spottiswoode—one of the few times that *two* directors had been fired off a film. Not surprisingly, the movie ultimately died an ugly death.

There are many productions for which writers remain on call to work on dialogue or elucidate a plot point, but filmmakers have learned the hard way that the script's basic structure must be in place, its characterizations clearly drawn, before a film can safely enter the crucible of production. To start earlier is to court disaster.

■

Filmmakers eager to rush into production may confront a dilemma even more frustrating than script problems—namely confusion about the underlying rights to their material. Producers occasionally elect to take what is deemed to be an acceptable risk in initiating a project without covering all their bases. In the case of so-called biopics, for example, they may decide to acquire the rights to a book or magazine article about an individual without clearances from the real person or his friends and relatives.

Warner Bros. started shooting *The Perfect Storm*, having acquired rights to the book by Sebastian Junger. The family of Billy Tyne, the captain of the swordfish boat, brought a lawsuit, claiming that the movie depicted real-life characters who had not granted their permission. "Fiction masquerading as fact is not protected free speech," the plaintiffs argued. The studio countered that the book and later the movie were accounts of an historic event and, as such, the law did not require such permissions. A federal judge in Florida upheld this argument and dismissed the suit in 2001, though appeals are still pending.

Another sort of conflict emerged from the CBS TV movie about the life of Linda McCartney. Though Paul McCartney, husband of the cancer victim, had not signed off on any rights, CBS felt confident that he would be cooperative once he learned that it was a highly sympathetic account and thought that he might even help out by allowing some of his music to be used. McCartney and his attorney refused repeated entreaties—they wouldn't even read the script.

When ABC decided to embark on a television movie on the life of Muhammad Ali, it acquired rights to *King of the World*, a biography by David Remnick, a respected journalist and editor of *The New Yorker*. (Ali had sold the rights to his life story to Columbia some years earlier—a deal that resulted in a rather dim movie called *The Greatest*.) The veteran John Sacret Young was hired to fashion a teleplay that would take Ali through the first Liston fight. If the movie went well, a sequel could be mounted dealing with the rest of his career. Some corporate synergy was even involved: ABC's sister network, ESPN, was about to air a show dealing with the fifty top athletes of the century, and the assumption was that Ali would grace the top of that list.

Coincidentally, Robert De Niro announced that his company, Tribeca Productions, had been developing a biopic for HBO. Like ABC, Tribeca did not have Ali's total cooperation. However, when HBO finally read the Tribeca script, it decided that it wasn't strong enough. ABC breathed a sigh of relief, but its respite was brief. Fox suddenly opted to pick up De Niro's project and rush it forward. Alarmed, ABC decided to propel its project forward, even buying spots on the Super Bowl to intimidate its prospective rivals. In the end ABC got there first, forcing Fox to push back. (Fox's picture has yet to be made.) The ABC show did well but was hardly a home run.

While producers are often frustrated by delays, the decision to trigger an early start date can be an expensive one. This is especially true if preparations are not complete or if the filmmaker is still ambivalent on key creative decisions. Jim Brooks delayed starting *I'll Do Anything* for some months until the studio persuaded him that the production would simply fall apart unless the cameras started rolling. Though Brooks had built a formidable reputation on his deft comedic touch, both in TV and film, reaching his zenith with *Terms of Endearment*, his newest film, *I'll Do Anything* was designed to be, of all things, a musical. At least that was the intent. Not far into production Brooks began to have second thoughts about his grand design, but he nonetheless persevered. His worst fears were realized in postproduction, and by the time he completed his test screenings, he was in a full retreat mode. The piece just didn't work as a musical. To the astonishment of Columbia executives, Brooks was suddenly recutting his show as a straight comedy. That didn't work either. The actors, led by Nick Nolte, Tracey Ullman and Albert Brooks, seemed to be waiting for the songs—the songs that never came. As a non-musical, the film bombed.

Just as a production can fade to black when a filmmaker loses his way, problems can be equally dire if the star turns against the material. Such was the case six weeks into the first *Batman* in 1988, when Jack Nicholson decided he didn't like his deal, his role or his work schedule. One night, still in makeup, his face frozen in the horrific leer of the Joker, Nicholson started ranting at the producers and anyone else within earshot. He'd been snookered, Nicholson shouted. He declared that everyone knew his part would run much longer than scheduled. Besides, life was too short to endure the hours of makeup. There was no placating him, but there was also no arguing with him because he was essentially in the right.

His deal had called for eight weeks of work; the problem was that the eight weeks weren't continuous, so he had to remain in damp, gray London for many weeks waiting for his intermittent scenes. Fortunately for the producers, Nicholson, a consummate pro, finished fulminating and went back to work. And thanks to his rich back-end deal, he ended up earning some $60 million from his labors on the film.

On an action film called *Double Team*, the problem wasn't that Jean-Claude Van Damme was quarrelsome, but rather that he simply wasn't there. Ironically, financiers had been skittish about the project from the start, not because of Van Damme, but because of his co-star, Dennis Rodman, the erratic six-foot-eight basketball rebounder. As it turned out, Rodman, eager to establish himself as an actor, was a model of good behavior. However, Van Damme, who was supposed to exert the calming influence, was a frequent no-show on shooting days, with stunt doubles substituted in some key scenes. *Double Team* ultimately was released—something of a mishmash and a box office disappointment.

■

On rare occasions, adversity perversely can actually be turned to the advantage of filmmakers. On the wide-screen Imax film *Everest*, the film crew was edging toward the peak, working on their own documentary, when they unexpectedly encountered a ragtag team of climbers who had run into foul weather and got separated from their companions. The film crew decided to shift its focus, telling instead the story of these lost climbers, some of whom were in dire straits. This story ultimately formed the basis for a book, *Into Thin Air*, as well as a movie of the week.

The worst-case scenario for filmmakers occurs when they have to cope with the death of actors in the middle of a shoot. Sometimes the film is simply canceled with the insurance company covering the damages. In other cases, however, the shrewd use of doubles and voice-overs has salvaged movies from extinction, much to the relief of their backers.

Oliver Reed, a celebrated but heavy-drinking British actor, died suddenly in Malta during production of *Gladiator*, leaving director Ridley Scott with a major hole in his film. According to the production schedule, Reed figured in two crucial scenes yet to be shot. With production shut down, a team of DreamWorks executives led by production chief Walter Parkes flew in from Los Angeles to meet with Scott and weigh their options. Clearly one alternative was to reshoot Reed's previous scenes and file an insurance claim that would total in excess of $25 million. But as Parkes and Scott walked the set and studied their outtakes, a second possibility suggested itself. The camera had caught some vivid moments involving Reed that could be excised from other scenes and digitally imposed into those that remained to be shot. Doubles could be introduced into these scenes and line readings lifted from previous moments in the film. Though all this required careful surgery, it nonetheless seemed less painful than reassembling hundreds of extras and reshooting all of Reed's previous work. Besides, Reed had been excellent in the film, and it seemed almost disrespectful to obliterate his final cinematic moments.

The results were seamless. Indeed, it is all but impossible for the casual moviegoer to detect Reed's absence from two of the film's most important scenes.

Another such celebrated incident occurred during production of *Brainstorm* in 1981 when Natalie Wood drowned with three weeks remaining in the schedule. The young director, Douglas Trumbull, found himself confronted with a devastated cast, which included Christopher Walken and Louise Fletcher, and also a panicky studio. To MGM, the only solution was to demand that Lloyds of London come up with the $18 million production cost and abandon the project. Lloyds of London drew a line in the sand, however, declaring that the existing footage could be salvaged. The insurer forced MGM to show the completed material to two other studios with this strategy in mind. Both agreed with Lloyds of London. Trumbull was a gifted pioneer in the field of special effects, it was reasoned. Surely he could come up with ways to shoot around his star. Trumbull concurred and so, eventually, did MGM.

One scene still to be shot showed Natalie Wood and Chris Walken devising a plan to outwit the bad guys, and Trumbull had an idea how to shoot around his star. But his task was made all the more eerie in view of the film's subject matter. The conceit of *Brainstorm* was that characters in the film had acquired the power to experience the sensations of another human being, to live their dreams and share their emotions. It now fell to Trumbull to find a way to design scenes that would convey this without showing Natalie Wood.

He brought it off superbly. The ultimate tab for the insurer was $6 million, not $18 million as first anticipated. And the film received felicitous reviews from major critics.

The Wood incident reminded industry old-timers of the death of Tyrone Power in the middle of *Solomon and Sheba* in 1958 when insurance paid for a fresh start with Yul Brynner taking the major role. Ray Walston took the place of Peter Sellers, who suffered a heart attack four weeks into the production of *Kiss Me, Stupid* in 1980. Some stars were rightly deemed irreplaceable. When Montgomery Clift was nearly killed in an auto accident during the filming of *Raintree County*, the movie simply shut down for months until he recovered, with the insurance company footing the bill.

Even short of death or violent accident, a film, once it has been plunged into the crucible of production, becomes something of a runaway train. No matter how careful the preparations, the film takes on a curious life of its own, following a course that seems somehow ineffable and self-determined. Its ultimate destiny will be a product of the convergence of the talents involved—artists whose career paths happened to collide at a particular moment in their lives. The circumstances and timing of this collision may be ideal for all involved. A unique chemistry may emerge that everyone will promptly attribute to the genius of the vision keeper. Such was clearly the case with Jack Lemmon and Walter Matthau in *The Odd Couple* or Robert Redford and Paul Newman in *Butch Cassidy and the Sundance Kid*. At the same time, the annals of filmmaking are replete with nightmare encounters. There are always filmmakers or casting directors who can propose combinations of actors who have the "right chemistry," but none can safely predict which actress will take an instant dislike to a particular leading man, or vice versa.

In reality, it is all in the hands of the gods—the movie gods, in this instance. The most that a producer or director or studio chief can do is monitor the film as it unfolds and try to minimize the damage.

"Rushes," or dailies as they are commonly called, provide the best vantage point for this monitoring process, but these, too, are fraught with danger. Every time the director decides to say, "That's a print," on the set, that particular fragment of celluloid will appear as part of that day's rushes. Customarily the director and his closest collaborators will see this material first, assessing the footage from the standpoint of performance, lighting and other criteria. The film editor will sit at the director's elbow, deliberating how these snippets of film will fit into the grand design. Some filmmakers willingly invite principal cast members and crew into these sessions, while others prefer privacy, arguing that stars become self-conscious when they see their work day by day. Often a director may be highly critical of his own work, deciding to shoot portions of the material again the next day. Others, by contrast, are renowned for falling in love with every frame of film and thus find the process of editing a torturous one.

By the time the production chief and his lieutenants see the film, he may already have heard rumors about its impact. "The scene is flat," someone may advise him. Again, the production chief's en-

tourage may consist of a wide circle of advisers or be limited to a select few, depending on the personality of the executive. The old-time
studio chiefs like Darryl F. Zanuck or Jack Warner always watched
dailies with an editor who was on their personal staff—a sort of personal editing guru. While watching reel after reel, they would take
phone calls and keep a running dialogue going with staff members.
All the while, the editor would be making careful notes, preparing
himself for the inevitable onslaught of questions. "It seems slow to
me," the studio chief might rant. "We've got to pick up the pace." In
point of fact, the old-line editors were proficient at predicting the final length of most films, warning their bosses that script pages must
be cut or scenes dropped. This tended to minimize the nasty surprises that today overtake less experienced regimes when their finished films time out in excess of two and a half or three hours.

The old-line studio czars also used dailies to resolve running arguments on script or cast. When pressure built to fire Robert Evans
from *The Sun Also Rises*—the young actor was cast in the unlikely
role of a bull fighter—Zanuck studied his dailies and uttered the
phrase, "The kid stays in the picture," which ultimately became the
title of Evans's famous memoir.

The evolution of the filmmaking process has lessened the value of
dailies, to be sure. Because more and more films rely on special effects,
it's increasingly difficult to evaluate a film scene by scene. A studio executive may find himself watching an actor standing alone, delivering
his lines in front of a blue screen. While other characters, live action or
animated, may later be "morphed" into the scene, only the effects wizard can predict if the moment carries its desired impact.

Watching the dailies for *Sleepy Hollow*, directed by Tim Burton,
was especially unsatisfying for its backers, given the absence of special effects and Burton's "trick" shots. The film seemed to lack energy
or point of view—elements that clearly came to light when Burton
incorporated all of this into his cut.

More important, most of the inhabitants of the executive offices have little, if any, on-the-set production experience and hence cannot effectively evaluate the material that they may see during their daily dose of rushes. Further, the tradition of the "staff editor" has long since been abandoned—a foolish economy, some feel. It's not uncommon, therefore, for some production chiefs today to pass up the opportunity to see dailies, delegating that responsibility to those junior to them who might be even less qualified to judge the product.

Given these practices, the showing of the so-called "first cut" or rough assembly becomes even more important, and potentially more traumatic. Suddenly it's all on the line—the epiphanies as well as the gross misjudgments, the brilliant gambles and the inadvertent miscalculations. The occasion is always a discomforting one. If the film has been independently made and is now being shown to potential distributors, the "suits" usually schedule the screening during the workday. Grim-faced, they file into the screening room as though attending a public execution. If it's a studio film, and the director has some weight in his profession, he may succeed in scheduling his screening for the evening, may even invite some friends or an audience of strangers who fit the film's ideal demographic—teens or middle-aged couples. He may even serve a drink first and try to ease the tension with some socializing.

Whatever the formalities, however, the end result is always the same. A small group of self-professed experts will enunciate their prediction as to how the particular film will be received by audiences worldwide, how many will pay to see it, how many video units may ultimately be sold or rented, how much will change hands for television rights, etc. A project's entire financial profile will be spewed forth in a few brief sentences, complete with an advisory or two—change the title, reshoot the ending, cut some scenes.

The work of two or three years will thus be reduced to two or three succinct pronouncements. The upshot may signal rewards in the millions of dollars, or it may sound like a harsh judgment that time and resources have been wasted. All those fretful hours in the crucible may have been for naught. At least until another self-professed expert says otherwise.

Yet even for those closest to the project, the movie that has finally emerged rarely matches the one first envisioned. It may be better in some ways, or worse, but never the same. The movie has taken on a life of its own in the crucible of production, one that cannot be anticipated by even the most resolute of control freaks. The experience of the shoot has created its own alchemy. No matter how firmly locked, the script has been forever changed through the interaction of the actors. The mood and morale of the players, the attitude of the crew, even the weather or other hardships of production—all have left their indelible impact.

Hence, amid all the screenings, the onslaught of comments and criticisms from the self-ordained experts, the audience tests and critiques, the vision keepers themselves must somehow set aside all their anxieties and come to terms with the reality of their own experience. They must say to themselves, Okay, this is what I have wrought. It didn't turn out the way I'd imagined, but such is the nature of art and such are the realities of the crucible. So here it is; now deal with it.

CUT TO: Peter Bart on George C. Scott

It had been raining on and off all day, and the winds were steadily picking up in intensity. We were two-thirds through our shooting schedule on *Islands in the Stream*, focusing now on a series of scenes that had to be shot on the open sea. The entire movie was being filmed on Kauai in the Hawaiian Islands, where the locals were friendly but the sea was hostile, even on a bright sunny day. We were now shooting a scene that would show the protagonist, a Heming-wayesque character portrayed by George C. Scott, piloting his small boat on a rescue mission. The camera crew was positioned on a raft-like vessel that was bolted to Scott's skiff. Even on calm days, the raft would be tossed around, but today the crew was having trouble standing and were ankle deep in water. I had been doing some ad-ministrative work in the production offices when I got a phone call from a Kauai native who was in charge of all the boats used on the film. "The seas are picking up, and I'm getting worried," he told me. A few minutes earlier I'd seen a weather forecast that warned of hurricane-force winds. "Why don't you shut them down?" I asked. "I tried but they ignored me, and they're still shooting," came the reply.

Concerned, I decided to summon a boat and head out to sea. I had been avoiding the water shoots because they were painstaking and boring to observe. The director, Franklin Schaffner, was a stickler for detail, and I didn't have the patience to watch him patch together his shots. Both Schaffner and his star were stern, rather distant men who were about as approachable as George S. Patton, the general Scott had re-created so brilliantly under Schaffner's direction. There was another reason as well: Standing on the camera raft as it bobbed in the waves for any period of time made me seasick.

As I hopped onto the raft now, I could sense the tension. It was raining hard and the weather forecast was proving to be correct. My man in charge of the boats looked very apprehensive as he whispered, "Mr. Schaffner is a very stubborn hombre. He's not backing off." In-deed, Schaffner barely acknowledged my presence. Scott meanwhile stood stalwart and flinty-eyed on his boat, rain cascading off him. He was in character and clearly wasn't giving ground. If Schaffner kept shooting, Scott would show that he was as tough as his director was.

Between takes, I walked over to Schaffner. "The weather forecast is predicting that things will get worse, and they're already pretty bad," I said. "Have you thought about calling it a day?"

"We've got a scene to get through," Schaffner said. "I don't want to come out here tomorrow."

Another wave jolted the raft, water pouring over our feet. "It's dangerous for the crew," I put in. "Think about it."

"Look at George," Schaffner said. "He's not worried."

I leaped over to Scott's boat to talk to the actor. Even in the best of times, this could prove dangerous to one's well-being. Prickly and opinionated, Scott was a tough fellow who took his stardom very seriously. "It's getting ugly out here, George," I said. "And it probably will get worse."

"If Schaffner wants to keep shooting, I'll match him," he snapped. Looking at him, I realized that the day's work had become a game of chicken between these two. There was mutual respect between them, but also a distinct tension, as though each was intent on proving he was more a man than the other. The contest probably had started on *Patton* and now I had inherited the results.

I pondered the standoff as I returned to the raft, noticing that the man who was reloading the camera was almost knocked overboard by another wave. The rain was picking up; Schaffner wasn't noticing.

I decided to bite the bullet. "I'm shutting you down," I called out to no one in particular. "It's getting too hairy out here."

Schaffner shot me a look of utter disdain. Scott seemed frozen in anger. The crew, however, greatly relieved, was already packing it in. Several craft already were circling to transport the crew and support personnel back to port. I expected to be on the receiving end of a tirade from my director for overriding his orders, but instead Schaffner tucked his script away, packed his things and headed for shore. I was glad; that was one confrontation I didn't need.

My relief was short-lived as I saw George C. Scott materialize at

my side. He was draped in a big yellow rain coat now and was swab-
bing his face with a towel. "I always wondered what producers do on
a movie," Scott intoned. "Now I've figured it out."

"What are you telling me?"

"Producers prevent you from drowning," Scott said. With that, he
turned to go ashore. The game of chicken was over. In the end, the
scene was cut from the movie.

CUT TO: Peter Guber on Fidel Castro

As the Oz, a super yacht, sailed toward Cuba in 1985, it required the
last-minute intervention by Secretary of State General Alexander
Haig with the U.S. Navy to prevent the boat from being seized—and
the producers aboard from being arrested. Our mission was the production of OceanQuest, an underwater adventure film, off the Cuban
coast. Upon penetration of the twelve-mile limit, the Oz and its companion workboat were circled by two Soviet PT-style gunboats. After
determining that our crafts had been invited, the gunboats accompanied us into Cuba's Hemingway Marina, formerly one of the busiest
pleasure-fishing destinations in the Caribbean. Now we were the
only vessels in port.

For nine days, the crew dived in these now-forbidden waters,
filming wrecks and reefs not visited by Hollywood since the late
1950s. On my last day, as I was preparing for a flight out of Cuba to
Mexico City and then home, we received word that Fidel Castro, a
diving aficionado, wanted to pay us a visit. "Cool Breeze"—the production team's code word for Castro—was coming. No one was
quite sure what to make of this "ten-minute" stopover. I didn't want
to miss my plane, but the Cuban officials politely "advised" me that
I really shouldn't leave now.

Two Russian-built limos roared up to the slip disgorging army officers, who fanned out as a third car make its way up to the *Moby*, on which the crew and cast had assembled. Castro himself moved quickly onto the gritty vessel.

Dressed in his familiar green fatigues and clutching his customary cigar, El Presidente cut a powerful figure. He shook everyone's hands, right down to the cook and boat's swabbie. He smiled when he met Shawn Weatherly, the former Miss USA and Miss Universe and star of this film. He even obliged her with a photo op. He fiddled with two remote diving submarines, steering one from the deck and watching its maneuvers on a TV monitor. Everyone seemed impressed by this illuminati's charm.

The ten minutes was long up but I still figured I could catch my plane when Castro and his entourage disembarked the workboat. As they started toward their limos, however, "Cool Breeze" stooped and pointed toward our yacht a hundred yards down the quay. He wanted to go aboard the Oz. Even though it was clear that his aides were trying to remind him of his schedule, he shrugged them off and charged on down the dock.

Seeing the "No Shoes" sign, he ordered all his men to take off their boots. Once on deck, Castro shooed off his men and sat with us, sharing his experiences of diving around Cuba. He knew his stuff. Then we took a brief tour of the yacht ending up in the owner's small stateroom. This time the conversation turned to movies. He was a fan, and he declared his favorite stars and films.

When he finally got ready to leave four hours later, I had resigned myself to the obstacles I'd have to face to get another flight out of the country the next day. But, El Presidente offered one of his cars to take me to the airport where the 727 waited. "Cool Breeze" had ordered the plane to wait. Amid the questioning stares and glares of the other passengers, I sat down. Chuckling to myself, I couldn't help but think, That's showbiz!

9.

The Dream Merchants

I espouse a totally Sartrean position. I only
look ahead commercially. I never look ahead
spiritually.

MEL BROOKS

Batman became a megahit. *The Phantom* couldn't earn
back its production costs. *X-Men* grossed $100 million
in its first two weeks. *The Adventures of Rocky and Bullwinkle* struggled to get past $20 million. *Gladiator,* released in 2000, grossed
more than $400 million worldwide at the box office. *The Fall of the
Roman Empire,* the 1964 epic that had the same story as well as several better performances, was a famous turkey.

It was William Goldman, the Oscar-winning screenwriter of *Butch
Cassidy and the Sundance Kid,* who argued that, in Hollywood, "Nobody knows anything." His declaration can apply, not just to picking
movies, but also to selling them. At the end of every summer, a
season in which 40 percent of Hollywood's revenues are generated,
everyone in the industry scratches their heads, and asks, "How did
that happen?"

Throughout the mid-1990s, the studios thought they had figured out a new surefire road to success, the special-effects extravaganza. Their confidence was misplaced. Though they'd pour $150 million into an effects-driven movie like *Speed 2: Cruise Control*, odd little hits kept popping out from unexpected places, like *Bean* and *The Full Monty*. And when the studios finally cranked out a genuine block-buster, it, too, seemed to come out of the blue. *Men in Black* wasn't based on a presold property, nor at the time did it offer a stellar cast (it made Will Smith a big star) yet ended up generating $590 million of worldwide box office gross. *Independence Day* had a no-star cast and a then-obscure German director in Roland Emmerich, yet it became Hollywood's first billion-dollar blockbuster. And finally there was *Titanic*, a movie with arguably the most negative advance buzz of any major studio film in recent history, but which went on to burst past the billion-dollar mark and become the most successful film of all time.

Paradoxically, despite these surprises, the press decided that it, too, could reliably forecast Hollywood's winners and losers. One magazine and newspaper after another, from *Time* and *Newsweek* to *Premiere* and the *Wall Street Journal*, boldly published its predictions for summer 1998, accompanied by projected grosses. There was near unanimity that the winner's circle would enshrine *Godzilla* and *The X-Files*, based on the hot TV series. In the end, both were disappointments. This is not because their ultimate financial results were anything to scoff at, but because the expectations had been set at such a high level. No one forecast that *There's Something About Mary* would become the sleeper hit of the summer, actually creeping rather than catapulting upon release into the number-one spot, after seven weeks on the top-ten list—an unprecedented achievement.

In light of these pricey surprises, the studios more and more turn to those who ostensibly are most knowledgeable about the process, their heads of advertising and distribution. These are the apparatchiks who supervise the massive marketing fusillades that launch every wannabe blockbuster. These, too, are the executives whose job it is to mobilize the marketing partners who also are by now deeply engaged in the big-stakes process: the fast food companies like McDonald's. Who best to figure out what was going right or wrong than the experts who run the show? Except they don't know much about making movies, and are quick to admit it. The whole cycle has gotten so mind-bogglingly out of control, that they, too, basically throw up their hands and say, "Take your best shot."

It wasn't always so. Though filmmaking, like everything else in our pop culture, from the outset remained an exercise in risk taking, the scale seemed within reason. During the 1930s and 1940s, the major studios had their key talent, including their top stars, under contract so that costs were relatively under control. At the same time the moguls also owned theater chains spanning the country, so they could basically force-feed even their least promising product to the moviegoing public.

And what a public it was. Nearly a third of the population considered themselves fairly frequent filmgoers. Thus a hit like *Gone With the Wind* could become a sort of cultural phenomenon, riveting the attention of the media. Its producer, David O. Selznick, didn't have to beg talk shows to book his stars. Virtually everyone seemed to be courting his cast and his filmmakers.

After World War II, antitrust laws stripped the studios of their oligopolies and television confiscated the "habit audience." By the 1960s the entire formula for opening a movie had been radically revamped. A promising new film like *Midnight Cowboy* or *Love Story* was opened in very limited situations, perhaps only four or five theaters in New York and Los Angeles, as film marketers sought to build "word of mouth" through good reviews and media attention. Initial marketing costs for a major release were limited to as little as $1 million. If a film failed to strike a chord with the public, its distributor could shift the campaign or even take his loss and retreat, but it was not unusual for a film to surprise its backers. No one really expected *Easy Rider* to become an instant cult film. When round-the-block lines formed outside theaters showing *Jaws*, the hierarchy at Universal was thunderstruck. Indeed two years earlier, that same studio was reluctant to release *American Graffiti*, deeming it an abject disaster, until teenagers at the sneak previews literally screamed their approval. Suddenly the studio did an about-face, striking prints, booking theaters and taking the credit.

Though distributors were experimenting with broader release platforms in isolated situations by the mid-1970s, it was not until the advent of the modern blockbuster that this strategy reached its present-day frenzy. Current formulas for launching movies have redefined the economics of the film industry and created a tail-wags-the-dog situation. In booking 3,000 or 4,000 screens, distributors must commit themselves to massive campaigns that are heavily dependent on multimillion-dollar television buys. The sheer cost of these campaigns in turn influences the sorts of films that are made. A film needs big stars to justify this size of investment. It needs an action-driven, effects-filled narrative whose ingredients can be conveyed in a TV spot or 90-second trailer. It needs shock value. With $50 million at stake just in marketing alone—a sum spent only on major summer tent-pole pictures—a studio must think twice before taking a chance on a new star or a character-driven plot or a subtle story line that may appeal primarily to the adult audience. A blockbuster must zero in on teens; it must not only lure them to theaters on opening weekend, but also bring them back for at least one return visit. If it's an action film, the action must be hot. If it's a comedy, it must have some shock value so that kids will talk it up in person and on the Internet. Preferably, it must have a semen joke, as in *There's Something About Mary*, or a penis joke, as in *Scary Movie*, or a machine-gun explosion of fart-and-feces gags, as in *Nutty Professor II: The Klumps*.

Given the high stakes, the selling of pop culture has clearly become something much more complex, expensive and, in some ways, insidious than the marketing of, say, packaged goods. The process of marketing toothpaste involves the relentless building of brand recognition. Awareness is enhanced through the tried-and-true formula of reach-and-repetition. A major soft drink like Pepsi Cola must be ubiquitous both in terms of brand and availability.

Movie marketers face a more complex universe, however. They have dozens of new products to introduce every year—480 feature films in 2000 vs. 467 a year earlier. The overall "brand," per se, whether it is Warners or Paramount or MGM, no longer represents added value. No one goes to see a film because Twentieth Century Fox released it—even the company name is an anachronism. Further, the simple hammering home of a title or logo does not in and of itself motivate anyone to buy a ticket. Rather, portentous though it may sound, the film must somehow be injected into the public's consciousness. The dream merchant must find a way of making that dream contagious. And he must mobilize every weapon under his command to do so. This entails press interviews, paid print and electronic ads, music videos, Internet sites, trailers in theaters and billboards on the streets. Wherever the potential filmgoer turns, he must somehow encounter some allusion to the movie. In Europe, where wireless communications are vastly more advanced than in the U.S., marketers foresee a time in the not too distant future when consumers will be watching mini-trailers on handheld devices that will be integrated with their mobile phones or handheld diaries. Hence they may find themselves involuntarily "reminded" of a given film even as they dial a number or check an appointment.

With some movies, this process seems to unfold effortlessly. It doesn't take a genius to "sell" the dinosaurs in *Jurassic Park*. The campaign was lavish and superbly mounted, but virtually every kid in the world, at that moment in time, seemed ready to adopt this lost species.

Similarly, it was hardly a momentous effort to "sell" *The Phantom Menace*, the 1998 prequel to *Star Wars*. A vast global audience, for whatever reason, had already psychically tuned in to the *Star Wars* saga, and had lifted it to mythic proportions. The principal task facing George Lucas and Twentieth Century Fox, his distributor, was to elicit the best terms possible in the market place (i.e., the cut of box office returns), surrounding it with the most profitable toys and other tie-ins imaginable. It became a question of setting things in motion, then getting out of the way.

By the year 2000, the major entertainment mega-companies began to sense a new type of "synergistic sell" to add to their marketing muscle. The Nickelodeon and MTV units of Viacom, for example, successfully launched feature films for Viacom's Paramount label by energizing their captive audiences. The *Rugrats* franchise received massive exposure among Kids on Nickelodeon. MTV's teens received their fill of promos for *Save the Last Dance*, as its sound track drummed into their sensibilities. Both films experienced banner openings, which signaled yet again the advantages of having cable and film units under one corporate roof. To business rivals, however, it also signaled the encroachment of semi-oligopolies. Just as independent producers in TV increasingly found network doors slamming in their faces because the networks wanted to showcase programs they themselves owned, would broadcasters now try to shut out those movies that were not hatched within the parent corporation? Bigness could be an immense advantage to some but could also be a weapon to stamp out other voices.

Given these forces, the marketing function has evolved to a point where it's become central to the production process rather than tangential to it. Marketing criteria determine what pictures are made and what TV shows get on the air. To a large degree, it is the marketing men who, more than any other corporate functionaries, deliver the synergies that justify the massive investments.

The people who run the studios and networks are mulling their marketing strategies from the moment of submission. A producer or filmmaker, in pitching his project, may strive to describe the "eureka" of the moment when his epiphany overtook him. In the 1960s that presentation by itself might have carried his project forward into production, but in the postmillennial era the focus is already on manipulating the audience. How can that vision be translated? Is it sufficiently fresh or, for that matter, sufficiently simple? The fabled dream machines won't market a dream unless it seems utterly contagious.

To the filmmaker or producer, the pivotal challenge is to somehow create a sense of momentum for his project that propels the marketing troops as well as those in production. That momentum may stem from the intrinsic "celebrity" of the material, be it a bestselling novel, a hit play or a script that has caught the fancy of a major star.

Sometimes this sense of "celebrity" itself may prove controversial. Warner Bros. forked out $1.1 million to acquire screen rights to Tom Wolfe's *The Bonfire of the Vanities* though many at the studio felt (correctly, it turned out) that the material wouldn't translate to the screen. On the other hand, the same skepticism trailed Jerzy Kosinski's satiric novel *Being There*—it's a studio axiom that satire doesn't work in movies, yet the movie, starring Peter Sellers, was both a financial and critical success. Likewise, Alice Walker's *The Color Purple* also was wrongly labeled a bad bet for the screen. Twentieth Century Fox was convinced that the celebrity of *The X-Files* TV show was of such magnitude that its cult audience would pay to see the movie even though the TV show was still airing. They were half right:

The film grossed $83.9 million in the U.S., but the movie failed to reach out beyond its core audience.

At times producers may wedge their way into a development slot and build momentum from there. In 1989, there was little interest from Warner Bros.' power players in the *Batman* comic strip, but over the course of a nine-year development process, it attracted the interest of some valuable allies. Dan Romanelli, the studio's merchandising pooh-bah, became enthusiastic about its licensing potential. Jeanette Kahn, who headed another Warners division, D C Comics, saw a whole new life for her asset along the lines of *Superman*, another comic strip hero brought back from the semi-comatose. The international distribution forces at the studio, always on the lookout for a marketable image that will travel across boundaries, began to rally to the side of *Batman* when Tim Burton signed on as director and Jack Nicholson was hovering in the wings. The soldiers of marketing were lobbying aggressively for what they then saw as a prospective franchise.

Ironically, the first marketing battle to break out usually involves the most obvious and basic element—the title. The trouble is great titles are in short supply. "It's like naming your baby, only worse," says Terry Press of DreamWorks. Once attached even on a temporary basis, this moniker is used by everyone, and it's damn difficult to get it out of the ether.

It is not mere coincidence that many of the biggest hits of all time carried inspired titles, at least on hindsight: *Jaws, Love Story, Star Wars*, and *Basic Instinct*. Of these, only *Jaws* originated with a prior work. Like *Jaws*, classics such as *Gone With the Wind* or *From Here to Eternity* take their memorable titles from established works. Ernest Hemingway, in particular, showed a genius at picking mythic titles, like *A Farewell to Arms* or *For Whom the Bell Tolls*. On rare occasions, a title was both obvious and mandatory: *Titanic* could really have been called nothing else unless its creators wanted to recycle the timeworn *A Night to Remember*. More often, however, coming up with a title represents pure torture. MGM released a high-profile picture starring Mel Gibson and Diane Keaton and titled *Mrs. Soffel*, mindful of the fact that this was a positively awful name for a film, but the dark prison romance simply didn't suggest something more intriguing. *The Shawshank Redemption* sounded like a religious ritual instead of the title for a serious prison drama. Castle Rock later acknowledged that it could have done better.

The question always is, does a great picture generate a great title, or the reverse? *Erin Brockovich* was a major hit despite its brain-dead title. Similarly *Forrest Gump* and *Rain Man* were hardly breakthrough titles. Even Spielberg could miss the mark: His title *Innerspace* misled the audience. Gimmicky titles sometimes yield paydirt, like *Honey, I Shrunk the Kids* or *Dr. No* or *Home Alone*. On occasion, studios, starved for inspiration, have gotten away with borrowing titles of popular songs: Hence "The Body" became *Stand by Me*. "Significant Other" was turned into *When a Man Loves a Woman*.

Though coming up with a title may seem simple, time and again Hollywood has hit cycles where dangerously similar titles appeared in close proximity. The word "dead" is not exactly attractive to audiences, but movies called *Dead Man*, *Dead Man Walking* and *Dead Man's Walk* were released within months of each other. A movie called *The Evening Star* appeared soon after *Lone Star*. And then there was a run of movies successively called *Bar Girls*, *Bad Girls* and *Showgirls*, not to mention *Bad Boys*, *The Jerky Boys*, *Boys on the Side* and *Tommy Boy*—all contributing to the great marketing blur!

Sometimes a muddy title can be salvaged with a sharp copy line or slogan. A classic example is the 1969 theatrical film *Goodbye, Columbus*. The movie was both funny and sexy, elements clearly not reflected in the title. The title portended neither excitement nor information as to subject matter. Steven Frankfurt, the youthful president of the Young & Rubicam ad agency, came up with the line,

"Every father's daughter is a virgin," which became tied to the title and was instrumental in helping it become a hit.

By contrast, the wordsmiths clearly struggled for a catchy line for the disastrous John Travolta movie *Lucky Numbers*. Their final copy promise: "When they put their heads together . . . it's a no brainer." So was their slogan.

Failure to come up with a decent copy line is often symptomatic of a deeper problem—that the movie, whatever its attributes, simply resists a "sell." A vivid example was *Almost Famous*, a poignant film written and directed by Cameron Crowe. The film cost $65 million but ended up with less than $32.5 million domestic, despite exultant reviews from critics and an extravagant ad campaign. The problem was one that often confounds even the most stalwart of dream merchants: Audience response may be enthusiastic, but getting them into the theaters is another matter. Various explanations were advanced: The movie's 1970s music didn't entice a young audience, yet its protagonist was a teenager and theoretically its prime market was in that age group. Moreover, even if the audience loved the film, there was difficulty explaining its narrative to someone else. It just didn't reduce to a simple line, which limited viral marketing.

■

In the movie business there is no sure way to forecast what sort of material may lend itself to momentum building. In mass marketing, for example, it is a given that sex sells. But even sex doesn't translate into automatic box office for movies. Films with a high sexual content have failed more often than not, witness Stanley Kubrick's lifeless final film, *Eyes Wide Shut*. A supposedly presold sex classic like *Tropic of Cancer*, based on the novel by Henry Miller, was a box office flop. Even the remarkably commercial Adrian Lyne, who flirted successfully with all facets of sexual content, directing such films as *Flashdance*, *Fatal Attraction*, and *9½ Weeks*, came up with the hugely expensive remake of *Lolita*, the Vladimir Nabokov classic. Independently financed, *Lolita* suffered premature rejection. No one wanted to touch it for distribution.

But there have also been inadvertent hits that captured this sexual "sell." In the early 1970s Columbia was in dire need of product. Almost Victorian in temper, the studio was hardly the place you'd expect to find any explicitly sexual material. The old-school corporate chief, Leo Jaffe, came from a financial background. Protecting the downside was central to his strategy.

Coincidentally, a young Columbia executive happened to be visiting Paris on business and, jet lagged and bored, found himself wandering down the Champs-Elysées late at night. The marquee for *Emmanuelle* flashed before him. It was a low budget, soft-core film that had been released in a few European cities with considerable success. North American distribution rights were still available. The problem: This was an X-rated film—NC-17 in today's parlance. Any film carrying that rating—for that matter, any sexy film—would surely be vetoed by the austere corporate chieftains in New York.

Columbia's young marketing executives agreed on a strategy. A screening was set up in New York, and the usual staffers involved in potential acquisitions were invited. Also invited, however, was the bright young advertising whiz, Steven Frankfurt. Frankfurt had earlier come up with eye-catching campaigns for *Love Story* ("Love means never having to say you're sorry") and *Rosemary's Baby* ("Pray for Rosemary's Baby").

Lo and behold, a simple mimeographed flyer that circulated with the title and a picture of the female lead, Sylvia Kristal, attracted a packed room. At the end of the screening no one dared to say whether he or she liked or disliked the movie, and everyone just filed out sheepishly. This provided an excuse to have another screening the next day. The word-of-mouth marketing that began at the watercooler among secretaries and junior executives produced an overflow crowd. Again the audience at the end was reluctant to signal approval. The moment of truth came the next day when Frankfurt produced the headshot of Kristal on the French poster and delivered his copy line: "X was never like this." Even the "suits" succumbed. The film was a big hit in its genre and reinforced the adage that sex sells, if handled shrewdly and discreetly.

Cinematic sex is a delicate balancing act, however, especially in the U.S. When *Body Heat* was first screened for the public, the buzz was that it was "hot." The trouble was that it was too explicit. Research showed that the audience was uncomfortable, men as well as women. Hence, some ten minutes of the "hot sex" was excised from the final U.S. version and the tone of the campaign brought in line with the research.

Often, too, movies that were not intended to be sexy ultimately benefited because of an inadvertency. *The Deep*, for example, set out to establish itself as an underwater action-adventure, based on a novel by Peter (*Jaws*) Benchley. A key element in casting *The Deep* was that all the stars had to agree to dive "live" in the ocean. No stunt doubles for the big close-ups. Serendipitously, Jacqueline Bisset was dressed in a white T-shirt for her dive because the director feared it would be hard for the audience to identify her down under without the white garment. Not until weeks later, when the first scenes were stitched together, did it become clear that the image of Bisset rising to the surface and emerging from the water in her well-filled T was worth far more than the buried loot she and Nick Nolte were ostensibly chasing. It was the ultimate "money shot," one that was widely heralded in the posters and that inspired wet T-shirt contests worldwide. Bisset at first wavered with her approval, but it proved to be a money shot for her as well, catapulting her acting fee from $175,000 per film to more than $1 million.

On the other hand, there is nothing more difficult for the dream merchant than to predict that a particular story or scene may strike an audience as sensual and romantic. A case in point was *Love Story*. The 1970 film starring Ali MacGraw and Ryan O'Neal as doomed young lovers had an ad campaign built around the catchy, if ambiguous, slogan, "Love means never having to say you're sorry." As directed by Arthur Hiller on a slim $1.3 million budget, the movie, as effectively as any other modern film, reduced the audience to tears. As such, it quickly became the nation's hottest "date" movie.

When marketing sex and romance, if the campaign is off-kilter even a little, confusion reigns. With *Proof of Life*, released by Warners in late 2000, the studio seemingly had everything going for it. Russell Crowe's *Gladiator* was picking up award steam, and Meg Ryan, his co-star, was an established star. However, prior to the film's release, the tabloids related in detail the stars' torrid romance and Meg Ryan's breakup with husband, Dennis Quaid. In *Proof of Life*, of course, the story had Crowe chasing down Meg's fictional kidnapped husband.

The early media strategy of capturing the titillating real-life romance between the actor and actress was a catastrophe. Its problems were exacerbated by having a hot on-camera sex scene between Crowe and Ryan, intercut with the story of her husband's escape from his jungle captors. At the moment of climax, a booby trap bamboo spear pierces the escaping husband's leg, and his scream merges with Meg Ryan's adulterous ecstasy. The audience rejected this; yet even when ten minutes of hot sex was expunged from the cut, the film emerged both sexless and senseless.

There have been occasions, of course, when the marketing team has benefited from offscreen peccadilloes. Elizabeth Taylor and Richard Burton's tumultuous affair was exploited by publicists on films like *The Sandpiper*. But while press agents can adjust their tactics day by day, their colleagues on the ad side already have committed to a campaign and don't have the flexibility to change the basic "sell" in midstream. If they get unlucky with the media, as in *Proof of Life*, they have no choice but to hunker down and hope for the best.

■

The decision to green light a project, once the preserve of powerful studio chiefs like Irving Thalberg or Jack Warner, now has become a committee function. Marketing teams are increasingly held accountable for the final decision to "go." As Stacey Snider, chairman of Universal, puts it, "I want those people who have to sell a picture to feel they have an investment in it. If they aren't convinced they can sell it, they shouldn't vote for it." From the summer of 2000 to Christmas, Universal successfully opened five number-one grossing films in a row. The upshot: Marc Shmuger, the head of advertising was promoted to vice chairman of the studio with expanded creative responsibilities.

Most studios ask marketing and distribution executives for performance projections even before green lighting a production, as well as a cost analysis as to how much must be committed to "open" the movie to achieve the projected box office. This, in turn, dictates how it's to be positioned in the marketplace, the number of screens, etc.

Studio marketing executives are a tough-minded and self-protective lot. They tend to be aggressive, yet cautious; articulate, yet reserved. In their world consensus is mandatory. A campaign must win the approval of the top production team, as well as the director and sometimes even the star. If a Mel Gibson doesn't like the way he is portrayed in posters or trailers or TV spots, his cooperation in selling the film will be sharply curtailed. "We are coalition builders," smiles Terry Press, DreamWorks marketing guru.

"When I first see a finished film, I have long steeled myself to see it merely as product," observes Buffy Shutt, for years one of the top marketing executives at TriStar and Universal. "I am not there to judge it. I am there to figure out how to market it. Even if my husband happens to be with me at the screening, I don't indulge myself by expressing my opinion to him. I won't say, 'This is an awful movie.' He may whisper to me, 'How did that thing ever get made,' but I won't answer. It's product and I am the one who's going to figure out how to find its audience."

■

From the standpoint of the vision keeper, there's no one in the studio hierarchy whose fealty is more important to gain than the dream merchants. A friendly ad staff will bring forth a range of possible options for a campaign. An unfriendly one will show the filmmaker a campaign, announce that it has "tested well" and close the discussion. Each side has its own weaponry to use in a creative shoot out. The shrewd marketing chief will hint that the studio is prepared to spend inordinate amounts of money on media buys, provided it's his preferred campaign. The tacit threat is that the budget will shrink if the studio is muscled into running a campaign that the marketers don't favor. An alert producer, of course, will leverage the prestige of his director or star. "Kevin doesn't like the thrust of the campaign," he will say. "If you want to sustain that relationship. . . ." That hint, too, carries incendiary implications. No studio wants to alienate a top star or a respected filmmaker over a disagreement on ads.

Nonetheless, it's a natural defense mechanism for ad executives to be secretive about their spending. Unless one has the clout of a Spielberg, it's virtually impossible for a filmmaker to elicit the precise figures. Though unwilling to admit it, some studios spend north of $50 million to massively launch their favorite films. Million-dollar Super Bowl spots, purchased well before the final cut is screened, are generally reserved for a Tom Hanks or a James Cameron blockbuster. By contrast, Miramax launched a more sophisticated project like *Shakespeare in Love* on relatively few screens in a few key cities, relying on print ads alone to herald it. If and when the movie generates favorable press and word of mouth, the distribution pattern is broadened in stages and TV advertising is added to support the increased screens.

"The prime question has to be, 'What do I spend and what do I get for that spending?'" says Arthur Cohen, Paramount's worldwide marketing president. His question is well advised: Media costs have risen astronomically in recent years, with ad budgets increasing accordingly. Between 2000 and 2001 alone, film marketing budgets jumped 11 percent to an average of $27.3 million per film for major studio releases, according to figures compiled by the Motion Picture Association of America. TV spending accounted for between 65 percent and 70 percent of total budgets. In that same period, however, actual admissions to theaters declined and, while total box office showed an uptick, the increase stemmed from higher ticket prices, not actual tickets sold.

The marketing momentum for a project often may stem not from the intrinsic merits of the film, but rather from the enthusiasm of the dream merchants for their own work. And despite the primacy of TV, the element that gets the marketing juices flowing usually surrounds the so-called "one sheet," whose basic image often accompanies, or occasionally haunts, a movie throughout its life span in theaters, on TV, in video and even inescapably on airplanes. The design of the one sheet has a pronounced impact on all that is to follow. Newspaper and magazine ads and even the billboards are but iterations of the one sheet. Their purpose is to turn the energy of information—i.e., "awareness"—into the emotion of "want to see." A vision keeper who fails to involve himself deeply in its design often regrets that lapse more than anything else in the process. The *Batman* icon established itself clearly and vividly in its one sheet. The Bisset wet tee image was firmly implanted in *The Deep*. Mega-lizards were front and center in the *Jurassic Park* campaign.

The shrewd marketers at DreamWorks knew they had a promising thriller on their hands in *What Lies Beneath*, for example, but didn't feel their two expensive stars, Michelle Pfeiffer and Harrison Ford, would appeal to the prime young demographic. The one sheet hence announced "nail biter," but the likenesses of the stars were absent—a major deviation from "accepted" strategy.

An even more complex problem confronted TriStar on the action thriller *Cliffhanger* with Sylvester Stallone, long an international star of the action genre. Carolco, the independent production company that marshaled the financing for *Cliffhanger*, had earlier been responsible for a string of highly remunerative action pictures, including *Terminator* and *First Blood*, the first Rambo movie, which also starred Stallone. By the time Carolco delivered *Cliffhanger* to its U.S. distributor, TriStar, Stallone's "Q" rating—the statistical measure of a star's box office draw—was in sharp decline. Alarmed, TriStar compelled the reluctant producers to hold a test screening, which confirmed its worst fears. Many of the key action scenes produced laughs rather than thrills.

While an editing team was hurried back to the cutting room, TriStar's ad executives presided over the creation of a one sheet that would emphasize suspense, not Stallone. The upshot: A poster that screamed the words "HANG ON" in towering letters. In smaller type, the title *Cliffhanger* sat inside the huge "O." Again, Stallone's face was nowhere to be seen. The film went on to box office success thanks in great part to this campaign, defying everyone's initial apprehensions.

The latitude to play with likeness or size of star names often is sharply inhibited by contractual commitments. Veteran ad executives are trained to perform all sorts of contortions so that star names appear in a specified size or place relative to the title or to other players. It is not a mere coincidence that Julia Roberts' name appears uniformly above the title of *Erin Brockovich*, and in almost the same size letters, or that Sean Connery's name adorns, also alone, *Finding Forrester*, in big block letters. A more complex configuration of the Redford and Newman names appeared over the title of *Butch Cassidy and the Sundance Kid*, because both had been promised top billing.

Even as the one sheet takes shape, the TV spots and trailers are subjected to intense step-by-step testing. Indeed, trailers are to TV ads what one sheets are to print advertising. Since they constitute arguably the most critical preopening advertising, each iteration is subject to the scrutiny of endless focus groups. Again, the filmmaker may look on in semi-horror as the testing gurus decide his fate. The most common complaint of the filmmaker is that, in the zeal to lure an audience, the dream merchants give away too much of the story, and their alarm bears some legitimacy. Over the years, trailers have become louder and longer. There's no subtlety in the trailers for effects films like *Deep Impact* or *The Perfect Storm*. The "big wave" was on display in both; there was no coy holding back. Similarly, trailers for action films look and sound dangerously similar, replete with cacophonous car chases and raucous gunfights. (Rarely does the audience have something memorable as a "take away.")

The impact of a trailer is greatly enhanced, to be sure, if it plays adjacent to a hit picture appealing to similar demographics. Customarily all this evolves as a result of intense negotiation between distribution chiefs. Clearly a studio would prefer to play its own trailers alongside its big hits, but if it doesn't have a suitable "match," it's open season for dealmaking. Money is not supposed to come into play but now and then it does. Jeff Blake, Sony's affable head of distribution, put $100,000 on the line to run a trailer for his comedy, *The Animal*, to accompany Universal's *The Mummy Returns*. In his mind, it was akin to placing an ad. As such, the economics of his "buy" were sound. Nonetheless Blake acknowledges that he "caught hell" for making this deal from his confreres in the industry and also from the press.

The "teaser," or abbreviated trailer, for *The Perfect Storm* was created long before the film finished shooting and started appearing in theaters seven months prior to release of the film. Marketing and distribution executives at Warner Bros. understood that a lot was riding on the success of their effort. The picture, based on a bestseller, had cost nearly $150 million to produce. Its star, George Clooney, had registered superbly with his audience in the *ER* television series, but his record in movies had been spotty at best. Moreover, *Storm* was opening on the Independence Day weekend of 2000 against another powerhouse movie, *The Patriot*, starring Mel Gibson. Adding to the pressure, Time Warner had just announced its merger with AOL, and the top corporate officers could hardly accept an embarrassment at the box office, which would then spill over into the media.

Given the prospect of a major shoot out, Warners loaded up early and large. The teaser, and later the trailer, was accompanied by a massive TV campaign, with the storm clearly emerging as the lead character, not George Clooney. The strategic aim was to match digital magic with marketing magic. The dream merchants prayed for clear sailing, but the portents forecast otherwise.

Indeed, Warner Bros. hubris about *The Perfect Storm* propelled the studio into a high-risk face-off on July 4, 2000, with Sony that produced a classic example of macho marketing. Sony was absolutely convinced it had a blockbuster on its hands in *The Patriot*, produced and directed by the same team responsible for *Independence Day*, and what better date to open a movie with that title than July 4? Meanwhile Warner Bros., too, felt *The Perfect Storm*, with all its bells and whistles, was invincible.

Still, industry pundits were shocked by the decision of the two companies to go head-to-head. It's a time-hallowed tradition that mega-budget films avoid these collisions. Besides *The Patriot* seemed to have so much going for it: Time and again Mel Gibson had proved

he could open a film. Director Roland Emmerich was a top-flight alchemist. Nonetheless, the Revolutionary War wasn't exactly material of the moment. Indeed, studios had systematically avoided the
period.

Warner Bros. insiders felt they had important weapons in their
arsenal for *Storm*. Their book had big-time celebrity. Their director,
Wolfgang Petersen, who'd made his name with *Das Boot* and *In the
Line of Fire*, was a distinguished craftsman. The PG-13–rated *Storm*,
seemed better matched to an Independence Day weekend launch—
in spite of the subject matter—than the R-rated *Patriot*, which also
had a considerably longer running time.

Reviewing his options, Daniel Fellman, the president of Warner
Bros. Distribution, nervously concluded he could not afford to
"blink." He had trumpeted his release date a year earlier; backing off
now would signal weakness to the industry and Warner's exhibitors.
A slight, wizened man who had labored up the ladder in his field for
some thirty years, Fellman understood full well that macho was an
important factor in his arcane business. He liked the July 4 weekend;
his many promotional partners who were helping to support his $40
million opening push liked it as well.

Even as he decided to stand firm, he couldn't help noticing the
concern on the faces of his colleagues. Early tracking studies were indicating that *The Patriot* commanded a far greater "awareness" factor
than *The Perfect Storm*. The public knew about Mel Gibson's film
and was expressing a preferential desire to see it. Fellman upped the
advertising ante in response to this intelligence but still could not
close the gap.

Finally, it was Sony that blinked, if ever so slightly. Serendipitously, the July 4 "weekend" in 2000 spanned six days, and Sony decided at the eleventh hour to move the opening of *The Patriot* to
Wednesday, June 28, rather than Friday July 1. "If you open on a
Wednesday and get poor or mixed reviews, they can haunt you for

six days," Fellman observed. If reviews came out Saturday, by contrast, they'd be too late to eat into weekend business. Fellman earmarked a new ad assault for the final days before release. His gut instinct proved correct. Gibson's star presence could not shoulder aside the wobbly reviews; opening day business was soft. By the end of the July 4 weekend *The Perfect Storm* had emerged from the shoot out unwounded, grossing $41.3 million to *The Patriot*'s $22.4. By the time the U.S. run for both films had come to a close, *The Storm* had blown away *The Patriot* by $183 million to $110 million. The Mel Gibson movie also encountered choppy waters in some of its international runs; audiences in England responded negatively to what they interpreted as an anti-Brit bias. The Warner Bros. team basked in satisfaction, but Dan Fellman acknowledged, "We had some monumental scares along the way."

Throughout the marketing process, distribution strategy is inextricably linked to marketing. Recognizing this, most of the major studios have recently placed both areas under the command of a single executive, a break with the long-standing tradition of having the ad people in their own fiefdom.

The exhibition contract between distributor and theater owner reads like a sort of prenuptial agreement in that, with all the cumbersome language, it's basically an invitation to endless renegotiation. The goal for the distributor is to get his hands on the best screens on the best terms with the largest guarantees. If that distributor has clout, he usually extracts what he wants. "Clout," in this context, stems from the weight of the stars, the buzz surrounding the film (if any) plus the strength of that company's future slate. Distribution executives keep up their harangue at the studio, asking for "event" pictures that can add distribution muscle to current films. It's a matter of leverage through perception. When United Artists distributed *Rain Man*, for example, it lacked a viable product flow and hence its "cut" of the box office from theater owners was on average nearly 10 percent lower than Warner Bros., where the project had started. All the creative back-end participants share in this pain. The collection process where distributors "pay up" is also easier for major studios. Smaller distributors often don't get paid their due.

Hence a distributor with muscle and a hot picture may demand a $200,000 guarantee and seek 90 percent of the box office, which would come after the theater owner recouped his overhead—a sum that could come to, say, $10,000 a week. During the course of the run, this percentage will change in favor of the exhibitor, but by the end of the run it may average out to only 54 percent for the distributor. If the film fails to pull an audience, the theater owner may start pulling screens, much to the exasperation of the filmmaker.

Many of the distribution executives are émigrés from exhibition, so the constant nattering and renegotiation takes on a ritualistic tone. Exhibitors understand that when a major film debuts, careers are on the line, perhaps even the future of a studio regime. The studio realizes, on the other hand, that exhibition as an industry is on shaky ground. Several of the most important theater circuits declared bankruptcy between 1999 and 2001, their financial distress stemming from overbuilding. So many glittering new mega-plexes were built with stadium seating and superior digital acoustics that they effectively eliminated the profitability of the older theaters. Thus while the pressure is on the studio soldiers to drive a hard bargain to support ballooning production costs, they also are wary of taking too great an advantage of a fragile situation. The studios need good deals, but no audience ever went to see a deal.

Despite this symbiosis, not uncommonly a movie comes along that drives a wedge between distributor and exhibitor. That's because the distributor may feel he's delivering God's gift to filmmaking while the theater owner, having seen all or part of the movie, feels the exercise is one of smoke and mirrors. Such was the case with *The Last Action Hero*, the Arnold Schwarzenegger epic that Columbia disgorged in 1993. On the surface this was a movie that seemed to have everything going for it. It was an action film with a star who all but owned the genre at the time. Its story was at once basic yet innovative. Indeed, both Mark Canton, the president of Columbia, and Schwarzenegger were so convinced that they had a blockbuster on their hands that they could not contain their excitement, forecasting its great success to the press. Even before production began, the release date of late June was set in stone. The objective was to capture the best date, when the largest audience was available to kick off the summer movie avalanche, and to defend it against all comers. Certainly that appeared to be the perfect strategy. The film would play long into the summer, which would pump up the ancillary values of cable and network sales, which were indexed to domestic box office results. This decision, however, set in motion a tsunami of angst. *Action Hero* proceeded to suck the air out of the studio and impact other films on its slate. It immediately became the lead vehicle for the studio at ShoWest, where all the distributors strut their stuff to exhibitors. Stars are shuttled to Las Vegas to bolster their territorial claims.

This film, it was preordained, would be the natural successor to Schwarzenegger's earlier triumphs, *Total Recall* and *Terminator 2*. No one at Columbia seemed intimidated by the fact that Universal was angling for the same date for its own potential blockbuster, Steven Spielberg's *Jurassic Park*.

The press smelled blood from the outset. Arnold against *T. rex* was a classic Hollywood shoot out. Columbia needed a hit and was persuaded that it had one. Jeff Blake, the studio's distribution chief, demanded and received top terms in corralling more than 2,000 screens nationwide, a very wide opening by standards of that year.

The studio's determination to make its release date was so intense that the apprehensions of its director, John McTiernan—or, for that matter, its star—over the script went unheeded. The basic conceit of the film was that Schwarzenegger would play himself—an indestructible superhero named Jack Slater who would pop in and out of reality. The script was steeped in in-jokes. At one point Slater's young charge asserts, "You can't die until the grosses go down," a jest which came back to haunt the movie when its grosses did plunge.

A twist like this requires a high degree of whimsy. A succession of writers, including the master Mr. Fix-It, William Goldman, were brought in to polish the script, with the rewriting continuing through production. All the while, studio press agents scurried to combat rumors that the film was well over budget. Even during the round-the-clock postproduction rush, the press carried reports of quarrels between exhausted filmmakers and the studio.

Meanwhile, the first one sheets emerging from the ad department only reinforced the suspicion that everyone had lost their sense of direction. The campaign suggested fantasy, not thrills; it seemed directed to young kids, not teens. There was internal strife among many of the key department heads over the focus of critical marketing components. One of the top ad executives stormed out of one meeting, shouting that he had washed his hands of this film. He held true to his threat, simply vanishing from the project.

Given the impending release date of June 22, just a few days after *Jurassic Park*, Columbia rushed its mandatory exhibitor screenings. The studio was eager to maintain high security at its screenings of the unfinished version. Some key special effects were still missing and further editing changes were under consideration. Some officials were becoming paranoid about public scrutiny. Never before had any film been so closely watched. Their worst fears were realized: Reporters had managed to infiltrate a "research screening" hosted by the studio. The *Los Angeles Times* published a story by a freelancer named Jeffrey Wells, criticizing the movie and describing the studio as worried by the decidedly mixed audience reaction.

The studio went ballistic, denouncing the story as "irresponsible and untrue." All *Times* reporters were banned from studio screenings. The studio even hinted that it might not advertise in the newspaper—an idle threat since the *Times* was a monopoly newspaper in Los Angeles.

The net effect was to make *Action Hero* the industry's hottest story. The studio's hysteria only fanned the flames. "Suddenly it seemed as though the town had a desire to see that film fail," observed Susan Lyne, then editor of *Premiere* magazine. Years later, Mark Canton reflected on the incident, acknowledging that "I just got caught up in the frenzy of the moment. I had brainwashed myself into thinking I had a megahit on my hands and we all got carried away with our hubris."

By opening day, everyone seemed resigned to failure.

No one was particularly surprised that the box office results were less than heroic. On its opening weekend, *Hero*'s $15.3 million was overshadowed by the $38.5 million for *Jurassic Park*, then in its second week. "Dinos Eat Arnold's Lunch," screamed the headline in *Daily Variety*. Its blood lust unsatiated, the press promptly hatched a series of stories speculating on how much the film would lose. Even the august *New Yorker* chimed in, claiming that *Hero* would rank as a bigger loser than even the fabled *Heaven's Gate*. Statements by Columbia that such estimates were ludicrous couldn't stem the tide. The finger pointing only fueled the frenzy.

All this off-screen drama even affected the international market and, although the film performed well overseas, it was still not up to Schwarzenegger's prior efforts. In the end the cash loss for the studio was not that daunting, and the film proved a valuable library asset for the company. Though the studio's prospects quickly perked up with the success of *Sleepless in Seattle* and *Philadelphia*, the story of *Action Hero* overwhelmed all that news and Columbia seemed permanently destabilized.

When a film is perceived as an anchor tenant of a studio's release schedule, it becomes a heat-seeking missile for media attention.

Laura Landro, who supervises showbiz and media coverage for the *Wall Street Journal*, feels that "business news rarely has an impact on a film," though she admits, "what starts out as business news leads to news about people, products and companies. If a film's budget is soaring this could have an adverse effect on the company's financial well-being. Once it's out in the business press, the consumer media gets it and value judgments about the film are made. The *Wall Street Journal* tries to stay away from making value judgments about a film, even though the *Journal* may highlight the buzz about the film."

The distinction between "buzz" and "news" remains a fuzzy one, however. The *Journal* was not above running a piece about the first *Batman* suggesting that the choice of Michael Keaton for the lead was puzzling, if not misguided. While Landro later argued that the article's intent was merely to "highlight the quirky concerns of *Batman* aficionados," the piece had a ripple effect in other newspapers around the world. Suddenly the choice of Keaton was a mini cause célèbre in the press—a controversy that quickly died down thanks to the movie's success at the box office.

The tendency of the press to second-guess even stretches to the domain of release dates. Whenever a film is delayed, conspiracy theories inevitably hit the newspapers—the studio is reediting the film, the star disagrees with the cut, etc.

In fact, final decisions about release dates involve a complex mix of ever-changing factors. What is the competition? Is it aiming at the same core audience? Can it survive a strong holdover from a prior release? What's coming up in the next two weeks? All these and a myriad of other considerations go into selecting the initial release date and number of screens.

In the case of Tim Burton's *Sleepy Hollow*, Paramount, the U.S. distributor, was determined to have an August release. By early summer, however, though the film had been booked into its U.S. slot, the effects were still not ready and Burton hadn't signed off on the final cut. Scott Rudin, the mercurial producer, was trying to prod his director toward agreeing to a tighter more accessible cut. Already the film was $20 million over budget.

The new release date—Halloween! Brilliant! Manna from heaven. There even was a pumpkin in the film. There would surely be no problem in making that date considering that the studio planned August from the get-go. Wrong! Again the movie wasn't ready. It premiered two weeks after Halloween. Paramount was devastated it had no film for that time slot. All the international territories also had to be reset. Despite all the arguments and misgivings, *Sleepy Hollow* opened to stellar business, grossing more than $200 million worldwide. Tim Burton had survived yet another of his high wire acts, and so had Paramount.

Ordeals like those experienced on *Sleepy Hollow* or *The Last Action Hero* make producers even more desperate to find dependable methods of pretesting their finished product before it hits the market. In fact, it's hard to think of any other industry that's as willing to turn on a dime based on this sort of instant analysis.

Tracking studies chart public awareness of a given film and are followed like gospel by studio executives despite their notorious inaccuracy. "I aged ten years during the week prior to the release of *Chicken Run*," confesses Jeffrey Katzenberg of DreamWorks, tracing his malaise to tracking research suggesting a dim reception for his film. The studies proved to be off by more than 35 percent.

Yet many filmmakers habitually put down tracking studies, placing their faith instead on previews, though even this methodology has changed radically in recent years. Until the mid 1980s, the common procedure for studios was to preview their movies before regular audiences at commercial theaters. While questionnaires would be distributed to the audience at the end of the screenings, most filmmakers would get caught up in the reaction of the moviegoers during the film itself—whispered conversation, the laughter, either sincere or derisive, the stirrings of restlessness. Sometimes the results of these previews could prove devastating. In the early 1970s, when Columbia Pictures previewed William Wyler's last movie, *The Liberation of L. B. Jones*, virtually the entire audience deserted the theater before the film had ended. The studio understandably decided not to bother to distribute survey cards under the circumstances.

A test screening of *An American Werewolf in London* ran into similar problems. Director John Landis' first cut was drenched in so much violence and bloodshed that many filmgoers fled during the course of the film. The studio had been nervous about audience response, but this extreme reaction was startling. It didn't take survey cards to point up the severity of the problem. The idea of a post-screening focus group was hastily abandoned when the visiting executives saw clusters of angry filmgoers surrounding their limousines. Ultimately the director repaired to the editing room to tone down the bloodletting. Everyone involved breathed a sigh of relief that news of the disastrous screening did not seep out to the press. Had the test screening taken place in the year 2000, the Internet would have been crackling with reports of the screening debacle.

In recent years, studios have sought to get more control over their audiences by shifting their "research screenings" to studio theaters on the lot and inviting their audiences. Many industry veterans distrust these practices. They argue that an audience—any audience—reacts differently when it's specially selected to see a film at a Hollywood studio rather than buying a ticket at a regular theater. These special test screenings have proven to be far from consistent in terms of predicting box office results.

Despite the reliance on test screenings over the past decade, there are still instances in which the entire process is done away with. After the three partners in DreamWorks viewed the finished cut of *American Beauty*, they promptly canceled their previews, taking the position that their film was both very special and very delicate. It would either play for audiences, or it would fail miserably. Previews would simply risk bad buzz from gossips and from self-styled critics on the Internet. The movie, of course, turned out to be a giant sleeper.

The late Alan Pakula confessed, after completing *Love and Pain (and the Whole Damn Thing)*, that his title summed up his feelings about opening day. "I wish I could make movies but never have to release them," he confided.

The rituals of previews and test screenings are supposed to ensure that filmmakers and studio pooh-bahs alike don't have any major surprises awaiting them on opening weekend. By the time a film finally hits the theaters, they should know exactly what to expect.

Except it doesn't work that way. Industry veterans love to relate war stories of opening-day surprises, cases in which long-ignored and scorned movies broke box office records and, conversely, projected blockbusters came crashing to earth.

George Lucas has delivered more shockers than most filmmakers. Universal disdained his 1973 film, *American Graffiti*, so intensely that it declined to release it even as a film for television (ultimately Universal changed its mind). The buoyant opening weekend numbers sent the studio's executive corps into therapy. Twentieth Century Fox was so cavalier about *Star Wars* that it negotiated away its merchandising rights. The opening numbers also sent them into shock.

The opening weekend process unfolds like this: As box office data trickles in on Friday night, distribution mavens are bent over their computers, churning out early projections. By late Friday the upshot is pretty clear, though it's usually not until the following night that major pronouncements start to fly. If a film is taking on water, word flashes to scale back TV spots and cut ad spending. These instant strategy changes cannot always be implemented. When Universal first saw the disappointing results of its 1999 Jim Carrey movie, *Man on the Moon*, an oddly disconcerting biopic about comedian Andy Kaufman, it promptly started canceling TV spots. However, TV stations around the country were so paranoid about Y2K foul-ups that they'd surrendered their capability to adjust to eleventh-hour changes. Most of the spots continued to run even as the studio admitted it had a turkey on its hands.

By the time that distribution chiefs start their round of calls to filmmakers and studio executives on Saturday, their descriptive lexicon shifts radically. To a star or filmmaker they'll soften the blow, advising, "The early results are less than encouraging." This will be followed by commiseration and assurances that the multiplexes are not canceling playdates. In the next call to a colleague on the production side, however, the message will be: "This one's a turkey. Let's cut our losses."

To be sure, filmmakers and production executives on the receiving end of these calls are cognizant of the fact that the data they are hearing will imminently be blasted out worldwide by the media. The "number-one" movie will be instantly enshrined as a box office winner—one that goes on the "must see" list. A film of far greater merit that happens to fall into the two or three spot well be stigmatized as an also ran—a fact that infuriates many industry insiders. They charge that the media is hell-bent on creating a contest of winners and losers. At the same time, of course, the studios, eager to capitalize on every possible advantage, will fan the flames of this competition when it favors their entry.

"There's no doubt the 'top three' horse race affects the want-to-see of a movie," concedes Joe Roth, who heads Revolution. "At the same time," he adds, "every movie company often practices 'misinformaton and disinformation' in feeding its numbers to the media." In other words, the dream merchants help further distort what is already a distorted process.

Further exacerbating the "opening night" tensions are the political pressures surrounding film ratings. Pitched battles between studios and their filmmakers on the ratings issue often continue through the opening of a picture. The ratings, ranging from G at one end to NC-17 on the other, are applied to films by the film industry's self-regulatory body. Indeed the basic ratings code was evolved by Jack Valenti, president of the Motion Picture Association of America, in the late 1960s. Its purpose ostensibly was to educate parents on film content so they could guide their children's moviegoing accordingly. By imposing its own ratings, the MPAA also warded off efforts of local states and communities to apply far more restrictive, indeed capricious, standards which would have the effect of limiting distribution channels. Even the industry's own ratings, however, represented a tacit form of censorship. Many newspapers around the country, for example, flatly decline to carry ads for films with an NC-17 rating. Further, theater leases in many malls restrict the exhibition of supposedly risqué films.

Studios, of course, prefer those ratings that invite the widest possible reach, and hence prod directors of NC-17 films to make edits to achieve an R, and directors of R pictures to cut them to qualify for PG-13. While some truly "tough" films like *The Exorcist* may deserve a restrictive rating, the industry's rigid criteria have also dispensed R ratings to benign films like *Almost Famous* and *Billy Elliot*. The criteria are basically technical: Too many "fucks" in *Billy Elliot*; a suggestion of drug use in *Almost Famous*.

No film stirred greater ratings turmoil than *Basic Instinct*, the Sharon Stone hit. Mario Kassar, the producer, and Paul Verhoeven, the Dutch director, were contractually obligated to deliver their picture with an R rating. To the ratings board, however, such a rating could only be achieved if Sharon Stone closed her legs. Verhoeven could argue himself blue in the face, but the ratings gurus knew what they saw—namely, the most private sector of Sharon Stone's anatomy. "We must have sat there in screening rooms and watched Sharon Stone cross and uncross her legs on film a thousand times during this battle," chortled Buffy Shutt, the marketing director in charge of the TriStar film.

Defending its director, the studio argued that this was not a sex scene but rather a dramatic encounter, a battle of wills between a strong woman and her police interrogators. The argument was bogus, of course; by flaunting her femininity, Sharon Stone had, in fact, transformed an interrogation into a sex scene. But, in the end, Paul Verhoeven won the day. Though snippets were removed from the scene to pacify the ratings board, the substance remained intact. And what had been visible to the board was still, in fact, visible to moviegoers.

The ratings battles have taken on even greater intensity as a result of stepped-up government pressure on marketing policies starting in the year 2000. While the rhetoric of the political attacks on Hollywood was windy, at its core was one key area of vulnerability: The dream merchants all too often were selling R-rated pictures on the back of family films. Trailers showing R movies were running at the front of PG-13 features, and TV ads for supposedly "restricted" films were broadcast during family viewing times.

While rejecting the broad-based attacks, many top filmmakers concurred with the specific marketing critiques. "I didn't care for the rhetoric, but the fact remains we were being careless about marketing practices," says Harvey Weinstein of Miramax. "There was definitely some house-cleaning to be done."

By agreeing to restrict the placement of ads for R films, the studios were implicitly creating even more pressure on filmmakers to avoid the R label. Given the new marketing inhibitions on R films, filmmakers had better have solid reasons to invite that more restrictive rating. Sony's top executives, for example, were all the more upset that a broad audience film like *The Patriot* was branded with an R because of its director's inclusion of a couple of very violent scenes.

By granting the right of final cut to a growing circle of directors, on the other hand, the Hollywood majors were surrendering control over these crucial decisions. What a studio may regard as a frivolous moment, a filmmaker may argue is essential to the integrity of the entire project—and he has the power to enforce his decree.

The demands of the ratings board often hinge on seemingly trivial criteria—the number of times the word "fuck" is used, for example. Is a fleeting crotch shot less "offensive" than one that is two seconds longer? Should children be barred from a movie that contains a sex act but permitted admission to one depicting violence and bloodshed? Often the debates over ratings rage through the final test screenings, with filmmakers still insisting that their work has been compromised by the final edits and studios arguing just as passionately that last-minute cuts would not hurt the movie but rather deliver a more favorable rating.

Even as these arguments are still raging, studio executives and filmmakers find themselves sitting side by side at festivals around the world trying to present a united front of peace and amity. Because of their set dates, festivals often show movies that are still works-in-progress, but marketing executives argue that festivals nonetheless present an excellent opportunity to showcase their product. The classic success stories were *M*A*S*H* (1970) and *E.T.* (1982), both dark horses, which received rapturous receptions at the Cannes Film Festival. In the case of *E.T.*, the festival filmgoers actually leapt to their feet to applaud. Steven Spielberg, then a still youthful filmmaker, was both shocked and touched. Yet *Moulin Rouge*, which was warmly received at Cannes in 2001, and which gleaned favorable worldwide publicity, enjoyed less-than-stellar business in the U.S. (It did better overseas.)

The advantages of the festival circuit are all but irresistible to film marketers. Mobs of reporters are hovering around, eager for a story. Photos of celebrities are dispatched to the world's media. What better chance to glom on to a free publicity ride?

But there's also the downside. Critics from around the world weigh in on every screening, and, given the vast menu of films, their critical assessments seem even more savage. While some fortunate movies gain a good "buzz" from festivals, others seem like cannon fodder. Eager to stir up attention for *The Last Action Hero*, Arnold Schwarzenegger held court at the Hotel du Cap d'Antibes and delivered a rapid-fire series of press interviews. It was an ill-fated exercise: Many of the press reports carried a negative tinge. Schwarzenegger, a man not renowned as self-effacing, even boasted to one reporter that he had done as many as thirty one-on-one interviews in a single day. Inevitably, the reporter remarked in his story that the star's quotes sounded "canned."

If the press can be the scourge of the studios, it can also be a helpful ally. Reporters from all over the U.S. routinely accept the hospitality of studios on press junkets to Hollywood, New York or even Honolulu, dutifully running the self-congratulatory quotes of stars as a "make-nice" for the free trip. Studio publicists can also count on a group of critics from obscure media who will summon up a felicitous quote for virtually any new movie, no matter how odoriferous. Hence Omar Lugones of Fox-TV can be depended upon to call a turkey like *Bicentennial Man*, "the most beautiful movie of the millennium." And Jacqueline Sonderling of KCAL in Los Angeles called Rob Reiner's truly soporific film, *The Story of Us*, "the most wonderful and romantic movie of the year." Diane Kaminsky of KHOU-TV Houston, said a dim thriller called *Switchback*, "will suck the air right out of your lungs."

Movie publicists know they can always find a critic to whom they can gently suggest a quote. What does the critic gain from complying with these requests? There are junkets to be attended, Christmas gifts to open and, besides, obscure writers in small cities enjoy seeing their names emblazoned across prestigious newspapers, even though their quotes might have been coaxed out of them. (Major newspapers discourage junkets and their reporters routinely return gifts valued at over $100.)

Though publicists have grown smug about their ability to control the celebrity press and to promulgate a steady outpouring of puff pieces, there are occasions when the whole exercise blows up in their faces. The most memorable such incident overtook TriStar and Woody Allen in 1993. Though Allen has steered away from the major studios through most of his career, preferring the autonomy of the independent world, he opted for a multiple picture deal with TriStar, a unit of Sony, hoping for wider distribution and better marketing. Indeed, the TriStar team venerated Allen. His audience was limited but loyal, and now and then he, too, created a breakout film like *Annie Hall*, which won the 1977 Oscars for best picture and best director, among others. TriStar determined not to meddle with his filmmaking prowess, but to support his work with marketing dollars and publicity.

They didn't realize how much publicity Woody Allen was about to get. No sooner had he completed the first film under his deal, ironically called *Husbands and Wives*, than the New York press was heralding the lurid details of his breakup with Mia Farrow, his affair with his adopted daughter, Soon-Yi Previn, and the melodramatic charges and countercharges that sprang from the imbroglio. This was clearly not the sort of publicity that would enhance public appreciation of his forthcoming comedy.

TriStar's spin doctors were all but paralyzed. Hours were spent debating strategy: Should they push back release of the movie a year or longer? What could they do to protect their asset?

Allen's response was to keep his head down and forge ahead. He was already preparing his next TriStar film, *Manhattan Murder Mystery*, even as the first blew up in his face. Nothing was going to derail him.

The studio, meanwhile, continued to take the buffeting. Sony's top executives in Japan even chimed in to express their alarm. To them, the entire situation was baffling. Why had the press leaped on Allen's problems? Why hadn't publicists contained the situation? The studio had no quick answers to explain a problem that had taken on cultural as well as financial repercussions.

Studios and producers have unleashed press agents for emergency damage control on many other projects, with decidedly mixed results. *Seven Years in Tibet* was close to release when an obscure newspaper in Austria touted the news that its true-life lead character had once been a member of the Nazi party before taking refuge in the Himalayas. Jean-Jacques Annaud, the director and co-writer, was horrified to see media outlets around the world pick up the story, which suggested that he had crafted his protagonist from a despicable character. This, of course, was true, and the whole point of the character arc of the film. Nevertheless, the reports were harmful to the box office results, though the film still did some $150 million worldwide.

Sometimes stunts carefully planned by press agents misfire. On *Gorillas in the Mist*, the publicist thought it would be a novelty to invite John Omirah Miluwi, a Rwandan tracker who appeared in the movie, to visit New York for meetings with the press. Having never been out of the Virunga Mountains, Miluwi was understandably confused when he arrived at Kennedy Airport at night and a day early to find no one was there to greet him. He *walked* from the airport to the Park Avenue apartment of the producer Arne Glimcher, only to be initially turned away by a suspicious doorman, who finally relented upon hearing Miluwi's amazing story. Glimcher returned home from a trip the next morning to find Miluwi sleeping in the back of his apartment house lobby under the emergency stairs. Fortunately, the good-natured tracker still obliged with his interviews and even told the story of his arrival with some relish.

When handling controversial projects, studio press agents customarily steel themselves for the worst. *The Godfather* was protested by Italian-American groups for the supposedly unfair depiction of their countrymen. Some gay activists protested *Philadelphia* because the principal male characters didn't seem to have much of a love life and that the script was all too dour.

In both these cases, damage control consisted of bringing community authority figures to the fore to defend the project. In the case of *The Godfather*, Paramount mobilized some friendly Italian-Americans who professed their fondness for the project (in fact, many senior Mafia figures quietly expressed their affirmation). On *Philadelphia*, prominent gay spokespeople defended the film and its depiction of the realities of gay life.

Whether in publicity or advertising, the message to marketers had become abundantly clear: The rules of the game had drastically changed. They now had more clout than ever before, but along with the clout came risk. More resources had been placed in their hands than their predecessors thought imaginable. As a result, they were positioned to accept credit for the triumphs and also blame for the failures. To an alarming extent, it had become their ball game—a mixed blessing if ever there was one.

And the ever-evolving and increasingly ubiquitous Internet would further complicate the lives of film marketers. Here was an entirely new frontier that demanded vastly different precepts. In one aspect the Internet harks back to the 1970s. The key to selling pop culture then was to build word of mouth. Get people talking about a new movie or TV show—that was the mantra of the moment. Now along comes the Internet, a medium ideally designed for just such a stratagem. If properly manipulated, surely it would become possible to build a veritable fervor among filmgoers to see a particular movie. There would be limitless possibilities for people to exchange enthusiasms. Word-of-mouth marketing became viral—faster, wider reaching and more insidious. The Net represented, after all, a revolutionary iteration of the storytelling food chain. What had once been a camp-fire had now become cyberspace. For the moment at least, no gate-keepers had achieved sufficient scale that they could control the way content was experienced, although the multinationals stood by, eager to control its ultimate distribution. The AOL Time Warners of the world would not be passive about protecting their turf, even if the nature of the turf remained undefined.

Every new movie now had its web site, albeit, the official sites might be little more than repositories of teasers and chat room–type exchanges. Were they helping to generate that magic word of mouth? Not really. Indeed, in some cases unofficial sites were spreading information that the filmmakers would have preferred to keep private. Rumors about casting and eleventh-hour script changes were regularly surfacing. Reports about the results of test screenings also became fodder for the proliferating new unofficial sites. Even screenplays appeared before they were either finished or shot. The second draft of Oliver Stone's script for "Beyond Borders" found its way onto the web, even though the film's start date had been regularly postponed. A month before the release of *Sleepy Hollow*, even as final edits were being made, a cut of the entire film appeared on the Internet. (Detective work revealed that it emanated from a site based in Korea, but originating in the San Fernando Valley of Los Angeles.) To moviemakers, the promise of the web seemed exhilarating, but frustrating. That is, until that bizarre exercise called *The Blair Witch Project* happened along.

In every sense, *Blair Witch* was amateurish and underfunded. It was a non-movie, yet it worked. It masqueraded as a documentary featuring a trio of filmmakers who disappeared while shooting the story of a legendary witch in the woods. By effectively using the Internet, the filmmakers were able to migrate their story through interstitial material, building the fantasy that they presumably died, letting the Internet audiences fill in the gaps. They built their web presence (www.blairwitch.com) to maximize the interactive potential of the medium. The site's tone and character created a reportage featuring extensive faux historical information, police reports and press interviews. What occurred was a truly participatory marketing experience that bled seamlessly into the film experience creating a kind of electronic word of mouth. This extended the media buy at very low cost and created personal attribution and support.

Whatever the alchemy at work here, *Blair*'s vision keepers, Eduardo Sánchez and Daniel Myrick, saw themselves as creating an experience, not a commodity. Their idea delivered an authentic fright to the audience that felt fresh and not manipulative.

The process represented an abandonment of all the conventional brick-and-mortar strategies to bring a film to market. In the spring of 1999 Artisan, *Blair Witch*'s distributor, dispatched a troop of more than one hundred guerrilla marketers and trendsetters to clubs, bookstores, cyber-cafés and trendy retailers where the target audience for this film entertained itself. They posted fliers as well as distributed comics and T-shirts, all designed to build word of mouth. These were hardly groundbreaking efforts—they'd been widely employed in the music industry and utilized even for conventional films. But when combined with other traditional marketing strategies and one of the most sophisticated web sites devised for a movie, the combination was stunning. It transformed the passive observer into a rabid fan before the film's debut.

It has been argued that the arcane nature of this film fit perfectly the qualities of the Internet. What is more to the point is that the dream merchant had a unique tool with the web in approaching and expanding an audience. Inevitably, the "new frontier" opened by *Blair Witch* proved a massive disappointment to many others who tried to exploit it. Movie after movie tried to follow the *Blair Witch* scenario, pouring resources into elaborate web marketing campaigns. A few, like *The Matrix* and *Lord of the Rings*, struck pay dirt. Most fell on their faces. Perhaps the most noticeable, and paradoxical, failure was that of *Blair Witch II*, the misbegotten, if inevitable sequel.

So what had seemed like new answers ended up stirring new questions as to what sort of fare was ideally suited for exploitation on the Internet. Subject matter was perhaps the key—or at least the way it was interpolated. Or perhaps the whole issue circled back to that frustrating question of uniqueness: Perhaps only a movie that was intrinsically unique and capable of building its own cult could be marketed successfully on the Internet. But if that were the case, would these projects have succeeded even without cyberspace? Would even *Blair Witch* have been a hit on its own?

It comes down to the fact that web marketers, like their more traditional brethren, are still at a loss to figure out why certain projects come with their own positive aura. With all their research, with all the weapons at their disposal, marketing gurus are still confounded by the basic mysteries of their trade. Indeed, this is also what keeps them in the hunt. They realize that, in the end, they are not selling toothpaste. No ad blitz, no matter how cosmic, will automatically generate market share. They are dealing with cultural forces beyond their control.

Beyond anyone's, fortunately.

CUT TO: Peter Bart on Hype

Show business is fueled by hype. Every picture is terrific. Every script is awesome. Every time a star reads a script, he's "excited." All of this is gross exaggeration, of course, but in Hollywood everyone is hustling everyone else, so it's taken as a matter of course.

When people get caught up in their own distortions, however, terrible things happen: Deals are broken, lawsuits get filed and friendships are scuttled.

I almost got trapped in the hype machine when I joined MGM as a senior vice president in the 1980s. A troubled project called "Road Show" was in preproduction. The salty veteran Martin Ritt was slated to direct it and pay-or-play deals had been concluded with Jack Nicholson and Tim Hutton. MGM's then president of production, Freddie Fields, loved the project and assured his colleagues it was a surefire blockbuster.

The trouble was, the script was lame. Its story focused on a maverick cattleman in the contemporary West who was besieged by creditors and infuriated by the outrageous prices demanded by truckers to transport his 250 head of cattle to Kansas City. Finally he decided on the ultimate act of defiance: He would drive his herd to market the old-fashioned way—a classic cattle drive that would traverse the turnpikes and Holiday Inns.

Fields was a strong-willed man who, after a long career as an agent, had produced some successful films including *Looking for Mr. Goodbar*. Like most agents, he was very persuasive. He could even persuade himself of virtually anything—a serious flaw. Though he was persuaded that "Road Show" was ready to shoot, no one else seemed to agree. Especially director Martin Ritt, who had become skittish about the impending start date. At sixty-three, Ritt felt he was getting too old for tough location shoots, especially when he had doubts about the script. Suddenly a legal letter arrived at Fields' office stating that Ritt was withdrawing from the film after consultation with his doctor.

Fields was shocked, but also secretly delighted. Though Ritt had long been attached to the project, Fields always knew that there was another gifted filmmaker who could make "Road Show" a classic—seventy-one-year-old Richard Brooks. Fields and Brooks had collaborated on *Goodbar*. "Brooks is the ideal director for the movie," Fields assured his colleagues at MGM. "Remember his work in *The Professionals*."

"That was in 1966," I protested. "If a director who's in his sixties withdraws from a project because it's too rigorous, why go to a man in his seventies?"

Fields wouldn't listen. He mounted a fusillade of publicity about Brooks' triumphant return. He met with his two stars, Nicholson and Hutton, and persuaded them that Brooks was the man for the job. Nicholson was grouchy, pointing out that he'd already taken himself off the market for nearly a year waiting for "Road Show" to start and didn't want further delays. Fields assured him there wouldn't be any.

But there would be. Upon moving onto the lot and dissecting the script, Brooks was getting increasingly worried. The basic premise didn't make sense, he felt. The conflicts were phony. The script needed work. He needed a writer.

A rewrite man was hired, and Brooks went off on a location scout. Shortly after he returned to Los Angeles, he disappeared. His aides on the film, now in advanced preproduction, were alarmed. His stars were perplexed. Fields quickly dispensed reassurances. Everything is on course, he said. Brooks was working on the script.

The trouble was that Brooks, in fact, was in intensive care having endured a heart attack. Fearful that his pricey package would fall apart, Fields nonetheless continued to sign up cast members, making yet another pay-or-play deal with Mary Steenburgen.

The news about Brooks filtered out, and the studio faced millions of dollars in pay-or-play deals. Fields came up with names of substitute directors. His actors turned them down. He offered Nicholson a substitute picture, but the star turned that down. Now Fields, in desperation, declared he was signing Michael Cimino, whose last movie was the disastrous *Heaven's Gate*, to replace Brooks. His boss, Frank Yablans, went ballistic. He notified the actors that "Road Show" had been abandoned because of Richard Brooks' disability. Pay-or-play commitments would no longer apply because of a legal technicality called force majeure, said studio attorneys. Trapped in his own hype, Freddie Fields retreated sheepishly to his office and canceled all his meetings. The actors filed lawsuits.

I felt shell-shocked. I'd admired Fields' dedication, but I always suspected the project would self-destruct. At one point Fields even assigned me to be its "project manager," but I'd begged off. I was asked to find a writer to help Brooks, but Brooks was too distracted to work with anyone. "This one's a slam dunk," Freddie Fields had kept assuring me. Maybe so, but in the end it was just a slam.

I learned a lot from "Road Show." Even in Hollywood, nothing can survive on hype alone.

CUT TO: Peter Guber on Envy

It was award season in Hollywood, 1974. *Midnight Express*, the little movie no one wanted to make, was suddenly "hot." Written by an unknown, directed by an unknown, starring an unknown and dealing with a subject no one ostensibly wanted to know about, the film was now every critic's darling. The normally raucous crowd at the Golden Globes banquet was downright reverent when *Midnight Express* was declared the winner for best picture and I was thrilled to accept it. I was barely back at my table, cradling the Globe in my arms, when the obvious question was raised. Will an Oscar be next? I was too freaked to respond. I just wanted to enjoy the moment.

But, of course, the Oscar would become an obsession. A Golden Globe is nice, but Oscar is the main event. To win an Academy Award would be a boon to my creative partners and also to my indie company. And there wasn't a strong list of competitors. In fact, only one film seemed to stand in the way. I had heard enthusiastic buzz about it but had not seen it myself. It was called *The Deer Hunter*, the work of a young filmmaker named Michael Cimino. I was in New York the following day, so the next night I steeled myself and paid my way into a theater on the East Side of Manhattan. It was packed. The film started. I was devastated. *The Deer Hunter* was pure magic. I was green with envy. As good as *Midnight Express* was, it paled by comparison in theme and scale. I could see the Oscar fading into the night . . . A prominent magazine journalist, eager to create controversy, goaded me into exposing my frustration with my Goliath competitor. Cimino won the day; he deserved to. I would be the runner-up. Rightly so. I realized later when I read my own reported remarks that no one raises their own reputation by trying to undermine another's. I dreamed that someday I would make my own *Deer Hunter*.

Reshoots

Two Snapshots:

David Lean, old and infirm, is dining with a couple of visitors at his beautiful home in the South of France. Someone asks him whether he ever imagined his films would reach such a vast audience around the world. He sips some wine, then replies: "Honestly, I made them for me. I suppose I hoped there were a lot of 'me's' out there."

Marcel Ophuls, sitting in the audience at the Academy Awards in 1972, hears himself summoned to the stage. He has just won an Oscar for *The Sorrow and the Pity*. As he climbs to the stage, he peers at his watch, then checks it again as he descends with his statuette. Fifteen seconds have elapsed. "Have I done all this work for fifteen seconds?" he asks himself. And then he realized, "No, it's about the journey. The journey is everything."

■

This book is about journeys. They are creative journeys. Also journeys of obsession.

And to what end? Their purpose was to communicate an idea or emotion. Or simply to tell a story, as with those ancient cave painters in France.

Today these journeys have become exponentially more costly and cumbersome. And, out of economic necessity, they must now be filtered through the prisms of corporate life. They must endure the power shoot outs that characterize virtually every aspect of our corporate and popular cultures. Inevitably, they will emerge as the product of both vision and accommodation.

And there is a lot at stake. The so-called "creative industries" are big business. The combined output of the core copyright business, such as film, music, media, advertising, etc., totals more than $2 trillion, which is between 6 percent and 7 percent of the global economy, according to *The Economist*. In the U.S. alone, it is larger than almost any other sector of activity.

The filmmaking process is a metaphor for a range of creative endeavors in our society. In a way it's a misleading, if colorful, metaphor because the payoff is so much greater, the process so much glitzier.

Yet the shoot outs of this process are virtually identical to those of advertising, publishing, deal making or even corporate acquisition. In each arena, there ultimately is a battle for proprietorship of the "ideas." Will the vision belong to those who fostered the idea or to those whose intent is to exploit and compromise it?

Hence the most urgent initial exercise for the vision keeper is one of self-definition and scale. Is my vision micro or macro? Am I driven to share it with millions or with no one? Will its illumination entail the expenditure of mega-millions, or will it merely dent Daddy's credit card?

David Lean bore no illusions about the scope of his vision. To get *Lawrence of Arabia* right, he shot for three years, not for three months. Though his view of his craft was megalomaniacal, his "voice" was as precise as it was personal.

At the start of this book, we stated that in the arts there are no rules, but you break them at your peril. Yet, there is, to be sure, one rule: the rule of survival.

Well into the production of *Midnight Express*, Alan Parker, then an ambitious young director, shot a riveting scene in which Billy Hayes, played by Brad Davis, breaks out of prison and walks free. He had endured the nightmare of a Turkish prison and beat the system.

His producers and the studio applauded Parker's work. Presumably he would now move on to the third act, as written by Oliver Stone. The protagonist would make his way across Turkey under close pursuit, hang on to the back of a fishing boat, slog through Greece, etc.

No, said Parker, the movie has just ended. It's not an action escape movie; that's not what it's about. It's about injustice, zealotry and the triumph of the spirit.

The producers were in shock. The studio was in rebellion. Why hadn't the filmmaker notified them earlier that he had no intention of shooting all of the action-filled third act? For once, executives were complaining about *not* having to spend money.

Parker was firm. He'd defined the film he wanted to make, and he'd made it. End of discussion.

Parker had survived his first major shoot out. He'd been given a script to shoot, and he shot as much of it as he saw fit. He understood the end game.

In so doing, he happened to make a brilliant film. To many laboring within the complex strata of our corporate culture, the creative accommodations are not so deftly achieved. The demands are greater, the dilution more extreme.

In the pop arts, the resources to create what is euphemistically called "content" increasingly are concentrated in global mega-companies such as AOL Time Warner, Vivendi Universal, News Corp., General Electric (which owns NBC), Sony and Disney. The reason these entities are in the "content" business is that they control vast distribution tentacles that circle the globe. In truth, the nature of their content is only marginally relevant. Their grand design is to establish hegemony over a particular distribution sector, whether that entails satellites or cable or the Internet. The payoff is not in the product, but in the ability to optimize control over a given market or medium. The incentive is not art but oligopoly.

Hence what were once dream factories to the moguls of old are now sources of concerns and consternation for the multinationals. Movies are expensive, risky and difficult to market. When a Rupert Murdoch owns two TV stations and a monopoly newspaper in a given market, he doesn't have to reinvent them every season. But each time he creates a movie or TV show, he starts from scratch, and too many are utter failures. Corporate executives are exasperated by failure. There's no line in the quarterly profit-and-loss statement labeled "failure."

Given this disdain for content, it is all the more paradoxical that these huge companies are stuck with what they are least comfortable with—nurturing creativity. They're not good at it. Their executives distrust it. There also is abundant evidence that their system isn't working.

In the music business, the stepped-up pace of consolidation has sharply inhibited the development of new artists, with more money instead being tossed at established "stars." The TV networks have fixated on so-called "reality programming" and quiz shows, thus curtailing conventional scripted dramatic shows like *ER* or *The West Wing*. Again, "reality" shows like *Survivor* or *Boot Camp* are dependent on voyeurism, not on the creative input of writer-producers. The film studios, meanwhile, have been sharply reducing the ranks of creative talent under contract and also cutting development. More and more, the studios are restructuring themselves as co-financiers and marketers, and they are becoming increasingly dependent on agents or independent contractors to assemble viable packages.

It's finally being acknowledged that the myriad echelons of corporate players are less than adept in dealing with the needs of the creative community. Breakthrough ideas do not survive the trek through layers of executive committees. The bolder the idea, the greater the risk; in the main, "suits" want presold ideas, not risky ones.

To compound the problem, it's become ever more apparent that the creative community is in rebellion against the way the revenue pie is being divided. This dissatisfaction was vividly dramatized during the labor unrest of 2001–2002, when virtually every sector of Hollywood's creative work force—actors, writers and directors—went to the barricades. At the core of the disagreements were issues of structure and philosophy, not simply numbers. The position of the megacompanies was that the profits from the production of TV and film product are wafer thin, having been eroded by soaring marketing and talent costs. The talent guilds argued that the companies with whom they were bargaining were no longer in the production business; they were, in fact, global distributors of content. Hence the discussion of profits had to be redefined to encompass all the revenue streams, past and prospective, as well as valuations of accumulated "libraries." Clearly Vivendi, the French conglomerate, didn't fret about wafer-thin profits in bidding $30 billion to acquire Seagrams, owner of Universal.

A productive co-existence between the corporate and creative communities, insiders feel, will never come to pass until basic structural changes are made. Talent must once again be allowed to function within smaller, more autonomous creative units that are more receptive to new ideas and more responsive to the incessant changes in style and taste within our pop culture. Though the multinational distribution entities will continue to have a substantial stake in these units, a greater ownership interest must redound to the creators themselves. A top filmmaker or star inevitably will want to achieve ownership over a substantial share of his own work—i.e., his personal oeuvre or library—mindful of the fact that, in so doing, he can truly share in the meaningful revenue streams, rather than being limited to the least important, which is its initial theatrical run. At the same time, more and more artists want to function actively not just in film but also in TV, commercials, music and the burgeoning universe of the Internet. Only by establishing their own mini corporate "pods" can they contribute creatively and benefit financially.

Technology is lending these mandates added urgency, opening new vistas to the combined poet-engineer. The Internet is stoking both his appetite and his imagination. Vast information banks and retrieval systems allow the storyteller to access a wondrous landscape of ideas and research. The wireless revolution is affecting every facet of the storytelling food chain. Digital filmmaking has opened up an entirely new universe of opportunity to neophyte vision keepers. Digital distribution of movies may enable independent filmmakers finally to gain access to those myriad screens in the multiplexes, thus helping the exhibition business emerge from its financial bloodbath. And while the bold, new power players of the wired world vie with one another to establish strategic choke holds, a combination of technological and economic turmoil may effectively keep them at bay.

In the end, technology may actually empower the poet-engineer as the shaman of the future—provided, that is, that his creative impulses are prompted, not by the lines of resolution on the television screen, but by the lines in the script. Even the techno-genius of the future must pay heed to the old bromide, "If it's not on the page, it's not on the stage." The word is still king. In the hands of the poet-engineer, movies will harness new tools to inspire emotion and passion. Vision keepers, as such, are in the emotional transportation business, and technology must bring the audience closer to the story, rather than distancing it.

For the vision keeper, the road is never easy. The world stage is populated by those who instinctively realize they will crash and burn one year, perhaps to return triumphant the next—artists who are willing to fail extravagantly, to risk the abyss on the off chance that it may actually be the summit. Losing a shoot out is a mere speed bump on the road to invincibility.

If you don't believe the vision keepers will win in the end, just ask them.

Bibliographical Note

We would like to acknowledge several books that may advance the understanding of those who wish to read further in this field. They include *Adventures in the Screen Trade* by William Goldman; *Which Lie Did I Tell?* also by William Goldman; *Final Cut* by Steven Bach; *Indecent Exposure* by David McClintick; *Directors Close Up*, edited by Jeremy Kagan; *Selznick*, by Bob Thomas; *Engulfed: The Death of Paramount Pictures and the Birth of Corporate Hollywood* by Bernard F. Dick; *Goldwyn* by A. Scott Berg; *Howard Hawks* by Todd McCarthy; *United Artists* by Tino Balio; *The Agency* by Frank Ross; and *Million and One Nights* by Terry Ramsaye.

Index

About the Authors

PETER BART became editor of weekly *Variety* in 1989 and, as vice president and editor in chief of Variety, Inc., also presides over its sister publications *Daily Variety* and *Daily Variety Gotham*. He also is a columnist for GQ.

Bart spent ten years as a staff reporter for the *Wall Street Journal* and the *New York Times* before entering the motion picture industry. He was also a consultant to the Ford Foundation and lecturer at the Salzburg Institute for American Studies.

Bart joined Paramount Pictures in 1967. In his eight years with the studio, he played a key role in developing and supervising such successful and influential films as *The Godfather, Paper Moon, Harold and Maude, True Grit* and *Rosemary's Baby*. He left Paramount in 1974, to form an independent production company, which produced *Fun With Dick and Jane* and *Islands in the Stream*.

During his tenure as president of Lorimar Films, beginning in 1977, the company produced *Being There* and *The Postman Always Rings Twice*. Subsequently, Bart served as senior vice president of MGM/UA.

Bart has published five books. The most recent include *Who Killed Hollywood?*, a compilation of Bart's columns, and *The Gross: The Hits, The Flops—The Summer that Ate Hollywood*. His previous books were *Fade Out: The Calamitous Final Days of MGM* plus two novels, *Destinies* and *Thy Kingdom Come*.

Bart was educated at Swarthmore College and the London School of Economics. He resides in Los Angeles with his wife, Leslie Bart. He has two daughters, Dilys Bart, a doctor, and Colby Bart-Centrella, a writer.

PETER GUBER is a thirty-year veteran of the entertainment industry. After receiving his bachelor of arts, master of law and Juris Doctor degrees—as well as admission to the New York and California Bars—he was recruited by Columbia Pictures in 1968 while pursuing an MBA degree at New York University's Graduate School of Business. Within three years he was made studio chief, and during his tenure at Columbia, the studio made such critically acclaimed box office hits as *Shampoo*, *The Last Detail*, *Tommy*, *The Way We Were*, *Taxi Driver* and *Close Encounters of the Third Kind*.

In 1976, Guber and Neil Bogart founded Casablanca Records and Filmworks. Their record operation included such superstars as Kiss, Donna Summer, the Captain and Tennille, the Village People and Parliament. Casablanca produced some of the era's most successful sound tracks, including the Academy Award–winning *Midnight Express*, Lionel Ritchie and Diana Ross' *Endless Love* and *Flashdance*, which sold more than 14 million albums.

Guber launched his career as an independent film producer with *The Deep*, which became one of Columbia's top-ten box office successes of all time. *Midnight Express* earned seven Academy Award nominations for Columbia including best picture, a Golden Globe for best picture and a place in film history, leading the National Association of Theater Owners to name Guber "producer of the year."

In 1979, Guber formed Polygram Filmed Entertainment where he was chairman and co-owner. He sold Polygram in 1983, and then formed and served as co-owner with Jon Peters of the Guber-Peters Entertainment Company, which established a major presence in motion pictures, television and music.

The films directly produced and executive produced by Guber, including *Rain Man* and *Batman*, have earned more than $3 billion in worldwide revenue and more than fifty Academy Award nominations, including four for best picture.

Guber's other personal box office and critical hits include Michael Apted's *Gorillas in the Mist*, Steven Spielberg's *The Color Purple* and *Innerspace*, George Miller's *The Witches of Eastwick*, *Flashdance*, Costa-Gavras' *Missing*, and John Landis' *American Werewolf in London*. In 1988, Guber-Peters became a public company with the acquisition of Barris Industries, and in 1989 it was sold to Sony Pictures Entertainment (SPE) where Guber became chairman of the board and chief executive officer.

Under Guber's leadership, the company reframed its entire exhibition circuit becoming the premier North American theatrical exhibition enterprise. During his tenure, 1989 to 1995, SPE's Motion Picture Group achieved an industry-best domestic box office market share averaging 17 percent as well as leading the industry in $100 million–plus blockbusters. Over its first four years, Sony Pictures led all competitors with a remarkable total of 120 Academy Award nominations, the highest four-year total ever for a single company.

After leaving Sony in 1995, Guber formed Mandalay as a multi-media entertainment vehicle (www.Mandalay.com) in motion pictures, television, sports entertainment and new media. Mandalay became one of the preeminent independent producers and financiers of major motion pictures for the global market. Successes include the box office smash *I Know What You Did Last Summer, Donnie Brasco, Seven Years in Tibet, Wild Things, Les Miserables, Sleepy Hollow, Enemy at the Gates* and *The Score.*

Mandalay's television projects have included top-rated network and cable series and more than twenty movies-of-the-week and mini-series.

Mandalay Sports Entertainment is a national sports entertainment provider with professional baseball and hockey teams, sports marketing and venue management. Among the professional sports franchises that are owned and operated by MSE are: the Las Vegas Stars, the Triple-A affiliate of the Los Angeles Dodgers; the Dayton Dragons, a Class-A affiliate of the Cincinnati Reds; and the Shreveport Swamp Dragons, the Double-A affiliate of the San Francisco Giants.

Guber is a full professor at the UCLA School of Theater, Film and Television, has been a member of the faculty for more than thirty years and is founding chairman of the Producers Program. He is also a member of the UCLA Foundation Board of Trustees, as well as the winner of UCLA's prestigious Service Award for his accomplishments and association with the school. He received his honorary doctorate in fine arts from the University of Connecticut; was named Albert Gallatin Fellow at New York University; is a recipient of Syracuse University's Arent's Award, the highest honor that can be given an alumnus, for his distinguished work in film; and is also a recipient of USC's Dean's Award for National Business Leadership.

Guber has been married to Lynda Guber for more than thirty-five years. They have four children: Jodi, Elizabeth, Samuel, and Jackson.